Investment Arbitration and National Interest

Investment Arbitration and National Interest

edited by Csongor István Nagy

Council on International Law and Policy
Indianapolis, 2019

This book was published in cooperation with the University of Szeged and the Iurisperitus Kiadó and with the generous support of the PADA Foundation (PADA Alapítvány).

Published by
Council on International Law and Politics LLC.
8409 Bay Colony Drive
Indianapolis, IN 46234, USA
http://www.cilpnet.com

Publications Coordinator: Kitti Kelemen and Ildikó Kovács

Printed by Iurisperitus Kiadó in Hungary and
Kindle Direct Publishing in USA

ISBN: 978-1-950137-00-8

TABLE OF CONTENTS

Csongor István Nagy[*]

INVESTMENT PROTECTION AND NATIONAL INTEREST

With the emerging wave of new-generation free trade agreements, investment arbitration, a more than half-century old pattern, came to be one of the central issues of the contemporary discourse on international economic relations.

Some argue that investment disputes are settled in the frame of intransparent *ad-hoc* arbitral proceedings devoid of any democratic legitimacy, which are inconsistent and unpredictable because of their *ad-hoc* and secretive nature. Critics assert that the current pattern of the settlement of investment disputes quite often strips national courts, including national constitutional courts, of their legitimate powers and vests *ad-hoc* and intransparent bodies with the competence to adjudicate public law questions. These questions include the validity of national legislation adopted by parliaments having democratic legitimacy; the review of the rationality of national regulatory decisions; the supervision of the fairness of national legal procedures and the exercise of contractual rights emerging from genuine commercial agreements.

The first bilateral investment treaty (Germany-Pakistan treaty of 1959) was meant to convert certain constitutional requirements e.g., expropriation, protection of legitimate expectations, into international obligations so as to guarantee them (guarantee function). The initial purpose of these treaties was to project certain constitutional requirements to the level of international disciplines as they were normally concluded between developed and developing countries and led by the concerns respecting the latter's legal system. The obligations were assumed to be, as a matter of courtesy, mutual i.e., reciprocal. However, these treaties did not aim at establishing higher, or in any sense different, standards for investment protection than the ones already part of the constitutional traditions of western democracies. The rationale was to convert the relevant constitutional rights and principles into international law guarantees in the form of bilateral agreements, so they could not be nullified unilaterally.

Nonetheless, there was no global agreement and especially no uniformity as to the investment protection standards. It is noteworthy that although goods, services and knowledge (intellectual property) are regulated in the global system of world trade (WTO), investment issues, including investment protection, were almost entirely left out, with the exception of the relatively insignificant provisions of TRIMs. The major turning point was when even developed democracies started concluding bilateral investment treaties.

---

[*] LL.M., Ph.D., S.J.D, dr. juris, professor of law and head of the Department of Private International Law at the University of Szeged, research chair and the head of the Federal Markets "Momentum" Research Group of the Hungarian Academy of Sciences, recurrent visiting professor at the Central European University (Budapest/New York), the Riga Graduate School of Law (Latvia) and the Sapientia University of Transylvania (Romania).

Today, investment protection became an integral part of new-generation free trade agreements, some of which are concluded between developed democracies (Canada, European Union, United States). With this, the guarantee function was put into the shade, and investment protection law fully detached from its original *raison d'être*.

Interestingly, investment protection, at least as far as substantive standards are concerned, has in essence remained bilateral, without a realistic chance to a multilateral system. During the last half-century, this pattern brought about a labyrinthine network of bilateral arrangements and investment protection took a life of its own. Instead of a duplicate it became an independent parallel system.

The major sources of uncertainty are the investment treaties' "treatment provisions" – fair and equitable treatment, security and protection, non-discrimination and national treatment. These principles center around fluid concepts, and confer on arbitral tribunals extremely wide powers to review national policy decisions and national administrative and judicial proceedings, entailing far-reaching consequences for states.

Furthermore, investor-state arbitration subjected genuine public-law disputes to an arbitral procedural pattern, initially designed for purely commercial disputes, which is devoid of democratic legitimacy due to its secrecy, intransparency and *ad-hoc* nature.[1]

The above developments were topped by new-generation free trade agreements, which are blamed for reinforcing these loose standards and the attached dispute settlement mechanisms lacking democratic legitimacy, thus making them part of the relations between developed democracies.

The first question which emerges in the context of bilateral investment protection treaties relates to their necessity. The reason is, obviously, the lack of appropriate standards and dispute settlement mechanism under (customary) international law concerning the protection of foreign investments.

The ontological analysis of investment protection treaty law inevitably raises the question whether the existence of this regime is warranted in the light of the constitutional standards of developed democracies and whether its maintenance is justified between developed democracies. Critics argue that the standards developed by investment tribunals are higher than the generally recognized constitutional standards of developed democracies and place a more onerous burden on national regulatory sovereignty than the burden accepted in a democratic society. An interesting gauge is the jurisprudence of the European Court of Human Rights – why should foreign investors enjoy a higher level of property protection than ordinary citizens? The contrasting of the case-law of investment tribunals and the constitutional practice of developed democracies, and the jurisprudence of the European Court of Human Rights, is susceptible of revealing whether the claim that in international investment protection treaty law investors are

---

[1] *Cf.* Joseph H.H. Weiler, *European Hypocrisy: TTIP and ISDS*, 25(4) European Journal of International Law 963 (2014) ("[T]he Bar that adjudicates them [investment disputes] is of a limited range [...], and dominated by arbitrators from private practice rather than public interest backgrounds [...]; and most damning of all, the substantive provisions of the investment treaties, when it comes to protecting societal interests, are woefully defective and inferior when compared with similar public interest provisions in trade agreements such as the WTO itself.").

"overprotected" and the clogs on national regulatory sovereignty are unduly onerous is valid.

One of the central questions of enforcement is access to the dispute settlement mechanism. Investment disputes are generally considered to be a mixture of private and public law, where a mechanism designed for the needs of the settlement of purely commercial disputes (arbitration) is used to adjudicate public law disputes.

International dispute settlement systems, as far as structure is concerned, range from *ad-hoc* mechanisms and permanent dispute settlement bodies to direct application by national courts. Investment protection law's dispute settlement mechanism concerns probably one of the politically most sensitive issues, given that this is the point where the international subjection of certain aspects of national regulatory sovereignty is perceived to crop out.

An important facet of enforcement is the consistency of the case-law and the role of precedents. Since investment arbitration has largely preserved its *ad-hoc* nature, where judgments have persuasive but no binding authority, critics have argued that this system is devoid of transparency and predictability. However, in relation to the new wave of free trade agreements, as to investment disputes, the creation of a permanent institution was proposed by the European Union.

The present volume addresses the above issues of investment arbitration in five sections.

The first section addresses the global debate and consists of two pieces.

The thought-provoking paper of Frank Emmert and Begaiym Esenkulova, "Balancing Investor Protection and Sustainable Development in Investment Arbitration – Trying to Square the Circle?", explores the mounting criticism against investment arbitration and analyzes possible solutions that may balance investment protection and sustainable development.

The paper of Dalma Demeter and Zebo Nasirova, "Trends and Challenges in the Legal Harmonisation of ISDS", examines the current landscape of international investment law consisting of thousands of different international agreements creating a fragmented legal framework and UNCITRAL's ongoing work in the field.

The second section deals with issues of legitimacy such as abuse, access, transparency and public participation.

The paper of Wasiq Abass Dar, entitled "'Abuse of Process' and Anti-Arbitration Injunctions in Investor-State Arbitration – an Analysis of Recent Trends and the Way Forward", deals with the abuse of procedural rights in investor-state arbitration employed by investors, such as multiple and parallel arbitral proceedings. His paper examines the concerns associated with this phenomenon, assesses the possible available remedies against abuse of process and proposes a balanced approach.

Rebecca Khan's paper "Third Party Participation by Non-Government Organizations in International Investment Arbitration – Transparency as a Tool for Protecting Marginalized Interests" examines a crucial question of public participation: whether non-disputing parties representing marginalized sectors may participate in international investment arbitration in an appropriate manner, channeling their interests in terms of impact of investment activities.

The paper of Bálint Kovács, "Access of SMEs to Investment Arbitration – Small Enough to Fail?" discusses the practical availability of investor-state dispute settlement mechanisms for small and medium-sized enterprises.

The third section addresses the regional perspectives of investment arbitration.

Dildar F. Zebari presents some key features of the developing case-law of the Energy Charter Treaty in his paper "The Promotion, Protection, Treatment and Expropriation of Investments under the Energy Charter Treaty – a Critical Analysis of the Case-Law".

Balázs Horváthy, in his paper entitled "Opinion 2/15 and the New Principles of Competence Allocation – a Solid Footing for the Future?", analyzes Opinion 2/15 of the Court of Justice of the European Union, which clarified the division of competences between the European Union and the Member States in relation to international trade policy in the context of the EU-Singapore Free Trade Agreement (EUSFTA).

Csongor István Nagy addresses various questions of BITs concluded between Member States and third countries in "Extra-EU BITs and EU law: Immunity, 'Defense of Superior Orders', Treaty Shopping and Unilateralism".

Pavle Flere's paper, entitled "Arbitrability of Competition Law Disputes in the European Union – Balancing of Competing Interests", addresses a classical issue of arbitration and arbitrability.

The fourth section deals with questions of enforcement and recovery.

In "Execution of ICSID Awards and Sovereign Immunity", Yue Ma addresses enforcement, a weak point of the life of ICSID arbitral awards. The paper analyzes the rationale of the ICSID's execution mechanism and evaluates the difficulties of enforcement under the recent backlash against investment arbitration.

The paper of Orsolya Tóth, entitled "The New York Convention – Challenges on Its 60th Birthday", addresses and analyzes some of the most recent challenges of the New York Convention in relation to arbitration involving a state.

The fifth and final section addresses institutional issues and consists of the paper of Zoltán Víg and Gábor Hajdu ("Investment Protection under CETA: a New Paradigm?"). This paper addresses one of the most exciting intellectual experiments of investment arbitration – the investment protection regime of the CETA, in particular the permanent international tribunal for the settlement of investment disputes.

The global debate

Frank Emmert[*] & Begaiym Esenkulova[**]

BALANCING INVESTOR PROTECTION AND SUSTAINABLE DEVELOPMENT IN INVESTMENT ARBITRATION – TRYING TO SQUARE THE CIRCLE?

Abstract

International investment arbitration is one of the most widely relied upon mechanisms of resolving disputes between investors and host states.[1] Since states typically do not like to submit to the jurisdiction of foreign courts, and investors often do not want to assume that they will be treated with complete neutrality and fairness by courts of states they are in a dispute with, arbitration in front of a neutral panel is the obvious alternative. The International Centre for Settlement of Investment Disputes (ICSID) and many other arbitral institutions provide a platform for hearing claims by foreign investors against host states.[2] ICSID alone has served as an administering institution for more than 500 investment cases to date.[3] Investors prefer arbitration not only because it is generally considered to offer an impartial forum for bringing claims against host states but also because it provides for an effective enforcement mechanism.[4] All of these characteristics of the arbitration process make it important and

---

[*] Prof. Dr. Frank Emmert, LL.M., FCIArb, is the John S. Grimes Professor of Law, and Director of the Center for Int'l & Comparative Law at Indiana University Robert H. McKinney School of Law in Indianapolis. He can be contacted at femmert@iupui.edu. For further information *see also* www.frankemmert.com, as well as https://www.research-gate.net/profile/Frank_Emmert2.

[**] Dr. Begaiym Esenkulova, LL.M., S.J.D., is an Associate Professor of the Law Division of the American University of Central Asia. She may be contacted at esenkulova_b@auca.kg.

[1] For a comprehensive analysis of the nature of investment arbitration *see* Andrea Bjorklund, *The Emerging Civilization of Investment Arbitration*, 113 Penn State Law Review 1269–1300 (2008–2009).

[2] In this regard, Reinisch and Malintoppi state that the ICSID system "...has known tremendous success, particularly over the last ten years, and is likely to grow further due to the increase in the number of Bilateral Investment Treaties ... all over the world". *See* August Reinisch and Loretta Malintoppi, *Methods of Dispute Resolution, in* The Oxford Handbook of International Investment Law 692 (Christoph Schreuer et al., eds, 2008); *See also* August Reinisch, *The Future of Investment Arbitration, in* International Investment Law for the 21st Century: Essays in Honour of Christoph Schreuer 894 (Christina Binder et al. eds, 2009).

[3] *UNCTAD*, ICSID Cases, 2018, http://investmentpolicyhub.unctad.org/ISDS/FilterByRulesAndInstitution accessed on Aug. 29, 2018; For the analysis of the work of ICSID *see* Ibironke Odumosu, *The Antinomies of the (Continued) Relevance of ICSID to the Third World*, 8 San Diego International Law Journal 345–385 (2007); Elizabeth Moul, *The International Centre for the Settlement of Investment Disputes and the Developing World: Creating a Mutual Confidence in the International Investment Regime*, 55 Santa Clara Law Review 881–916 (2015).

[4] *See* Muthucumaraswamy Sornarajah, The International Law on Foreign Investment 217 (2012) ("Arbitration, in a neutral state before a neutral tribunal, has traditionally been seen as the best method of securing impartial justice... [for investors]"); Herfried Wöss et al., *Valuation of Damages in International Arbitration, in* Damages in International Arbitration under Complex Long-Term Contracts 259 (Loukas Mistelis ed., 2014) ("...[G]overnmental opportunism is restrained ... by the potential financial penalties associated with ... misbehaviour arising

often indispensable for the protection of investors' rights. Yet, despite all the advantages of arbitration as a dispute resolution system, there is now a rising backlash against it. This article explores the mounting criticism against investment arbitration and discusses possible solutions to address this criticism to balance investor protection and sustainable development in investment arbitration.

I. The Legitimacy Crisis in International Investment Arbitration

Investment arbitration is being criticized for becoming an alarmingly all-too powerful system which threatens the sovereignty of states. In the early decades of investment arbitration, cases were often about expropriation, and the question was less whether the state should pay compensation, but how much would be adequate. In a way, this period built a momentum in favor of investors, with almost a presumption that a state may have been within its rights to expropriate or nationalize an investment, but generally had to do so for a public purpose and with payment of prompt, adequate, and effective compensation.

In more recent years, states are less in the business of taking away an entire investment; the focus has shifted in many cases to regulatory interventions by host states that are interfering with business plans or profit expectations of investors. Since many bilateral and multilateral investment protection agreements are quite broad when it comes to obligations of host states, countries are increasingly concerned with the impact that investment arbitration provided in most of these international investment agreements may have on their right to regulate and undertake other measures in the public interest.[5] States have faced multi-million and multi-billion dollar arbitration claims by investors for the alleged violation of investment protection standards.[6] For instance, in *Micula v.*

---

from ... arbitral awards"); Vladimir Pavić, *"Non-Signatories" and the Long Arm of Arbitral Jurisdiction, in* Resolving International Conflicts: Liber Amicorum Tibor Várady 213 (Peter Hay at al. eds., 2009) ("[A]rbitration promises a relatively relaxed, flexible procedural surrounding, swift delivery of the final award and very limited opportunities for review"); Stephan Schill, *Private Enforcement of International Investment Law: Why We Need Investor Standing in BIT Dispute Settlement, in* The Backlash against Investment Arbitration: Perceptions and Reality 33 (Michael Waibel et al. eds., 2010) ("The existence of investor-state dispute settlement mechanisms is ... crucial for investors to hold host states to their original commitments, whether given in contractual or statutory form or in an international treaty, and thus to ensure stability and predictability in investor-state cooperation").

5 Karl Sauvant and José Alvarez, *International Investment Law in Transition, in* The Evolving International Investment Regime: Expectations, Realities, Options xxxviii (*José Alvarez* et al. eds., 2011). For a comprehensive analysis of the growing backlash against the international investment law regime *see* Asha Kaushal, *Revisiting History: How the Past Matters for the Present Backlash against the Foreign Investment Regime*, 50 Harvard International Law Journal 491–534 (2009).

6 An example of a developed country facing investment arbitration is Germany. A Swedish investor filed arbitration claims against Germany with respect to its adoption of laws on phasing out of nuclear power plants by 2022. *See Vattenfall AB, Vattenfall Europe AG, Vattenfall Europe Generation AG v. Federal Republic of Germany I.* ICSID Case No. ARB/09/6, Mar. 11, 2011, http://investmentpolicyhub.unctad.org/ISDS/Details/329 accessed on Aug. 15, 2018 (the investor claimed 1400.00 mln. USD as compensation; the case was settled); *Vattenfall AB and others v. Federal Republic of Germany II.* ICSID Case No. ARB/12/12, 2012,

Romania (2013), Romania was held liable for breaching the Sweden-Romania bilateral investment treaty (BIT) due to its revocation of economic incentives offered to investors under its national law.[7] The tribunal ruled in favor of the investor even though Romania was required to repeal its law in order to comply with EU state aid obligations, and the investor was from Sweden, another Member State of the EU bound by EU state aid rules, just like Romania.[8] It is interesting that the European Commission has adopted a decision ordering Romania *not* to pay the compensation awarded to investors by the ICSID tribunal.[9] The Commission has also submitted that the Micula award is "...illegal and unenforceable under E.U. law" and that "....as a matter of E.U. law, Romania is squarely prohibited from complying with the Award".[10] At present, enforcement proceedings are pending in the United States. It remains to be seen whether the award will be enforceable. Similarly, in *Eiser v. Spain* (2017), the tribunal found Spain liable to pay compensation in the amount of 128 million Euro to the investor.[11] According to the tribunal, Spain violated the fair and equitable treatment standard under the Energy Charter Treaty[12] due to its adoption of measures that reduced the level of subsidies paid to investors in the Concentrated Solar Power sector and other renewable generators.[13] The European Commission has instructed Spain *not* to pay investor-state awards in this and several other solar energy cases, on EU state aid grounds.[14]

Investment arbitration is being criticized by states for being overly protective of investors' rights and not adequately considering state interests. One example is the recent case of *Bear Creek v. Peru* (2017). Bear Creek Mining Corporation was successful in an arbitration against Peru under the Free Trade Agreement between Canada and Peru.[15] Bear Creek, a Canadian company, invested in the Santa Ana Mining Project in Peru.[16] The

---

http://investmentpolicyhub.unctad.org/ISDS/Details/467 accessed on Aug. 15, 2018 (the investor claimed 4700.00 mln. EUR as compensation; the case is currently pending).

[7] *Ioan Micula, Viorel Micula and others v. Romania*. ARB/05/20, Dec. 11, 2013, https://www.italaw.com/sites/default/files/case-documents/italaw3036.pdf accessed on Aug. 29, 2018.

[8] *Ioan Micula v. Romania.*

[9] EU Commission, Decision on State Aid SA.38517 (2014/C) (ex 2014/NN) implemented by Romania –Arbitral Award Micula v Romania of 11 December 2013, 2015/1470, Mar. 30, 2015, https://www.italaw.com/sites/default/files/case-documents/italaw9152.pdf accessed on Aug. 25, 2018.

[10] EU Commission, Brief for Amicus Curiae the Commission of the European Union in support of Defendant-Appellant in the Case of Ioan Micula, European Food S.A., S.C. Starmill S.R.L., Multipack S.R.L., Plaintiffs-Appellees v. Government of Romania, at 10, https://www.italaw.com/sites/default/files/case-documents/italaw9198.pdf accessed on Aug. 24, 2018.

[11] *Eiser Infrastructure Limited and Energia Solar Luxembourg S.À R.I. v. Kingdom of Spain*. ICSID Case No. ARB/13/36, May 4, 2017, https://energycharter.org/fileadmin/DocumentsMedia/Disputes/ISDSC-043en.pdf accessed on Aug. 29, 2018.

[12] *See* 1994 Energy Charter Treaty, Article 10(1), https://energycharter.org/process/energy-charter-treaty-1994/energy-charter-treaty/ accessed on Aug. 25, 2018.

[13] *Eiser v. Spain*.

[14] Douglas Thomson, *EU Warns Spain not to Pay Solar Awards*, Jan. 19, 2018, https://globalarbitrationreview.com/article/1152912/eu-warns-spain-not-to-pay-solar-awards accessed on Aug. 29, 2018.

[15] *Bear Creek Mining Corporation v. Republic of Perú*. ICSID Case No. ARB/14/21, Nov. 30, 2017, https://www.italaw.com/sites/default/files/case-documents/italaw3036.pdf accessed on Aug. 29, 2018.

[16] *Bear Creek v. Perú*, at paras 150–151.

mining project turned out to be highly contentious. Local communities, in particular, were against it due to environmental and various other concerns.[17] The protests resulted in the burning of a mining camp in 2008[18] and continued with anti-mining marches, massive demonstrations, strikes, and other activities through 2011.[19] In May of 2011 the number of protesters grew to 13,000 people in Puno with protests becoming violent and resulting in the looting of governmental institutions and destruction of commercial establishments.[20] According to the *Amici* submissions, the Bear Creek Mining Corporation "... did not do what was necessary to understand the doubts, worries and anxieties of the Aymara culture and religiosity...".[21] Moreover, the expert report states that "... Bear Creek did not engage in sufficient efforts to inform all the communities within its area of influence of the effects and benefits the project could bring".[22] As a result of the intense protests against the mining project, the Peruvian government revoked Supreme Decree 083[23] which entitled the investor to "... acquire, own and operate the...mining concessions and to exercise any rights derived from the ownership".[24] At the time of the revocation, Claimant Bear Creek had not yet secured 99 agreements for the use of land and still had to have its Environmental and Social Impact Assessment approved.[25] Apart from this, according to witness testimony, it would have been highly unlikely for the investor's mining project to continue amidst the strong anti-mining protests.[26] Despite Bear Creek's lack of permits and widespread protests against its mining project, the Tribunal decided that Peru had indirectly expropriated Bear Creek's investment and ordered it to pay damages in the amount of US$ 18,237,592, as well as reimburse 75% of Claimant's arbitration costs.[27] This case shows the problem investment arbitration proceedings have with the adequate consideration of state and local community interests.

Another criticism directed against investment arbitration is the problem of uncertainty and unpredictability.[28] For example, in *Yukos v. Russia* (2014), the tribunal applied a 25% reduction in damages for contributory fault, lowering the amount of damages from

[17] *Bear Creek v. Perú*, at paras 152–153.

[18] *Bear Creek v. Perú*, at para 155.

[19] *Bear Creek v. Perú*, at paras 169–178 and 182.

[20] *Bear Creek v. Perú*, at paras 189–190.

[21] *Bear Creek v. Perú*, at para 218.

[22] Antonio Alfonso Peña Jumpa, *Expert Report as part of the Case on Bear Creek Mining Corporation v. Republic of Perú*, Oct. 6, 2015, at para 96, https://www.italaw.com/sites/default/files/case-documents/italaw4476.pdf accessed on Aug. 29, 2018.

[23] *Bear Creek v. Perú*, at para 202.

[24] *Bear Creek v. Perú*, at para 149.

[25] *Bear Creek v. Perú*, at para 201.

[26] *Bear Creek v. Perú*, at para 265. *See also* Philippe Sands QC, *The Partial Dissenting Opinion in Bear Creek Mining Corporation v. Republic of Perú,* Sep. 12, 2007, at para 38, https://www.italaw.com/sites/default/files/case-documents/italaw3036.pdf accessed on Aug. 29, 2018 ("[T]he nature and extent of the opposition made it clear that there was no real possibility of the Project soon obtaining the necessary 'social license'").

[27] *Bear Creek v. Perú*, at paras 416 and 738.

[28] *See generally* August Reinisch, *The Future of Investment Arbitration, in* INTERNATIONAL INVESTMENT LAW FOR THE 21st CENTURY: ESSAYS IN HONOUR OF CHRISTOPH SCHREUER 904 (Christina Binder et al. eds, 2009) ("It is an open secret that there are awards and decisions of highly variable quality" with some of them not fulfilling "...expectations

around 66 billion USD to approximately 50 billion USD.[29] It is not clear how the tribunal arrived at this percentage for contributory fault. The tribunal simply noted that it had a wide discretion in such cases.[30] The "discretion" in this particular case resulted in a difference of a staggering amount of around 16 billion USD. Similarly, in *Occidental v. Ecuador* (2012) the tribunal applied a 25% reduction in damages for contributory fault,[31] but it did not explain how it arrived at this percentage. The tribunal stated that it had "...a wide margin of discretion in apportioning fault".[32] It is important to note that one of the arbitrators wrote a dissenting opinion in this case, arguing that the tribunal greatly underestimated Claimants' contribution to damages and should have applied a 50% reduction in damages for contributory fault.[33] The difference between a reduction by 25% and a reduction by 50% was about 589 million USD! One of the key problems, as illustrated by these cases, is predictability.

Similar uncertainty arises in cases regarding regulatory expropriation for public purposes. There have been various extreme and some more balanced positions taken so far. Some tribunals have adopted the sole effect doctrine, disregarding the purpose of the measure but looking only at its effect from the investor point of view.[34] For example, an ICSID tribunal ordered Costa Rica to pay 16 million USD as compensation for a regulatory expropriation which took place after Costa Rica passed a decree taking the property of investors.[35] Although the decree was enacted in order to expand the territory of a national park for the purpose of conserving endangered feline species, including pumas and jaguars, the investment arbitration tribunal did not take this public

of the users of the system…"). For an analysis of related problems in international arbitration *see also* LOUKAS MISTELIS ED., PERVASIVE PROBLEMS IN INTERNATIONAL ARBITRATION (2006).

29 *Yukos Universal Limited (Isle of Man) v. The Russian Federation*. Permanent Court of Arbitration (PCA), Case No. AA 227, July 18, 2014, at para1637, https://www.italaw.com/sites/default/files/case-documents/italaw3279.pdf accessed on Aug. 29, 2018.

30 *Yukos v. The Russian Federation*, at para1637.

31 *Occidental Petroleum Corporation, Occidental Exploration and Production Company v. The Republic of Ecuador*. ICSID Case No. ARB/06/11, Oct. 5, 2012, at para 687, https://www.italaw.com/sites/default/files/case-documents/italaw1094.pdf accessed on Aug. 29, 2018 ("Having considered and weighed all the arguments which the parties have presented to the Tribunal in respect of this issue, in particular the evidence and the authorities traversed in the present chapter, the Tribunal, in the exercise of its wide discretion, finds that, as a result of their material and significant wrongful act, the Claimants have contributed to the extent of 25% to the prejudice which they suffered when the Respondent issued the *Caducidad* Decree").

32 *Occidental v. Ecuador*, at para 670.

33 Brigitte Stern, *Dissenting Opinion in Occidental Petroleum Corporation, Occidental Exploration and Production Company v. The Republic of Ecuador*, Sep. 20, 2012, at paras 7-8, https://www.italaw.com/sites/default/files/case-documents/italaw1096.pdf accessed on Aug. 26, 2018.

34 Supportive, for example, Ben Mostafa, *The Sole Effects Doctrine, Police Powers and Indirect Expropriation under International Law*, 15 267 (2008). A more nuanced approach with an endorsement of the kind of proportionality test applied by the European Court of Justice and the European Court of Human Rights is advocated by Ursula Kriebaum, *Regulatory Takings: Balancing the Interests of the Investor and the State*, 8 717 (2007).

35 *Compañía del Desarrollo de Santa Elena, S.A. v. The Republic of Costa Rica*, ICSID Case No. ARB/96/1, at para 111, Feb. 17, 2000, https://icsid.worldbank.org/ICSID/FrontServlet?requestType=CasesRH&actionVal=showDoc&docId=DC539_En&caseId=C152 accessed on Aug. 18, 2018.

purpose into account.[36] According to the tribunal, "...[e]xpropriatory environmental measures – no matter how laudable and beneficial to society as a whole – are...similar to any other expropriatory measures that a state may take in order to implement its policies: where property is expropriated, even for environmental purposes, whether domestic or international, the state's obligation to pay compensation remains".[37] Although every act of expropriation must be followed by compensation, the arbitral tribunal's insensitivity to the public purpose behind the measure illustrates the tension between broad investment protection standards and states' right to regulate in the public interest.

States are also becoming increasingly concerned with arbitral tribunals reaching diametrically opposed decisions in similar cases.[38] There have been a number of cases, where different tribunals have interpreted the same standard in the same treaty as having a different meaning. For instance, in *Glamis Gold v. USA* (2009), the tribunal interpreted FET in the NAFTA Agreement as a standard requiring an "egregious," "shocking," and "gross" denial of justice,[39] whilst in *Bilcon v. Canada* (2015), the tribunal interpreted the same standard in the same treaty as requiring that the conduct of the host state be merely "arbitrary" and "unjust",[40] noting that "...there is no requirement in all cases that the challenged conduct reaches the level of shocking or outrageous behaviour."[41] As it may be seen, there is currently a lack of uniformity in arbitral decisions. In some cases, this has gone as far as tribunals issuing blatantly conflicting awards on similar issues.

---

36 *Santa Elena, S.A. v. Costa Rica*, at para 18.

37 *Santa Elena, S.A. v. Costa Rica*, at para 72.

38 Pia Acconci, *Most-Favoured-Nation Treatment, in* The Oxford Handbook of International Investment Law 367 (Christoph Schreuer et al. eds., 2008) ("ICSID is criticized by some developed and developing countries that are no longer satisfied with the increasingly frequent recourse to its arbitration by private investors, resulting in increasingly complex amounts of inconsistent case-law"). It is also important to note the writings of Prof. Tibor Várady on this issue. While Várady affirms that it is not likely that the pro-arbitration stance will change to the negative towards international commercial arbitration, he is not as certain with respect to international investment arbitration due to „existing reservations (or 'hostility') towards...investment arbitration...". *See* Tibor Várady et al., International Commercial Arbitration: A Transnational Perspective 81 (2015). For further analysis of these issues *see also* William McElhiney, *Responding to the Threat of Withdrawal: On the Importance of Emphasizing the Interests of States, Investors, and the Transnational Investment System in Bringing Resolution to Questions Surrounding the Future of Investments with States Denouncing the ICSID Convention*, 49 Texas International Law Journal 601–619 (2014); August Reinisch and Loretta Malintoppi, *Methods of Dispute Resolution, in* The Oxford Handbook of International Investment Law 719 (Christoph Schreuer et al. eds, 2008) ("...[W]ith a significant growth experienced by investment arbitration over the last two decades...a number of inconsistent and partially conflicting decisions have been produced"); Nassib Ziadé, *Challenges and Prospects Facing the International Centre for Settlement of Investment Disputes, in* The Evolving International Investment Regime: Expectations, Realities, Options 120–124 (José Alvarez et al. eds., 2011).

39 *Glamis Gold, Ltd. v. United States of America*. International Centre for Settlement of Investment Disputes [ICSID], June 8, 2009, at paras 612, 616 and 828-829, https://www.italaw.com/sites/default/files/case-documents/ita0378.pdf accessed on Aug. 29, 2018.

40 *William Ralph Clayton, William Richard Clayton, Douglas Clayton, Daniel Clayton and Bilcon of Delaware, Inc v. Government of Canada*. Permanent Court of Arbitration [PCA], Case No. 2009-04, March 17, 2005, at paras 442-444 and 591-592, https://www.italaw.com/sites/default/files/case-documents/italaw4212.pdf accessed on Aug. 29, 2018.

41 *Bilcon v. Canada*, at para 444.

The above factors contribute to states' overall uncertainty as to the outcomes of their regulatory decisions.

Apart from traditional investment arbitration claims, countries are nowadays also facing situations, where investors threaten to bring arbitration claims against almost any new law, regulation or similar measure they perceive in any way burdensome. This results in a "regulatory chill",[42] i.e. states deciding not to adopt new rules for fear of costly arbitration claims.[43]

The controversial nature of international investment arbitration largely stems from its dealings both with private and public law matters. It is the latter aspect that triggers a variety of legitimacy related arguments against investment arbitration.[44] In this respect,

---

[42] It is not easy to say who coined the term. For example, *see* Julia G. Brown, *International Investment Agreements: Regulatory Chill in the Face of Litigious Heat?*, 3 Western Journal of Legal Studies 1-25 (2013); Stephan W. Schill, *Do Investment Treaties Chill Unilateral State Regulation to Mitigate Climate Change?*, 24 Journal of Int'l Arbitration 469–477 (2007); and Kyla Tienhaara, *Regulatory Chill and the Threat of Arbitration: A View from Political Science*, in Evolution in Investment Treaty Law and Arbitration 606 (Chester Brown & Kate Miles, eds., 2011).

[43] For further analysis of this problem *see* Howard Mann, *Reconceptualizing International Investment Law: Its Role in Sustainable Development*, 17 Lewis and Clark Law Review 527 (2013).

[44] One of these arguments takes issue with tribunals frequently omitting any serious explanation of the calculation and valuation of damages. *See* Joshua Simmons, *Valuation in Investor-State Arbitration: Toward A More Exact Science*, 30 Berkeley Journal of International Law 196, 214 (2012) ("Although investor-state decisions are moving toward better explanations of valuation, deficient discussions of specific calculations remain a common exception to the trend. The failure to explain calculations in detail is perhaps justified in rare cases in which investors claim relatively small amounts. In most cases, however, the failure to explain valuation adequately hints at a failure to address the issue methodically, thus exposing an award to greater skepticism"). One concrete illustration of this problem is the case of *Maritime International v. Guinea*, where the ICSID ad hoc committee annulled the previously issued arbitral award for the failure to state reasons in the calculation of damages. *See Maritime International Nominees Establishment v. Republic of Guinea*. ICSID Case No. ARB/84/4, Decision for Partial Annulment of the Arbitral Award, Jan. 6, 1988, at paras 6 and 109, https://www.italaw.com/sites/default/files/case-documents/italaw8608.pdf accessed on Aug. 1, 2018. For issues related to the rising cost of investment arbitration *see* Susan Franck, *Rationalizing Costs in Investment Treaty Arbitration*, 88 Washington University Law Review 769–852 (2011). For arguments related to the lack of proper balancing of interests in the current system of investment arbitration *see generally* Aaron Cosbey, *The Road to Hell? Investor Protections in NAFTA's Chapter 11, in* International Investment for Sustainable Development: Balancing Rights and Rewards 168 (Lyuba Zarsky ed., 2005) ("...[I]t is inappropriate that the balancing of public policy priorities such as health and safety, the environment and economic growth be conducted outside of government and with few of the procedural safeguards that help ensure legitimacy, transparency and accountability"); Stephan Schill, *Enhancing International Investment Law's Legitimacy: Conceptual and Methodological Foundations of a New Public Law Approach*, 52 Virginia Journal of International Law 57, 69 (2011) ("The system of international investment law...[is facing and will]... most likely continue to face demands for increased transparency, openness, predictability, and fair balance between investors' rights and public interests"); Susan Franck, *The Legitimacy Crisis in Investment Treaty Arbitration: Privatizing Public International Law through Inconsistent Decisions*, 73 Fordham Law Review 1521–1625 (2004–2005); Thomas Schultz and Cédric Dupont, *Investment Arbitration: Promoting the Rule of Law or Over-Empowering Investors? A Quantitative Empirical Study*, 25 European Journal of International Law 1147–1168 (2014). For criticism of arguments voiced against investment arbitration *see* Charles Brower and Stephan Schill, *Is Arbitration a Threat or a Boon to the Legitimacy of International Investment Law?* 9 Chicago Journal of International Law 471–498 (2008–2009); Irene Ten Cate, *The Costs of Consistency: Precedent in Investment Treaty Arbitration*, 51 Columbia Journal of Transnational Law 418–478 (2012–2013); Stanimir Alexandrov, *On the Perceived Inconsistency in Investor-State Jurisprudence, in* The Evolving International Investment Regime: Expectations, Realities,

addressing the negative outcomes of international arbitration for host states, Gus Van Harten rightfully observes that "....flaws in the system [are] a consequence of the unhappy marriage of international arbitration and public law".[45] This "unhappy marriage" has already resulted in "divorce" for some states, as they have taken the decision to leave ICSID.[46] In particular, Bolivia denounced ICSID in 2007,[47] Ecuador withdrew from ICSID in 2009,[48] and Venezuela did likewise in 2012.[49] Strong criticism of investor-state Dispute Settlement (ISDS) is also being made by developed states. For instance, after facing an investment arbitration claim by Philip Morris Company against its new tobacco packaging requirements,[50] Australia decided not to include investment arbitration as a means of dispute resolution in a number of its newer FTAs[51] and has even officially announced that it is against signing investment agreements that will limit its right to regulate in the public interest.[52]

OPTIONS 60–69 (José Alvarez et al. eds., 2011); Susan Franck, *Considering Recalibration of International Investment Agreements: Empirical Insights, in* THE EVOLVING INTERNATIONAL INVESTMENT REGIME: EXPECTATIONS, REALITIES, OPTIONS 73–94 (José Alvarez et al. eds., 2011).

45 GUS VAN HARTEN, INVESTMENT TREATY ARBITRATION AND PUBLIC LAW 153 (2008).

46 L. Yves Fortier, *Canadian Approach to Investment Protection: How Far We Have Come!, in* INTERNATIONAL INVESTMENT LAW FOR THE 21st CENTURY: ESSAYS IN HONOUR OF CHRISTOPH SCHREUER 543 (Christina Binder et al. eds, 2009) (discussing some States leaving ICSID); *See also* Ilija Mitrev Penusliski, *A Dispute Systems Design Diagnosis of ICSID, in* THE BACKLASH AGAINST INVESTMENT ARBITRATION: PERCEPTIONS AND REALITY 507, 520–526 (Michael Waibel et al. ed., 2010); Anne van Aaken, *The International Investment Protection Regime though the Lens of Economic Theory, in* THE BACKLASH AGAINST INVESTMENT ARBITRATION: PERCEPTIONS AND REALITY 550–551 (Michael Waibel et al. eds., 2010); Timothy Nelson, *"History Ain't Changed": Why Investor-State Arbitration Will Survive the "New Revolution", in* THE BACKLASH AGAINST INVESTMENT ARBITRATION: PERCEPTIONS AND REALITY 573–575 (Michael Waibel et al. eds., 2010) (noting several of South American countries' actions or threats regarding leaving the ICSID and analyzing their consequences); Susan Franck, *Development and Outcomes of Investment Treaty Arbitration*, 50 Harvard International Law Journal 435–489 (2009) (noting states that argued against the legitimacy of the investment arbitration system and analyzing the link between the development status of countries and arbitration).

47 Oscar Garibaldi, *On the Denunciation of the ICSID Convention, Consent to ICSID Jurisdiction, and the Limits of the Contract Analogy, in* INTERNATIONAL INVESTMENT LAW FOR THE 21ST CENTURY: ESSAYS IN HONOUR OF CHRISTOPH SCHREUER 252 (Christina Binder et al. eds, 2009).

48 Nicolle Kownacki, *Prospects for ICSID Arbitration in Post-Denunciation Countries: An Updated Approach*, 15 UCLA Journal of International Law and Foreign Affairs 529, 532 (2010).

49 Federico Lavopa et al., *How to Kill a BIT and Not Die Trying: Legal and Political Challenges of Denouncing or Renegotiating Bilateral Investment Treaties*, 16 Journal of International Economic Law 869, 871 (2013); For additional analysis of states' withdrawing from investment arbitration *see* Muthucumaraswamy Sornarajah, *The Retreat of Neo-Liberalism in Investment Treaty Arbitration, in* THE FUTURE OF INVESTMENT ARBITRATION 291–293 (Catherine Rogers and Roger Alford eds., 2009).

50 *Philip Morris Asia Limited v. The Commonwealth of Australia*. Permanent Court of Arbitration (PCA), Case No. 2012-12, Dec. 17, 2015, http://www.pcacases.com/web/sendAttach/1711 accessed on Aug. 19, 2018.

51 *Australia – United States of America Free Trade Agreement, May 18, 2004, http://investmentpolicyhub.unctad.org/Download/TreatyFile/2682 accessed on Aug. 3, 2018; Malaysia – Australia Free Trade Agreement, May 22, 2012, http://investmentpolicyhub.unctad.org/Download/TreatyFile/2634 accessed on Aug. 3, 2018.*

52 Australian Government, the Department of Foreign Affairs and Trade, Investor-State Dispute Settlement, http://dfat.gov.au/trade/topics/Pages/isds.aspx accessed on Aug. 3, 2018 ("The Australian Government is opposed to signing up to international agreements that would restrict Australia's capacity to govern in the public interest – including in areas such as public health, the environment or any other area of the

It is also important to note the EU's criticism of ISDS. In *Achmea v. Slovakia* (2018) the arbitral tribunal found Slovakia liable for violating the 1992 Agreement on Encouragement and Reciprocal Protection of Investments with the Kingdom of the Netherlands due to its reversal of the liberalization of the private sickness insurance market and ordered it to pay damages to the investor in the amount of approximately 22 million Euro.[53] Slovakia moved to set the award aside in Germany, and the Federal Court of Justice (Bundesgerichtshof) submitted a request to the European Court of Justice (CJEU) for a preliminary ruling under Article 267 TFEU regarding the compatibility of the arbitration clause in the BIT with EU law.[54] In response, the CJEU has ruled that EU law precludes "...a provision in an international agreement concluded between Member States, such as Article 8 of the Agreement on encouragement and reciprocal protection of investments between the Kingdom of the Netherlands and the Czech and Slovak Federative Republic, under which an investor from one of those Member States may, in the event of a dispute concerning investments in the other Member State, bring proceedings against the latter Member State before an arbitral tribunal whose jurisdiction that Member State has undertaken to accept".[55] The implication of the *Achmea* decision is that courts in the EU will be able to set aside arbitral awards rendered under intra-EU BITs, thereby reinforcing the EU's critical stance against the existing investor-state arbitration model.[56]

As can be seen, there is a rising backlash against ISDS. This backlash is understandable considering that the outcome of investment disputes may affect not only the business operations of a particular company but also livelihoods of entire communities, the work of governments, and national budgets.[57] One cannot but agree with Gottwald that "... even a single successful investor claim could wreak havoc on [a state's] economy, weaken its capacity to regulate in the public interest, and damage its reputation as a desirable investment location".[58] How should this growing criticism of international investment arbitration as a system for settlement of disputes be addressed? If the international investment arbitration system is to remain successful, it needs to be aligned with sustainable development goals!

---

economy"). For further analysis *see* Jürgen Kurtz, *Australia's Rejection of Investor-State Arbitration: Causation, Omission and Implication*, 27 ICSID Review – Foreign Investment Law Journal 65 (2012).

53 *Achmea B.V. v. The Slovak Republic*. Permanent Court of Arbitration (PCA), Case No. 2008-13, Dec. 7, 2012, at para 352, https://www.italaw.com/sites/default/files/case-documents/italaw3206.pdf accessed on Aug. 29, 2018.

54 *See* the Judgment in Case C-284/16 *Achmea*, ECLI:EU:C:2018:158.

55 The Judgment in Case C-284/16 *Achmea*, ECLI:EU:C:2018:158, at para 62.

56 For a critical review of the Achmea decision *see* Csongor István Nagy, *Intra-EU Bilateral Investment Treaties and EU Law After Achmea: "Know Well What Leads You Forward and What Holds You Back"*, 19 German Law Journal 981 (2018).

57 As noted by Moss, "[t]he community may be affected by the outcome of the dispute, for example where considerable payments have to be made from the public budget, or where regulatory measures or administrative practices have to be changed or adapted to accommodate an award." *See* Giuditta Cordero Moss, *Commercial Arbitration and Investment Arbitration: Fertile Soil for False Friends*? *in* International Investment Law for the 21st Century: Essays in Honour of Christoph Schreuer 793 (Christina Binder et al. eds, 2009).

58 Eric Gottwald, *Leveling the Playing Field: Is it Time for a Legal Assistance Center for Developing Nations in Investment Treaty Arbitration*? 22 American University International Law Review 237, 239 (2007).

II. Balancing Investor Protection *and* Advancement of Sustainable Development in Investment Arbitration as the Way Forward

As the world is approaching the end of the second decade of the 21st century, there is an increasing recognition of the need for a modern legal framework of investment that provides not only for the protection of investors' rights but also properly addresses the investments' wider social, economic, and environmental effects.[59] Historically the emphasis of investment law was placed primarily on investment protection.[60] However, such an asymmetrical treatment of foreign direct investment (FDI) is slowly but steadily giving way to a new generation legal framework of FDI, the objective of which is not only to promote and protect investment but also to advance host states' sustainable economic, social and environmental development.[61] According to the 2015 UNCTAD Investment

---

[59] *See generally* Marie-Claire Cordonier Segger and Avidan Kent, *Promoting Sustainable Investment through International Law, in* Sustainable Development in World Investment Law 774 (Marie-Claire Cordonier Segger et al. eds., 2011) ("Instead of regarding international investment law as an isolated regime, an integrated approach should be adopted, one that will require the promotion of sustainable development law and principles through the legal framework of international investment law. The only way in which the two may co-exist and support each other is through reconciliation, beginning with recognition of the stake that each regime has in the other").

[60] Most international investment agreements signed and ratified in the 20th century and early 2000s provide only for investors' rights, failing to specify their obligations, and contain very broad investment protection standards, such as indirect expropriation, the fair and equitable treatment standard, full protection and security, and others. For analysis of the predominantly one-sided nature of these agreements *see generally* Muthucumaraswamy Sornarajah, *A Law for Need or a Law for Greed?: Restoring the Lost Law in the International Law of Foreign Investment*, 6 International Environmental Agreements 329, 331 (2006) ("International investment law is …the law of greed simply because of the fact that it is built on accentuating only one side of the picture of foreign investment so as to benefit the interests of multinational corporations which exist to seek profits for their shareholders"); Mehmet Toral and Thomas Schultz, *The State, a Perpetual Respondent in Investment Arbitration? Some Unorthodox Considerations, in* The Backlash Against Investment Arbitration: Perceptions and Reality 588 (Michael Waibel et al. eds., 2010) ("…IIAs seem to fail to impose clear obligations on investors that would allow dispute settlement bodies to adequately address the issues raised in areas such as human rights and sustainable development"); Tarcisio Gazzini, *Bilateral Investment Treaties, in* International Investment Law: The Sources of Rights and Obligations 107 (Eric De Brabandere et al. eds., 2012); Helene Bubrowski, *Balancing IIA Arbitration through the Use of Counterclaims*, Improving International Investment Agreements 216 (Armand de Mestral et al. eds., 2013); Jan Wouters et al., *International Investment Law: The Perpetual Search for Consensus, in* Foreign Direct Investment and Human Development: The Law and Economics of International Investment Agreements 48 (Olivier De Schutter, et al. eds., 2013); Genevieve Fox, *A Future for International Investment? Modifying BITs to Drive Economic Development*, 46 Georgetown Journal of International Law 229, 232–236 (2014).

[61] *See generally* UNCTAD, World Investment Report on "Towards A New Generation of Investment Policies" (United Nations, 2012), http://unctad.org/en/PublicationsLibrary/wir2012_embargoed_en.pdf accessed on Aug. 1, 2018; *Columbia Center on Sustainable Investment and the World Association of Investment Promotion Agencies*, Report of the Findings of the Survey on Foreign Direct Investment and Sustainable Development 4 (2010), http://ccsi.columbia.edu/files/2013/12/fdi.pdf accessed on Aug. 3, 2018. The most widely accepted definition of the term "sustainable development" is the one provided in the Brundtland Report: "Sustainable development is development that meets the needs of the present without compromising the ability of future generations to meet their own needs". *See* Report of the World Commission on Environment and Development on "Our Common Future", U.N. G.A. Res. A/43/427, Aug. 4, 1987, at 54, www.un-documents.net/wced-ocf.htm accessed on Aug. 3, 2018.

Law Policy Framework for Sustainable Development, "... 'new generation' investment policies place inclusive growth and sustainable development at the heart of efforts to attract and benefit from investment".[62] Similarly, the Report on "Investment Promotion Agencies and Sustainable FDI: Moving toward the Fourth Generation of Investment Promotion" emphasizes the current move to the promotion of not simply any kind of FDI, but *sustainable* FDI.[63] The underlying idea is to ensure a proper balance between the protection of investors' rights and those of other relevant stakeholders. Efforts at reforming the legal framework of FDI in line with this paradigm shift in investment law are still fragmented. However, it is clear that sustainable development has emerged as the foundation of this new generation legal regime of FDI. Accordingly, investment law reforms must be aligned with goals broadly associated with sustainable development. Failure to achieve this paradigm shift may destroy ISDS as we know it. How is it possible to align international investment arbitration with sustainability objectives? The sections below advance both substantive and procedural solutions.

a) New Generation International Investment Agreements (IIAs)

One obvious way to address the balance between investor protection and sustainable development is the negotiation and implementation of new generation investment treaties and the re-negotiation of old generation treaties in line with sustainable development goals. This is important, as it is the language of these treaties that ultimately shapes the outcome of arbitral proceedings. In this regard, Brigitte Stern, currently one of the most frequently appointed arbitrators by respondents in investor-state arbitration proceedings,[64] is correct when noting that "...if states do not include provisions [advancing sustainable development]...in their investment treaties..., arbitration can only play a very marginal, or even non-existent role, in making investments foster sustainable development".[65] Indeed, arbitrators have to apply existing rules. If these rules provide

[62] UNCTAD, Investment Policy Framework for Sustainable Development (United Nations, 2015), at 3, http://investmentpolicyhub.unctad.org/Upload/Documents/INVESTMENT%20POLICY%20FRAMEWORK%20 2015%20WEB_VERSION.pdf accessed on Aug. 4, 2018; *See also* UNCTAD, World Investment Report on "Towards A New Generation of Investment Policies" 14 (United Nations, 2012), http://unctad.org/en/PublicationsLibrary/wir2012_ embargoed_en.pdf accessed on Aug. 1, 2018. The Organisation for Economic Co-operation and Development (OECD) has also placed sustainable development at the forefront of its analysis of investment. In its key recent work on investment, the OECD states that "...[s]ustainability and responsible investment are integral parts of a good investment climate and should be factored in from the beginning and not as an after-thought". *See* OECD, Policy Framework for Investment 18 (OECD, 2015), http://www.oecdilibrary.org/docserver/download/2014041e. pdf?expires=1459242455&id=id&accname=guest&checksum=E28BFF7350ED92EB93C8124B79A8B987 accessed on Aug. 1, 2018; *See also OECD*, Guidelines for Multinational Enterprises, 2011, http://www.oecd.org/ daf/inv/mne/48004323.pdf accessed on Aug. 5, 2018.

[63] *Columbia Center on Sustainable Investment and the World Association of Investment Promotion Agencies*, Report of the Findings of the Survey on Foreign Direct Investment and Sustainable Development, 2010, at 4, http://ccsi. columbia.edu/files/2013/12/fdi.pdf accessed on Aug. 3, 2018.

[64] UNCTAD, Information on Arbitrator Appointment, 2018, http://investmentpolicyhub.unctad.org/ISDS/FilterByArbitrators accessed on Aug. 1, 2018.

[65] Brigitte Stern, *The Future of International Investment Law: A Balance between the Protection of Investors and*

for, or at least allow, a balance between the protection of investors' rights and those of other stakeholders, then such balanced considerations will be reflected in arbitral tribunal awards.

Older investment treaties are increasingly being criticized for being one-sided, since they provide investors with many protection standards but generally fail to stipulate investor obligations towards host states.[66] This concern is valid as most of the investment treaties in force today do not have provisions that would help protect the environment or stimulate sustainable social and economic development. Apart from that, vague and unqualified investment protection standards, such as the fair and equitable treatment standard,[67] the indirect expropriation standard, and similar open-ended standards shaped in a different investment age, have been challenged for their ability to "... impede, discourage, or even prohibit government measures to ensure the sustainable development".[68] Indeed, while old generation investment treaties do accord protection

---

the States' Capacity to Regulate, in The Evolving International Investment Regime: Expectations, Realities, Options 175 (José Alvarez et al. eds., 2011). In a contrarian view, the constraints of existing treaties are largely dismissed because the Vienna Convention on the Law of Treaties supposedly allows a new interpretation of the vague language often found in BITs and MIAs. *See* Katharina Berner, *Reconciling Investment Protection and Sustainable Development: A Plea for an Interpretative U-Turn*, in Shifting Paradigms in International Investment Law – More Balanced, Less Isolated, Increasingly Diversified (Steffen Hindelang & Markus Krajewski eds., 2016), 177–203. Unfortunately, the present authors are not so optimistic about the interpretative potential of the old generation agreements.

66 In particular, Taillant and Bonnitcha have voiced criticism with respect to the one-sided nature of BITs in the following way: "BITs do not place obligations on foreign investors nor do they set out the rights of stakeholders. BITs focus exclusively on the protection of the interests of foreign investors. Again, third party stakeholders, particularly vulnerable groups whose human rights could be violated by circumstances deriving from upholding BITs, while they may have an important stake in the outcomes of the execution of activities covered by a BIT, are left to fend for themselves if their rights are violated as a consequence". *See* Jorge Daniel Taillant and Jonathan Bonnitcha, *International Investment Law and Human Rights, in* Sustainable Development in World Investment Law 65 (Marie-Claire Cordonier Segger et al. eds., 2011). For criticisms of existing investment agreements *see also* Louis Wells, *Preface, in* The Evolving International Investment Regime: Expectations, Realities, Options xix (José Alvarez et al. eds., 2011) ("To be completely accepted by developing countries...an investment regime should also impose behavioral rules on foreign investors"); Tarcisio Gazzini, *Bilateral Investment Treaties, in* International Investment Law: The Sources of Rights and Obligations 107 (Eric De Brabandere et al. eds., 2012) ("[T]he manifestly asymmetrical nature of...[bilateral investment treaties]... with all obligations incumbent upon the host state and virtually all rights granted to the foreign investor, has often been criticized"); Helene Bubrowski, *Balancing IIA Arbitration through the Use of Counterclaims*, Improving International Investment Agreements 216 (Armand de Mestral et al., eds., 2013) ("...IIAs are asymmetrical," as they "produce obligations for host states and corresponding rights for investors"); Andrew Newcombe and Marie-Claire Cordonier Segger, *An Integrated Agenda for Sustainable Development in International Investment Law, in* Sustainable Development in World Investment Law 113 (Marie-Claire Cordonier Segger et al. eds., 2011); Howard Mann, *Civil Society Perspectives: What Do Key Stakeholders Expect from the International Investment Regime? in* The Evolving International Investment Regime: Expectations, Realities, Options 27 (José Alvarez et al. eds., 2011).

67 For discussion *see* Roland Kläger, *Revising Treatment Standards – Fair and Equitable Treatment in Light of Sustainable Development*, in Shifting Paradigms in International Investment Law – More Balanced, Less Isolated, Increasingly Diversified (Steffen Hindelang & Markus Krajewski eds., 2016), 65–80.

68 Andrew Newcombe and Marie-Claire Cordonier Segger, *An Integrated Agenda for Sustainable Development in International Investment Law, in* Sustainable Development in World Investment Law 103 (Marie-Claire Cordonier Segger et al. eds., 2011). *See also* Anthony VanDuzer et al., Integrating Sustainable Development into International

to investors, they do not properly consider the interests of other relevant stakeholders. In this regard, one cannot but agree with Taillant and Bonnitcha that this problem "...is largely due to the fact that...international investment law evolved as a specialized regime (with specialized actors) primarily concerned with protecting foreign investment from unfair interference by host states in unstable economies" and, therefore, "[t]he public interest in terms of the social, environmental, or economic negative externalities of large foreign investments, was simply not part of the objectives pursued in the evolution of... [the] investment legal framework".[69] This observation is accurate. Investment treaties were created to protect investors from nationalization and other risks in developing states. That was traditionally the main goal and, indeed, often the only goal.

It has been shown that the very structure of international investment law that seemed appealing in the 1980s and 90s is no longer fully answering the call of modern times in terms of advancement of sustainable development, with due regard being given to the rights of all relevant stakeholders. Indeed, many states have started reconsidering their investment agreements to ensure that they reflect their interests both as capital-exporting and capital-importing states.[70] A leading example in this regard is the case of the United States of America. The USA's Model BIT of 1984 was pro-investor.[71] Alvarez stated that it was "...the most investor-protective in the world," utilizing "...every lawyerly device imaginable to achieve a single unitary object and purpose: to protect the foreign investor".[72] The obvious thinking was that the investor would most likely be an American entity, whilst the host state would most likely be a developing nation, rather than the other way around. Although the direction of the investment flows covered by U.S. BITs has not really changed in recent years,[73] the United States revised its Model BIT in 2004 and

---

Investment Agreements: A Guide for Developing Country Negotiators (2013); Markus Gehring and Avidan Kent, *Sustainable Development and IIAs: from Objective to Practice, in* Improving International Investment Agreements 302 (Armand de Mestral and Céline Lévesque eds., 2013); Graham Mayeda, *Sustainable International Investment Agreements: Challenges and Solutions for Developing Countries, in* Sustainable Development in World Investment Law 542 (Marie-Claire Cordonier Segger et al. eds., 2011).

[69] Jorge Daniel Taillant and Jonathan Bonnitcha, *International Investment Law and Human Rights, in* Sustainable Development in World Investment Law 59 (Marie-Claire Cordonier Segger et al. eds., 2011). *See also* Mahnaz Malik, *The IISD Model International Agreement on Investment for Sustainable Development, in* Sustainable Development in World Investment Law 565 (Marie-Claire Cordonier Segger et al. eds., 2011) ("The international investment law regime, with few exceptions, has been solely focused on the legal aspects of facilitating cross-border investment flows and protecting foreign investors").

[70] Karl Sauvant and José Alvarez, *International Investment Law in Transition, in* The Evolving International Investment Regime: Expectations, Realities, Options xxxix-xli (*José Alvarez* et al eds., 2011); *See also* Rainer Geiger, *Multilateral Approaches to Investment: The Way Forward, in* The Evolving International Investment Regime: Expectations, Realities, Options 155 (*José Alvarez* et al eds., 2011) (Geiger notes that when developed countries were capital-exporting, they "...were setting rules that were incorporated into bilateral investment treaties, and as a result strong and almost unqualified investment protection backed by investor-state arbitration was predominant". However, this has changed, as the "...same countries today follow a more cautious approach, as they have become hosts of foreign investment").

[71] U.S. Model Treaty Concerning the Reciprocal Encouragement and Protection of Investment, Feb. 24, 1984, http://scholarship.law.berkeley.edu/cgi/viewcontent.cgi?article=1042&context=bjil accessed on Aug. 3, 2018.

[72] José Alvarez, *The Return of the State*, 20 Minnesota Journal of International Law 223, 231 (2011).

[73] U.S. BITs are in force mainly with developing nations, such as Azerbaijan, Cameroon, Congo, Ecuador,

again in 2012.[74] The most recent iteration, in particular, provides clear mandates for the host state authorities to pursue environmental goals (Article 12),[75] as well as protection of labor rights (Article 13).[76] By contrast, as recently as 2008, Germany published an updated Model BIT that is a classic old generation treaty and refers only to investor rights and not at all to any other stakeholders or public interest concerns.[77]

However, before calling the Germans backward and praising the U.S. for its more progressive approach, the application of the treaties in practice has to be examined as well. Indeed, out of 40 BITs currently in force for the U.S., 38 are based on the old generation model of 1984, and 2 have some modest mention of environmental and labor rights as per the 2004 revision, while not a single BIT has so far been concluded that follows the most progressive standards adopted in the 2012 Model BIT.[78] This nicely illustrates the problem – hundreds of BITs negotiated by dozens of countries over decades are largely in place for the relationships, where investment flows are significant and protection is potentially needed. They will not easily and quickly be replaced with more modern versions, since it always takes (at least) two to tango.[79]

A faster route to getting investments covered by more progressive treaties would seem to be the multilateral approach. Instead of having to negotiate or re-negotiate a multitude of bilateral treaties, a single multilateral treaty could potentially cover an entire phalanx of bilateral relations. An example of this approach would be the 2009 ASEAN Comprehensive Investment Agreement.[80] Unfortunately, the ASEAN Agreement does not contain such clear language as found in the 2012 U.S. Model BIT. However, it does

---

Egypt, Honduras, Kazakhstan, Kyrgyzstan, Moldova, Mongolia, Mozambique, Rwanda, Senegal, Sri Lanka, Tunisia, Turkey, and Ukraine. For a full list of countries *see*: https://tcc.export.gov/Trade_Agreements/Bilateral_Investment_Treaties/index.asp.

[74] U.S. Model Treaty Concerning the Encouragement and Reciprocal Protection of Investment, 2004, http://www.state.gov/documents/organization/117601.pdf accessed on Aug. 3, 2018; U.S. Model Treaty Concerning the Encouragement and Reciprocal Protection of Investment, 2012, https://ustr.gov/sites/default/files/BIT%20text%20for%20ACIEP%20Meeting.pdf accessed on Aug. 3, 2018. The 2012 Model BIT is also available in World Trade and Investment Law – Documents 113 (Frank Emmert ed., 2018).

[75] Article 12(5) provides that "[n]othing in this Treaty shall be construed to prevent a Party from adopting, maintaining, or enforcing any measure otherwise consistent with this Treaty that it considers appropriate to ensure that investment activity in its territory is undertaken in a manner sensitive to environmental concerns".

[76] A clear legacy of the Obama years, this article refers to obligations under ILO Conventions and the ILO Declaration on Fundamental Principles and Rights at Work. Unsurprisingly, the 2012 Model BIT has so far not been used with any of the U.S.'s trading partners.

[77] *See* http://investmentpolicyhub.unctad.org/Download/TreatyFile/2865. *See also* World Trade and Investment Law – Documents 94 (Frank Emmert ed., 2018).

[78] U.S. Department of State, United States Bilateral Investment Treaties, https://www.state.gov/e/eb/ifd/bit/117402.htm accessed on Aug. 29, 2018.

[79] For discussion *see* Karsten Nowrot, *Termination and Renegotiation of International Investment Agreements*, in Shifting Paradigms in International Investment Law – More Balanced, Less Isolated, Increasingly Diversified (Steffen Hindelang & Markus Krajewski eds., 2016), 227–265.

[80] *See* Asean Comprehensive Investment Agreement, http://www.asean.org/storage/images/2013/economic/aia/ACIA_Final_Text_26%20Feb%202009.pdf accessed on Aug. 29, 2018. *See also* World Trade and Investment Law – Documents 495 (Frank Emmert ed., 2018).

contain an almost verbatim reproduction of Article XX of the GATT 1947. Thus, Article 17 of the ASEAN Agreement, entitled "General Exceptions", provides that

> *"[s]ubject to the requirement that such measures are not applied in a manner which would constitute a means of arbitrary or unjustifiable discrimination between Member States or their investors where like conditions prevail, or a disguised restriction on investors of any other Member State and their investments, nothing in this Agreement shall be construed to prevent the adoption or enforcement by any Member State of measures: (a) necessary to protect public morals or to maintain public order; (b) necessary to protect human, animal or plant life or health; (c) necessary to secure compliance with laws or regulations which are not inconsistent with this Agreement, including those relating to: (i) the prevention of deceptive and fraudulent practices to deal with the effects of a default on a contract; (ii) the protection of the privacy of individuals in relation to the processing and dissemination of personal data and the protection of confidentiality of individual records and accounts; (iii) safety; (d) aimed at ensuring the equitable or effective imposition or collection of direct taxes in respect of investments or investors of any Member State; (e) imposed for the protection of national treasures of artistic, historic or archaeological value; (f) relating to the conservation of exhaustible natural resources if such measures are made effective in conjunction with restrictions on domestic production or consumption".*[81]

The present authors do not have insider information with respect to whether considerations of sustainable development and other public interest concerns were actively discussed in the negotiations that led to the ASEAN Agreement and the heavy reliance on the GATT provision was the ultimate acceptable compromise, or whether the inclusion of the GATT provision with minimal editing was the result of a lazy drafter looking for a suitable model at a time when the 2012 U.S. Model BIT was not yet available. Be that as it may, it will be exciting to watch whether and to what extent arbitration tribunals called to apply the ASEAN Agreement will look for inspiration in the case law of the GATT and WTO.

The ultimate horror scenario arguing against reliance on multilateralism in this regard, however, is the effort by the OECD to come up with a Multilateral Agreement on Investment, commonly referred to as "the MAI". After efforts extending over half a century, the 1998 Draft is potentially more comprehensive than any other and is also more ambitious with regard to scope and coverage. However, it is also riddled with disagreement and alternative proposals, making it virtually certain that a final and widely acceptable draft will never see the light of day.[82]

---

[81] With regard to the "public order", the Article contains an official note to clarify that the provision "may be invoked by a Member State only where a genuine and sufficiently serious threat is posed to one of the fundamental interests of society".

[82] The text is available at http://www1.oecd.org/daf/mai/pdf/ng/ng987r1e.pdf. *See also* World Trade and Investment Law – Documents 161 (Frank Emmert ed., 2018). For commentary *see*, inter alia, Lance Compa,

If 34 of the most developed nations in the world, under the umbrella of the OECD, cannot agree upon a multilateral investment treaty, although they should have many interests in common, it is not surprising that the only multilateral treaty currently in force that is not a regional treaty, is anything but ambitious. The WTO Agreement on Trade-Related Investment Measures (TRIMs) can be neatly reproduced on three pages[83] and mostly refers back to the GATT, in particular with regard to exceptions. Indeed, Article 3 of the TRIMs Agreement states that "[a]ll exceptions under GATT 1994 shall apply, as appropriate, to the provisions of this Agreement". This is nothing but a circumlocutory reference to Article XX of the GATT 1947. It can only be speculated whether this was the only acceptable compromise for the states negotiating in the Uruguay Round, or whether the drafters of the TRIMs were even lazier than the drafters of the ASEAN Agreement. Nevertheless, the provision is there, and 164 countries around the world are bound by it!

In concluding our observations on the propagation of sustainable development goals and other public interest topics via the negotiation of new generation or re-negotiation of old generation investment treaties, we may say that any progress in this direction will be "...a strong and slow boring of hard boards" as Max Weber observed for politics more generally.

If new and better treaties remain *de lege ferenda* and will not be available any time soon, however, this makes it more urgent to be more creative in using the existing treaty provisions. To this end, some innovative proposals that may be achievable *de lege lata* will be discussed.

b) Public Interest Attorneys

One of the key problems, whilst seeking a better representation of sustainable development goals in ISDS, is the lack of a good advocate for the laudable cause. A good solution could be the involvement of a public interest attorney to represent sustainable development goals in general, even if the investor does not bring them up for lack of interest, and the host state does not bring them up because they do not know how to or otherwise choose not to. The model of the "Advocate General" who is an independent member of the European Court of Justice and represents *the European interest* in cases

---

The Multilateral Agreement on Investment and International Labor Rights: A Failed Connection, 31 Cornell International Law Journal 683 (1998); Riyaz Dattu, *A Journey from Havana to Paris: The Fifty-Year Quest for the Elusive Multilateral Agreement on Investment*, 24 Fordham International Law Journal 275 (2000–2001); Peter T. Muchlinski, *The Rise and Fall of the Multilateral Agreement on Investment: Where Now?*, 34 International Law Journal 1033 (2000); Daniel Egan, *The Limits of Internationalization: a Neo-Gramscian Analysis of the Multilateral Agreement on Investment*, 27(3) Critical Sociology 74 (2001); Katia Tieleman, *The Failure of the Multilateral Agreement on Investment (MAI) and the Absence of a Global Public Policy Network*, UN Vision Project on Global Public Policy Networks, available at http://citeseerx.ist.psu.edu/viewdoc/download?doi=10.1.1.627.7992&rep=rep1&type=pdf. *See also* Stephen Young and Ana Teresa Tavares, *Multilateral Rules on FDI: Do We Need Them? Will We Get Them? A Developing Country Perspective*, 13(1) Transnational Corporations, (April 2004).

[83] *See* https://www.wto.org/english/docs_e/legal_e/18-trims_e.htm. *See also* FRANK EMMERT (ED.), WORLD TRADE AND INVESTMENT LAW – DOCUMENTS (2018), at 607.

before the CJEU and makes recommendations for the judges how a case should be decided, has proven extremely successful.[84] The Advocate General is able to consider the impact of a particular case on a broader scale, removed from the self-interest of the parties and the more narrow considerations that may inform the judges. His or her recommendations address not only the arguments advanced by the parties but also other arguments that could or should be taken into account to get the best possible outcome from a broader perspective of European integration, all Member States, and all peoples of the EU. In many cases, the Opinions of the Advocate General make for more interesting reading than the judgments adopted later. Indeed, the CJEU follows the recommendations of its Advocate Generals in more than 80% of its decisions.[85]

The problem is, of course, that investors are quite happy with the way things are in ISDS and have no reason to agree to the involvement of a public interest attorney unless such an involvement is mandated by a new generation investment treaty. Thus, it is highly unlikely that a systematic involvement of independent voices for the advancement of sustainable development in front of investment arbitration tribunals will be seen any time soon.

However, this does not have to be the death sentence to the idea. First, if an investment treaty provides any language in support of balancing investor rights with state and public interest considerations, arbitral tribunals could appoint experts to analyze the public interest dimension of a dispute.[86] Even if arbitrators should shy away from taking such an approach for fear of not being appointed in future cases, there is no reason why the respondent state could not bring in the expert as a party appointed expert or even as a member of the legal team. In particular, if the respondent is a developing country, often, the government does not have highly qualified lawyers to represent it in arbitration.[87] Some countries have, therefore, outsourced the work and brought in expensive representation from well-known international law firms. However, it is by no means clear that money spent on this kind of counsel is well spent because from the perspective of the law firm, there is little incentive to work beyond the call of duty. Old generation investment treaties seem to favor the investor, the law firm cashes in regardless of outcome, and the respondent state is unlikely to become a repeat customer. Creative arguments, for example that the exceptions based on Article XX of the GATT should be taken into consideration even if they are not mentioned in the BIT because both parties to it are also Contracting Parties of the WTO and bound by the TRIMs Agreement, are rarely seen in these kinds of cases. This does not have to be the

---

[84] For discussion of the CJEU *see*, inter alia, Noreen Burrows & Rosa Greaves, The Advocate General and EC Law (2007); for more general considerations about public interest advocates at court *see* Cyril Ritter, *A New Look at the Role and Impact of Advocates-General – Collectively and Individually*, 12 Colum. J. Eur. L. 751 (2005–2006).

[85] For further analysis *see also Frank Emmert*, Der Europäische Gerichtshof als Garant der Rechtsgemeinschaft (1998), https://www.researchgate.net/publication/259848618_Der_Europaische_Gerichtshof_als_Garant_der_Rechtsgemeinschaft accessed on Aug. 28, 2018.

[86] This option is specifically provided by Article 32 of the 2012 U.S. Model BIT.

[87] The authors have seen this in their own practical experience, although other factors play an important role in the apparent bias of investor-state arbitration procedures against less developed host states. For comprehensive analysis *see* Daniel Behn, Tarald Laudal Berge & Malcolm Langford, *Poor States or Poor Governance? Explaining Outcomes in Investment Treaty Arbitration*, 38 Nw. J. Int'l L. & Bus. (2018), 333–389.

case, and there are certainly experts available in academia and NGOs that would make more passionate and unconventional arguments to try to tip the scale toward a better representation of sustainable development goals.

c) Amicus Submissions

The 2012 U.S. Model BIT provides in Article 28(2) that "[a] non-disputing Party may make oral and written submissions to the tribunal regarding the interpretation of this Treaty". Thus, in a dispute between an investor and a host country, the home country of the investor would be entitled to make submissions as well, if a BIT based on the 2012 Model were in force.[88] Unfortunately, it is not very likely that the home country of the investor would take "the other side" and advocate for a limitation of the investor's rights and an expansion of public interest considerations in the host country.

More interesting in this regard may be the provision in Article 28(3) of the same 2012 U.S. Model BIT pursuant to which "[t]he tribunal shall have the authority to accept and consider amicus curiae submissions *from a person or entity that is not a disputing party*" (emphasis added). The U.S. did not invent this rule, however. It is taken almost verbatim from the ICSID Rules of Procedure for Arbitration Proceedings after their 2006 amendment. The big difference is that under the ICSID Rules, the tribunal has the authority only "[a]fter consulting both parties" and if certain conditions are met, including "a significant interest" of the non-disputing party in the proceeding.[89] An example, where the conditions were met is *AES Summit v. Hungary* (2010).[90] The investor claimed that the introduction of certain price control measures in the Hungarian electricity market violated their rights protected by the Energy Charter. The EU Commission requested and, after consultation of the parties, was allowed to file limited observations regarding the application of EU competition or antitrust law. However, for lack of agreement by the parties, the EU Commission did not get access to the written submissions of the parties.[91] Happ observes that there is an inherent conflict in Rule 37 of the ICSID Rules.[92] On the one hand, Rule 37(2)(a) requires that "...the non-disputing party submission would assist the Tribunal in the determination of a factual or legal issue related to the

---

[88] As we have outlined above, so far the U.S. has not actually entered into BITs based on the 2012 Model. However, this may still happen in future. Other countries could also craft BITs of their own and include similar language.

[89] *See* Rule 37(2) of the ICSID Rules of Procedure for Arbitration Proceedings. For discussion *see* Filip Balcerzak, *Amicus Curiae Submissions in Investor – State Arbitrations*, 12 Common Law Review 66 (2012); as well as Eugenia Levine, *Amicus Curiae in International Investment Arbitration: The Implications of an Increase in Third-Party Participation*, 29 Berkeley Journal of International Law 200 (2011); and A. Saravanan & S.R. Subramanian, *The Participation of Amicus Curiae in Investment Treaty Arbitration*, 5 Journal of Civil and Legal Sciences 21 (2016).

[90] *AES Summit Generation Limited and AES-Tisza Erömü Kft. v. Republic of Hungary (II)*. ICSID Case No. ARB/07/22, Sep. 23, 2010, http://investmentpolicyhub.unctad.org/ISDS/Details/279 accessed on Aug. 29, 2018.

[91] *AES Summit Generation Limited v. Hungary*, at para 3.22.

[92] *See* Richard Happ, *ICSID Rules*, *in* Institutional Arbitration Article-by-Article Commentary on ... ICSID ... 923–1005, at para 206 (Rolf A. Schütze (ed.) 2013).

proceeding by bringing a perspective, particular knowledge or insight that is *different* from that of the disputing parties" (emphasis added). On the other hand, unless the disputing parties give broad consent, the non-disputing party will have very limited rights and even more limited access. But how are the *amici* supposed to know what they might be able to add beyond what is already presented to the tribunal by the disputing parties, if they do not have access to the files?

An even more pertinent example may be *von Pezold and others v. Zimbabwe* (2015).[93] The investors were various owners of tobacco, tea and coffee farms that were expropriated in the course of land reforms undertaken by the Zimbabwean government. The European Center for Constitution and Human Rights, as well as four indigenous communities of Zimbabweans applied for leave to participate as *amici curiae* on behalf of the host state. However, since the investors objected, the tribunal denied the request,[94] although it seems clear that the petitioners had a genuine interest in the matter, since they were the beneficiaries of the land reforms. The argument made by the tribunal is quite striking, namely that "the circumstances of the petition gave rise to legitimate doubts as to *the independence and neutrality* of the Petitioners" (emphasis added). Therefore, supposedly, the applicants did not meet the criteria of the ICSID Rules for third party participants.[95] It is not clear, where in the Rules the tribunal would locate a requirement that *amici* need to be independent and neutral. In light of the fact that Rule 37(2)(c) requires, *expressis verbis*, that the non-disputing party must have "a significant interest in the proceeding", the opposite would seem to be the case.

What these examples show, unfortunately, is ambiguity inside the ICSID Rules which leads, once again, to unpredictable outcomes. The authors are not aware whether the drafters of the 2012 U.S. Model BIT dropped the conditions for participation of *amici* for these very reasons to ensure a better integration of sustainable development and other public policy considerations in the future, or whether it is just a fortuitous coincidence. One can only hope that the 2012 U.S. Model does not remain merely a Model much longer. Until then, however, the parties to a dispute may have to bring their *amici* on the official ticket.

d) A Multilateral Investment Court

As traditional ISDS is facing mounting criticism, another procedural solution advanced by commentators is the call for the establishment of an international investment court.[96] For

---

[93] *Bernhard von Pezold and others v. Republic of Zimbabwe*. ICSID Case No. ARB/10/15, July 28, 2015, http://investmentpolicyhub.unctad.org/ISDS/Details/376 accessed on Aug. 29, 2018.

[94] *Bernhard von Pezold v. Zimbabwe*, at paras 36–38.

[95] *Bernhard von Pezold v. Zimbabwe*, at para 38.

[96] For a comprehensive analysis of this issue *see* Rob House, *Designing a Multilateral Investment Court: Issues and Options, in* Yearbook of European Law, Volume 36 209–236 (Albertina Albors-Llorens et al., eds, 2017). *See also* David Howard, *Creating Consistency through a World Investment Court,* 41 Fordham International Law Journal 1 3–52 (2017); Louis Wells, *Backlash to Investment Arbitration: Three Causes, in* The Backlash against Investment Arbitration: Perceptions and Reality 349 (Michael Waibel et al. ed., 2010); Ilija Mitrev Penusliski, *A Dispute Systems Design Diagnosis of ICSID, in* The Backlash against Investment Arbitration: Perceptions and Reality

example, Asif Qureshi calls for a "...Supreme Investment Court ... [to be]...set up as such, or as part of a chamber in the ICJ..."[97] in order to "...contribute to greater transparency, accountability, and legitimacy in the adjudicative process; deal with the asymmetry in the manner in which different types of investment are currently dealt with; and provide certain safeguards".[98] Similarly, Gus Van Harten states that "...the lack of an appellate body to review awards makes it difficult, if not impossible, to unify the jurisprudence into a stable system of state liability".[99] Therefore, he proposes "...an international court with comprehensive jurisdiction over the adjudication of investor claims".[100] These ideas for reforming the current system of international investment arbitration may be good to implement in order to advance greater consistency in the arbitral process. The problem is, as before, that the ideas need to be implemented via treaties and those have to be drafted, negotiated, supported and ratified by home states *and* host states, and preferably many of them.

The biggest proponent of the idea of an investment court system has been the EU. Already in 2015, the EU Commission proposed providing for a permanent investment court in all of the EU's investment agreements.[101] The idea behind this has been the need to create an independent, predictable, comprehensive, cost-effective, and transparent dispute resolution system, with a permanent institution authorized to hear investment claims instead of having only arbitration tribunals set up on a case-by-case basis.[102] As a result, a number of the EU's investment agreements already provide for an investment court. For example, the EU-Singapore Investment Protection Agreement establishes a tribunal of first instance and an appeal tribunal.[103] The tribunal consists of two members nominated by the EU, two members nominated by Singapore, and two members jointly nominated by the EU and Singapore who are not to be nationals of any Member State of the EU or Singapore.[104] It is interesting to note that the Parties have indicated knowledge or experience in public international law as one of the key criteria for appointment, along with having qualifications similar to those required to become a judge in the respective

---

529–531 (Michael Waibel et al. ed., 2010); Debra Steger, *Enhancing the Legitimacy of International Investment Law by Establishing an Appellate Mechanism, in* IMPROVING INTERNATIONAL INVESTMENT AGREEMENTS 247–264 (Armand de Mestral et al. eds., 2013); For criticism of the idea of a multilateral investment court *see* Charles Brower and Jawad Ahmad, *From the Two-Headed Nightingale to the Fifteen-Headed Hydra: The Many Follies of the Proposed International Investment Court*, 41 Fordham International Law Journal 791, 792–820 (2018).

[97] Asif Qureshi, *An Appellate System? in* THE OXFORD HANDBOOK OF INTERNATIONAL INVESTMENT LAW 1165 (Christoph Schreuer et al. eds., 2008).

[98] *Id.* at 1167.

[99] GUS VAN HARTEN, INVESTMENT TREATY ARBITRATION AND PUBLIC LAW 152 (2008).

[100] *Id.* at 180.

[101] EU Commission, A MULTILATERAL INVESTMENT COURT, http://trade.ec.europa.eu/doclib/docs/2017/september/tradoc_156042.pdf accessed on Aug. 29, 2018.

[102] *Id.*

[103] EU-Singapore Investment Protection Agreement, Ch.3, http://trade.ec.europa.eu/doclib/docs/2018/april/tradoc_156731.pdf accessed on Aug. 23, 2018, Ch.3, Article 3.9, 3.10; For analysis of the tribunal under the EU-Singapore Investment Protection Agreement *see* Leon Trakman, *Enhancing Standing Panels in Investor-State Arbitration: The Way Forward?* 48 Georgetown Journal of International Law 1145, 1146–1195 (2017).

[104] EU-Singapore Investment Protection Agreement, Ch.3, Article 3.9, Section 2.

countries or having qualifications required to be jurists of recognized competence.[105] The appointment is made for an eight-year term.[106] Although the Agreement establishes the dispute resolution system on a bilateral basis, it also provides for the possibility of a multilateral dispute settlement mechanism.[107]

Similarly, the Comprehensive Economic and Trade Agreement (CETA) between the EU and Canada provides for a tribunal and an appellate tribunal.[108] The tribunal is to have fifteen members with five members being nationals of EU Member States, five members being nationals of Canada, and five members being nationals of third countries.[109] The appointment is made for a five-year term.[110] The Agreement also specifies "...demonstrated expertise in public international law" as one of the key criteria to be appointed as the member of the tribunal[111] which stands in stark contrast to the existing ISDS, where arbitrators do not necessarily have to possess any knowledge of public international law. The Agreement also notes that the "...Parties shall pursue... the establishment of a multilateral investment tribunal and appellate mechanism for the resolution of investment disputes".[112]

Apart from including the provision on an investment court in these investment agreements, the EU has been actively promoting its proposal of a multilateral investment court as "...a logical next step in the approach to set up a more transparent, coherent and fair system to deal with investor complaints under investment protection agreements".[113] The EU Council of Ministers has issued "negotiating directives" for a Convention establishing a multilateral court for the settlement of investment disputes.[114] The negotiations are to take place under the auspices of the United Nations Commission on International Trade Law (UNCITRAL).[115] The Convention is to establish a multilateral

---

[105] EU-Singapore Investment Protection Agreement, Ch.3, Article 3.9, Section 4.

[106] EU-Singapore Investment Protection Agreement, Ch.3, Article 3.9, Section 5.

[107] EU-Singapore Investment Protection Agreement, Ch.3, Article 3.12 ("The Parties shall pursue with each other and other interested trading partners, the establishment of a multilateral investment tribunal and appellate mechanism for the resolution of international investment disputes. Upon establishment of such a multilateral mechanism, the Committee shall consider adopting a decision to provide that investment disputes under this Section will be resolved pursuant to that multilateral mechanism, and to make appropriate transitional arrangements").

[108] Comprehensive Economic and Trade Agreement between the EU and Canada, Ch. 8, Article 8.27, 8.28, http://ec.europa.eu/trade/policy/in-focus/ceta/ceta-chapter-by-chapter/ accessed on Aug. 29, 2018. For an analysis of the dispute settlement mechanism under CETA *see* David Schneiderman, *International Investment Law's Unending Legitimation Project*, 49 Loyola University Chicago Law Journal 229, 249–254 (2017).

[109] Comprehensive Economic and Trade Agreement between the EU and Canada, Article 8.27, Section 2.

[110] Comprehensive Economic and Trade Agreement between the EU and Canada, Article 8.27, Section 5.

[111] Comprehensive Economic and Trade Agreement between the EU and Canada, Article 8.27, Section 4.

[112] Comprehensive Economic and Trade Agreement between the EU and Canada, Article 8.29.

[113] EU Commission, A Multilateral Investment Court, http://trade.ec.europa.eu/doclib/docs/2017/september/tradoc_156042.pdf accessed on Aug. 29, 2018.

[114] Council of the European Union, Negotiating Directives for a Convention Establishing a Multilateral Court for the Settlement of Investment Disputes, Mar. 1, 2018, http://data.consilium.europa.eu/doc/document/ST-12981-2017-ADD-1-DCL-1/en/pdf accessed on Aug. 29, 2018.

[115] Council of the European Union, Negotiating Directives for a Convention Establishing a Multilateral Court for the

investment court in the form of a tribunal of first instance and an appeals tribunal.[116] The Directives stipulate that members of the multilateral court must be "...subject to stringent requirements regarding their qualifications and impartiality," "...appointed for a fixed, long and non-renewable period of time and enjoy security of tenure" and have to "...receive a permanent remuneration".[117]

Although having a multilateral court instead of the existing ISDS system would be a step forward, widespread implementation of this idea may be very difficult in practice due to opposition both to ISDS and to a multilateral investment court coming from various countries around the world. For example, Brazil does not allow investors to have direct recourse to investment arbitration in its investment agreements. Brazil's 2015 Cooperation and Facilitation Investment Agreement provides for a Joint Committee to "...resolve any issues or disputes concerning investments of investors of a Party in an amicable manner".[118] It also establishes a National Focal Point or "Ombudsman" to support the investor and to "...seek to prevent differences in investment matters, in collaboration with government authorities and relevant private entities".[119] The Model Agreement only gives Parties a right to state-to-state arbitration.[120] Another example of a state that opposes international investment arbitration is South Africa.[121] South Africa's domestic law provides investors with recourse to mediation instead of arbitration.[122]

The topic of reforming ISDS and the possible creation of a multilateral investment court is now being discussed as part of UNCITRAL Working Group III.[123] It remains to be seen whether this idea will be implemented. Even if it is implemented, the multilateral investment court per se may not be able to solve all problems related to the current imbalance between the protection of investors and advancement of sustainable

SETTLEMENT OF INVESTMENT DISPUTES, Mar. 1, 2018, para 4, http://data.consilium.europa.eu/doc/document/ST-12981-2017-ADD-1-DCL-1/en/pdf accessed on Aug. 29, 2018.

116 Council of the European Union, NEGOTIATING DIRECTIVES FOR A CONVENTION ESTABLISHING A MULTILATERAL COURT FOR THE SETTLEMENT OF INVESTMENT DISPUTES, Mar. 1, 2018, para 10, http://data.consilium.europa.eu/doc/document/ST-12981-2017-ADD-1-DCL-1/en/pdf accessed on Aug. 29, 2018.

117 Council of the European Union, NEGOTIATING DIRECTIVES FOR A CONVENTION ESTABLISHING A MULTILATERAL COURT FOR THE SETTLEMENT OF INVESTMENT DISPUTES, Mar. 1, 2018, para 11, http://data.consilium.europa.eu/doc/document/ST-12981-2017-ADD-1-DCL-1/en/pdf accessed on Aug. 29, 2018.

118 Model Cooperation and Facilitation Investment Agreement of the Federative Republic of Brazil, 2015, Article 17, http://investmentpolicyhub.unctad.org/Download/TreatyFile/4786 accessed on Aug. 29, 2018.

119 Model Cooperation and Facilitation Investment Agreement of the Federative Republic of Brazil, 2015, Article 18, http://investmentpolicyhub.unctad.org/Download/TreatyFile/4786 accessed on Aug. 29, 2018.

120 Model Cooperation and Facilitation Investment Agreement of the Federative Republic of Brazil, 2015, Article 24, http://investmentpolicyhub.unctad.org/Download/TreatyFile/4786 accessed on Aug. 29, 2018.

121 *See* Sean Woolfrey, *The Emergence of a New Approach to Investment Protection in South Africa*, in SHIFTING PARADIGMS IN INTERNATIONAL INVESTMENT LAW – MORE BALANCED, LESS ISOLATED, INCREASINGLY DIVERSIFIED (Steffen Hindelang & Markus Krajewski eds., 2016), 266–290.

122 Trishna Menon and Gladwin Issac, DEVELOPING COUNTRY OPPOSITION TO AN INVESTMENT COURT: COULD STATE-STATE DISPUTE SETTLEMENT BE AN ALTERNATIVE? Feb. 17, 2018, http://arbitrationblog.kluwerarbitration.com/2018/02/17/developing-country-opposition-investment-court-state-state-dispute-settlement-alternative/ accessed on Aug. 29, 2018.

123 UNCITRAL, WORKING GROUP III, http://www.uncitral.org/uncitral/en/commission/working_groups/3Online_Dispute_Resolution.html accessed on Aug. 29, 2018.

development. Therefore, the negotiation and renegotiation of BITs and IIAs in line with sustainable development goals remains indispensable.

III. Concluding Observations

International investment arbitration is one of the most widely relied upon forms of alternative dispute resolution, as it offers a neutral and impartial forum for resolving disputes between foreign investors and host states. However, despite all the advantages of arbitration, there is now a mounting criticism against investment arbitration due to problems related to inconsistency of arbitral awards, lack of transparency and other issues. If the international investment arbitration system is to remain successful, it needs to be aligned with sustainable development goals. Failure to achieve this paradigm shift may destroy ISDS as we currently know it. The traditional approach to investment protection favoring investor rights and ignoring those of other stakeholders has already become unsustainable. It is the hope of the authors that both substantive and procedural solutions advanced in this article will be applied in practice – and very soon – in order to balance investor protection and sustainable development in investment arbitration. As Jack Welch famously said, "change before you have to."

Dalma Demeter* & Zebo Nasirova**

TRENDS AND CHALLENGES IN THE LEGAL HARMONISATION OF ISDS

Abstract

The creation of international law has moved from the traditional state-centred model to a multilateral process where states, judiciary, private tribunals, international organizations and other non-state actors all jointly contribute to the development of international law across a range of fora. The combined roles of government and non-state actors and their interaction within the legislative development process become especially apparent in the growing area of international investment law and investment disputes.

The current landscape of international investment law consists of thousands of different international trade and investment agreements with differing provisions, resulting in a fragmented legal framework that hinders the development of uniform principles in the field and leads to the criticism the system faces today. As a result, the UNCITRAL has been given a broad mandate to identify and address concerns regarding ISDS. The different stakeholders directly or indirectly affected by the system create a tension in the harmonised regulation of the field, the current work on the ISD reform nicely reflecting the correlation between the top-down approach and a bottom-up influence over legal harmonisation, which today appears to have taken a rather multidimensional shape.

I. Introduction

International law has traditionally been just that: international. It mainly consists of a set of legal rules and institutions and it governs relationships among states.[1] According

* Ms Dalma Demeter is assistant professor at the University of Canberra. She earned her LLB (Bachelor of Laws) at the "Babes-Bolyai" University and the Christian University "Dimitrie Cantemir" (joint degree) in 1997, her LLM (Master of Laws) in International Business Law and her SJD (Doctor of Juridical Science) in International Business Law at the Central European University in 2004 and in 2011. She has the certificate from the Emory World Law Institute (earned in 2004), a Total Law Diploma in Advanced European and Global Legal Practice earned at the Central European University in 2007 and a Graduate Certificate in Tertiary Education earned at the University of Canberra in 2013.

** Mrs. Zebo Nasirova is a PhD candidate at the University of Canberra (Australia), with an LLB (2005) and LLM (2008) from the University of World Economy and Diplomacy (UWED) in Uzbekistan. Zebo also acquired a second LLM from the University of Canberra in 2014, starting her PhD in 2015. She is currently teaching and researching in international business law, international e-commerce and contracts, with her PhD focussing on the interpretation of international law through the lens of domestic law, with special focus on the uniform interpretation of the CISG.

1 Joseph Gabriel Starke, *Monism and Dualism in the Theory of International Law*, 17 British Yearbook of International Law 66 (1936).

to the traditional rules of international law, only when a state exercised diplomatic protection and implemented the claims of its subjects in an international arena could the claims of individuals or entities reach the international level. [2]

The traditional model of international law as distinct from the domestic domain represents the domestic issues the international legal system sought to address, specifically the enabling of state-to-state cooperation and the treatment of one state's nationals by another state.[3]

Nowadays, international law is made in a large number of fora, including multilateral processes, tribunals and the bodies of international organizations.[4] Although countries continue to be the main producers of international law, they are joined by other participants such as international organizations and legal bodies which are significant in the making of international law, including non-state actors as well as non-governmental organizations (NGOs).[5] These activities are increasingly disparate, with different rules and practices being developed in different areas, by a number of entities, with little by way of coordination and this reflects the decentralized approach to the making of international law.[6]

Contemporary international law is often the product of a subtle and evolving interplay of law-making instruments and it is made through a wide variety of processes and by a growing number of entities and individuals.[7] The deficiency of a unified approach to the creation of international law has meant that law-makers have increasingly felt less controlled by standing practices and procedures. This has allowed larger room for novelty, as states and other entities involved in law-making, pursue to set rules for definite problems or aspects of international existence.[8] International organisations and institutions have become a vital aspect in international law-making processes due to a few features, such as the knowledge gained in their spheres of activities, the proliferation of international institutions and the interconnection between various spheres of international law.[9] Transnational corporations, different legal bodies and institutions in contemporary international law are no longer considered as simply consultants and spectators to international law-making but they have become dynamic actors by playing a vital role in almost every field of international law and regulation.[10]

---

2 Harold Hongju Koh, *Is International Law Really State Law*, 111 Harvard Law Review 1824 (1997).

3 Louis B. Sohn, *The New International Law: Protection of The Rights of Individuals Rather than States*, 32 American University Law Review 1 (1982).

4 Eyal Benvenisti, & George W. Downs, *The Empire's New Clothes: Political Economy and the Fragmentation of International Law*, 60(2) Stanford Law Review 595 (2007).

5 Non-state Actors in International Relations (Bas Arts, Math Noortmann & Bob Reinalda eds., Ashgate Publishing, 2001); A. Dan Tarlock, *The Role of Non-Governmental Organizations in the Development of International Environmental Law*, 68 Chicago-Kent Law Review 61 (1992).

6 John Boli, & George M. Thomas, *World Culture in the World Polity: A Century of International Non-Governmental Organization*, 62(2) American Sociological Review 171–190 (1997).

7 Alan Boyle & Christine Chinkin. The Making of International Law (OUP 2007).

8 *Id.*

9 Arnold N. Pronto, *Some Thoughts on the Making of International Law*, 19(3) European Journal of International Law 601 (2008).

10 Alan Boyle & Christine Chinkin. The Making of International Law (OUP 2007).

II. The Role of Different Actors in Creating International Law

There is increasing discussion within the discipline of international law about the trends and the legal and political challenges in the legal harmonization of international law. The relations between the concepts of globalization, harmonization, implementation and international law raise complex issues about the primary structures of international law that need further exploration.[11]

Discourses of globalization demonstrate that the impact of non-state actors and different legal institutions on the international legal arena is progressively moving out of its borders, in the direction of broader involvement in the formation of international norms and in the functioning of international law. The number of legal bodies and non-state actors is visible in the international arena, especially in United Nations (UN) agencies and processes, and continues to develop as frameworks of international law are gradually adapting to accept this phenomenon.[12] The different potentials for legal bodies to get involved in the governance processes of international law across the world exemplify the strains that exist about the degree, value and merits of the involvement of these actors in the international arena and the insufficiencies of present structures and processes of international law.[13]

The participation of legal bodies and non-state actors in the international arena creates a more multifaceted, multidimensional image of international law than that of the traditional state-centered archetype.[14] Old-style state-centric models of international law continue to express and limit the boundaries of the international legal agenda but no longer efficiently and successfully mirror the level of international institutions and non-state actors' participation in the international arena. In contemporary international law, however, the active role of non-state actors, such as international organizations, different non-governmental bodies, entities or transnational corporations has altered the way international law is being created, developed, implemented and applied.[15] Non-state actors have become a constant factor in modern international relations and they play a vital role in almost every field of international law and regulation, albeit not always in a clearly visible role.

In any legal system the subjects of law are the persons, national and juridical, upon whom the law awards rights and imposes duties. In international law, these persons are normally states. The terms legal bodies/entities or non-state actors include all those actors in international relations that are not states and include different entities

---

[11] Anne-Marie Slaughter Burley, *International Law and International Relations Theory: a Dual Agenda, in* The Nature of International Law 11–46 (Gerry Simpson ed., Routledge, 2017).

[12] Alan Boyle & Christine Chinkin. The Making of International Law (OUP 2007).

[13] Kenneth W. Abbott & Duncan Snidal, *Hard and Soft Law in International Governance*, 54(3) International Organization 421–456 (2000); *see also* Eyal Benvenisti & George W. Downs, *The Empire's New Clothes: Political Economy and the Fragmentation of International Law*, 60(2) Stanford Law Review 595 (2007).

[14] José E. Alvarez, *International Organizations as Law-Makers* (OUP, 2005); *see also* Duncan B. Hollis, *Why State Consent Still Matters-Non-State Actors, Treaties, and the Changing Sources of International Law*, 23 Berkeley Journal of International Law 137 (2005).

[15] Kenneth N. Waltz, Theory of International Politics (Waveland Press 2010).

such as international organizations, corporations, non-governmental organizations ('NGOs'), trade associations and transnational corporations.[16] Non-state actors do not possess official or government authorities and powers and do not have institutional and financial relationships with states.[17] They are considered as potentially new subjects of international law even though they have not been recognized as traditional objects of it.[18] According to one definition, "the concept of non-state actors is generally understood as including any entity that is not actually a state, often used to refer to armed groups, terrorists, civil society, religious groups or corporations".[19]

Organizations having a different juridical nature from the states composing them, may and have become subjects of international law. It is today largely standard in a variety of treaties and otherwise, that international public bodies composed of states hold an international character or nature and as such are subjects of international law.[20] Individuals, on the other hand, possess international legal personality only in a limited scope given to them expressly or by implication and not always accompanied by corresponding procedural capacity. Nevertheless, different legal bodies and institutions are progressively functioning as participants in the direct formation, application and administration of international law. Changes in domestic business values and dogma consistent with the elimination of barriers to trade activity are enhancing commercial authority.[21] Corporations are receiving rights through new practices of domestic legal documents[22] as governments are also actively engaging in the expansion of corporate rights and powers. With states playing "an indispensable enabling role in the globalization of capital ... governments have facilitated global firms' operations and profits with suitably constructed property guarantees, currency regulations, tax regimes, labour laws and police protection".[23]

---

[16] Richard Higgott, Geoffrey RD Underhill & Andreas Bieler, *Introduction: Globalisation and Non-State Actors, in* NON-STATE ACTORS AND AUTHORITY IN THE GLOBAL SYSTEM (Richard Higgott, Geoffrey RD Underhill & Andreas Bieler eds., Routledge, 2000). *See also* ANDREW CLAPHAM, HUMAN RIGHTS OBLIGATIONS OF NON-STATE ACTORS 211 (OUP, 2006): "The concept of non-state actors is generally understood as including any entity that is not actually a state, often used to refer to armed groups, terrorists, civil society, religious groups or corporations".

[17] Richard Higgott, Geoffrey RD Underhill & Andreas Bieler, *Introduction: Globalisation and Non-State Actors, in* NON-STATE ACTORS AND AUTHORITY IN THE GLOBAL SYSTEM (Richard Higgott, Geoffrey RD Underhill & Andreas Bieler eds., Routledge, 2000).

[18] Janne E. Nijman, *Non-State Actors and the International Rule of Law: Revisiting the 'Realist Theory' of International Legal Personality 1., in* NON-STATE ACTOR DYNAMICS IN INTERNATIONAL LAW 91–124 (Cedric Ryngaert & Math Noortmann eds., Routledge, 2016) ("[N]on-state actors are subject or persons of international law. The conception of non-state actors as an object of international law does, however, not sufficiently explain its present-day position in the international law... In the other words, power and influence of non-state actors in many cases goes far beyond that of entities to which international law has traditionally accorded to object states.").

[19] ANDREW CLAPHAM, HUMAN RIGHTS OBLIGATIONS OF NON-STATE ACTORS 211 (OUP 2006).

[20] KENNETH N. WALTZ, THEORY OF INTERNATIONAL POLITICS (Waveland Press 2010).

[21] Jan Aart Scholte, *Global Capitalism and the State*, 73(3) International Affairs 427–452 (1997).

[22] Carl J. Mayer, *Personalizing the Impersonal: Corporations and the Bill of Rights, 41* Hastings Law Journal 577 (1989); *see also* Chris Tollefson, *Corporate Constitutional Rights and the Supreme Court of Canada*, 19 Queen's Law Journal 309 (1993).

[23] Jan Aart Scholte, *Global Capitalism and the State*, 73(3) International Affairs (1997).

Even though there seems to be a great deal of acknowledgement of the greater power of transnational corporations, it is unaccompanied by effective efforts to control them. In many aspects, international law is silent.[24] There is no binding, compulsory and universal international commercial code regulating the practices of transnational corporations. Most issues are dealt with under domestic structures of commercial and private international law principles.[25] The hard work of international organizations and private business as well as business associations have formed several mechanisms that try to adjust corporate behaviour but they have a tendency to have a 'soft law' nature,[26] leaving a disparity between the governing power corporations have and the principles they are subjected to transnationally.

It is important to highlight the non-state actors, which hold some form of legal capacity under international law and hence it is certainly possible that non-state actors may also be granted the status of right-holders and of duty-holders. This feature differentiates non-state actors from states which as a rule own full legal capacity. To the extent non-state actors are concerned, this legal capacity may take on manifold levels, depending on and restricted by the purpose of a non-state actor in the international legal order.[27] The participation of non-state actors may not be seen as being still limited to a quite insignificant role or to the status of bystander: non-state actors are increasingly partaking, directly or indirectly, in international discussions and in the systematization of international law, in international litigation. The most explicit example is the distinctive role played by NGOs in the institutional process of international law-making in three particular circumstances:

1) the UN 1992 Rio Conference on Environment and Development;[28]
2) the negotiations of the Convention on the Prohibition of the Use, Stockpiling, Production and Transfer of Anti-Personnel Mines and on Their Destruction;[29]
3) the Rome Statute of the International Criminal Court.[30]

---

[24] Daniel K. Tarullo, *Norms and Institutions in Global Competition Policy*, 94(3) American Journal of International Law 478–504 (2000).

[25] Notes of Cases, *The Multinational and the Antiquities of Company Law*. 47 The Modern Law Review 87–92 (1984).

[26] Fleur Johns, *The Invisibility of the Transnational Corporation: an Analysis of International Law and Legal Theory*, 19 *Melbourne University Law Review* 893 (1993).

[27] Klaus Dieter Wolf, *11 Private Actors and the Legitimacy of Governance Beyond the State, in* GOVERNANCE AND DEMOCRACY: COMPARING NATIONAL, EUROPEAN AND INTERNATIONAL EXPERIENCES 200 (Arthur Benz & Yannis Papadopoulos eds., Routledge, 2006).

[28] United Nations Conference on Environment & Development Rio de Janerio, Brazil, 3 to 14 June 1992; *see also* BERTRAM IRWIN SPECTOR, GUNNAR SJÖSTEDT & I. WILLIAM ZARTMAN, NEGOTIATING INTERNATIONAL REGIMES: LESSONS LEARNED FROM THE UNITED NATIONS CONFERENCE ON ENVIRONMENT AND DEVELOPMENT (UNCED) (Graham & Trotman/Martinus Nijhoff 1994).

[29] Convention on The Prohibition of the Use, Stockpiling, Production and Transfer of Anti-Personnel Mines and on their Destruction, 1997; *See also* Shawn Roberts, *No Exceptions, No Reservations, No Loopholes: The Campaign for the 1997 Convention on the Prohibition of the Development, Production, Stockpiling, Transfer, and Use of Anti-Personnel Mines and on Their Destruction*, 9 Colorado Journal of International Environmental Law & Policy 371 (1998).

[30] Rome Statute of the International Criminal Court, 17 July 1998.

Nevertheless, the input of private actors in the advance of international standards of commercial conduct (*lex mercatoria*) might also be considered as an example of involvement of non-state actors in the process of formation of international law.[31] Of course, at the international level the significant influence of non-state actors on normative results does not make them the formal law-maker but it shows their significance in this process. Besides law-making power, non-state actors also participate in adjudication processes. This means that non-state actors may be a party to international judicial proceedings by having direct access to a number of international tribunals and may directly enforce their claims[32] and submit *amicus curiae* briefs before international courts.[33]

It has been some decades since the idea of non-state actors made its entrance into the sphere of international law. Shifting the fora of treaty negotiations from ad hoc conferences to international institutions increased the influence of various non-state actors such as NGOs, international civil servants and experts in the treaty-making process.[34] Non-state actors do not hold authorized or government powers and controls, besides they do not have official and economic relations with states.[35] Intrinsically, they have not commonly been recognized as customary objects of international law but, as an alternative, have become potentially new subjects of it. "… Non-state actors are subject or persons of international law. The concept of non-state actors as an object of international law does, however, not sufficiently explain its present-day position in the international law… In other words, power and influence of non-state actors in many cases goes far beyond that of entities to which international law has traditionally accorded to object states".[36]

To have legal character, a legal body is required to have rights in consort with obligations within a legal system. There are international mechanisms which have enumerated several rights and obligations for non-state actors, depending on the content and intent of the mechanism.[37] There are disputes and doubts about the consequences of the recognition of non-state actors' legal personality. "There is a fear that one 'legitimizes' actors by giving them human rights obligations and implies a power which they may themselves erode, rather than enhancing, human freedom and autonomy".[38] One of the substantial causes for not awarding 'legal personality' to non-state actors is the outdated

---

31 Bhupinder S Chimni, *International Institutions Today: an Imperial Global State in the Making*, 15(1) European Journal of International Law 1–37 (2004).

32 Antarctic Resources Policy: Scientific, Legal and Political Issues (Francisco Orrego-Vicuna ed., Cambridge University Press 1983).

33 Thomas Buergenthal, Dinah L. Shelton & David Stewart, International Human Rights in a Nutshell (West 2009).

34 Jose E Alvarez, *The new treaty makers*, 25 Boston College International and Comparative Law Review 213 (2002).

35 Roderick Arthur William Rhodes, *The New Governance: Governing Without Government*, 44(4) Political Studies 652–667 (1996).

36 Janne E. Nijman, *Non-State Actors and the International Rule of Law: Revisiting the 'Realist Theory' of International Legal Personality 1.*, *in* Non-State Actor Dynamics in International Law 91–124 (Cedric Ryngaert & Math Noortmann eds., Routledge, 2016).

37 Duncan B. Hollis, *Why State Consent Still Matters-Non-State Actors, Treaties, and the Changing Sources of International Law*, 23 Berkeley Journal of International Law 137 (2005).

38 Andrew Clapham, Human Rights Obligations of Non-State Actors 46 (OUP, 2006).

state-centred or state-focused ideology of international law and consequently, the unwillingness of the states to share their powers and authorities with non-state actors.[39]

The adoption of two main treaties, the Rome Statute of the International Criminal Court[40] and the Ottawa Convention on the ban of landmines[41], showed the role of non-state actors and NGOs and their participation in the international law-making process. These are prominent examples of this tendency for the obvious and important role that non-state actors have played in their formation.[42]

Another notable role of non-state actors is their involvement in international law adjudication processes. This refers to the opportunity that non-state actors be involved in international judicial proceedings. For example, until recently an entity's lack of standing before international tribunals has been used as a reason to deny the entity's subjectivity under international law.[43]

Law-making and adjudication process are not the only power they have as non-state actors may also effectively participate in law enforcement processes. For example, non-state actors, particularly NGOs can ensure the compliance with agreements such as multilateral environmental[44] or human rights agreements in which non-state actors may control or inspect the implementation of international law standards. They can directly or indirectly participate in monitoring activities and may activate instruments of compliance or implementation. Their power to collect data and deliver expertise makes non-state actors authoritative players in the implementation of international law. This is especially evident in contemporary international investment law.[45]

The combined roles of government and non-state actors and their interaction within the legislative development process is relevant to assess the correlation between the formal top-down legal harmonisation of international law and the reality of bottom-up development initiatives impacting on the same. These influences become especially apparent in the growing area of international investment law and investment disputes.

---

[39] *Id.*

[40] United Nations, *Rome Statute of the International Criminal Court*, 26 Social Justice 125–143 (1999).

[41] Kenneth Anderson, *The Ottawa Convention Banning Landmines, the Role of International Non-Governmental Organizations and the Idea of International Civil Society*, 11(1) European Journal of International Law 91–120 (2000).

[42] Thomas Risse-Kappen, *Bringing Transnational Relations Back In: Introduction, in* Bringing Transnational Relations Back In: Non-State Actors, Domestic Structures and International Institutions 3 (Thomas Risse-Kappen ed., Cambridge University Press 1995).

[43] Antarctic Resources Policy: Scientific, Legal and Political Issues (Francisco Orrego-Vicuna ed., Cambridge University Press 1983).

[44] Astrid Epiney, *The Role of NGOs in the Process of Ensuring Compliance with MEAs, in* Ensuring Compliance with Multilateral Environmental Agreements 319–352 (U. Beyerlin, Peter-Tobias Stoll & Rüdiger Wolfrum eds., Brill, 2006).

[45] Thomas Risse-Kappen, *Bringing Transnational Relations Back In: Introduction, in* Bringing Transnational Relations Back In: Non-State Actors, Domestic Structures and International Institutions 3 (Thomas Risse-Kappen ed., Cambridge University Press 1995).

III. ISDS – Where It Came from and Where It Is Heading

As mentioned above and under the traditional rules of international law, claims of individuals could reach the international level only when a state exercised diplomatic protection and adopted the claims of its nationals in an international forum.[46] Historically, there was no right for an individual or a corporation who had been wronged to sue a host state for a breach of customary international law. The aggrieved party would have to petition its government to espouse the claim on its behalf.[47] If a state decided to pursue the claim it meant that it assumed the claim under its own name, thereby granting the aggrieved party diplomatic protection, subject to certain requirements. The investor had to be a national of the state granting diplomatic protection and must have been a national to the state continuously from the time of the injury until the claim is presented to the state, or possibly even until the dispute has been settled. The investor must have also exhausted all local remedies in the host state prior to diplomatic protection being granted.

The investor had no right to diplomatic protection and it was up to the discretion of the investor's home state government to decide whether diplomatic protection would be granted to the investor.[48] As confirmed by the ICJ, "the state must be viewed as the sole judge to decide whether its protection will be granted, to what extent it is granted and when it will cease. It retains in this respect a discretionary power the exercise of which may be determined by consideration of political or other nature, unrelated to the particular case".[49] Considering this, it is quite clear that from the investor's perspective the diplomatic channel is not a desirable system of investment protection and dispute resolution.

From the perspective of the state, there are also some serious disadvantages with granting diplomatic protection. The most important of these is a possible disruption in international relations, which could lead to prolonged disputes and in extreme cases even armed conflict – even though the use of armed force is not a permitted means of protecting the rights of a foreign investor.[50]

Apart from the diplomatic avenue, a foreign investor would usually depend on the host state's courts in case of a dispute regarding its investment, unless there is an international agreement saying otherwise, as conflict of law rules will most often point to the courts in the state in which the investment is made. From the investor's perspective this is quite undesirable as there is a risk that the judiciary might be biased or even controlled by the state. Especially when dealing with states where the legal system is not as well-developed, or the political regime is too authoritarian or unstable, this risk is imminent. In addition, even if the court would decide in favour of the investor, the

---

[46] *Mavromatis Palestine Concessions* (*Greece v. Gr. Brit.*), 1924 P.C.I.J. (ser. A) No. 2, at 12 (Aug. 30).

[47] Nigel Blackaby & Constantine QC Partasides, Alan Redfern & Martin Hunter, Redfern and Hunter on International Arbitration 441 (OUP, 2015).

[48] Rudolf Dolzer & Christoph Schreuer. Principles of International Investment Law 22–23 (OUP, 2012).

[49] *Barcelona Traction, Light and Power Co Ltd* (*Belgium v. Spain*), Judgement, 5 February 1970, ICJ Reports (1970) para 44.

[50] Rudolf Dolzer & Christoph Schreuer. Principles of International Investment Law 232–233 (OUP, 2012).

executive branch of the host government might ignore the court's decision.[51] The home state of the investor will usually lack jurisdiction over a dispute arising from a foreign investment as the investment is made in another state. Even if a domestic court other than the court of the host state would have jurisdiction, rules of state immunity are a serious obstacle to overcome, rendering most lawsuits arising from investment disputes in another country unsuccessful, unless there is a waiver of immunity from the host state.[52]

Due to these disadvantages and problems both in regard to diplomatic protection and the use of domestic courts, alternative methods were developed to settle disputes, most notably international investment arbitration. This development was made possible by reforms in the dispute settlement provisions of Bilateral Investment Treaties (BITs) and by the conclusion of the ICSID convention.[53] International investment arbitration deals with the issue of biased courts by providing a forum that is more neutral both in a political and a procedural regard.[54] Developed from the concept of commercial arbitration as an alternative dispute resolution system, one prerequisite for investment arbitration is, as with any other form of arbitration, that there is an agreement to arbitrate, with consent being required from both state and investor. Consent by a state can be given through a direct agreement with the investor, by adopting national legislation which gives a general consent to arbitration, or by concluding a BIT or another international trade and investment agreement with an ISDS provision offering ISDS protection to all investors who are nationals of the other contracting state.[55] Since the ICSID convention, states became more open to include ISDS provisions in BITs and regional trade agreements, granting investors the right to seek direct recourse for their claims through investment arbitration.[56]

The increasing number of trade agreements led to a multitude of varying ISDS provisions globally, but the main investor-state dispute resolution method remained either ICSID or *ad hoc* arbitration, keeping both the sovereign state and the private commercial investing entity on equal procedural footing and with balanced rights in seeking resolution to their dispute. The net of relationships became more complicated in Europe after the Lisbon Treaty entered into force in December 2009, when the competence to conclude trade and investment agreements was transferred into concurring competence, giving both the EU Member States and the EU itself authority to enter into such agreements. This tension has further escalated through the recent landmark Achmea decision,[57] in which the Court of Justice of the European Union (CJEU) decided that the arbitration clause contained in an intra-EU BIT is incompatible with

---

[51] *Id.* at 235.

[52] *Id.* at 232–33.

[53] Nigel Blackaby & Constantine QC Partasides, Alan Redfern & Martin Hunter, Redfern and Hunter on International Arbitration 443 (OUP, 2015).

[54] William W. Park & Alexander A. Yanos, *Treaty Obligations and National Law: Emerging Conflicts in International Arbitration*, 58 Hastings Law Journal 251, 327 (2006).

[55] Rudolf Dolzer & Christoph Schreuer. Principles of International Investment Law 254–258 (OUP, 2012).

[56] Nigel Blackaby & Constantine QC Partasides, Alan Redfern & Martin Hunter, Redfern and Hunter on International Arbitration 444 (OUP, 2015).

[57] Case C-284/16 *Slovak Republic v. Achmea* B.V.

EU law. While the CJEU decision is not binding upon investment treaty tribunals, it is likely to have serious consequences on the inclusion and application of ISDS in BITS concluded within the EU and consequently on ISDS in any trade relationships including EU Member States.

The changing landscape of intra-EU investment disputes is reinforced by the EU Commission's view that intra-EU BITs are anyway unnecessary as there are EU remedies available to resolve investment disputes between Member States. This may both disrupt or lead to a harmonised legal approach for investment from and into the EU and ultimately impact investment treaties and disputes globally. A harmonised approach would benefit foreign investors as the standardisation of legal rules would provide one single and simplified route into the whole EU market. At the same time, even in international investment there is no one size fits all (procedural) solution to all disputes and this dichotomy is at the core of the current review of ISDS.

The current landscape of international investment law consists of thousands of different international trade and investment agreements with differing provisions. This fragmented legal framework creates legal uncertainty for investors, which then leads to inconsistent arbitral awards and complicates the development of uniform principles in the area of international investment law. It is not surprising, therefore, that ISDS is considered to "lack many of the basic protections and procedures of the justice system normally available in a court of law. There is no appeals process. There is no oversight or accountability of the private lawyers who serve as arbitrators, many of whom rotate between being arbitrators and bringing cases for corporations against governments".[58] While some of these claims are true, insofar as there is usually no appeals process in arbitration, other criticisms such as the statement that investment arbitration lacks basic procedural protections, is incorrect. Arbitration is a highly structured and formal process which operates through specific rules and procedures, although these might vary depending on what arbitration rules govern the proceedings. Some of the formalities and procedural technicalities common in domestic legal systems and court proceedings might not exist in arbitration, but arbitration must always conform with a minimal standard of justice and due process that is common to all developed legal systems in the world.[59] Both the ICSID and the UNCITRAL Arbitration Rules governing *ad hoc* investment arbitrations contain multiple control mechanisms to ensure the procedural fairness of any awards, including a possibility to dismiss arbitrators which are perceived to be biased.[60]

ISDS has proved to be a very effective way of settling dispute in international investment law and as a result, the amount of ISDS claims has increased sharply over the past decades. With this increase of claims there have also been other developments. Litigants have started to engage in strategic considerations about where and how to bring their cases, 'forum shopping' and trying to pursue their claims in multiple fora with different courts and tribunals.[61] Multiple and parallel proceedings, however, come with

---

[58] Alliance for Justice, Letter Opposing ISDS.

[59] Jeswald W. Salacuse, The Law of Investment Treaties 369–370 (OUP, 2010).

[60] Article 56–58, ICSID Convention, Article 12, UNCITRAL Procedural Rules.

[61] Marc L. Busch, *Overlapping Institutions, Forum Shopping, and Dispute Settlement in International Trade*, 61(4) International Organization 735–761 (2007).

a number of drawbacks, multiplying costs and resources and potentially straining states financially. The availability of various fora may also lead to investors utilising harassing and oppressive litigation tactics, forcing the state to defend itself. The greatest risk, however, is the risk of inconsistent outcomes across the field of investment relations and disputes overall.

One of the most fundamental values of a system based on the rule of law is predictability. If investment tribunals render conflicting judgments on similar or same issues, then there will be poor predictability in the ISDS system. The issue of inconsistent outcomes is not only an issue when there are parallel proceedings but also when there are separate cases which have a similar background or fact pattern.[62] That the awards of investment tribunals are inconsistent and unpredictable is not very surprising, considering that the awards are based on a framework of public international law that is decentralised and non-hierarchic and consists of thousands of different investment agreements. There is no formally binding principle of *stare decisis* or precedent in public international law or international arbitration. In regular international commercial arbitration, the award is usually kept confidential, which makes inconsistencies and fact discrepancies hard to detect. Awards rendered in investment disputes are, however, to a large extent published which makes it easy to detect inconsistencies and deviations from established rules and principles.[63] Inconsistent outcomes in ISDS mean not only that independent investment tribunals have divergent views on legal issues or on how to assess the facts of the case, but are also impacting on the uniform interpretation of public international law principles, therefore hindering the intended purpose of texts serving legislative harmonisation. This fragmented legal framework produces legal ambiguity for investors, which in turn perplexes the growth of uniform principles in international investment law and leads to the criticism the system faces today. As a result, the UNCITRAL[64] Working Group III (WGIII)[65] has been given a mandate to identify and address concerns regarding ISDS. This mandate and the resulting work beautifully reflect the role of the different actors in developing international law and the correlation between the top-down approach and a bottom-up influence over legal harmonisation.

The UNCITRAL mandate made it clear that discussions within the working group are meant to be government-led, with a broad mandate to review the system before recommending any amendments to it. Due to the transparent nature of WG processes, the reform about the future of ISDS raised interest for the prospect of a more systemic

---

[62] Susan D. Franck, *The Nature and Enforcement of Investor Rights Under Investment Treaties: Do Investment Treaties Have a Bright Future*, 12 UC Davis Journal of International Law & Policy 47 (2005).

[63] Kaj Hobér, *Investment Arbitration and the Energy Charter Treaty*, 1(1) Journal of International Dispute Settlement 153–190 (2010).

[64] The United Nations Commission on International Trade Law (UNCITRAL) was established by the United Nations General Assembly by its Resolution 2205 (XXI) of 17 December 1966 "to promote the progressive harmonization and unification of international trade law".

[65] The 35th session of Working Group III of the United Nations Commission on International Trade Law (UNCITRAL) took place April 23–27, 2018, in New York to continue discussions on possible reform of investor-state dispute settlement (ISDS). WGIII started its work in the 34th session which took place from 27 November to 1 December 2017. http://www.uncitral.org/uncitral/en/commission/working_groups/3Investor_State.html, accessed on June 1, 2018.

reform. Nevertheless, the review is limited to the procedural aspects of dispute settlement, not including substantive issues that affect the overall perception of ISDS effectiveness – issues that are also more politically charged.

WGIII started its work in the 34th session in 2017, with the key points for review being identified as the duration of proceedings, overall costs, allocation of costs, security for costs, third party funding, transparency and early dismissal mechanisms.[66] The overarching issue discussed in this session was the concern over the legitimacy of the system, where some states supported a fact-based analysis of ISDS, while others emphasised the necessity to address wider public perceptions of the system. The 35th session, although bearing the potential to produce a versatile plan for ISDS, did not lead to harmony. It is difficult to identify cohesion at this stage in either the nature of the perceived issues associated with the current system of ad hoc arbitration, or on how those issues might be resolved. While on a global level, states are divided on whether investment claims would be better heard by *ad hoc* arbitral bodies or a permanent investment court, on a domestic level ISDS has evidenced serious tensions within some states, resulting in a firm repulsion towards the system overall. Consequently, in the 35th session, two general issues emerged: whether states should be concerned with facts and perceptions, or just facts, and whether some of the issues identified were systemic in nature and, accordingly called for systemic solutions.

The systemic concerns regarding ISDS derive from the interaction of multiple elements of the current system. The issues identified as needing reform range from the lack of consistency and predictability across decisions, limited systemic checks on correctness and consistency in the absence of an effective appeal mechanism, the nature of the appointment process impacting the outputs of the adjudicative process, significant costs and a lack of transparency[67]. The contemporary investment regime is described by repeat disputes, relative indeterminacy and vertical relationships in a context of public international law and public law situations. The international society and states have preferred to produce permanent standing bodies to adjudicate disputes in the context of such regimes.[68]

At the time of writing this paper, it is likely that there will be at least one more session before the working group makes any recommendations on the reform of ISDS. There is still need for multilateral reform as different responses from different countries to address problems that largely affect all countries, and thus, there is momentum to engage in discussions to multilaterally reform investment dispute settlement and need to work on realizable objectives that have a broad positive impact for all. It is necessary to consider a new framework for investment dispute resolution which is permanent, independent and recognised as legitimate by citizens, not only law-makers.

---

[66] http://www.uncitral.org/uncitral/en/commission/working_groups/3Investor_State.html, accessed on June 1, 2018.

[67] United Nations Commission on International Trade Law Working Group III (Investor-State Dispute Settlement Reform) Thirty-fifth session New York, 23–27 April 2018. https://documents-dds-ny.un.org/doc/UNDOC/LTD/V17/088/32/PDF/V1708832.pdf?OpenElement, accessed on June 1, 2018.

[68] *Id.*

IV. Conclusion – Top-Down or Bottom-Up?

The correlation between the formal top-down legislative process and the often bottom-up role of non-state actors is especially important in the regulation of investment disputes involving public interest in a private process.[69] The different stakeholders directly or indirectly affected by the system create a tension in the harmonised regulation of the field. Several generations of legal theorists[70] traditionally agreed that "law is something handed down to the populace by high officials following professional norms and the citizenry is obligated to follow the rules simply because they are the rules handed down by the duly established mechanisms for handing down rules"[71]. This perception has been radically changed to a currently more accepted view that law "often percolates up from 'the bottom,' from communities of citizens who experience the world or law in a certain way".[72] The communities shaping the development of investment law and investor-state dispute resolution range from directly interested stakeholders composed of corporations to NGOs representing public interests affected by foreign investment and the state regulations impacting those investments.

An easy-to-recognize example of such corroborated net of interests is visible through the Phillip Morris v Australia saga, in which the Australian Tobacco Plain Packaging legislation[73] aimed to protect public health triggered a series of investment claims from Philip Morris, among others[74], through investment arbitration[75]. While the tribunal decided that it does not have jurisdiction to hear the case[76], this being the first investment claim formulated against Australia, the mere existence of the claim had such an initial impact on the public opinion and consequently the government's position towards ISDS, that Australia introduced a flat exclusion policy of ISDS provisions from all its treaties[77]. The policy has since been reversed with the change of government, yet again reflecting how exposed a state's approach to regulating ISDS is to bottom-up pressures and influences.

Whether the current ISDS reform globally will successfully address the underlying reasons triggering the need for reform in the first place, part of which are not procedural but substantive, is yet to be seen. The way this reform is happening, however, is worthy

[69] Anthea Roberts, *Clash of Paradigms: Actors and Analogies Shaping the Investment Treaty System*, 107(1) American Journal of International Law 45–94 (2013), available at https://ssrn.com/abstract=2033167, accessed on June 1, 2018.

[70] Like the formalists, the realists, and the legal process thinkers.

[71] William N. Eskridge Jr., *Public Law from the Bottom Up*, 97 West Virginia Law Review 141, 142 (1994).

[72] *Id.* at 148.

[73] *Tobacco Plain Packaging Act 2011* (NO. 148, 2011).

[74] Two constitutional challenges in 2012: *British American Tobacco Australasia Limited and Ors v. Commonwealth of Australia, and J T International SA v. Commonwealth of Australia*; and WTO panels established at the request of Ukraine (on 28 September 2012), Honduras (on 25 September 2013), Indonesia (on 26 March 2014), Dominican Republic (on 25 April 2014) and Cuba (on 25 April 2014).

[75] *Philip Morris Asia v Australia*, ad hoc arbitration under the UNCITRAL Rules.

[76] Decision of 18 December 2015, available at https://www.cio.org.au/assets/27887028/Decision%2018%20December%202015%20a.pdf, accessed on June 1, 2018.

[77] DFAT, Gillard Government Trade Policy Statement: Trading Our Way to More Jobs and Prosperity, April 2011, Canberra 14 (2011).

of its own analysis. The formal structure of legal harmonisation processes through the UNCITRAL involves the UNCITRAL Commission (currently comprising 60 UN member states) identifying topics for work, which are then assigned to a certain working group. The working groups consist of delegates of the member states who are experts in the field but are also representing their governments' position – an aspect that is specifically relevant in the current work of WG III, expressly flagged as government-led. Once assigned a topic, a working group is generally left to complete its substantive task without intervention from the Commission, but only within the Commission's mandate. In this sense, legal development and harmonisation through the UNCITRAL is essentially top-down development: it is formulated at the level of the UN Commission, creating a mandate for the working group experts to work out the technicalities to be approved (or not) by the Commission, so that they can become model laws, conventions, or technical guidelines for states to adopt. Based on the top-down model, individuals and businesses in the adopting countries are then supposed to simply accept and operate under the legislative framework developed under the aegis of international harmonisation.

Nevertheless, the initial source of the mandate reaching the member states sitting on the Trade Commission and the influences reaching the work of the working groups, frequently originate from non-state actors. Practical changes to legal development seem to consistently start from the lowest common denominator i.e., the lowest level at which participants are being involved in the process. The Phillip Morris experience shows that public interest is pushing states to adapt their approach to ISDS overall, due to the political capital and its associated risks attached to policies impacting on public interest. The impact public pressure can have on governments' position with regard to the need for ISDS reform is currently reflected by the differentiation within the WG III review between analysing only the facts of the system or both the factual reality and the perception of that reality. If 'perception' is formally recognised as a relevant factor leading to the level of reform of a system that may, otherwise, be found to be objectively efficient, the regulation of ISDS through an UN-driven legislative development process will, in fact, be officially admitted to be a bottom-up process.

Given that the UN itself is an international organisation established to protect public interest globally,[78] such a process conducted through a non-state actor itself, may not be surprising. Given that the UN and consequently the UNCITRAL, is composed of member states that possess the sovereign power to create legislation regulating ISDS, the correlation between the state and non-state actors becomes more convoluted and the previously perceived top-down or bottom-up vertical processes seem to be of a rather multidimensional shape.

---

[78] *See* the Preamble and Chapter I on Purposes and Principles of the UN Charter, available at http://www.un.org/en/charter-united-nations/index.html.

Legitimacy issues: abuse, access and public participation

Wasiq Abass Dar[*]

'ABUSE OF PROCESS' AND ANTI-ARBITRATION INJUNCTIONS IN INVESTOR-STATE ARBITRATION – AN ANALYSIS OF RECENT TRENDS AND THE WAY FORWARD

Abstract

The abuse of procedural rights in investor-state arbitration is often employed by investors as a strategy to maximize the possibility of a favorable decision. Initiating multiple or parallel arbitral proceedings, at times under different bilateral investment treaties, for the same or related claims is one such manifestation of abuse of process. In response, host states usually prefer to approach national courts for obtaining a relief against the abuse of process in form of an anti-arbitration injunction. Though a popular tool for state parties in investor-state arbitration, anti-arbitration injunctions granted by national courts, inter alia, are often criticized for being an interference with the arbitral tribunal's authority to decide on matters of admissibility and jurisdiction. This article examines the concerns associated with the notion of abuse of process in the context of investor-state arbitration and evaluates possible remedies against the abuse of process. While focusing on the practice of national courts to grant anti-arbitration injunctions, the article, based on recent trends, assesses the varying positions of national courts on the issue. Taking into account the concerns and apprehensions raised by both investors and host states, the article proposes a balanced approach where the scope of national courts is narrowed down when it comes to issuing anti-arbitration injunctions and only the supervisory courts are authorized to grant such injunctions.

I. Introduction

Investors, more often than not, have a perception that the national courts of a host state will have a sense of loyalty towards the host state and, therefore, will inevitably be partial while deciding the dispute.[1] This opinion, which may not always be incorrect, is one of the most significant driving forces influencing investors to opt for impartial international arbitration proceedings as a dispute settlement mechanism – instead of conventional litigation before the courts of the host state.

One of the peculiar features of investor-state arbitration is that it is a product of a treaty between states (the home state of the investor and the host state) that allows the investor to initiate international arbitration proceedings against the host state. Once the

---

[*] S.J.D. Candidate, Department of Legal Studies, Central European University, Budapest. Email: Dar_Wasiq@phd.ceu.edu.

[1] Christoph Schreuer, *Interaction of International Tribunals and Domestic Courts in Investment Law, in* Contemporary Issues in International Arbitration and Mediation: The Fordham Papers 71 (A.W. Rovine ed., Boston, 2010).

parties to a dispute consent to arbitration, it automatically means that all other remedies to settle the dispute are excluded as a rule.[2] This does not, however, suggest that the national courts or conventional litigation completely disappear from the prospect.

Growth in investor-state arbitration has also given rise to instances of litigation in related issues. One of the by-products of the surge in investor-state arbitration, owing to the large stakes involved, has been the increasingly creative strategies resorted to by the parties to a dispute, be it before the arbitral tribunal or before a national court.[3]

Perverse abuse of procedural rights is one such strategy that parties, at times, have relied upon, in order to increase the chances of getting a favorable decision. Such abuse of procedural rights is often challenged by the aggrieved party on the basis of the doctrine of 'abuse of process'. This article looks into the concerns that the notion and practice of 'abuse of process' has raised in the world of investor-state arbitration – in particular, the manner in which the investors rely upon a strategy of initiating multiple or parallel arbitration proceedings for the same claims - with the objective of increasing the chances of favorable decisions and jeopardizing the position of the host state.

This article also examines the practice of granting anti-arbitration injunctions by various national courts, at the request of state parties – safeguarding their interests against the alleged abuse of process. Anti-arbitration injunctions, particularly in investor-state arbitration, have found great support from state parties – in situations where investors with the aim of multiplying the chances of a favorable award go for multiple or parallel proceedings by way of abusing procedural rights.[4]

However, in the recent past, the international legal community, more specifically some of the stakeholders in investor-state arbitration, have raised their concerns on national courts' authority on issuing such anti-arbitration injunctions.[5] One of the principle arguments put forth is that the arbitral proceedings should not get frustrated by the interventionist approach of a court, as such uncalled for interventions deny the tribunals the competence to decide on issues like abuse of process.[6] It is also argued that an anti-arbitration injunction issued by a court of a host state can well be seen as an attempt to deny justice to the investor – which, in itself, may amount to a breach of the investment treaty.[7]

In light of the raised concerns, the article analyzes recent trends on how anti-arbitration injunctions have been used by national courts in order to remedy the issue of abuse of process. The article also investigates the imperative questions as to whether the national courts should at all be issuing anti-arbitration injunctions and if yes, then

---

2 *Id.* at 76.

3 Emmanuel Gaillard, *Abuse of Process in International Arbitration*, 32(1) ICSID Review 17, 18 (2017).

4 Sharad Bansal and Divyanshu Agarwal, *Are Anti-Arbitration Injunctions a Malaise? An Analysis in the Context of Indian Law*, 31 Arbitration International 615 (2015).

5 Julian Lew, *Does National Court Involvement Undermine the International Arbitration Process?*, 24 Am. U. Int'L. Rev. 489 (2009).

6 Christoph Schreuer, *Interaction of International Tribunals and Domestic Courts in Investment Law, in* Contemporary Issues in International Arbitration and Mediation: The Fordham Papers 87 (A.W. Rovine ed., Boston, 2010).

7 Richard Garnett, *National Court Intervention in Arbitration as an Investment Treaty Claim*, 60 International and Comparative Law Quarterly 491 (2011).

where do the national courts derive the authority to issue such injunctions? Also, in the well-known disparity in practice, which national court(s) should intervene and grant such orders enjoining arbitral proceedings?

II. 'Abuse of Process' – Concept and Concerns

Abuse of process, in most lucid terms, is use of a procedural right which on its own is perfectly valid under law but the exercise of which is perverse because it is used with an objective to cause injury to other party and to maximize the possibility of getting a favorable decision.[8] The notion of 'abuse of process' finds its application in both private law as well as public international law. Not only has it been recognized by various national legal systems, its application is also acknowledged by various international forums, including the International Court of Justice and the WTO Tribunals.[9] Owing to such recognition and application, the principle of abuse of process is well accepted as a general principle of international law.[10]

Interestingly, various scholarly writings and tribunals have argued that the doctrine of abuse of process finds its roots in abuse of rights, suggesting that abuse of procedural rights goes against the fundamental principle of good faith that parties are expected to adhere to while engaging in proceedings before an international tribunal.[11] Parties ought to be discouraged from undertaking any such actions that can have the potential of frustrating the proceedings resorted to, or to gain any unwarranted advantage as a result of exercise of bad faith.

The significance of observing the principle of good faith, in order to avoid any attempt at abuse of procedural rights, while initiating a claim was highlighted by the tribunal in *Phoenix Action Ltd. v. Czech Republic*[12]. The arbitral tribunal pointed out that:

> *"The principle of good faith has long been recognized in public international law, as it is also in all national legal systems. The principle requires parties "to deal honestly and fairly with each other, to represent their motives and purposes truthfully, and to refrain from taking unfair advantage..." This principle governs the relations between states, but also the legal rights and*

---

[8] Eric De Brabandere, *"Good Faith", "Abuse of Process" and the Initiation of Investment Treaty Claims*, 3(3) Journal of International Dispute Settlement 620 (2012); *see also*, Emmanuel Gaillard, *Abuse of Process in International Arbitration*, 32(1) ICSID Review 17 (2017).

[9] Yuval Shany, The Competing Jurisdictions of International Courts and Tribunals 257 (OUP, 2003); *see also*, Eric De Brabandere, *"Good Faith", "Abuse of Process" and the Initiation of Investment Treaty Claims*, 3(3) Journal of International Dispute Settlement 618 (2012).

[10] Zimmermann et al. The Statute of International Court of Justice: A Commentary 831-832 (OUP, 2006); *see also*, Emmanuel Gaillard, *Abuse of Process in International Arbitration*, 32(1) ICSID Review 17, 33 (2017).

[11] Michael Byers, *Abuse of Rights: An Old Principle, A New Age*, 47 McGill Law Journal 441 (2002), *see also*, Eric De Brabandere, *"Good Faith", "Abuse of Process" and the Initiation of Investment Treaty Claims*, 3(3) Journal of International Dispute Settlement 610 (2012); *see, Abaclat and others v. Republic of Argentina*, ICSID Case No. ARB/07/5, Decision on Jurisdiction and Admissibility, 4 August 2011, paras 647-649.

[12] *Phoenix Action Ltd. v. Czech Republic*, ICSID Case No. ARB/06/5, Award, 15 April 2009.

> *duties of those seeking to assert an international claim under a treaty. Nobody shall abuse the rights granted by treaties, and more generally, every rule of law includes an implied clause that it should not be abused."*[13]

Similarly, the Delhi High Court in a recent decision while dealing with the issue of 'abuse of process' delved into the principle of good faith and abuse of rights. It observed that abuse of process basically finds its origin in the notion of good faith and the related concept of abuse of rights, which have roots in private law as well as public international law and as such is well recognized in various national legal systems.[14]

In *Abacalt and others v. Argentine Republic*[15], whilst drawing and highlighting the connection between good faith and abuse of process, the tribunal observed that:

> *"The theory of abuse of rights is an expression of the more general principle of good faith. The principle of good faith is a fundamental principle of international law, as well as investment law. As such, the Tribunal holds that the theory of abuse of rights is, in principle, applicable to ICSID proceedings".*[16]

Lauterpacht, in his seminal work, recognized the possibility of abuse of rights, including procedural rights, highlighted the option of a remedial action against such abuse, and stated that: 'there is no right however well established, which could not, in some circumstances, be refused recognition on the ground that it has been abused'.[17]

The doctrine of abuse of process is often invoked to question the admissibility of a claim.[18] A significant difficulty that arbitrators or courts face in such a situation is to ascertain the claim of abuse of process. What makes it even more challenging is that abuse of procedural rights, as a strategy, is not illegal per se because it does not violate any legal rule – nonetheless it has the potential of causing significant harm to the party against whom it is directed.[19]

The courts or the tribunals seized with the assessment of admissibility of a claim may understandably deny admission of such claim, to avoid abuse of process, by exercising their inherent powers.[20] Owing to the fact that establishing abuse of process requires sufficient subjective analysis of the relevant facts and circumstances, the tribunals or

---

13 *Id.* at para 107; footnote omitted

14 *Union of India v. Vodafone Group PLC United Kingdom & Anr*, Delhi High Court, 7 May 2018, paras 106 and 108.

15 *Abaclat and others v. Republic of Argentina*, ICSID Case No. ARB/07/5, Decision on Jurisdiction and Admissibility, 4 August 2011.

16 *Id.* at para 646.

17 HERSCH LAUTERPACHT, THE DEVELOPMENT OF INTERNATIONAL LAW BY THE INTERNATIONAL COURT 164 (CUP, 1982).

18 YUVAL SHANY, THE COMPETING JURISDICTIONS OF INTERNATIONAL COURTS AND TRIBUNALS 255 (OUP, 2003).

19 Emmanuel Gaillard, *Abuse of Process in International Arbitration*, 32(1) ICSID Review 17, 18 (2017); *see also*, Eric De Brabandere, *"Good Faith", "Abuse of Process" and the Initiation of Investment Treaty Claims*, 3(3) Journal of International Dispute Settlement 620 (2012).

20 *Waste Management v. United Mexican States*, ICSID Case No. ARB (AF)/98/2, 2000, para 49; *see also, Phoenix Action Ltd. v. Czech Republic*, ICSID Case No. ARB/06/5, Award, 15 April 2009, paras 142-144; *see also, S.H. Sabbagh v. W.S. Khoury & Others*, [2018] EWHC 1330 (Comm), paras 17-18.

courts generally prefer to exercise restraint and deny admissibility of claims only when absence of good faith is manifest.

III. Abuse of Process and Investor-State Arbitration

In the context of international arbitral proceedings, the principle of good faith is taken into account when allegations of abuse of rights or abuse of process are leveled against one of the parties. To understand and examine the role of abuse of process in investor-state arbitration, it is crucial to study the application of the doctrine of abuse of process in the context of investor-state arbitration and also to assess the possible consequences – in particular the possible remedy against abuse of process in the form of anti-arbitration injunctions. For the purpose of discussion in this article, recourse to abuse of process on the part of investors before arbitral tribunals will be examined.

In the recent past, from the beginning of the 21st Century, there has been a tremendous surge in the number of investment related claims that have been filed against host states. There has also been a correlated increase in the number of allegations against the investors/claimants for abuse of process to maximize favorable results. Instances of abuse of process or potential of such abuse have generated some reservations and apprehensions in the minds of state parties with regard to the efficiency and efficacy of investor-state arbitration as a dispute resolution mechanism.[21]

One of the major concerns for state parties, in disputes arising out of investment treaties, has been the way foreign investors, on several occasions, have exploited the option of launching multiple or parallel arbitration proceedings against the host state under the garb of different investment treaties. It should be kept in mind that it is not the initiation of different arbitral proceedings against the respondent under different investment treaties that, per se, amounts to abuse of process.[22] Instead, it is the simultaneous initiation of multiple or parallel proceedings for the same claim, with an objective of increasing the chances of a favorable award, that is understood as abuse of process.

There are different strategies that investors may rely upon, which later on might end up being challenged by the host states on the ground of abuse of process. One of the strategies, as already pointed out, can be to initiate more than one proceeding before different arbitral tribunals for the same claim, by banking upon different investment treaties. The other strategy can be splitting of the claims and presenting those before different arbitral tribunals. In both scenarios, the respondent is strained to undergo extreme inconvenience of defending itself before different arbitral tribunals – not only costing it more time and money but also running the risk of dissimilar outcomes.[23]

---

[21] Eric De Brabandere, *"Good Faith", "Abuse of Process" and the Initiation of Investment Treaty Claims*, 3(3) Journal of International Dispute Settlement 611 (2012).

[22] *British Caribbean Bank Ltd. v. The Government of Belize*, Caribbean Court of Justice, 10 December 2013, para 41.

[23] Emmanuel Gaillard, *Abuse of Process in International Arbitration*, 32(1) ICSID Review 17, 23-24 (2017).

a) Corporate Restructuring and Abuse of Process

Corporate restructuring, of late, has evolved as one of the more popular mechanisms that investors resort to in order to file the same or similar claims before multiple arbitral tribunals, under different investment treaties. The objective is to maximize the possibility of getting favorable results. It is worth mentioning that corporate restructuring on its own does not lead to a conclusion that the investor intended to abuse the process. An investor may be held liable for abuse of process only if such corporate restructuring is done with an aim of gaining access to a dispute resolution mechanism under a particular investment treaty whilst the dispute was not yet crystallized but the result was clearly foreseeable.[24]

In *Phoenix Action Ltd v. Czech Republic*[25], a Czech national transferred the shares of his Czech company in favor of an Israeli company owned by the wife of the Czech national. The move was made in order to find a remedy in a domestic dispute by raising a claim before an international arbitral tribunal under the relevant Bilateral Investment Treaty. The tribunal while recognizing abuse of process observed that:

> *"All the elements analyzed lead to the same conclusion of abuse of rights. The abuse here could be called a "detournement de procedure", consisting in the Claimant's creation of a legal fiction in order to gain access to an international arbitration procedure to which it was not entitled... The conclusion of the Tribunal is therefore that the Claimant's initiation and pursuit of this arbitration is an abuse of the system of international ICSID investment arbitration... It is the duty of the tribunal not to protect such an abusive manipulation of the system of international investment protection under the ICSID Convention and the BITs".*[26]

Similarly, in *Philip Morris Asia Limited (Hong Kong) v. The Commonwealth of Australia*[27], Australia raised an objection that corporate restructuring by the investor was done on purpose for bringing a claim under the Hong Kong – Australia BIT and therefore amounted to abuse of process. The Tribunal, rejecting the argument of the claimant observed that 'it would not normally be an abuse of rights to bring a BIT claim in the wake of a corporate restructuring, if the restructuring was justified independently of the possibility of such a claim', which was far from true in the instant case.[28]

In *Renee Rose Levy and Gremcitel SA v. Republic of Peru*[29], a family owning a group of companies had acquired shares of a local company called Gremcitel. Right before a

[24] Eric De Brabandere, *"Good Faith", "Abuse of Process" and the Initiation of Investment Treaty Claims*, 3(3) Journal of International Dispute Settlement 612 (2012).

[25] *Phoenix Action Ltd. v. Czech Republic*, ICSID Case No. ARB/06/5, Award, 15 April 2009.

[26] *Id.* at paras 143-144.

[27] *Philip Morris Asia Limited (Hong Kong) v. The Commonwealth of Australia*, PCA Case No. 2012-12, Award on Jurisdiction and Admissibility (2015).

[28] *Id.* at para 570.

[29] *Renee Rose Levy and Gremcitel SA v. Republic of Peru*, ICSID Case No. ARB/11/17, Award (2015).

resolution of the Peruvian government that could have adversely affected the investment, the family transferred the majority interest of Gremcitel to one of the members of the family – Renee Levy, a French national. Once the Peruvian government passed the resolution, ICSID arbitration was initiated under the France-Peru BIT. The Tribunal held that though the claimant was well within its rights to initiate the arbitral proceedings and all the jurisdictional requirements were met, the manner and timing in which shares were transferred to Ms. Levy suggested that the purpose was to abuse the process. The tribunal observed that 'the corporate restructuring by which Ms. Levy became the main shareholder of Gremcitel…constitutes an abuse of process'[30] and the tribunal accordingly, decided to decline jurisdiction.

Similar opinions of arbitral tribunals, on abuse of process, can be found in cases where investors have either tried to change their nationality to take advantage of an investment treaty or where some of the shareholders of a corporate structure have attempted to benefit from filing separate claims. For example, in *Pac Rim Cayman LLC v. El Salvador*[31], the Tribunal was of the opinion that an abuse of process may exist if a change of nationality occurs 'when the relevant party can see an actual dispute or can foresee a specific future dispute as a very high probability and not merely as a possible controversy'.[32]

In *Rachel S. Grynberg and Others v. Grenada*[33], the claim filed by the investor was rejected by the ICSID Tribunal[34], following which the investor initiated annulment proceedings. However, pending annulment proceedings some of the shareholders initiated a new claim against the host state. The Tribunal, upholding the findings of the first tribunal, observed that the claim was made in bad faith.

b) Abuse of Process – An Issue of Admissibility

It is important to clarify that when an allegation of abuse of process is raised that it is not the jurisdiction of the tribunal to entertain a claim that is directly challenged but it is the admissibility of the claim that is questioned.[35]

In case of 'jurisdiction' the tribunal or court decides whether the claim can be entertained for the purposes of rendering a decision over it, whereas, in the case of 'admissibility', the tribunal or court may decide to refuse to proceed on grounds of certain procedural requirements.[36]

---

30 *Id.* at para 195.

31 *Pac Rim Cayman LLC v. El Salvador*, ICSID Case No. ARB/09/12, Decision on the Respondent's Jurisdictional Objections (2012).

32 *Id.* at para 2.99.

33 *Rachel S. Grynberg and Others v. Grenada*, ICSID Case No. ARB/10/6 (2010).

34 *RSM Production Corporation v. Grenada*, ICSID Case No. ARB/05/14, Award, 2009.

35 *SGS Societe Generale de Surveillance v. Republic of the Philipines*, ICSID Case No. ARB/02/6, Decision of the Tribunal on Objections to Jurisdiction (2004), para 171.

36 Shabtai Rosene, *International Courts and Tribunals, Jurisdiction and Admissibility of the Inter-State Applications, in* Max Plank Encyclopedia of Public International Law 2 (Rudiger Wolfrum ed., OUP, 2012); *see also* Andrew

For example, the tribunal will lack jurisdiction in a case if investor X files a claim against state Y and it later turns out that there was no investment made in the first place. However, in the case of admissibility – despite there being an investment and jurisdiction of the tribunal to proceed with the claim – the tribunal may still decline to entertain the claim if it has a reason to believe that such a claim was initiated in bad faith and that admitting the claim would result in abuse of process.[37]

The fundamental difference, in terms of consequences, is that the claimant cannot resubmit the claim in case of denial of jurisdiction where as in case of inadmissibility, the tribunal may entertain the claim once the reason of inadmissibility ceases to exist at the time of resubmission. The distinction is highlighted by the tribunal in *SGS v. The Philippines*, which noted

> *"Normally a claim which is within jurisdiction but inadmissible ... will be dismissed, although this will usually be without prejudice to the right of the claimant to start new proceedings if the obstacle of admissibility has been removed".*[38]

In practice, the tribunal decides on the question of jurisdiction and admissibility at the same time, though in theory, the decision on jurisdiction precedes the ascertainment of admissibility of the claim.[39] The issue of admissibility, at least in theory, is different from jurisdiction – in practice, the effect of inadmissibility precludes the tribunal to exercise its jurisdiction over a claim. As a result the tribunal is not in a position to entertain the claim on grounds of inadmissibility.

The question arises as to what happens if the investor initiates multiple or parallel proceedings for same claim and the tribunal(s) fails to recognize or ignores the abuse of process and ends up admitting the claim? More importantly, what are the options with the host state in a scenario where an abuse of process exists and the host state not only decides not to submit before the arbitral tribunal(s) but also considers stopping the tribunal(s) from initiating or continuing the arbitral proceedings?

There is no single answer to these questions. Remedies may vary depending upon the facts and circumstances of the case and more likely upon the host state's choice of forum, which maybe approachable for relief. Typically, the host state may either contest the admissibility before the tribunal(s) itself or before a national court, on the ground of abuse of process and by relying on the doctrine of *Lis Pendens*. Alternatively, it may rely on the doctrine of *Forum Non Conveniens* and request that the national court grants a stay against the proceedings before the inappropriate forum. In any case, if the state

---

Newcombe, *Investor Misconduct: Jurisdiction, Admissibility or Merits?*, *in* Evolution in Investment Treaty Law and Arbitration, 194 (C. Brown and K. Miles eds., CUP, 2011).

37 Eric De Brabandere, *"Good Faith", "Abuse of Process" and the Initiation of Investment Treaty Claims*, 3(3) Journal of International Dispute Settlement 617 (2012).

38 *SGS Societe Generale de Surveillance v. Republic of the Philipines*, ICSID Case No. ARB/02/6, Decision of the Tribunal on Objections to Jurisdiction (2004), para 171.

39 Eric De Brabandere, *"Good Faith", "Abuse of Process" and the Initiation of Investment Treaty Claims*, 3(3) Journal of International Dispute Settlement 618 (2012).

party chooses to approach a national court, the relief sought would inevitably be an order enjoining the challenged arbitral proceedings.

IV. Anti-Arbitration Injunctions – A Remedy Against Abuse of Process?

Obtaining anti-arbitration injunctions from national courts is a popular tool that aggrieved parties resort to in order to disallow abuse of process. Anti-arbitration injunctions are issued either before the commencement of arbitration or during the course of arbitration proceedings – either against the parties or/and against the arbitral tribunal itself. National courts have on several occasions intervened to prohibit abuse of process in context of investor-state arbitration by issuing anti-arbitration injunctions. Anti-arbitration injunctions particularly come into the picture to handle the situation of multiple or parallel proceedings.[40]

However, various stakeholders of investor-state arbitration have for a long time questioned the authority of national courts to intervene and issue anti-arbitration injunctions.[41] The authority of national courts to enjoin arbitral proceedings is often seen as a measure not only thwarting the arbitral process but also going against the essence of bilateral investment treaties.

Though the national courts in certain jurisdictions continue to claim that they do enjoy the authority to intervene and issue anti-arbitration injunctions, there are questions that persist including from where do these courts derive such authority and which courts, if any, should intervene when an allegation of abuse of process is raised?

Looking at the relationship of anti-arbitration injunctions with the New York Convention[42] shows that it has been anything but clear. Art. II (3) of the New York Convention suggests that, by virtue of the *Kompetenz- Kompetenz* principle, the arbitrators should get priority over the courts in deciding the jurisdiction. This, of course, remains subject to annulment and enforcement proceedings at a later stage.[43] Although there is no direct mention or even a suggestion for allowing national courts to issue anti-arbitration injunctions, the counter-argument has been that the New York Convention does not also expressly prohibit it – particularly if one takes into account the case of an arbitration agreement being null and void or inoperative or incapable of being

---

[40] Gabrielle Kaufmann-Kohler, *How to Handle Parallel Proceedings: A Practical Approach to Issues such as Competence-Competence and Anti-Suit Injunctions*, 2(1) Dispute Resolution International 111 (2008).

[41] Julian Lew, *Does National Court Involvement Undermine the International Arbitration Process?*, 24 American University International Law Review 489 (2009); *see also* Winnie Ma, *Parallel Proceedings and International Commercial Arbitration: The International Law Association's Recommendations for Arbitrators*, 2 Contemporary Asia Arbitration Journal 53 (2009).

[42] Convention on Recognition and Enforcement of Foreign Arbitral Awards, June 1958.

[43] Robin F. Hansen, *Parallel Proceedings in Investor-State Treaty Arbitration: Responses for Treaty-Drafters, Arbitrators and Parties*, 73(4) The Modern Law Review 531 (2010); *see also*, Winnie Ma, *Parallel Proceedings and International Commercial Arbitration: The International Law Association's Recommendations for Arbitrators*, 2 Contemporary Asia Arbitration Journal 53 (2009); *see also*, Peter Schlosser, *Arbitral Tribunals or State Courts: Who Must Defer to Whom?*; *in* ARBITRAL TRIBUNALS OR STATE COURTS: WHO MUST DEFER TO WHOM? 15, 29 (Pierre A. Karrer ed, ASA Special Series No. 15, 2001).

performed.[44] However, reading of the New York Convention through a pro-arbitration prism would most likely side with the voices that oppose anti-arbitration injunctions.[45]

Similarly, Art. 41(1)[46] of the ICSID Convention[47], which governs most of the modern day investor-state arbitrations, authorizes the tribunal to decide on its competence, as does Article 23(1)[48] of the UNCITRAL Arbitration Rules. Moreover, the ICSID Convention also suggests that the domestic courts should defer to the findings of the ICSID tribunals.[49] The question is whether this is leaving any scope for the national courts to intervene in case of deciding admissibility or jurisdiction.

In such prevailing uncertainty and lack of clarity over the issue, an overwhelming majority of scholarship in the arbitration world has favoured a position against anti-arbitration injunctions.[50] Scholars like Stephen Schwebel have gone to the extent of opining that granting anti-arbitration injunctions not only goes squarely against the New York Convention but the principles of international law as well. He argues that, 'The object and purpose of the New York Convention is to ensure that agreements to arbitrate and the resultant awards – at any rate, the resultant foreign awards – are recognized and enforced. It follows that the issuance by a court of an anti-suit injunction that, far from recognizing and enforcing an agreement to arbitrate, prevents or immobilizes the arbitration that seeks to implement that agreement, is inconsistent with the obligations of the state under the New York Convention'.[51]

The afore-mentioned arguments give rise to a more pertinent question – whether courts should at all be approached when the abuse of process pertains to arbitration? Why not let the forum, whose process is under abuse, decide on the matter? The principle of *Kompetenz-Kompetenz*, undeniably, is of profound importance when it comes to determining the jurisdiction of an arbitral tribunal. Though, as discussed above, abuse of process is considered a ground to deny 'admissibility' rather than jurisdiction, the consequence, however, is that the inadmissibility precludes the jurisdiction of the tribunal to proceed with arbitration, if abuse of process is established. Since the issue indirectly affects the jurisdiction of the tribunal, it can be argued that the arbitral tribunal should be the deciding authority when a claim of abuse of process is raised. In such a

---

44 Sharad Bansal and Divyanshu Agarwal, *Are Anti-Arbitration Injunctions a Malaise? An Analysis in the Context of Indian Law*, 31 Arbitration International 620 (2015).

45 Gary Born. International Commercial Arbitration 1053 (Kluwer Law International, 2009).

46 Article 41 (1): 'The Tribunal shall be the judge of its own competence'.

47 The International Centre for Settlement of Investment Disputes (ICSID) – Convention on the Settlement of Investment Disputes between States and Nationals of Other States, 1966.

48 Article 23(1): 'The arbitral tribunal shall have the power to rule on its own jurisdiction, including any objections with respect to the existence or validity of the arbitration agreement'.

49 Christoph Schreuer, *Interaction of International Tribunals and Domestic Courts in Investment Law, in* Contemporary Issues in International Arbitration and Mediation: The Fordham Papers 87 (A.W. Rovine ed., Boston, 2010).

50 Stephen Schwebel, *Anti-Suit Injunctions in International Arbitration – An Overview, in* Anti-Suit Injunction in International Arbitration 5 (E. Giallard ed., Juris Publishing, 2005); *see also*, Pierre A. Karrer, *Anti-Arbitration Injunctions: Theory and Practice, in* ICCA Congress Series No. 13 228 (Kluwer Law International, 2007); *see also*, Gary Born. International Commercial Arbitration 1053 (Kluwer Law International, 2009).

51 Stephen Schwebel, *Anti-Suit Injunctions in International Arbitration – An Overview, in* Anti-Suit Injunction in International Arbitration 10-11 (E. Giallard ed., Juris Publishing, 2005).

scenario, resorting to courts for an anti-arbitration injunction would, understandably, be in contravention to the well-established principle of *Kompetenz-Kompetenz*. Furthermore, if the state party is aggrieved with the decision of the tribunal, it will always have the option of approaching the seat court for relief. The argument is essentially grounded on the principle of minimal curial intervention, as propounded by the Model Law.[52]

However, as of today, this approach has not found many takers – particularly in common law countries. It is evident from practice, national courts have on several occasions preferred to intervene and issue anti-arbitration injunctions – irrespective of being a supervisory court or a non-supervisory court.

a) National Courts and Anti-Arbitration Injunctions

The role of national courts in investor-state arbitration cannot be completely ruled out as there are situations where involvement of a court in the overall arbitral process becomes inevitable – particularly in case of non-ICSID investor-state arbitrations. This, however, does not negate the fact that what makes a difference in ensuring the success of inter-state arbitrations is whether the court involvement is complementing or impeding the process of arbitration.[53]

When it comes to the practice of national courts, as far as issuing anti-arbitration injunctions is concerned, a comparative study of civil law and common law jurisdictions suggests that the former are more unenthusiastic to issue such injunctions in comparison to the later.[54] In France, for example, the law directs that tribunals should get preference over courts in deciding disputes except where the arbitration agreement itself is manifestly invalid.[55] Similarly, Switzerland has a clear stand that anti-arbitration injunctions are contrary to the Swiss legal system, as such injunctions go squarely against the *Kompetenz-Kompetenz* principle.[56] The Swiss court, taking a strong position, has gone to the extent of suggesting that owing to the *Kompetenz-Kompetenz* principle, courts can neither issue anti-arbitration injunctions nor can enforce any such injunctions in Switzerland, if issued by a foreign court.

Civil law jurisdictions, in general, prefer to resort to the doctrine of *Lis pendens* while handling issues of parallel proceedings. For example, courts of EU Member States, as a general rule, because of the Brussels Regulation (Recast) on Jurisdiction

[52] Nicholas Poon, *The Use and Abuse of Anti-Arbitration Injunctions – A Way Forward for Singapore*, 25 Singapore Academy of Law Journal 287 (2013).

[53] Julian Lew, *Does National Court Involvement Undermine the International Arbitration Process?*, 24 American University International Law Review 490 (2009).

[54] Gabrielle Kaufmann-Kohler, *How to Handle Parallel Proceedings: A Practical Approach to Issues such as Competence-Competence and Anti-Suit Injunctions*, 2(1) Dispute Resolution International 111 (2008).

[55] Article 1458 of the French New Code of Civil Procedure; *see also*, Savage & Gaillard. Fouchard Gaillard and Goldman on International Arbitration 407 (Kluwer Law International, 1997).

[56] *Air (PTY) Ltd. v. International Air Transport Association (IATA) and CSA in Liquidation*, Case No C/1043/2005-15SP, Republic and Canton of Geneva Judiciary, Court of First Instance (2005); *see also*, Matthias Scherer & Werner Jahnel, *Anti-Suit and Anti-Arbitration Injunctions in International Arbitration: A Swiss Perspective*, 4 International Arbitration Law Review 66 (2009).

and enforcement,[57] restrain from enjoining a party if proceedings are already initiated in a court of another Member State.[58] The Regulation, though, makes an exception in case of arbitration by allowing the courts of a Member State to determine whether or not an arbitration agreement is null and void, inoperative or incapable of being performed; it excludes the decision made on such issues from the ambit of the Regulation.[59] Therefore, providing less inducement to the parties willing to resort to abuse of process by way of initiating proceedings before a court of a Member State, as the decision will not have the support of the Regulation for the purpose of recognition in other Member State(s). Furthermore, Art. 73(2) of the Regulation provides precedence to the New York Convention over the Regulation, therefore, ensuring that a Member State can enforce an award despite there being a contrary judgment in some other Member State.

Common law courts, on the other hand, are of the opinion that they can intervene and issue, when appropriate, anti-arbitration injunctions. They generally resort to the authority sourced in their equity powers. The common law system does not have an established position on the principle of abuse of rights but it has not prevented the courts from exercising their inherent powers to stop a party from abusing procedural rights.[60] Extending this argument to the right to arbitrate under investor-state arbitrations means the courts have intervened and restrained international arbitrations when convinced that abuse of legal process was involved.

English courts, for instance, do not shy away from granting such injunctions, though it is done with reluctance. Courts in England have consistently been of the opinion that they derive the power to issue anti-arbitration injunctions from Sec. 37 of the Supreme Court Act of 1981.[61] However, the courts have clarified that anti-arbitration injunctions should be granted only when the court is fully convinced that arbitration proceeding would be oppressive, vexatious, or result in abuse of process.[62]

In the United States, as well, though with relatively more restraint, courts have granted anti-arbitration injunctions in exercise of their inherent powers.[63] However, there have been instances where the courts in the US have opted for a completely diverging opinion.

---

[57] Regulation (EU) No. 1215/2012 of the European Parliament and the Council on Jurisdiction and Recognition and Enforcement of Judgments in Civil and Commercial Matters (Recast), 12 December 2012.

[58] *See*, Article 29 and Recital 21 & 22 of the Brussels Regulation (Recast); *see also*, Gabrielle Kaufmann-Kohler, *How to Handle Parallel Proceedings: A Practical Approach to Issues such as Competence-Competence and Anti-Suit Injunctions*, 2(1) Dispute Resolution International 112 (2008).

[59] *See*, Recital 12 of the Brussels Regulation (Recast).

[60] Emmanuel Gaillard, *Abuse of Process in International Arbitration*, 32(1) ICSID Review 17, 32 (2017); *see also*, *Union of India v. Vodafone Group PLC United Kingdom & Anr*, Delhi High Court, 07 May 2018, paras 107 and 110.

[61] *Welex A.G. vs. Rosa Maritime Ltd*, APP.L.R. 07/03 (2003), paras 34-40; *see also*, *S.H. Sabbagh v. W.S. Khoury & Others*, [2018] EWHC 1330 (Comm), paras 17-18.

[62] *Claxton Engineering Services Ltd v TXM Olaj-es Gazkutato KTF*, [2011] EWHC 345 (Comm), paras 34 and 36; *see also*, *Elektrim SA v. Vivendi Universal SA*, [2007] EWHC 571 (Comm); *Republic of Kazakhstan (ROK) v. Istil Group Inc. (Istil)*, [2007] EWHC 2729 (Comm); *J. Jarvis & Sons Ltd. v. Blue Circle Dartford Estates Ltd.*, 2007, para 40.

[63] *Satcom International Group PLC v. Orbcomm International Partners, LP.*, 49 F Supp. 2d 331 (SDNY) 1999; *see also*, Jennifer Gorskie, *US Courts and Anti-Arbitration Injunction*, 28 Arbitration International 307 (2012).

For example, in *Republic of Ecuador v. Chevron Corporation*[64], the US court declined the request to issue an anti-arbitration injunction citing strong US policy of facilitating arbitration and absence of any express provisions under the New York Convention that would support such injunctions.

Indian courts have also on multiple occasions, expressed their opinion in favour of having inherent authority to issue anti-arbitration injunctions.[65] Following a lead from the courts in England, the Indian courts also claim to be courts of both law and equity and thus are empowered to provide equitable relief to aggrieved parties in the form of anti-suit or anti-arbitration injunctions. However, the courts have highlighted that such jurisdiction should be exercised with extreme caution and only under compelling circumstances e.g. presence of apparent abuse of process.[66]

b) Anti-Arbitration Injunction – An Exception and Not a Rule

Courts, while dealing with a request for granting an anti-arbitration injunction, must carefully weigh the competing interests of upholding the sanctity of the arbitral process and ensuring that investors do not take undue advantage of the same arbitral process by engaging in abuse of process.[67]

National courts, across the jurisdictions, have more often than not shown extreme caution while handling the requests for issuing anti-arbitration injunctions.[68] For example, the Caribbean Court of Justice in *British Caribbean Bank Ltd. v. The Government of Belize* when deciding on the issue whether courts in Belize have the authority to enjoin investment treaty arbitration proceedings, held in affirmative.[69] It observed that courts in Belize can issue anti-arbitration injunction – as authorized by Section 106A (8) of the Supreme Court of Judicature Act.[70] However, the court also pointed out that such injunctions might be issued only in exceptional circumstances, with extreme hesitation.[71] The court observed that

> *"...the court must re-double the caution it normally exercises in restraining foreign proceedings because of the importance of recognizing and enforcing*

[64] 638 F. 3d 384, Court of Appeals, 2nd Circuit CA (2011).

[65] *World Sport Group (Mauritius) v. MSM Satellite Singapore*, SC 968, AIR (2014); *see also, Union of India v. Vodafone Group PLC United Kingdom & Anr*, Delhi High Court, 07 May 2018.

[66] *Modi Entertainment Network v. W.S. G. Cricket Pvt. Ltd.*, 4 SCC 341(2003); *Union of India v. Vodafone Group PLC United Kingdom & Anr*, Delhi High Court, 07 May 2018.

[67] Nicholas Poon, *The Use and Abuse of Anti-Arbitration Injunctions – A Way Forward for Singapore*, 25 Singapore Academy of Law Journal 290 (2013); *see also*, Sharad Bansal and Divyanshu Agarwal, *Are Anti-Arbitration Injunctions a Malaise? An Analysis in the Context of Indian Law*, 31Arbitration International 629 (2015).

[68] *Elektrim SA v. Vivendi Universal SA*, [2007] EWHC 571 (Comm), para 39.

[69] *British Caribbean Bank Ltd. v. The Government of Belize*, Caribbean Court of Justice, 10 December 2013, para 14.

[70] *Id.* at para 30.

[71] *Id.* at paras 38 and 40.

> *the agreement of parties to the mechanism for dispute resolution and the accepted principle of international law that the arbitral tribunal should not be subject to the control of the domestic courts before it makes an award".*[72]

Similarly, the Delhi High Court, taking a cue from the international practice of restrained approach in granting anti-arbitration injunctions, noted that

> *"...the jurisdiction to grant an anti-arbitration injunction must be exercised with caution and granted only if the arbitral proceedings are vexatious or oppressive or inequitable or abuse of process. After all, one must not lose sight of the fact that a legislation or action that is perfectly lawful under the national law could nonetheless trigger a successful investment claim under the bilateral investment treaty...In fact the approach to arbitration agreements contained in investment treaties is for the court to support, so far as possible, the bargain for international arbitration. It is only with extreme hesitation that the Court would interfere with the process of arbitration".*[73]

V. Seat Court - The Appropriate Forum for Granting Anti-Arbitration Injunction

Although rare, it is quite evident from the practice that some national courts do issue anti-arbitration injunctions in order to prevent investors from resorting to abuse of process. A more complex concern that has been debated with no concrete solutions has been to identify the court(s), which should have the authority to issue anti-arbitration injunctions in case a claim of abuse of process is raised.

It is plausible to suggest that only the seat court or the supervisory court should be approached in order to avoid potential misuse of the option of such injunctions at the hands of state parties and to foster some sort of uniformity in practice.[74] Not only do seat courts enjoy jurisdictional standing over the arbitration process but, from a practical point of view, the seat court's decision will come across as impartial and command more respect from the tribunal.

The International Law Association Recommendations on *Lis Pendens* and Arbitration[75], while dealing with issue of parallel arbitral proceedings, did not provide a direct solution. However, some valid observations and suggestions were made. In the case of pending parallel proceedings before the supervisory court, the tribunal is expected to exercise its jurisdiction with caution, as a contrary decision to that of the supervisory court can run the risk of annulment.[76] In the case of proceedings pending before a non-supervisory court,

---

[72] *Id.* at para 41.

[73] *Union of India v. Vodafone Group PLC United Kingdom & Anr*, Delhi High Court, 07 May 2018, paras 114-115.

[74] Jennifer Gorskie, *US Courts and Anti-Arbitration Injunction*, 28 Arbitration International 295 (2012).

[75] *ILA, International Law Association Recommendations on Lis Pendens and Arbitration*, Conf. Res. No. 1/2006, Annex 1, at 1 (June, 2006).

[76] *Id.*, Recommendation No.3, para 5.8; *see also*, Winnie Ma, *Parallel Proceedings and International Commercial*

it is recommended that the tribunal should proceed with arbitration, as the decisions of such courts may not have any immediate adverse impact on the proceedings or the decision of the tribunal.[77]

Based on the afore-mentioned analogy, it can be inferred that the ILA recommendations do place the decisions of the supervisory courts on a higher pedestal in comparison to those of non-supervisory courts, as far as the impact on arbitral tribunals and arbitral proceedings is concerned. Therefore, it can be argued that an anti-arbitration injunction issued by the seat or supervisory court is more likely to be effective. On the other hand, when a non-supervisory court issues an anti-arbitration injunction, it not only comes across as an attack on the competence of the tribunal to decide on its jurisdiction but it challenges the authority of the supervisory court as well.[78] And if the non-supervisory court happens to be a national court of the host state, then the decision enjoining arbitral proceedings raises more questions.

Moreover, it is pertinent to note here that an arbitral tribunal, generally, is not under any obligation to necessarily abide by anti-arbitration injunctions.[79] It may well decide to continue with the arbitral proceedings, more so when the injunction is issued by a non-supervisory court as in that case the award will not run the risk of being set-aside. For example, in *SGS v. Pakistan*, the Supreme Court of Pakistan tried to intervene and deny the jurisdiction of the tribunal. However, the tribunal continued with the proceedings and observed:

> *"Although the Supreme Court Judgment of July 3, 2002 is final as a matter of the law of Pakistan, as a matter of international law, it does not in any way bind this tribunal".*[80]

It is also argued that the supervisory court is the most appropriate forum for granting anti-arbitration injunction because of the two natural advantages it enjoys in comparison to any non-supervisory court: It would be in a better position to interpret the *lex arbitri* – that would be relevant in deciding the existence of abuse of process, and it will discourage the possibility of forum shopping which the state party may resort to, in order to maximize the chances of obtaining an anti-arbitration injunction.[81]

Arbitration: The International Law Association's Recommendations for Arbitrators, 2 Contemporary Asia Arb. Journal 58 (2009).

77 ILA, *International Law Association Recommendations on Lis Pendens and Arbitration*, Conf. Res. No. 1/2006, Annex 1, at 73, *Recommendation No. 4, para 5.9; see also*, Winnie Ma, *Parallel Proceedings and International Commercial Arbitration: The International Law Association's Recommendations for Arbitrators*, 2 Contemporary Asia Arb. Journal 59 (2009).

78 Gabrielle Kaufmann-Kohler, *How to Handle Parallel Proceedings: A Practical Approach to Issues such as Competence-Competence and Anti-Suit Injunctions*, 2(1) Dispute Resolution International 112 (2008).

79 *SGS Société Générale de Surveillance SA (SGS) v. Islamic Republic of Pakistan*, ICSID Case No. ARB/01/13, Procedural Order 02, (2002); *see also, Saipem S.P.A v. The People's Republic of Bangladesh*, ICSID Case No.ARB/05/07, Decision on Jurisdiction (2007), para 31.

80 *SGS Société Générale de Surveillance SA (SGS) v. Islamic Republic of Pakistan*, ICSID Case No. ARB/01/13, Procedural Order 02, (2002) 299.

81 Jennifer Gorskie, *US Courts and Anti-Arbitration Injunction*, 28 Arbitration International 317 (2012); *see also*

VI. Conclusions

There is no denying that investor-state arbitration, as a dispute resolution mechanism, evolved keeping in mind the vulnerability of investors as against the might of host states. There is also no disagreement on the fact that investors, at times, have attempted to abuse the relative advantage they enjoy by virtue of the structure and operation of the investor-state arbitration regime.

There have been instances where investors, resorting to abuse of procedural rights, initiated parallel or multiple proceedings in connection with the same or related claims with an aim of maximizing the possibility of a favorable decision. Such moves prejudice the host state, not only in terms of cost and time, but also the risk of contradictory decisions.[82] Abuse of process, though, does not per se result in violation of any legal rule, nevertheless, ought to be discouraged when identified.[83]

One of the ways that host states have preferred, while grappling with the issue of abuse of process, has been to seek relief from national courts in the form of anti-arbitration injunctions. However, anti-arbitration injunctions issued by national courts are often criticized for being a direct interference with the authority of the arbitral tribunals to decide on admissibility and jurisdiction.[84]

Despite the longstanding and persistent debate on whether national courts should intervene and remedy abuse of process, the fact remains that it is very unlikely that the national courts – particularly in common law jurisdictions – will be keen to give up their authority to grant anti-arbitration injunctions. In defense of the national courts, sometimes circumstances do arise where judicial intervention becomes inevitable to prevent abuse of process.

There are genuine apprehensions that even the anti-arbitration injunctions can become instruments of abuse of process. Anti-arbitration injunctions issued by the national courts of host states can very well have obstructionist and parochial undertones. Such trepidations call for some sort of uniformity in practice. Narrowing down the scope of national courts to issue anti-arbitration injunctions and more importantly authorising only specific national courts to grant anti-arbitration injunctions – when required – can go a long way in settling the concerns of both investors as well as the state parties.

Anti-arbitration injunctions should be granted with caution. The recent trends, discussed in this article, show that national courts may enjoin arbitral proceedings only in exceptional circumstances, like manifest abuse of process. And as far as the question of the appropriate national court is concerned, the seat or supervisory court should be approached. It will ensure minimal judicial interference, which compliments the larger pro-arbitration policy.

Julian Lew, *Does National Court Involvement Undermine the International Arbitration Process?*, 24 American University International Law Review 494 and 510 (2009).

[82] Robin F. Hansen, *Parallel Proceedings in Investor-State Treaty Arbitration: Responses for Treaty-Drafters, Arbitrators and Parties*, 73(4) The Modern Law Review 528-529 (2010).

[83] Emmanuel Gaillard, *Abuse of Process in International Arbitration*, 32(1) ICSID Review 17, 18 (2017).

[84] H. Seriki, *Anti-Suit Injunctions and Arbitration: A Final Nail in the Coffin?*, 23(1) Journal of Arbitration International Arbitration 25 (2006).

Rebecca E. Khan[*]

THIRD PARTY PARTICIPATION BY NON-GOVERNMENT ORGANIZATIONS IN INTERNATIONAL INVESTMENT ARBITRATION: TRANSPARENCY AS A TOOL FOR PROTECTING MARGINALIZED INTERESTS

Abstract

In recent years, a palpable move towards increased transparency in investment arbitration has resulted in the revision of institutional arbitral rules, a set of rules devoted entirely to transparency and even a convention. Consequently, arbitral tribunals have gradually become more receptive to utilizing mechanisms for third party participation, including open hearings and the acceptance of written submissions by amici curiae.

Two particular sectors have sought to avail themselves of these participation mechanisms with limited success: indigenous peoples and environmental groups. These two groups are often at odds with foreign investors in extractive industries and other investment activities performed in environmentally critical areas; they assert an interest to participate in ongoing investment disputes, often with the aid of non-governmental organizations. This paper will examine whether the procedural mechanisms for participation of non-disputing parties in international investment arbitration cases adequately provide particular marginalized sectors with recourse to protect their interests from the impact of investment activities.

I. Introduction

In 2016, opposition against the construction of the Dakota Access Pipeline made news headlines in the United States and around the world. Protesters from the Standing Rock Sioux tribe were joined at the protest encampment by members of other Native American nations, campaigning against an oil project that potentially imperils indigenous sacred lands and poses a threat of contamination to the Missouri River. This massive demonstration has brought public attention to the clash between indigenous rights and the interests of extractive industries, as well as the government's role in mediating between these diverging concerns. While the Dakota Access Pipeline is a project of a US company and is therefore a domestic investment, the well-publicized conflict surrounding it is illustrative of past and prospective international investment disputes where the activities of foreign investors are met with opposition by indigenous and/or environmental groups and the governmental actions in response consequently become the subject of investment treaty claims. In investor-state disputes involving extractive activities near protected lands,

[*] Rebecca E. Khan is an international arbitration and litigation practitioner. She may be reached at rkhan@law.gwu.edu.

indigenous peoples are not parties to a legal process that has an impact on their rights. Considering that their interests are often in direct conflict with those of claimant investors, and inadequately represented by the sovereign respondent, appropriate avenues must be identified through which indigenous peoples and environmental groups can assert rights and be heard by investment tribunals.

Indigenous peoples and non-governmental organizations (NGOs) have sought to avail themselves of third-party participation mechanisms in investment arbitration with limited success. Often at odds with foreign investors in extractive industries, indigenous groups have frequently insisted that mining activities on their ancestral lands have a detrimental impact on their heritage and way of life. NGOs focusing on environmental concerns have tried to intervene in many investment cases that impact ecosystems affected by investment activity. Thus, these affected indigenous peoples assert an interest to participate in ongoing investment disputes, sometimes with the aid of non-governmental organizations.

In the investment arbitration cases in recent years wherein these interest groups sought to make written submissions as non-disputing parties, the response of tribunals can be described as lukewarm or even dismissive. Requests to access arbitration documents or attend hearings have generally been denied. By reviewing these particular cases, the present study will examine the reasoning of the arbitral tribunals to understand the considerations that factored into allowing or denying non-disputing party participation, with a view to assessing whether the promises of an increased transparency regime will eventually benefit indigenous peoples and environmental groups seeking to participate in these disputes, depending on how their requests for intervention are framed.

A review of cases involving indigenous peoples seeking to intervene in investor-state disputes reveals that the claimants in these cases are involved in extractive industries, particularly mining. That extractive activities are at the core of these particular disputes is, perhaps, a direct function of indigenous peoples' rights and cultural heritage being inextricably linked to their sacred lands and ancestral domain. A significant development spurring the recognition of the rights of indigenous people under international law is the adoption of the United Nations Declaration on the Rights of Indigenous Peoples (UNDRIP) in 2007.[1] This important international law instrument recognizes the "distinctive spiritual relationship" that indigenous peoples have with their territories and accords them the "right to the lands, territories and resources which they have traditionally owned, occupied or otherwise used or acquired."[2] Another relevant international law instrument is the International Labour Organization (ILO) Convention No. 169 Concerning Indigenous and Tribal Peoples in Independent Countries, which recognizes the right of indigenous

---

1 United Nations Declaration on the Rights of Indigenous Peoples (UNDRIP), G.A. Res. 61/295, UN Doc. A/RES/61/295 dated 13 September 2007; Valentina Vadi, Cultural Heritage in International Investment Law and Arbitration, 204 (Cambridge University Press, 2014),; Christina Binder, *Investment, Development and Indigenous Peoples, in* International Investment Law and Development – Bridging the Gap 427–428 (Stephan W. Schill, Christian J. Tams and Rainer Hofmann, eds. 2015).

2 UNDRIP, Arts. 25, 26; Christina Binder, *Investment, Development and Indigenous Peoples, in* International Investment Law and Development – Bridging the Gap 427 (Stephan W. Schill, Christian J. Tams and Rainer Hofmann, eds. 2015).

peoples to decide their development priorities in relation to their beliefs and their lands.[3] Indeed, cultural rights and land rights of indigenous peoples are interconnected and interdependent with each other.[4]

This special relationship with their sacred lands means that indigenous peoples should be deemed to meet the "significant interest" requirement[5] for being allowed to make non-party submissions in investment arbitration cases where the investment in dispute involves activity that impacts their lands. Some scholars have noted that the scope of investment disputes provides minimal opportunity for indigenous peoples to intervene, but it is imperative that they be able to participate in decision-making processes that directly affect them.[6] The importance of taking into account public interest considerations when analyzing investment activities taking place in proximity to sacred lands is underscored by the duty of states to undertake environmental and social impact assessments for activities that may potentially affect indigenous peoples, as well as share the benefits of these investment activities with indigenous peoples.[7]

Environmental groups can similarly find their footing bolstered by international legal instruments establishing liability for environmental harm as an international law norm and, arguably, an enforceable right. For example, the 1992 Rio Declaration on Environment and Development exhorts governments to "endeavour to promote the internalization of environmental costs and the use of economic instruments, taking into account the approach that the polluter should, in principle, bear the cost of pollution with due regard to the public interest and without distorting international trade and investment."[8] The general acceptance of this principle internationally is shown by its use as a preamble in several other international environmental law instruments, such as the Kiev Protocol on Liability for Pollution of Transboundary Waters and Lakes (2003); the London Protocol on Preparedness, Response and Co-operation to Pollution Incidents by Hazardous and Noxious Substances (2000); the UNECE Convention on the Transboundary Effects of Industrial Accidents (1992); and the Oil Pollution Preparedness and Response Convention (1990).[9] This "polluter pays principle" can translate into an "an actionable standard for the host

---

3 Federico Lenzerini, *Foreign Investment in the Energy Sector and Indigenous Peoples' Rights, in* Foreign Investment in the Energy Sector – Balancing Private and Public Interests 194 (Eric De Brabandere and Tarcisio Gazzini, eds. 2014) 194.

4 *Id.*

5 A requirement for third-party participation. *See* UNCITRAL Rules on Transparency, Article 4(3)(a); ICSID Arbitration Rule 37(2)(c); Statement of the Free Trade Commission on Non-Disputing Party Participation dated 7 October 2003, paraB(6)(c).

6 Valentina Vadi, Cultural Heritage in International Investment Law and Arbitration, 206 (Cambridge University Press, 2014).

7 Alessandro Fodella, *Indigenous Peoples, the Environment and International Jurisprudence, in* International Courts and the Development of International Law – Essays in Honour of Tullio Treves 360 (Nerina Boschiero, Tullio Scovazzi, Cesare Pitea, Chiara Ragni, eds. 2013).

8 Declaration on Environment and Development, 13 June 1992, UN Doc. A/CONF.151/26, Principle 16, *cited in* Zachary Douglas, *The Enforcement of Environmental Norms in Investment Treaty Arbitration, in* Harnessing Foreign Investment to Promote Environmental Protection: Incentives and Safeguards 440 (Pierre-Marie Dupuy and Jorge E. Viñuales, eds. 2013).

9 Zachary Douglas, *The Enforcement of Environmental Norms in Investment Treaty Arbitration, in* Harnessing Foreign Investment to Promote Environmental Protection: Incentives and Safeguards 440 (Pierre-Marie Dupuy and Jorge E. Viñuales, eds. 2013).

state's transnational tort claim against the investor".[10] Environmental groups can invoke this public interest in their interventions, among other environmental law principles.

Below, in two separate sections, are examinations of cases where (1) indigenous peoples, and (2) environmental groups sought to participate in investment treaty claims. A third section follows, analyzing the responses of investment arbitration tribunals towards third-party participation by these groups.

II. Indigenous Peoples

To better understand the factors affecting tribunal decisions regarding the intervention of indigenous peoples or their representatives in investment arbitration cases, a review of past and pending cases may prove enlightening. Four investment arbitration cases are relevant to the discussion: (1) the NAFTA case *Glamis Gold v. USA*, decided in 2009; (2) The Permanent Court of Arbitration (PCA) case *Chevron v. Ecuador*, decided in 2011; (3) the ICSID Case *Von Pezold v. Zimbabwe*, decided in 2015; and (4) the currently ongoing ICSID case *Bear Creek v. Peru*. The first two cases were conducted pursuant to UNCITRAL Arbitration Rules, while the latter two used the ICSID Arbitration Rules. Indigenous Peoples were allowed to participate as *amici curiae* in *Glamis Gold* and *Bear Creek*, whereas the tribunals in *Chevron v. Ecuador* and *Von Pezold v. Zimbabwe* ruled against allowing the Indigenous Peoples to intervene. Thus there is a sample of cases where intervention was allowed under the UNCITRAL Rules and the ICSID Rules and also cases following those arbitration rules where third-party participation was not allowed.

a) Glamis Gold v. USA

The case of *Glamis Gold, Ltd. v. United States of America* (hereafter "*Glamis Gold v. USA*") was brought by a Canadian mining company pursuant to Chapter 11 of NAFTA,[11] in accordance with the UNCITRAL Arbitration Rules before the ICSID Additional Facility. The dispute involved a mining project on federal land in southeastern California, located "near to – but not a part of – designated Native American lands and areas of special cultural concern".[12] Claimant alleged violations of its rights as an investor under NAFTA because of regulations imposed by the state of California requiring backfilling and site recontouring of mining sites.[13] Glamis alleged that these regulations amounted to an indirect expropriation of its investment by the United States because the economic value of its investment had been destroyed through these measures.[14]

This case is significant because it allowed an indigenous group to participate as *amicus curiae*. The Quechan Indian Nation (hereafter "Quechan") cited three reasons it should

[10] *Id.* at 439–440.

[11] *Glamis Gold v. USA*, Award dated 8 June 2009, at para 1.

[12] *Id.* at para 10.

[13] *Glamis Gold v. USA*, Notice of Arbitration dated 9 December 2003, at paras 11–23.

[14] *Id.* at paras 23 and 25.

be allowed to intervene in the investment dispute: (1) being constitutionally recognized as a sovereign government,[15] its interests cannot be adequately represented by another sovereign, i.e. the United States government, nor could its interests be represented by the Canadian claimant; (2) the claimant's interests are adverse to that of the Quechan, and the respondent's agencies may be biased in defending some of its actions; and (3) only the Quechan has the expertise and authority regarding the cultural, social and religious value of the indigenous sacred lands involved in the dispute, or the severity of impacts to the area and the Quechan.[16]

In deciding to allow the Quechan to make a non-disputing party submission, the Tribunal relied heavily on the Free Trade Commission's Statement on Non-Disputing Party Participation and also considered that neither claimant nor respondent objected to such submission.[17]

Despite the participation of the Quechan, however, the Tribunal was rather categorical in stating that their submission had no bearing on the resolution of the issues. With respect to the *amicus* filings, the Tribunal declared at the outset of its award that the Tribunal deemed its task to be limited to addressing those filings "to the degree that they bear on decisions that must be taken."[18] However, the Tribunal maintained that its holding with respect to the claims in the dispute "does not reach the particular issues addressed" by the *amicus* submissions.[19] Ultimately, the Tribunal ruled that the measures adopted by California did not breach the obligations of the United States under NAFTA. Thus, while the resulting Award was favorable to the rights of the Quechan in that the California regulations according protection to their sacred lands were upheld, their concerns and asserted rights in their third-party submission did not impact the reasoning of the arbitral tribunal.[20]

b) Chevron v. Ecuador

Another case wherein representatives of an indigenous community tried to intervene is a case brought before the Permanent Court of Arbitration (PCA), *In the Matter of an Arbitration under the UNCITRAL Arbitration Rules between Chevron Corporation and Texaco Petroleum Company and the Republic of Ecuador* (hereafter "*Chevron v. Ecuador*").[21] The case was filed in

---

[15] The United States Supreme Court has "consistently recognized that Indian tribes retain 'attributes of sovereignty over both their members and their territory'". *California v. Cabazon Band of Mission Indians*, 480 U.S. 202 (1987), at 207, citing *United States v. Mazurie*, 419 U.S. 544, 557 (1975).

[16] *Glamis Gold v. USA*, Quechan Indian Nation Application for Leave to File a Non-Party Submission dated 19 August 2005, at 3–4.

[17] *Glamis Gold v. USA*, Decision on Application and Submission by Quechan Indian Nation dated 16 September 2005, at para 9.

[18] *Glamis Gold v. USA*, Award dated 8 June 2009, at para 8.

[19] *Id.*

[20] Christina Binder, *Investment, Development and Indigenous Peoples, in* International Investment Law and Development – Bridging the Gap 432 (Stephan W. Schill, Christian J. Tams and Rainer Hofmann, eds. 2015).

[21] PCA Case No. 2009-23.

2009 by claimants Chevron Corporation ("Chevron") and Texaco Petroleum Company ("TexPet") alleging a breach of the BIT between Ecuador and the United States in relation to a class action litigation for environmental harm instituted by Ecuadorian plaintiffs against Chevron in the courts of Ecuador.[22] The US-based claimants in the investment arbitration alleged that the sovereign respondent colluded with the plaintiffs in the court case, such that Ecuador's various state organs were involved in a coordinated effort to shift liability for environmental impact to Chevron, for harm caused by "government-sanctioned colonization and agricultural and industrial exploitation of the Amazonian region" resulting from previous activities carried out by a consortium comprised of Ecuador's state-owned oil company and TexPet, wherein allocation of liability had already been the subject of settlement agreements between TexPet and the Ecuadorian government.[23]

In 2010, the Fundación Pachamama and the International Institute for Sustainable Development (IISD) sought to participate as *amici curiae* in the case before the PCA.[24] The Fundación Pachamama is an Ecuador-based non-governmental organization (NGO) which assists indigenous communities in preserving traditional ways of life and asserting self-determination, while the IISD is an international NGO geared towards sustainable development.[25] In their petition to intervene, the NGOs sought leave to (1) "file a written submission with the Tribunal regarding matters within the scope of the dispute;" (2) attend the oral hearings and present their submission therein, or in the alternative, to attend as observers or reply to specific questions of the Tribunal regarding their written submission; and (3) access the key arbitration documents, subject to redaction of confidential or privileged information that is not relevant to the concerns of the NGOs as non-disputing parties.[26]

Since the arbitration at the PCA was instituted pursuant to UNCITRAL Arbitration Rules, the NGOs relied on Articles 15[27] and 25[28] thereof, noting that "[p]revious tribunals have

---

22 *Chevron v. Ecuador*, Claimant's Notice of Arbitration dated 23 September 2009, at 1–2.

23 *Id.*

24 *Chevron v. Ecuador*, Petition for Participation as Non-Disputing Parties dated 22 October 2010. The Tribunal in that case noted that communications from the NGOs, including the submission of the Petition and the accompanying written submission, was coursed through EarthRights International. (Procedural Order No. 18 dated 18 April 2011).

25 *Id.* at paras 1.2, 3.2 and 3.3.

26 *Id.*

27 Because the case was initiated prior to the 2010 UNCITRAL Rules, the NGO Petition refers to the 1976 version, wherein Article 15 states as follows:
"1. Subject to these Rules, the arbitral tribunal may conduct the arbitration in such manner as it considers appropriate, provided that the parties are treated with equality and that at any stage of the proceedings each party is given a full opportunity of presenting his case.
2. If either party so requests at any stage of the proceedings, the arbitral tribunal shall hold hearings for the presentation of evidence by witnesses, including expert witnesses, or for oral argument. In the absence of such a request, the arbitral tribunal shall decide whether to hold such hearings or whether the proceedings shall be conducted on the basis of documents and other materials.
3. All documents or information supplied to the arbitral tribunal by one party shall at the same time be communicated by that party to the other party."

28 The NGOs cited Article 25 in consideration of "the Tribunal's powers over oral hearings". The 1976 version

interpreted Article 15(1) to allow such submissions," specifically referring to the *Methanex* case. [29] The NGOs conceded, however, that the UNCITRAL Arbitration Rules did not outline any procedure for making *amicus curiae* submissions.[30]

With respect to their interest in the arbitration, the NGOs expressed that the case presented "issues of vital concern to specific indigenous communities and peoples in Ecuador and other indigenous communities and individuals living in areas potentially affected by foreign investments in Ecuador and elsewhere."[31] Citing the mandates and activities of their respective organizations, the NGOs asserted that they could advise the Tribunal on the implications of the BIT interpretation pushed by the claimants in the arbitration, including "the particular rights of indigenous peoples under international law to be able to access judicial remedies for environmental and human rights damages."[32]

The Tribunal allowed the parties to comment on the NGOs' petition to participate in the proceedings.[33]

In the meantime, since the hearing on jurisdiction and admissibility was a short time away, the Tribunal sent notice to the NGOs that it was declining their application to attend the oral hearings, as it was required to do so pursuant to Article 25(4) of the 1976 UNCITRAL Arbitration Rules which mandated that "[h]earings shall be held in camera" unless the Parties to the arbitration have "agreed otherwise".[34] During the hearing, which the NGOs were not allowed to attend, the Tribunal further discussed the *amicus* petition with the parties, which by then had submitted written comments on the petition.[35]

In its written comment, the claimants opposed the intervention of the NGOs, for both attendance at the hearing as well as the submission of an *amicus* brief, alleging that these two organizations "have a longstanding record of asserting baseless claims against Chevron" and

---

of the UNCITRAL Rules provides as follows:

"1. In the event of an oral hearing, the arbitral tribunal shall give the parties adequate advance notice of the date, time and place thereof.

2. If witnesses are to be heard, at least fifteen days before the hearing each party shall communicate to the arbitral tribunal and to the other party the names and addresses of the witnesses he intends to present, the subject upon and the languages in which such witnesses will give their testimony.

3. The arbitral tribunal shall make arrangements for the translation of oral statements made at a hearing and for a record of the hearing if either is deemed necessary by the tribunal under the circumstances of the case, or if the parties have agreed thereto and have communicated such agreement to the tribunal at least fifteen days before the hearing.

4. Hearings shall be held in camera unless the parties agree otherwise. The arbitral tribunal may require the retirement of any witness or witnesses during the testimony of other witnesses. The arbitral tribunal is free to determine the manner in which witnesses are examined.

5. Evidence of witnesses may also be presented in the form of written statements signed by them.

6. The arbitral tribunal shall determine the admissibility, relevance, materiality and weight of the evidence offered."

[29] *Chevron v. Ecuador*, Petition for Participation as Non-Disputing Parties dated 22 October 2010, at para 2.1.

[30] *Id.* at para 2.2.

[31] *Id.* at para 3.1.

[32] *Id.* at para 3.4.

[33] *Chevron v. Ecuador*, Procedural Order No. 8 dated 18 April 2011, at para 4.

[34] *Id.* at para 5.

[35] *Id.* at paras 4, 6 and 16.

were thus "not genuine 'friends-of-the-court'".[36] The claimants also requested, in the event that the Tribunal would allow the intervention, a complete disclosure by the NGOs of their affiliations.[37] On the other hand, the sovereign respondent did not interpose any objections to the attendance of the NGOs at the hearing and had no comment with respect to the substance of the *amicus* petition.[38] However, the respondent asserted that submissions by non-parties on purely legal issues regarding the scope of the tribunal's jurisdiction were unlikely to assist the Tribunal.[39]

Ultimately, the Tribunal did not allow the petitioners to participate in the jurisdictional phase of the proceeding, citing its discretion under Article 15(1) of the UNCITRAL Arbitration Rules.[40] In declining to allow the intervention, the Tribunal noted that both parties "do not believe that the *amicus* submissions will be helpful to the Tribunal and neither side favours the participation of the petitioners during the jurisdictional phase of the arbitration, in which the issues to be decided are primarily legal and have already been extensively addressed by the Parties' submissions."[41]

c) Von Pezold v. Zimbabwe

Another case involving an attempted intervention by indigenous peoples' groups is the case of *Bernhard von Pezold and Others v. Republic of Zimbabwe*, an ICSID case filed pursuant to the BITs of Germany and Switzerland with Zimbabwe.[42] Initiated in 2010, this case falls under the revised ICSID Arbitration Rules which contain provisions allowing for the participation of *amici curiae*. This case involved a dispute triggered by land policies put into place following Zimbabwe's independence from colonial rule in 1980.[43] These land policies favored the "black indigenous population" of the country formerly known as Rhodesia, reversing the land policies of the colonial era which favored the white minority.[44]

The European Centre for Constitution and Human Rights (ECCHR) and four indigenous communities of Zimbabwe petitioned to participate as *amici curiae* in the case, seeking to: (i) file a written submission; (ii) access the key arbitration documents; and (iii) attend the oral hearings and reply to any specific questions of the Tribunal on the written submissions.[45]

The ECCHR described itself as an "independent, non-profit legal and educational organization dedicated to protecting human rights,"[46] with an interest in the arbitration

[36] *Id.* at para 14.

[37] *Id.*

[38] *Id.* at para 15.

[39] *Id.* at para 13.

[40] *Id.* at para 20.

[41] *Id.* at para 18.

[42] ICSID Case No. ARB/10/15 (hereinafter "*Von Pezold v. Zimbabwe*").

[43] *Von Pezold v. Zimbabwe*, Award dated 28 July 2015, at paras 2–3.

[44] *Id.*

[45] *Id.* at para 36; Procedural Order No. 2 dated 26 June 2012, at para 14.

[46] *Von Pezold v. Zimbabwe*, Procedural Order No. 2 dated 26 June 2012, at para 17.

because of its "mission to develop the strategic use of legal actions for corporate human rights responsibilities."[47]

The indigenous communities consisted of the Chikukwa, Ngorima, Chinyai and Nyaruwa peoples, living in the areas on which the claimants' properties are located.[48] In the *amicus* petition, the indigenous communities asserted that they each have "a distinct cultural identity and social history which is inextricably linked to their ancestral lands."[49] Specifically, they submitted that the indigenous communities' "collective and individual rights" would be: (i) affected by any outcome of the arbitration that would determine rights and access to land inhabited by them, "which may impede their enjoyment of their internationally recognized rights to land and to consultation in relation to their ancestral lands; and (ii) prejudiced by not being able to participate in or contest the decisions of the arbitral Tribunal".[50]

In asserting that the indigenous communities have rights under international law in relation to the lands subject of the investor-state dispute, the petitioners posited that both claimant and respondent have incurred shared responsibilities toward the indigenous communities.[51] The petitioners urged the Tribunal to adopt the legal perspective that the "interdependence of international investment law and international human rights law" mandates the consideration of international human rights norms – in this case, the rights of the indigenous communities – in arriving at a decision in the dispute.[52] The petitioners cited Article 26 of the 2007 United Nations Declaration on the Rights of Indigenous Peoples, which requires states to give legal recognition and protection to the lands, territories and resources possessed by indigenous peoples by reason of traditional ownership and other traditional occupation or use, and upholds the right of indigenous peoples to own, use, develop and control these lands.[53]

The claimants opposed the petition on several grounds, arguing that: (1) the petitioners are not independent of the respondent, citing the appointing and dismissing authority of the country's President of the chiefs of the indigenous groups, as well as a connection between the petitioners and an organization allegedly involved in "invasions" of the claimants' lands in dispute; (2) the submissions proposed by petitioners do not relate to the legal and factual issues in the proceedings; (3) the proposed legal submissions on the law of indigenous peoples does not concern the applicable law; (4) if the applicable law does include the law of indigenous peoples, the petitioners have not proven that they are "indigenous" peoples; (5) the petitioners will not provide knowledge or insight that is different from respondent; (6) human rights are not at issue in the proceedings; and (7) "investment treaty tribunals should not adjudicate as to who are indigenous peoples, what are their rights, and what obligations they are owed (if any). States should be the first-line decision makers on these issues."[54]

---

[47] *Id.* at para 22.

[48] *Id.* at para 17.

[49] *Id.* at para 21.

[50] *Id.*

[51] *Id.* at para 25.

[52] *Id.* at para 26.

[53] *Id.* at para 27.

[54] *Id.* at paras 29 and 31–44.

Additionally, noting that the parties had previously agreed that no non-disputing party submissions would be made, the claimants argued that the Tribunal "had no residual discretion under Article 44 of the ICSID Convention to admit any such submissions into the record."[55] The respondent, on the other hand, admitted that the parties had agreed to the non-application of the ICSID Arbitration rule on *amici curiae*, but stated that it had not anticipated at the time that any person or organization other than the parties could have an interest in the case.[56] Thus, the respondent did not interpose any objection to the participation of the NGO and indigenous groups, provided that the written submissions "fell within the scope of ICSID Arbitration Rule 37(2), and did not impinge on or amount to a challenge to the sovereignty and territorial integrity of Zimbabwe."[57]

Disagreeing with the claimants' position regarding Rule 37(2) of the ICSID Arbitration Rules, the Tribunal maintained that it has the discretion, upon consulting with the parties, to allow a non-disputing party to make a submission, provided that the criteria outlined in said Rule were met.[58]

The Tribunal also disagreed with the averments of claimant that the indigenous communities were not independent of the state; the Tribunal reasoned that the functions of the chiefs of the communities were not attributable to the Republic of Zimbabwe, and the appointment and dismissal power of the President of Zimbabwe over the chiefs was constrained by criteria set out in the relevant domestic statute.[59]

However, the Tribunal took note of previous incidents cited by claimants wherein members of the indigenous communities allegedly "invaded" the claimants' lands and "wish to permanently occupy" parts of the estate.[60] The Tribunal opined that since the indigenous communities appear to lay claim over some of the lands which claimants' assert "a right to full, unencumbered legal title and exclusive control," the petitioner communities "appear to be in conflict with the claimants' primary position in these proceedings."[61] Also in relation to these "invasions", the Tribunal considered the claimants' allegation of support provided by the organization that instigated these acts and the head of the latter organization's well-documented support for the respondent state's land reform policies.[62]

This conflict of interest and questionable independence led the Tribunal to deny the petition for the ECCHR and the indigenous communities to participate as *amici curiae*,[63] reasoning that legitimate doubts as to the independence or neutrality of the petitioners caused them to fall short of the criteria in Rule 37(2) for allowing non-disputing party participation.[64]

---

[55] *Von Pezold v. Zimbabwe*, Award dated 28 July 2015, at para 37.

[56] *Id.*

[57] *Id.*

[58] *Von Pezold v. Zimbabwe*, Procedural Order No. 2 dated 26 June 2012, at para 48.

[59] *Id.* at paras 52 and 53.

[60] *Id.* at para 51.

[61] *Id.*

[62] *Id.* at paras 54–56.

[63] *Id.* at para 56.

[64] *Id.*

With respect to the potential contributions such a non-disputing party submission would have made, the Tribunal was of the view that the legal and factual issues subject of the petition to intervene were unrelated to the matters before the Tribunal. The Tribunal agreed with claimants' submission that "the reference to 'such rules of general international law as may be applicable' in the BITs does not incorporate the universe of international law into the BITs or into disputes arising under the BITs."[65] The Tribunal went on to underscore the role of the Parties, in framing the issues to be considered by the Tribunal, to rule that the submission proposed by the petitioners would be outside the scope of the dispute: "neither Party has put the identity and/or treatment of indigenous peoples, or the indigenous communities in particular, under international law, including international human rights law on indigenous peoples, in issue in these proceedings."[66] The Tribunal also rejected the petitioners' view that international investment law and international human rights law are interdependent, maintaining that consideration of international human rights norms was not part of the Tribunal's mandate under either the ICSID Convention or the applicable BITs.[67]

d) Bear Creek v. Peru

Whereas the indigenous groups in the cases discussed above were denied the opportunity to participate in the arbitral proceedings, a recent case is significant for allowing an indigenous group to attend the hearing on the merits as well as make a written submission. The case of *Bear Creek Mining Corporation v. Republic of Peru*[68] was filed pursuant to the Free Trade Agreement (FTA) between Canada and the Republic of Peru.[69] The Canadian mining company alleges that the aforementioned investment treaty was breached when the Peruvian government enacted a decree revoking claimant's concession to operate a mining project in Peru, resulting in cessation of its operations at the mine and a significant loss of its investment.[70] For its part, the respondent state alleges that the claimant unlawfully acquired its mining concession by violating nationality requirement laws for ownership; the respondent also attributed claimant's losses to its own failure to obtain community support for the mining project.[71]

The mining concession in dispute is located in the territories inhabited by the indigenous peoples called the Aymara and the Quechua.[72] In their *amicus* submission, the organization representing these indigenous groups aimed to demonstrate that "the

65 *Id.* at para 57.

66 *Id.* at paras 57 and 60.

67 *Id.* at paras 58–59.

68 ICSID Case No. ARB/14/21 (hereinafter "*Bear Creek v. Peru*").

69 *Bear Creek v. Peru*, Claimant's Memorial on the Merits dated 29 May 2015, at 1.

70 *Id.* at paras 6–12.

71 *Bear Creek v. Peru*, Respondent's Counter-Memorial on the Merits and Memorial on Jurisdiction dated 6 October 2015, at 9–32.

72 *Bear Creek v. Peru*, Amicus Curiae Brief Submitted by the Association of Human Rights and the Environment – Puno and Mr Carlos Lopez PhD, dated 9 June 2016, at 1.

negative impacts of mining, together with Bear Creek's poor management of the project and its relations with the communities, were the direct causes of the social conflict" in the area of the mining concession that led to the events subject matter of the investment arbitration between Bear Creek and Peru.[73] The new insight offered to the Tribunal by way of the intervention was "information on the events from the point of view of the Aymara peasant communities (indigenous peoples) as they consider it important that the Arbitral Tribunal should be aware of the perspective of those involved in the social movement regarding the Santa Ana project."[74]

In agreeing to allow the participation of the petitioners, the Tribunal looked to Art. 836.4(a) of the Canada – Peru FTA which provided that non-disputing party submissions could be allowed if such "would bring a perspective, particular knowledge or insight that is different from that of the disputing parties."[75] Notably, however, the Tribunal provided the caveat that allowing the petitioners to make a written submission was "[w]ithout prejudice as to whether the submissions of the Applicants will finally be considered relevant for the Tribunal in drawing its conclusions in this case".[76]

The case drew to a close on 30 November 2017. In its Award, the Tribunal devoted a significant number of pages summarizing the facts as presented in the *amici* submissions,[77] the claimant's response to the *amici* submissions,[78] and the respondent's response to the *amici* submissions.[79] However, the Tribunal expressly stated that these summaries were "presented without prejudice as to the relevance of these facts for the decisions of the Tribunal."[80] The Tribunal did make findings on the issue of social unrest – which was the focus of the *amici* submissions – and concluded that there was no proven causal link to claimant's conduct.[81] In reaching this conclusion, however, the Tribunal made absolutely no reference to the *amici* submissions. After the summary of the *amici* submission and the parties' responses thereto, no reference to the *amici* submission appears again for the remainder of the Award.

The *amici* submissions did get a nod of approval, however, in the Partial Dissenting Opinion of the respondent-appointed arbitrator, Philippe Sands. Partly disagreeing with the majority, the dissenting arbitrator was of the view that "the Claimant did not do all it could have done to engage with all the affected communities."[82] The arbitrator stated that "[t]his conclusion is confirmed by the helpful *amicus curiae* submission of DHUMA."[83] The arbitrator also elaborated as follows: "local communities of indigenous

---

[73] *Id.* at 1–2.

[74] *Id.* at 2.

[75] *Bear Creek v. Peru*, Procedural Order No. 5 dated 21 July 2016, at para 39, see also Emmert & Esenkulova, above, 15–16.

[76] *Id.* at para 40.

[77] *Bear Creek v. Peru*, Award dated 30 November 2017, 218–230.

[78] *Id.* at 231–250.

[79] *Id.* at 251–266.

[80] *Id.* at 217.

[81] *Id.* at 411, *et seq.*

[82] *Bear Creek v. Peru* – Partial Dissenting Opinion of Professor Philippe Sands QC dated 12 September 2017, at 35.

[83] *Id.* at 36.

and tribal peoples also have rights under international law, and these are not lesser rights. In my view, DHUMA assisted the Tribunal 'by bringing a perspective, particular knowledge or insight that is different from that of the disputing parties.' Its participation in these proceedings was helpful and polite at all times, and added to perceptions of the legitimacy of ICSID proceedings of this kind."[84]

III. Environmental Groups

a) Pac Rim v. El Salvador

In the recently concluded case of *Pac Rim Cayman LLC v. Republic of El Salvador*,[85] a public invitation for third-party participation was made in accordance with CAFTA,[86] to which the Center for International Environmental Law (CIEL) responded, accompanied by several community-based NGOs. The Tribunal in this case allowed CIEL *et al.* to participate and make written submissions in both the jurisdictional and merits phases of the dispute, for which the NGOs had to file separate applications. The Tribunal considered the arguments put forth by the *amici* in its Decision on Jurisdiction; however, it appears that the Tribunal did not directly rely on these arguments.[87] As for the merits, however, the Tribunal explicitly stated in its October 2016 Award that it did not address the CIEL submission because: (1) parties did not agree for CIEL to access the evidence or attend the hearing; and (2) the case could be decided on issues unrelated to the CIEL brief.

In its *Application for Permission to Proceed as Amici Curiae*, CIEL represented a number of member organizations of the Mesa Nacional Frente a la Mineria Metálica de El Salvador (the El Salvador National Roundtable on Mining), described as "a coalition of community organizations, research institutes environmental, human rights, and faith-based nonprofit organizations who collectively aim to improve public policy dialogue concerning metals mining in El Salvador."[88] The Application averred that these organizations were "uniquely qualified to offer the Tribunal a broad contextual understanding – and defense – of the substance and historical significance of the government's response to the democratic debate over metals mining and sustainable development in El Salvador."[89] Furthermore, CIEL alleged that the investment claim was not actually between Claimant and the Republic of El Salvador, but rather between the Claimant and the

[84] *Id.* at 36.

[85] ICSID Case No. ARB/09/12 (hereinafter "*Pac Rim v. El Salvador*").

[86] On 2 February 2011, ICSID released a "news release" on its website, inviting non-disputing parties to make a written application to the Tribunal in the aforementioned case, for permission to file submissions as *amici curiae*, citing Article 10.20.3 of CAFTA, as well as ICSID Arbitration Rule 37(2). *Pac Rim v. El Salvador*, Procedural Order Regarding *Amici Curiae* dated 2 February 2011.

[87] Mariel Dimsey, *Article 4. Submission by a Third Person, in* Transparency in International Investment Arbitration: A Guide to the UNCITRAL Rules on Transparency in Treaty-Based Investor-State Arbitration 157 (Dimitrij Euler, et al., eds. 2015).

[88] *Pac Rim v. El Salvador*, Application for Permission to Proceed as *Amici Curiae* dated 2 March 2011, at 1.

[89] *Id.* at 2.

independently-organized communities who have risen up against Claimant's mining projects.[90]

The Claimant expressed that it had no objection to the submission of *amicus* briefs by the aforementioned applicants, but asked the Tribunal to establish procedural standards for the acceptance of these submissions.[91] Furthermore, Claimant opined that the allegations that the Applicants made regarding Claimant's activities have no connection to the issues to be decided by the Tribunal.[92]

The Respondent, on the other hand, urged the Tribunal to accept the *amicus* submission, stating that the organizations are devoted to the protection of the environment and represent "a significant segment of civil society that lives in the vicinity of the proposed mine" subject of the arbitration and thus "have genuine and unique concerns that the parties to the dispute are not in a position to convey to the Tribunal."[93]

The Tribunal allowed the *amicus* submission, stating that it should be limited to the jurisdictional issues raised by the Parties and should not address the merits. The arbitration was in its jurisdictional stage and the Tribunal stated that another application could be made if the case proceeded to the merits.[94]

The case did proceed to the merits phase. When CIEL made an application to make a written submission during this phase, the Tribunal again admitted CIEL.[95] This written submission was completely disregarded by the Tribunal, however, which stated: that it considered it "unnecessary" to fully address CIEL's case, for two reasons: (1) CIEL did not have access to the mass of factual evidence presented in the arbitration (which was attributable to a lack of consent from the disputing parties to allow such access); and (2) "the Tribunals' decisions in this Award do not require the Tribunal specifically to consider the legal case advanced by CIEL [...]".[96] Ultimately, CIEL's participation did not contribute to the outcome of the case. Notably, the relevance of its participation – or rather, lack thereof, in the eyes of the Tribunal – was pinned to CIEL's lack of access to the arbitration documents.

b) Infinito Gold v. Costa Rica

The currently pending case of *Infinito Gold Ltd. v. Republic of Costa Rica*[97] is an ICSID arbitration wherein the tribunal allowed an NGO to make a written submission, and granted the NGO's request to access arbitration documents – albeit with clearly defined limits. However, the tribunal denied the NGO's requests to attend the oral hearings.

---

[90] *Id.*

[91] *Pac Rim v. El Salvador*, Claimant's Response to the Amicus Curiae Application dated 18 March 2011, at 1–2.

[92] *Id.*

[93] *Pac Rim v. El Salvador*, Respondent's Response to the Amicus Curiae Application dated 18 March 2011, at 2.

[94] *Pac Rim v. El Salvador*, Procedural Order No. 8 dated 23 March 2011.

[95] *Pac Rim v. El Salvador*, Award dated 14 October 2016, at para 1.48.

[96] *Id.* at para 3.30.

[97] ICSID Case No. ARB/14/5 (hereinafter "*Infinito Gold v. Costa Rica*").

In September 2014, the Asociación Preservacionista de Flora y Fauna Silvestre (APREFLOFAS) filed a *Petition for Amicus Curiae Status* in the aforementioned case.[98] The petitioner described itself as "a well-established Costa Rican non-governmental organization" with a mission to protect the environment,[99] particularly for "promoting the conservation of Costa Rican tropical forests."[100] In its Petition, APREFLOFAS disclosed that it has a history of legal disputes with the Claimant in the ICSID case.[101] The NGO averred that Costa Rican courts had determined that the open-pit metallic mining concession granted to Claimant was void and contrary to the laws of Costa Rica, as "apparent corrupt acts had occurred in granting permits to the Claimant".[102]

Asserting that APREFLOFAS could contribute significantly to the ICSID arbitration proceedings as *amicus curiae*, the NGO stated that it possessed important information regarding the following "public interest concerns" involved in the ICSID case: (1) "the protection of the environment in Costa Rica," and (2) "the manner in which governmental processes were apparently corrupted to the detriment of the environment."[103] Most significantly, the petitioner NGO suggested that the Claimant failed to disclose relevant facts about the investment case to the Tribunal, arguing that "[t]here is no discussion in the Claimant's submissions to the Tribunal of the existing legal dispute between APREFLOFAS, the Claimant and the government of Costa Rica."[104] The petitioner pointed out that it was this very dispute that forms the underlying basis for the investment claim, as it was the proceeding that led the Costa Rican courts to find that the Claimant's concession rights were awarded illegally.[105] Thus, APREFLOFAS maintained that it was in a position to inform the Tribunal about this legal proceeding and should be allowed to make an *amicus* submission.[106]

The Tribunal invited the Claimant and Respondent to file their submissions on APREFLOFAS's Petition.[107] The Parties filed their submissions on 29 April 2016.[108]

Infinito Gold opposed APREFLOFAS's request for non-disputing party status, anchoring its objection on three points: (1) the NGO did not meet the test for disputing party status; (2) its participation would disrupt the proceedings and unduly burden the Claimant; and (3) the request was premature.[109]

---

98 *Infinito Gold v. Costa Rica*, APREFLOFAS Petition for Amicus Curiae Status, 15 September 2014.

99 *Id.* at 2.

100 *Id.* at 3. The petition also states that the NGO's principal objectives are "the prevention of deforestation and illegal plant-trafficking, illegal hunting of wild animals and contamination of national rivers."

101 *Id.* at 4.

102 *Id.* The petition also states that several criminal proceedings have been initiated thanks to the NGO's efforts, including criminal prosecutions against the former Minister of Environment and former President of Costa Rica.

103 *Id.* at 4.

104 *Id.* at 6.

105 *Id.* at 6–7.

106 *Id.* at 7.

107 *Infinito Gold v. Costa Rica*, Procedural Order No. 2 dated 1 June 2016, at para 2, *citing* Procedural Order No. 1 dated 17 February 2015.

108 *Infinito Gold v. Costa Rica*, Procedural Order No. 2 dated 1 June 2016, at para 6.

109 *Id.* at para 17.

Conversely, Respondent Costa Rica submitted that the Tribunal should grant APREFLOFAS's requests to make a written submission and to access the Parties' key submissions.[110] However, the Respondent suggested that the Tribunal defer decision on APREFLOFAS's request to attend the oral hearing.[111] Respondent argued that "[d]ue to its participation in the domestic judicial proceedings and given its environmental expertise, APREFLOFAS would provide information that could assist the Tribunal when ruling on Costa Rica's jurisdictional objections."[112]

The Tribunal accorded weight to the fact that APREFLOFAS was the plaintiff in cases in Costa Rican courts that resulted in the cancellation of Infinito Gold's concession and said cancellation being among the very measures upon which the Claimant anchors its BIT claims.[113] Noting that APREFLOFAS was the successful plaintiff against both the Claimant and Respondent in those domestic court cases, the Tribunal ruled that the NGO "may provide a perspective different from that of the parties" and ruled that APREFLOFAS's input may assist the Tribunal in understanding "certain factual and legal aspects which may impact its jurisdiction and possibly the merits of the claims."[114]

On the point that APREFLOFAS could provide information on ongoing corruption and criminal proceedings against former Costa Rican government officials, the Tribunal noted that neither Party has made any allegations of corruption.[115] However, the Tribunal pointed out that the BIT involved in the case contained the language defining a protected investment as that made in accordance with the laws of the host state.[116] Thus, the Tribunal stated that it cannot rule out the relevance of corruption allegations during the early stages of the ICSID proceeding, as it could possibly have some role in the Tribunal's assessment of the dispute.[117]

With respect to environmental matters, the Tribunal observed that APREFLOFAS "does not appear to seek to provide information regarding environmental law or environmental concerns", but that APREFLOFAS's submission may shed light on whether the measures disputed in the investment claim fall under a provision in an annex of the BIT that allows a host state to adopt, maintain or enforce a measure "to ensure that investment activity in its territory is undertaken in a manner sensitive to environmental concerns."[118]

Ruling on APREFLOFAS's request to be granted access to the principal arbitration documents, the Tribunal decided that the extent of such access depended on the information required for the NGO to effectively discharge its task of providing the Tribunal with "a useful and particular insight on facts or legal questions relevant to its jurisdiction."[119] To avoid a redundant or useless submission from APREFLOFAS, the

[110] *Id.* at para 22.

[111] *Id.*

[112] *Id.* at para 23.

[113] *Id.* at para 31.

[114] *Id.*

[115] *Id.* at para 33.

[116] *Id.*

[117] *Id.*

[118] *Id.* at para 34, *citing* Article III(1) of Annex 1 of the 1998 Costa Rica – Canada BIT.

[119] *Infinito Gold v. Costa Rica*, Procedural Order No. 2 dated 1 June 2016, at para 43.

Tribunal reasoned that the NGO ought to know what information has already been submitted to the Tribunal.[120] Thus, the Tribunal ordered that the Respondent's Memorial on Jurisdiction, selected portions of the Claimant's Memorial on the Merits and the exhibit lists attached to these memorials be made available by the ICSID Secretariat to APREFLOFAS.[121] The Tribunal also ordered APREFLOFAS not to communicate these materials to third parties or use them outside the ICSID arbitration.[122]

The NGO's request to attend the oral hearings was denied by the Tribunal, citing ICSID Arbitration Rule 32(2), noting that the Claimant had expressly objected to APREFLOFAS's participation in any hearing.[123]

IV. Legal Perspectives Affecting Acceptance or Denial of Applications of Non-Disputing Parties to Participate as Third Parties in Investment Disputes

a) Tribunal Deference to Disputing Party Opposition

A review of the cases discussed above demonstrate that tribunals still exert a hefty amount of discretion when deciding whether to grant applications for non-disputing party participation, even under a regime of increased transparency in investor-state arbitration promoting the participation of third parties. This gatekeeper function is even supported by the UNCITRAL Rules on Transparency, which, when compared to the ICSID Arbitration Rules and NAFTA FTC guidelines, proposes the least hurdles to third-party participation. These three texts, examined earlier, still suggest or require consultation with the parties before allowing a third party to make a written submission. Notably, in the cases of *Chevron v. Ecuador* and *Von Pezold v. Zimbabwe*, where the parties expressed opposition to the participation of the indigenous groups, the Tribunals made special note of this fact in their decisions denying the applications for third-party participation.[124] In the cases of *Glamis Gold v. USA*, the Tribunal took into account that neither Claimant nor Respondent objected to such submission.[125] In *Bear Creek v. Peru*, the Claimant objected to the application for third-party participation, while the Respondent supported it. The Tribunal addressed the Claimants' concerns point by point in deciding to allow the written submission.[126]

Party opposition to other aspects of third-party participation also sway Tribunal decisions, such as access to documents, or attendance of hearings. The Tribunal in *Pac Rim v. El Salvador* essentially disregarded the written submission made by CIEL during

---

[120] *Id.*

[121] *Id.* at para 44.

[122] *Id.*

[123] *Id.* at paras 47–48.

[124] *Chevron v. Ecuador*, Procedural Order No. 8 dated 18 April 2011, at para 8; *Von Pezold v. Zimbabwe*, Procedural Order No. 2 dated 26 June 2012, at para 51.

[125] *Glamis Gold v. USA*, Decision on Application and Submission by Quechan Indian Nation dated 16 September 2005, at para 9.

[126] *Bear Creek v. Peru*, Procedural Order No. 5 dated 21 July 2016, at para 31 *et seq.*

the merits phase because CIEL could not address matters pertaining to the evidence or issues raised during the hearing, even if it was the Parties lack of consent to give access that placed CIEL in this situation. Meanwhile, in *Infinito Gold v. Costa Rica*, the Tribunal could not allow APREFLOFAS to attend the oral hearing over the objection of the Claimant in that case.

b) Non-Recognition of Indigenous Rights as a "Significant Interest" or "Perspective or Insight Different from That of the Disputing Parties"

With respect to intervention by indigenous peoples in particular, one obstacle that has not been overcome is the perception of tribunals of what might constitute a "significant interest" in the proceedings, as well as "a perspective, particular knowledge or insight that is different from that of the disputing parties" from an indigenous rights standpoint. In *Von Pezold v. Zimbabwe*, for example, the Tribunal rejected the notion that international human rights law was interdependent with international investment law and maintained that its mandate as an ICSID Tribunal did not include the consideration of international human rights norms.[127] In *Chevron v. Ecuador*, where the NGOs proposed lending their expertise on the particular rights of indigenous peoples in relation to the interpretation of the bilateral investment treaty, the Tribunal decided that the NGOs had nothing to contribute in the jurisdictional phase of the arbitration because only legal matters were involved.[128] It would appear that international law on indigenous rights was not deemed to be relevant by the Tribunals in these two cases. This leads to the observation that international investment law revolves exclusively around the economic impact of foreign investment, without regard to non-economic or cultural concerns.[129]

c) Conflicting International Obligations

International law is increasing in complexity with the development of many specific areas of international lawmaking and adjudication and thus it becomes inevitable that various international obligations and sources of law may come into conflict with one another, or at least be irreconcilable.[130] This reflects both on the inability of indigenous peoples to intervene in investment cases by asserting indigenous rights and it also applies to sovereign respondents caught between obligations under bilateral investment

[127] *Von Pezold v. Zimbabwe*, Procedural Order No. 2 dated 26 June 2012, at paras 58–59.

[128] *Chevron v. Ecuador*, Petition for Participation as Non-Disputing Parties dated 22 October 2010. at para 2.1; Procedural Order No. 8 dated 18 April 2011, at para 18.

[129] Valentina Vadi, Cultural Heritage in International Investment Law and Arbitration, 205–206 (Cambridge University Press, 2014).

[130] *See generally*, Mosche Hirsch, *Conflicting Obligations in International Investment Law: Investment Tribunals' Perspective, in* The Shifting Allocation of Authority in International Law: Considering Sovereignty, Supremacy and Subsidiarity 323–343 (Tomer Broude and Yuval Shany, eds. 2008).

treaties on the one hand and environmental and human rights treaties on the other.[131] It is this latter scenario that paved the way for the participation of indigenous groups in the cases of *Glamis Gold v. USA* and *Bear Creek v. Peru*, where measures taken by the sovereign respondents to protect indigenous peoples and their lands became the basis for the filing of investment claims. Likewise, in *Infinito Gold v. Costa Rica*, the NGO was allowed to intervene in the event that it could shed light on the environmental protection dimensions of the governmental measures that gave rise to the investment claim.

d) Definition of the Issues in Dispute

In *Glamis Gold v. USA* and *Bear Creek v. Peru*, the submissions by the indigenous peoples touched on factual matters relating the sacred nature of the land involved in the dispute, as well as the activities carried out in the area of their sacred lands. In this sense, the participation of the indigenous peoples as third parties was limited by what the claimant and respondent had put in issue in the cases. The "perspective, particular knowledge or insight that is different from that of the disputing parties" is ironically circumscribed by the disputing parties' definition of the issues.

e) Lack of Obligation to Consider the Third-Party Submission

It is also worth noting that the Tribunal in *Glamis Gold* categorically stated that the submission by the Quechan did factor into their decision in favor of the sovereign respondent.[132] In *Bear Creek*, the Tribunal stated that, while it had allowed the organization representing the Aymara and the Quechua to file a written submission, it was not obligated to consider the submission in drawing its conclusions in the case.[133] In *Pac Rim*, the Tribunal likewise stated that "the tribunal's decisions in this Award do not require the Tribunal specifically to consider the legal case advanced by CIEL."[134] By allowing interest groups to make a written submission in investment arbitrations, tribunals have already fulfilled the promise of transparency embodied in arbitral rules and jurisprudence, but are not constrained in their decision-making. Indeed, some commentators have expressed the view that allowing *amicus curiae* briefs is but a political response to the criticisms against the legitimacy of the investor-state dispute settlement system.[135]

---

[131] Christina Binder, *Investment, Development and Indigenous Peoples, in* International Investment Law and Development – Bridging the Gap 430–431 (Stephan W. Schill, Christian J. Tams and Rainer Hofmann, eds. 2015); Mosche Hirsch, *Conflicting Obligations in International Investment Law: Investment Tribunals' Perspective, in* The Shifting Allocation of Authority in International Law: Considering Sovereignty, Supremacy and Subsidiarity 324 (Tomer Broude and Yuval Shany, eds. 2008).

[132] *Glamis Gold v. USA*, Award dated 8 June 2009, at para 8.

[133] *Bear Creek v. Peru*, Procedural Order No. 5 dated 21 July 2016, at para 40.

[134] *Pac Rim v. El Salvador*, Award dated 14 October 2016, at para 3.30.

[135] Nigel Blackaby & Caroline Richard, *Amicus Curiae: A Panacea for Legitimacy in Investment Arbitration?*, *in* The Backlash Against Investment Arbitration: Perceptions and Reality 274 (Michael Waibel, et al., eds. 2010).

Bálint Kovács*

ACCESS OF SMEs TO INVESTMENT ARBITRATION – SMALL ENOUGH TO FAIL?

Abstract

This paper discusses investor-state dispute settlement mechanisms and the way these mechanisms are able to serve SMEs.

I. SMEs in Foreign Direct Investment

Small and Medium-Sized Enterprises (SMEs) are recognized as playing a major role in most economies and thus have an important contribution to the global economy.

In developed countries, SMEs employ the majority of the workforce and make the biggest contribution to GDP. In the European Union, SMEs make up 99.8% of enterprises, out of which over 92% are microenterprises. SMEs account for 67% of employment and 57.5% of gross value added[1]. It is the category which gives birth to large enterprises and also becomes their competition. It is where entrepreneurs start when they get into the world of business. It is also where most people find their first job and start climbing the ladder towards new jobs. As such, it is a business category which overflows with potential in foreign direct investment (FDI).

So which companies qualify as SMEs? According to the European Commission, the category of small and medium-sized enterprises is made up of enterprises which employ less than 250 people and have an annual turnover not exceeding EUR 50 million and/or an annual balance sheet total not exceeding EUR 43 million. Within this category, a small enterprise is defined as an enterprise which employs less than 50 persons and whose annual turnover and/or annual balance sheet total does not exceed EUR 10 million. Finally, a microenterprise is defined as an enterprise which employs less than 10 persons and its annual turnover and/or annual balance sheet total does not exceed EUR 2 million.[2]

* Bálint Kovács is an adjunct professor at Sapientia University of Transylvania, and a PhD Student at Debrecen University. He obtained his LLB in 2013 at Babeş-Bolyai University (Romania) and has obtained an M.A. in Private Law of the European Union at the same institution in 2014, subsequently attaining an LL.M. degree in European and International Business Law in a joint program of Debrecen University and Sapientia University of Transylvania. The author would like to express his gratitude to Professor Csongor István Nagy for the invitation to publish and Dr. Víg Zoltán for his useful remarks related to this paper.

1 Statistics on small and medium-sized enterprises. Available at: http://ec.europa.eu/eurostat/statistics-explained/index.php/Statistics_on_small_and_medium-sized_enterprises, accessed on 29 April 2018.

2 Commission Recommendation Concerning the Definition of Micro, Small and Medium-Sized Enterprises (2003/361/EC).

The definition of an SME changes country by country. For example, in the United States of America, or Canada, SME refers to businesses with fewer than 500 employees. In Romania, the officially accepted definition is the recommendation of the European Commission, cited above.

The acceleration of globalization, aided by the rapid development in information and communication technologies; improved transport facilities and tariff reductions presents opportunities and challenges to SMEs. SMEs, with their active participation in the global economy,have the opportunity to attain financial stability, increase productivity and expand their markets. Cooperation within a network of upstream and downstream partners can enhance a firm's status, information flows and learning possibilities as well as introduce new business practices and more advanced technology. SMEs' involvement in value chains demands greater managerial and financial resources, the ability to meet international standards and the protection of in-house intellectual property.[3]

Domestic policies play an important role in supporting SMEs in their internationalization strategies. Entrepreneurship policies, business start-ups' support and the promotion of research and development are crucial for making SMEs "fit" for cooperation with transnational enterprises (TNEs) and multinational enterprises (MNEs); for deriving maximum benefit out of this collaboration and minimizing associated risks, as well as for preparing SMEs to become foreign investors in their own right.[4] Other important measures of governments in support of SME international ventures are export promotion, through export guarantees, assistance in the establishment of business contacts, and the provision of information about foreign markets. Investing abroad can carry heavy costs and gathering information can also be time consuming, so investment guarantees, preferential public loans, and information services about foreign business opportunities, are some of the measures which can support SMEs which have reached a point at which they are willing to invest abroad.[5]

Many internal and external barriers continue to prevent SMEs from being able to access foreign markets.[6] The particular situation of SMEs when planning, implementing and operating an investment abroad, can be quite challenging. Internal barriers in this sense are faced when operating in foreign markets, which, more often than not, requires experience and knowledge in particular fields, which add to the cost of the venture. SMEs can also face managerial and financial constraints, with added language problems. More importantly, investing in a foreign country requires knowledge of the legal system and knowledge of the protection system that their venture might fall under, which automatically implies knowledge of international investment agreements and principles surrounding international investment law. External barriers have to do with cultural

---

[3] Integrating Developing Countries' SMEs into Global Value Chains – UNCTAD – 2010. Available at http://unctad.org/en/Docs/diaeed20095_en.pdf, accessed on 29 April 2018.

[4] Joachim Karl, *The Treatment of Small and Medium-Sized Enterprises in International Investment Law, in* Small and Medium-Sized Enterprises in International Economic Law 242 (Thilo Rensmann ed., OUP, 2017).

[5] *Id.*

[6] Martina Lodrant and Lucian Cernat, *SME Provisions in Trade Agreements and the Case of TTIP, in* Small and Medium-Sized Enterprises in International Economic Law 167 (Thilo Rensmann ed., OUP, 2017).

challenges, market circumstances or government policies and practices but also trade and investment regimes.[7]

Mostly, due to their size, SMEs have a weaker bargaining power than MNEs, which puts them in a more vulnerable position, making it almost impossible for them to negotiate with the authorities of the host country. In my view, this affects the ability of SMEs to secure the best possible conditions for their investment. This being the situation, SMEs are left vulnerable and in need of better opportunities to protect their investments. In many cases, policies of the host state might not even be discriminatory with regards to the size of the company or the "person" of the investor but can nevertheless affect SMEs disproportionately.

Many SMEs, especially in developing countries, do not wish or are not able to establish business relations abroad. This being the case, their concerns do not lie with the ways they may face the challenges of becoming foreign investors, rather, they are more interested in how they can become suppliers of MNEs at home, in industries where they have comparative advantages e.g., agriculture, agro-processing, small-scale manufacture and services.[8] Nevertheless, such "first contact" with MNEs is important for enterprises to get a taste of the international market, prompting them to become foreign investors in the long run.

Recognizing the importance of boosting SMEs willingness to go global, countries have started incentivizing export and foreign investment for this category of companies. These policies have also been transposed in some ways into international trade and investment agreements. These agreements are being negotiated in such ways as to include specific provisions concerning investment promotion for SMEs.[9] More sophisticated mega-regional agreements have also put into perspective the setting up of dedicated bodies which would assist SMEs throughout the implementation of the agreement, as was the case of the TTIP.[10] The challenges faced by SMEs have resulted in the establishment of numerous projects worldwide, aimed at assisting SMEs in their global development. These projects establish programs for networking and cooperation, legal and taxation assistance but also financial aid. There is a general aim to establish incubators and development centers, which would assist in technological innovation, development, establishment of partnerships etc. All in all, these programs have been established in order to help with the internationalization of SMEs.[11]

---

[7] *Id.*

[8] Joachim Karl, *The Treatment of Small and Medium-Sized Enterprises in International Investment Law, in* Small and Medium-Sized Enterprises in International Economic Law 242 (Thilo Rensmann ed., OUP, 2017).

[9] For example: Comprehensive and Enhanced Partnership Agreement between the EU and Armenia – Available at: http://investmentpolicyhub.unctad.org/Download/TreatyFile/5669, accessed on 29 April 2018, but also treaties enumerated by Martina Lodrant and Lucian Cernat, *SME Provisions in Trade Agreements and the Case of TTIP, in* Small and Medium-Sized Enterprises in International Economic Law 170 (Thilo Rensmann ed., OUP, 2017).

[10] Martina Lodrant and Lucian Cernat, *SME Provisions in Trade Agreements and the Case of TTIP, in* Small and Medium-Sized Enterprises in International Economic Law 178 (Thilo Rensmann ed., OUP, 2017).

[11] For more details on some of these programs: Joachim Karl, *The Treatment of Small and Medium-Sized Enterprises in International Investment Law, in* Small and Medium-Sized Enterprises in International Economic Law 242 (Thilo Rensmann ed., OUP, 2017).

The advantages of SMEs as foreign investors are those that are inherent to their existence – being small. While MNEs tend to face a level of opposition from local business or politicians, SMEs can easily fly under the radar and conduct business by blending into the crowd. Many countries have a minimum value threshold for reporting FDIs, this having the added advantage for SME investments to not really stick out. Although SMEs are sometimes in a better position to adapt to changes in the host state, they can also be left more exposed by changes. In some situations SMEs might be forced to just exit, which can often result in losses which endanger the existence of the company itself, thus incurring a greater loss, in comparison with incidental costs of adaptation which can be better absorbed by MNEs.

The most important international policy instruments dealing with foreign investments are international investment agreements (IIAs) and bilateral investment treaties (BITs). Their main objective is to promote and protect foreign investors in the host country. To this purpose, IIAs and BITs shield investors against certain political risks, in particular the risk of discrimination, expropriation, and capital transfer restrictions. Most IIAs and BITs also allow foreign investors to start international arbitration against the host state in case of an alleged violation of treaty obligations. Their core provisions (the principle of non-discrimination, fair and equitable treatment, protection against expropriation or nationalization, capital transfer rights, dispute settlement) protect foreign investors independent of their size. Arguments have been laid down for special provisions for SMEs, due to their more vulnerable situation and these include the acknowledgement of the special situation of SMEs in the preamble of some agreements; defining investment (supporting non-equity forms of investment); investment promotion and facilitation and setting up of agencies in the host country which deal specifically with SMEs.[12] It is also important for IIAs and BITs to avoid language and provisions which might be detrimental for SME development, such as performance requirements, establishment rights, access to land, state support measures etc.[13]

In the last 60 years, since IIAs have been popping up all over the world in the form of bilateral investment treaties (BITs), plurilateral treaties, regional agreements and other treaties with investment provisions (TIPs) account for a total of 3.325 treaties, out of which 2.671 treaties are in force today.[14] The treaties have resulted in more than 650 cases having been registered at the principal ISDS forum, which is the International Centre for Settlement of Investment Disputes (ICSID).[15]

For all the disadvantages faced by SMEs in international markets, change is slowly starting to gain momentum. Industrialized, developed countries, which are most capable of engaging in capital exports and have a strong SME sector, have started to seek strong investment promotion and protection provisions in the treaties they are signing.[16]

---

[12] Joachim Karl, *The Treatment of Small and Medium-Sized Enterprises in International Investment Law, in* Small and Medium-Sized Enterprises in International Economic Law 242 (Thilo Rensmann ed., OUP, 2017).

[13] *Id.*

[14] http://investmentpolicyhub.unctad.org/IIA, accessed on 29 April 2018.

[15] https://icsid.worldbank.org/en/Documents/resources/ICSID%20Web%20Stats%202018-1(English).pdf, accessed on 29 April 2018.

[16] Joachim Karl, *The Treatment of Small and Medium-Sized Enterprises in International Investment Law, in* Small

This paper discusses the issue of investor-state dispute settlement (ISDS) mechanisms used in the resolution of international investment related disputes and the way these mechanisms are able to serve SMEs.

II. Investor-State Dispute Settlement

The reason why the first international investment agreements were signed and the ICSID was created was to protect foreign direct investments from arbitrary actions of host countries.

It is highly important for SMEs to have access to investor-state arbitration, just like MNEs. It is a question of the aims of international investment agreements, the direction they are going in and the way they are fulfilled.[17]

IIAs have the aim of furthering cross-border economic prosperity and development, through the liberalization and stimulation of foreign direct investment. Investment agreements advance these aims by establishing substantive standards of investment protection that legally bind host states. Investor-state arbitration is essential for the policing of host state compliance with the protection standards that have been set up, sanctioning negative host state conduct where needed.[18]

Most investors prefer international arbitration over domestic litigation. This is because of a perceived bias in host states' courts. In such cases, if SMEs are not provided with the opportunity to choose international arbitration, and are only left with domestic litigation, foreign direct investments on their part would be highly discouraged. Not to mention that it would be discriminatory to reserve such opportunities only for larger enterprises, not SMEs.

There is also a historical perspective of the importance of having access to international arbitration, instead of seeking local remedies. An institution which can provide support for international private investment in an independent way, treating investors and host countries without interest, represents a great incentive for companies to go international, making their risk a bit more calculable. Before ISDS, when a domestic court did not fully compensate an investor for losses incurred by fault of the host state, the situation might have caused the investor to seek their government's assistance in vindicating its rights through the politicized process of espousal. The way for a foreign investor to seek remedy was to go through the host state's domestic court system or prove that exhausting all domestic remedies was of no use, after which they would lobby their own government to seek remedy on a political or diplomatic path. This had huge shortcomings: whenever there was a commercial situation to be discussed, it could be put up against a military or other foreign policy decision. In such a way, politics and diplomacy would mix with business even though the situations had absolutely no relation to each other. International investment agreements have created a less politicized, more

AND MEDIUM-SIZED ENTERPRISES IN INTERNATIONAL ECONOMIC LAW 250 (Thilo Rensmann ed., OUP, 2017).

[17] *Id.*

[18] *Id.*

"judicialized" process of dispute settlement, named investor-state arbitration, which would solve the problems posed by the process of espousal.[19]

When reading bilateral investment treaties, more or less the same dispute resolution methods can be easily identified. There is initial consultation between the parties concerned, this being the attempt at getting parties to amicably solve the case and, if the first method did not work, the dispute is to be sent for settlement to national courts or to international arbitration.

Whenever either litigation or arbitration ensues, typically there are three means of going forward contained in most IIAs. The first way is for the claimant to start proceedings before the competent courts of the contracting party in breach of the treaty (meaning litigation in front of national courts). The second is that the claimant can refer the case to the International Centre for the Settlement of Investment Disputes (ICSID) and finally the claimant may start proceedings for arbitration following more general rules, or the rules set forth in this regard by the United Nations Commission on International Trade Law (UNCITRAL), in case the signatories of the BIT are not signatories of the ICSID Convention. The second and third possibilities belong to the realm of international arbitration.

The ICSID has become one the most utilized institutions for the settlement of investment disputes, in large part due to the recognition and enforcement provisions accepted by signatory states. Parties to the treaty have an obligation to recognize awards granted in ICSID proceedings as binding, and enforce the awards granting pecuniary obligations as final domestic judgments. For obvious reasons, countries are keen on using legally binding means of arbitration and with the general language used to formulate most BITs, the majority of cases in front of the ICSID stem from the different BITs which accord it jurisdiction.[20] Due to its importance, the paper proceeds with presenting the ICSID's take on the settlement of investment disputes brought by SMEs.

III. ICSID and SMEs

The International Centre for Settlement of Investment Disputes is the largest and most prestigious international institution devoted to international investment dispute settlement. It was established under the World Bank by the Convention on the Settlement of Investment Disputes Between states and the Nationals of Other states of 1965 (ICSID Convention), with the aim of promoting international investment. As of January 2018 it accounts for 162 signatory states.[21] Despite its vast experience and large case number, resulting in quite a serious jurisprudence, the ICSID has also often been criticized. The

[19] *Id.*

[20] Over 60%, as shown in the 2018 ICSID Caseload Statistics, available at:https://icsid.worldbank.org/en/Documents/resources/ICSID%20Web%20Stats%202018-1(English).pdf, accessed on 29 April 2018.

[21] List of contracting states and other signatories of the convention (as of January 11,2018) https://icsid.worldbank.org/en/Documents/icsiddocs/List%20of%20Contracting%20States%20and%20Other%20Signatories%20of%20the%20Convention%20-%20Latest.pdf, accessed on 29 April 2018.

critiques faced by the ICSID are in many cases applicable to the domain of ISDS in general, as well[22].

a) Costs Paid

One of the main critiques launched against the ISDS systems has to do with the enormous costs attached to the settlement of a dispute. These costs stem not only from the cost of the legal expertise needed to conclude such dispute settlement but the disputing parties also have to fund the costs of the arbitral tribunal consisting of the fees and expenses of the arbitrators, administrative expenses of the tribunal, including stenography, translation and secretarial services among others. The average overall cost of ISDS proceedings is of approximately US $8 million, and in exceptional cases can rise to US $30 million.[23] Within the ICSID there have been cases where arbitration costs as high as US$7,623,693 were awarded in ADC v. Hungary[24] (ICSID Case No. ARB/03/16) Award of October 2, 2006, or 60% of EUR 6,053,443.78 in Spyridon Roussalis v. Romania (ICSID Case No. ARB/06/1) Award of December 7, 2011.

Such costs are made even more unbearable due to the long time it takes for the tribunal to render an award, usually four to five years[25]. Additional time is needed for the enforcement of the award[26] in case the investor argues its case successfully. For SMEs, such costs can quite easily prove unbearable, especially after the host state, via its actions, has left the SME investor in serious financial difficulty.

The costs incurred by SMEs seeking an award at the ICSID hinder their willingness to turn to the institution, even though there is theoretically no impediment for SMEs to make use of the ICSID Convention. This might be one of the reasons for which the number of SMEs that resorted to international dispute settlement mechanisms is only about 15 per cent[27]

[22] For details concerning the specific effects of ICSID arbitration in South America and the solutions proposed by UNASUR, *see* Manuel A. Gomez, *The South American Way: Sub-Regional Integration Under ALBA and UNASUR and International Dispute Resolution, in* Missed and New Opportunities in World Trade (Csongor István Nagy & Zoltán Víg (eds.), Akadémiai Kiadó, Budapest, 2017) / Vol. 58, No. 3 Hungarian Journal of Legal Studies (2017) available at: https://akademiai.com/doi/10.1556/2052.2017.58.4.6.

[23] Alexander Gebert, *Legal Protection for Small and Medium-Sized Enterprises Through Investor-State Dispute Settlement: Status Quo, Impediments, and Potential Solutions, in* Small and Medium-Sized Enterprises in International Economic Law 294 (Thilo Rensmann ed., OUP, 2017).

[24] Csongor István Nagy, *Hungarian Cases Before ICSID Tribunals: The Hungarian Experience with Investment Arbitration* Vol. 58, No. 3 Hungarian Journal of Legal Studies, 291-310 (2017). Available at SSRN: https://ssrn.com/abstract=3110264.

[25] Alexander Gebert, *Legal Protection for Small and Medium-Sized Enterprises Through Investor-State Dispute Settlement: Status Quo, Impediments, and Potential Solutions, in* Small and Medium-Sized Enterprises in International Economic Law 295 (Thilo Rensmann ed., OUP, 2017).

[26] *See* the complicated case of the Micula brothers against Romania, where the enforcement of the award has been hindered by the intervention of the European Commission. (ICSID Case No. ARB/05/20).

[27] The number seems to be higher among investors from the United States, where SMEs are the predominant users of investor-state dispute settlement. – According to Martina Lodrant and Lucian Cernat, *SME Provisions in Trade Agreements and the Case of TTIP, in* Small and Medium-Sized Enterprises in International Economic Law 185 (Thilo Rensmann ed., OUP, 2017).

of all disputes between 2008 and 2013, according to a preliminary research done by UNCTAD.[28]

One of the factors which contribute to the high costs is the exclusivity of legal expertise in this field.[29] The investment arbitration market is in the hands of a few large law firms[30] which have billing hours that can objectively be considered as being astronomical. Such prices can only be afforded by big companies, not by SMEs. The issue is that without professional legal expertise, the endeavors of an SME in trying to recoup losses incurred due to abuses of the host state can be seriously hindered. This could leave the SME facing even more costs and with no damages granted.

The high costs of litigation have also resulted in a new industry – litigation finance. Litigation financiers analyze and choose on a case-by-case basis, just as they would do in the case of any other investment. SMEs can turn to such investors in order to cover their litigation costs. It looks like a win-win situation but given that the financiers change 30-50% of any award, this is rather an effect of the problem and not a solution in itself.[31]

The real solution for such issues lies with provisions which grant a reduction of financial burdens for SMEs, like in the case of CETA.[32]

b) An Issue of Interpretation

In a case heard in 2001 called *Salini v. Morocco* (ICSID Case No. ARB/00/4), an ICSID tribunal held that the "investment requirement" of Article 25 (1) has objective content limiting ICSID jurisdiction. Article 25 (1) of the ICSID Convention gives ICSID jurisdiction over "any legal dispute arising directly out of an investment, between a Contracting state … and a national of another Contracting state, which the parties to the dispute consent in writing to submit to the Centre."[33] The text of the Convention, although not setting a limit to what an investment means, and also not excluding any investment dispute due to the size of it,[34] practically puts up serious impediments for some actors to enjoy the services and the protection of the Centre, especially after some of the interpretations it has faced in the *Salini case*.[35]

---

[28] Joachim Karl, *The Treatment of Small and Medium-Sized Enterprises in International Investment Law, in* SMALL AND MEDIUM-SIZED ENTERPRISES IN INTERNATIONAL ECONOMIC LAW 242 (Thilo Rensmann ed., OUP, 2017).

[29] Lee M. Caplan, *Making Investor-State Arbitration More Accessible to Small and Medium-Sized Enterprises. in* THE FUTURE OF INVESTMENT ARBITRATION (Catherine A. Rogers, Roger P. Alford eds., Oxford University Press 2009).

[30] This small monopoly is also used to formulate one of the main critiques against the existing ISDS system, which is the lack of regulation of conflict of interest.

[31] Juridica Investments Ltd. is such a company, which is also publicly traded.

[32] CETA Text: http://trade.ec.europa.eu/doclib/docs/2014/september/tradoc_152806.pdf, accessed on 29 April 2018.

[33] The text of the Convention: http://icsidfiles.worldbank.org/icsid/icsid/staticfiles/basicdoc/partA-chap02.htm accessed on 29 April 2018.

[34] As the author observes in Alexander Gebert, *Legal Protection for Small and Medium-Sized Enterprises Through Investor-State Dispute Settlement: Status Quo, Impediments, and Potential Solutions, in* SMALL AND MEDIUM-SIZED ENTERPRISES IN INTERNATIONAL ECONOMIC LAW (Thilo Rensmann ed., OUP, 2017).

[35] *Salini Costruttori SpA v. Kingdom of Morocco*, ICSID Case No. ARB/00/4, Decision on Jurisdiction (23 July

The Tribunal stated the following:

> *"The doctrine generally considers that investment infers: contributions, a certain duration of performance of the contract and a participation in the risks of the transaction* [...]. *In reading the Convention's preamble, one may add the contribution to the economic development of the host state of the investment as an additional condition.*
> *In reality, these various elements may be interdependent. Thus, the risks of the transaction may depend on the contributions and the duration of performance of the contract. As a result, these various criteria should be assessed globally even if, for the sake of reasoning, the Tribunal considers them individually here."*

Even though the Tribunal had called for a global assessment of these criteria, later tribunals have generally attributed to the *Salini case* the creation of a four-part test.[36] The author of the above cited Chapter, Mr. Perry S. Bechky, criticizes the fourth part of the so-called *Salini test*, which requires an investment to "contribute to the economic development of the host state" as a condition of access to ICSID arbitration. This development prong has been criticized before but when looked at through the lens of microinvestment (a concept introduced by Mr. Bechky), it reveals new problems: it imposes a backdoor size requirement that inhibits access to ICSID by microinvestors who may have the greatest need for such access, thereby harming ICSID's ability to fulfill its objectives, including development promotion.[37]

A microinvestment dispute is a legal dispute arising directly out of a microinvestment, between a state and a foreign investor. A microinvestment, in turn, is an investment worth less than US$5 million, made by an individual, a micro-enterprise, or a small or medium-sized enterprise.[38] A microinvestment dispute shall not be mistaken with a small claim. It is of the nature of the microinvestment that it is crucial for the SME, giving rise to a "bet the company"-type litigation for many companies, as opposed to an "ordinary business dispute" for larger companies.[39] In this sense, microinvestment dispute excludes claims by large businesses. As such, Mr. Bechky concludes that the definition is tied to the size of both the investment and the investor, not to the amount in controversy, in theory. In practice, though, data about the size of the investment and the investor is often unavailable and the amount in controversy serves as a proxy for the (claimed) value of the investment, because most cases allege the taking or (nearly) complete destruction of the investment.

2001) Available at: https://www.italaw.com/sites/default/files/case-documents/ita0738.pdf, accessed on 29 April 2018.

36 Perry S. Bechky, *Microinvestment Disputes, in* SMALL AND MEDIUM-SIZED ENTERPRISES IN INTERNATIONAL ECONOMIC LAW (Thilo Rensmann ed., OUP, 2017).

37 *Id.*

38 *Id.*

39 *Id.*

In the above cited article, Mr. Bechky brings as an example two cases where the *Salini test*, including the development prong, had been used to decide on two microinvestments: *Mitchell v. DR Congo* and *Malaysian Historical Salvors v. Malaysia*.

In the case of *Mitchell v. DR Congo*, the claim was brought to the ICSID under the BIT signed between the United States and Congo, by Patrick Mitchell, a US citizen, the owner of a small law firm in Congo called Mitchell & Associates. In 1999 the Congolese authorities had sealed the law firm's premises, seized documents and other items and detained two attorneys for more than eight months. This resulted in effectively putting the law firm out of business.[40]

The claim brought by Mitchell was successful in the first phase; the ICSID tribunal ruling in favor of Mitchell, stating that Mitchell had been the victim of an expropriation.

In 2006, an *ad hoc* committee annulled the tribunal award,[41] giving way to the arguments brought by Congo, according to which Mitchell had not made an investment within the meaning of Article 25 of the ICSID Convention.[42]

In the case of *Malaysian Historical Salvors v Malaysia,*[43] the Malaysian Government hired the Malaysian Historical Salvors, a marine salvage company, to find and salvage the cargo of a British ship that sank in the Strait of Malacca in 1817. The case was brought before a sole arbitrator who, by analyzing the contract came to the conclusion that it required Salvors 'to utilize its expertise, labour and equipment to carry out the salvage operation, and to invest and expend its own financial and other resources, and assume all risks of the salvage operation'. Salvors also assumed the risk of not being paid in case it did not salvage the ship's cargo.[44] Salvors managed to recover much of the cargo but had not been paid in full by the Malaysian Government, finally filing an ICSID case under the Malaysia-UK BIT.[45] In short,[46] the tribunal held that the capital invested was not of a substantial amount, that the size of the contribution was insufficient, that the contribution to development was not significant and also that the duration of the project did not satisfy the duration prong in the *Salini test*. The tribunal dismissed the case for lack of jurisdiction, not discussing the merits of the case but just by interpreting the meaning of the term investment within Article 25 of the ICSID Convention. Salvors subsequently requested the annulment of the award and won.

What is noteworthy about these two cases is the fact that the tribunals chose to apply a restrictive interpretation of the term investment, which highly endangers the chances of SMEs seeking effective remedies before this institution. The *Salini test* risks the introduction of a size requirement in the ICSID Convention even though there is

---

40 *Id.* at 277.

41 *Mitchell v Democratic Republic of Congo*, ICSID Case No ARB/99/7.

42 A detailed analysis of the case can be found in Perry S. Bechky, *Microinvestment Disputes, in* Small and Medium-Sized Enterprises in International Economic Law (Thilo Rensmann ed., OUP, 2017).

43 *Malaysian Historical Salvors, SDN, BHD v Malaysia*, ICSID Case No ARB/05/10.

44 Perry S. Bechky, *Microinvestment Disputes, in* Small and Medium-Sized Enterprises in International Economic Law 281 (Thilo Rensmann ed., OUP, 2017).

45 *Id.* at 281.

46 A more extensive review of the case can be found in Perry S. Bechky, *Microinvestment Disputes, in* Small and Medium-Sized Enterprises in International Economic Law (Thilo Rensmann ed., OUP, 2017).

no such explicit requirement in the Convention itself. Due to the way in which most of the BITs are constructed, as shown above, where jurisdiction of ICSID is established by default between contracting states which are signatories to the ICSID Convention, the risk of small investments being excluded from the procedure could leave SMEs without an effective remedy.

Furthermore, it must be pointed out that the purpose and object of the ICSID Convention should not be interpreted in such a way as to limit the jurisdiction of the tribunals. Also, the negotiating history of the ICSID Convention reveals that proposals excluding small disputes and small investments from the reach of ICSID have been rejected expressly.[47] What is more, the term investment has not even been defined in the ICSID Convention, so that it would not spark unnecessary debates.

Cases, such as the ones briefly presented above, can also act as a deterrent for SMEs in seeking remedies in front of the ICSID, due to the costs they might incur in cases where their claims are dismissed. As a result, litigation financiers would consider such cases to be of high risk and subsequently refuse to invest in microinvestment claims, if cases such as the above will grow in numbers.What the above cases also show us is the ways in which ICSID has shown its limits in handling the complexity reached by some FDIs.

IV. General Criticism Faced by the Current ISDS Systems

BITs started appearing after World War II as a way for more developed economies to ensure their interests in developing countries. The concept behind BITs is simple – poor countries need capital in order to develop, which could be provided by foreign investments. In turn, foreign investments need legal certainty and a measure of political stability. International investment agreements and international arbitration are meant to shield investors from political instability, securing investments without having to go through the long process of establishing the same rule of law mechanisms which exist in developed countries.

The lack of legal certainty and political stability are put in question in cases where, for example, an American company would invest in Angola, so as to grant it the much needed protection against arbitrary expropriation, or in case the state violated the principle of fair and equitable treatment. Nonetheless, the issue has now become that developed countries have begun concluding BITs. A French company might sue the USA for any internal policy decision which might be serving the public interest but also puts their investment in danger.[48] This has evolved into a situation where companies starting procedures in front of arbitral tribunals are interfering with the states' value-judgments, causing potential restrictions in policymaking, via free trade agreements. This certainly is an intrusion into national regulatory sovereignty.[49]

---

[47] *Id.* at 267.

[48] *E.g. The Philip Morris v. Australia* case (plain packaging of cigarettes), or the *Vattenfall* Case.

[49] Csongor István Nagy, *Free Trade, Public Interest and Reality: New Generation Free Trade Agreements and National Regulatory Sovereignty*, Vol. IX Czech Yearbook of International Law , 197–216 (2018). Available at SSRN: https://ssrn.com/abstract=3172064.

Obviously, there are mechanisms in place to prevent claimants from abusing their rights. This however does not prevent actors from forwarding claims and starting very expensive arbitration procedures. Also, until abusive cases play out, they have been known to affect the willingness of governments to adopt policies in certain areas. This is called regulatory chill.[50] The right to regulate in certain areas, especially public health, public safety or consumer protection, should be provided for expressly in future agreements.

Another important aspect is the fact that arbitrators are not tenured, in contrast to judges in national judicial systems or in some international courts. The public finds this to be quite unsettling, due to the fact that it is perceived as not granting security against conflict of interest situations which may arise. This has to do with the perception of independence of the professionals involved in ISDS cases, undermining one of the most important traits the ISDS system has.

Transparency or the lack thereof, is something that is brought up quite often in discussions about ISDS, as a factor which hinders the fair and efficient resolution of investment disputes. In fact, the lack of transparency has been considered to be such a serious issue that the United Nations Commission on International Trade Law (UNCITRAL) has drafted a Convention on Transparency in Treaty-Based Investor-State Arbitration (also known as the Mauritius Convention on Transparency).[51]

With lack of transparency, it is also quite hard to criticize the actual merits of the existing ISDS system. Information about the existence of disputes, the procedure which they have undergone, not to mention the details of the case, such as the state of affairs, or the ruling itself, have only been published in a limited number. This being the case, the current ISDS system, by its nature, has hindered the means with which it should be reformed. Although ICSID has been around for five decades, only in the last twenty years has it started making serious contributions to the development of ISDS. Yet, even the limited case-law has already provided arguments for the reformation of this highly fragmented system.

The existence of a multitude of BITs, multilateral treaties and regional treaties also impacts the coherence and consistency of the ISDS systems. The question of nationality of the claimant plays a highly important role in this, as do most favored nation clauses.[52]

Without violation of due process provisions in the treaties governing the ISDS procedure or other highly restrictive provisions, parties do not have the right to appeal the decisions, making this, in combination with the lack of coherence and consistency a highly risky venture for investors. In such circumstances it is quite obvious why SMEs would rather stay away from the existing ISDS system.

---

[50] Eckhard Janeba, *Regulatory Chill and the Effect of Investor State Dispute Settlement*, Available at https://papers.ssrn.com/sol3/papers.cfm?abstract_id=2887952, accessed on 29 April 2018. Zoltán Víg & Gábor Hajdu, *CETA and Regulatory Chill*, *in* A Szellemi Tulajdonvédelem és a Szabadkereskedelem Aktuális Kérdései 48 (Márta Görög & Péter Mezei eds., Iurisperitus Kiadó 2018).

[51] United Nations Convention on Transparency in Treaty-based Investor-State Arbitration: https://www.uncitral.org/pdf/english/texts/arbitration/transparency-convention/Transparency-Convention-e.pdf.

[52] Christoph Schreuer, *Coherence and Consistency in International Investment Law*, available at: http://www.univie.ac.at/intlaw/wordpress/wp-content/uploads/2014/01/Coherence-and-Consistency-in-International-Investment-Law.pdf, accessed on 29 April 2018.

The above issues, though having a general validity in the ISDS universe, disproportionately affect SMEs. Fixing them is even more urgent from an SME point-of-view.

V. Proposed Solutions and Conclusions

It must be kept in mind that in finding general dispute settlement solutions, resolutions meant for SMEs must be not only affordable but also quicker than the existing ones, due to the vulnerability of these business actors.

Mediation and conciliation could be sought by SMEs as a way to avoid litigation and arbitration. These means are quicker, incomparably less expensive and a less formal way of finding an amicable solution to a litigious situation.[53] The issue here could be the fact that SMEs are less flexible when it comes to the losses they have incurred. If an SME loses money because of the illegal actions of a host state, it can easily be put in a betting-the-company situation, which might not leave it with any other choice but to pursue damages for all losses incurred. Without the real, viable possibility of cutting some of its losses and recovering a portion of them, which is something a conciliation and mediation process might entail, SMEs are left with no other choice but to go through arbitration or litigation.

Conciliation and mediation provisions can be found in the EU-Canada Comprehensive Economic and Trade Agreement (or CETA) but also in a lot of BITs, as standard provisions.

CETA has made use of a very welcomed concept in the ISDS universe – institutionalized dispute settlement. The European Union has been a pioneer of such treaties, establishing the Investment Court System within CETA and within the BIT signed with Vietnam. These institutionalized systems also include tenured judges.

The Investment Court System comes with a roster of 15 Tribunal members, named by the parties to the Agreement. The new System also comes with an appeal mechanism, which is highly welcome in order to ensure the consistency and predictability of the system. For investors generally, this goes a long way in making a calculated decision but for SMEs especially it will represent a great feature in risk aversion.

CETA also has provisions which give the Investment Court the possibility to reduce the financial burdens on SMEs, as mentioned above, while also maintaining the 'loser pays' rule. Jurisprudence will reveal how this provision will play out.

The Investment Court of CETA, just as the ICSID, represents institutionalized dispute settlement mechanisms. This could mean that, theoretically, costs could be reduced more easily and also a pro-bono legal assistance program for SMEs could be developed. Within the ICSID, although it had been discussed as a "pro bono advisory service", no concrete steps have been made since the Secretary General has talked about it in 2005.[54]

---

[53] Joachim Karl, *The Treatment of Small and Medium-Sized Enterprises in International Investment Law, in* Small and Medium-Sized Enterprises in International Economic Law 242 (Thilo Rensmann ed., OUP, 2017).

[54] https://www.oecd.org/investment/internationalinvestmentagreements/36053800.pdf, accessed on 29 April 2018.

The best chance for SMEs is for key institutional players to establish a formal framework of assistance aimed at providing consistent, coordinated and reliable support to SMEs facing the burdens of investor-state arbitration. Such a framework would have two principle aims. The first would be to reduce costs wherever and as much as possible. The second would be to educate SMEs and their legal counsel on how to enforce their rights under international investment treaties through investor-state arbitration.[55]

The European Union, together with UNCITRAL, have been pioneers in promoting reforms which will bring about changes in the world of ISDS. International institutions have to take the lead in reforming the dispute settlement system, which has become one of the most politically sensitive subjects in free-trade.[56] In March 2018, the Council of the European Union gave a mandate to the European Commission for the negotiation of directives for a Convention establishing a multilateral court for the settlement of investment disputes. Such a court has been envisaged by professionals in the field of international investment law as being one of the most effective methods of correcting the shortcomings of the current system.[57] The mandate has been given by the Council to UNCITRAL just half a year after such a project had been announced in the 2017 state of the Union address.[58] The mandate of the Council to UNCITRAL is a new opportunity to better cover the needs of SMEs in a Multilateral Investment Court.

Institutions set up pursuant to these proposals will further international investment law and investor-state arbitration. They are in a position to regulate SME access to investment arbitration in the near future. The possibility of filing low-value claims, decided by tenured judges at a lower cost, could also offer them protection against high cost/high risk procedures.

The dispute settlement mechanisms adopted by IIAs should ensure investors are covered against the risks posed by the inconsistencies of host states, through investment arbitration. It is certain that investment arbitration must be available to all investors. SMEs should benefit from more favorable measures so that they are able to make use of dispute settlement mechanisms, when in need. Uncertainty in such matters just adds to the general uncertainty of cross-border business.

---

[55] Lee M. Caplan, *Making Investor-State Arbitration More Accessible to Small and Medium-Sized Enterprises. in* The Future of Investment Arbitration (Catherine A. Rogers, Roger P. Alford eds., Oxford University Press 2009).

[56] Csongor István Nagy, *Free Trade, Public Interest and Reality: New Generation Free Trade Agreements and National Regulatory Sovereignty*, Vol. IX Czech Yearbook of International Law 197–216 (2018). Available at SSRN: https://ssrn.com/abstract=3172064.

[57] Christoph Schreuer, *Coherence and Consistency in International Investment Law*, 8. Available at: < http://www.univie.ac.at/intlaw/wordpress/wp-content/uploads/2014/01/Coherence-and-Consistency-in-International-Investment-Law.pdf, accessed on 29 April 2018.

[58] http://europa.eu/rapid/press-release_IP-17-3182_en.htm, accessed on 29 April 2018.

Regional perspectives

Dildar F. Zebari*

THE PROMOTION, PROTECTION, TREATMENT AND EXPROPRIATION OF INVESTMENTS UNDER THE ENERGY CHARTER TREATY – A CRITICAL ANALYSIS OF THE CASE-LAW

Abstract

This paper analyses the case law of article 10 (promotion, protection and treatment of investments) and article 13 (expropriation) of the Energy Charter Treaty (ECT).

I. Introduction

This essay discusses the case law of the Energy Charter Treaty (ECT), in relation to its articles 10 (promotion, protection and treatment of investments) and 13 (expropriation). However, it is necessary to give a general overview of these two articles before exploring the case law.

The first paragraph of Article 10 states that:

> *"(1) Each Contracting Party shall, in accordance with the provisions of this Treaty, encourage and create stable, equitable, favourable and transparent conditions for Investors of other Contracting Parties to make Investments in its Area. Such conditions shall include a commitment to accord at all times to Investments of Investors of other Contracting Parties fair and equitable treatment. Such Investments shall also enjoy the most constant protection and security and no Contracting Party shall in any way impair by unreasonable or discriminatory measures their management, maintenance, use, enjoyment or disposal. In no case shall such Investments be accorded treatment less favourable than that required by international law, including treaty obligations. Each Contracting Party shall observe any obligations it has entered into with an Investor or an Investment of an Investor of any other Contracting Party."*

This is the first clear statement in the ECT that explicitly spells out the contracting parties' intention of protecting each other's investments and banning the use of

* Dildar F. Zebari is currently a PhD student at the Law Faculty of the University of Szeged, Hungary. His field of study is investment and energy law. He has an LLM from University of East London, United Kingdom and a B.A. in Law from the College of Law and Politics, Dohuk University, Iraq. He has previously worked as legal adviser for the national oil company (Iraqi Crown) and taught civil law at Duhok Polytechnic University, Iraq.

discriminatory or otherwise unreasonable measures that would impair or hinder foreign investors.

The ECT establishes, in Article 10 (2) and (3), the Most Favoured Nation (MFN) standard of treatment for investors belonging to the contracting parties, in relation to the areas covered by the ECT. Furthermore, Article 10 (4) mandates the creation of a supplementary treaty, which obliges its signatories to expand the scope of the ECT MFN treatment to select other parties.

In Article 10 (5), the contracting parties commit to limiting exceptions to MFN treatment to a minimum and also agree to progressively remove existing restrictions affecting the investors of other contracting parties, in relation to the areas covered by the ECT. Furthermore, besides the general treatment provision in (2) and (3), Article 10 (7) specifically extends the MFN standard to management, maintenance, use, enjoyment, disposal (or other related activities) of investments covered by the scope of the ECT.

However, the MFN standard does not apply to the protection of intellectual property, as noted by Article 10 (10), which instead refers the subject to the applicable international agreements for the protection of intellectual property rights.

Finally, Article 10 (12) contains an enforcement provision that mandates each contracting party to ensure that its domestic law provides effective means for the assertion of claims and the enforcement of rights with respect to investment and investment agreements.

Continuing with Article 13, this article is fundamentally about expropriation, nationalization and equivalent measures, as shown here:

> *"(1) Investments of Investors of a Contracting Party in the Area of any other Contracting Party shall not be nationalized, expropriated or subjected to a measure or measures having effect equivalent to nationalization or expropriation (hereinafter referred to as "Expropriation") except where such Expropriation is:*
> *(a) for a purpose which is in the public interest;*
> *(b) not discriminatory;*
> *(c) carried out under due process of law; and*
> *(d) accompanied by the payment of prompt, adequate and effective compensation."*

To be specific, Article 13 (1) (d) posits that all legitimate expropriation is to be accompanied by the payment of prompt, adequate and effective compensation. This provision thus establishes the Hull standard of compensation. The second part of Article 13 (1) mandates that such compensation is to amount to the fair market value of the investment expropriated at the time immediately before the expropriation or impeding expropriation became known in such a way as to affect the value of the investment (the valuation date). Finally, the ECT also mandates that, at the request of the foreign investor, this fair market value is to be expressed in a freely convertible currency on the basis of the market rate of exchange existing for that currency on the valuation date. This compensation should also include interest at a commercial rate established on a market basis from the date of expropriation until the date of payment.

II. ECT Case Law Concerning Articles 10 and 13

One of the very first cases was the *Nykomb Synergies Technology Holding AB* (the Claimant) versus Republic of Latvia (the Respondent).[1] In this case, the Claimant, a Swedish company, acquired 100% ownership of Latvian owned company SIA Windau in September 2000 which produced electric power and heat.[2] A Latvian state owned company named Latvenergo, formed in 1991, entered into a contract in 1997 with Windau to build a power plant and produce energy and heat to be distributed and delivered to the Bauska municipality. The power plant was completed and a contract was entered for Nykomb to sell the energy and heat at a double tariff rate for the first eight years of production. An amendment to the Latvian Energy Law on 3 August 2000 made energy not privatizable as it was a national economic object of the state economy. This made Latvenergo a state monopoly on energy control, regulation and pricing. It changed the multiplier from the double tariff rate, to a multiplier of 0.75. The Claimant then halted production and demanded the original contractual rate of double tariff rate, which Latvenergo refused.[3]

The Claimant argued that the Respondent, by not paying the double tariff rate as agreed by the contract and while paying other Latvian energy companies the double tariff rate, had breached its contractual obligations under the ECT. It applied for relief for all loss of income incurred from the halt of production of energy and heat while the double tariff rate was not being paid, in addition of future losses incurred. It claimed the Respondent violated Article 10(1) and 13(1) for fair and equitable treatment and most favoured nation treatment, by unreasonable and discriminatory measures and actions equivalent to expropriation.[4]

The Respondent argued that Latvenergo's conduct was not attributable to Latvia, that the government had not contravened its obligations under Part III of the Treaty; that Nykomb had not suffered any loss warranting compensation and that all costs of the Arbitration should be borne by the Claimant. Essentially their argument was that changes in Latvian law are not attributable to Latvenergo on the grounds that acts of Parliament cannot be construed to be acts by Latvenergo. By amending the Latvian Energy Act, Latvenergo was merely to enforce any changes in tariff rates that the Latvian Energy Council were to recommend.[5]

The Arbitral Award held, *inter alia*, that the Respondent did violate its obligations under Article 10(1) and 13(1) of the ECT. Changes in the average sales price are allowed to be made but the multiplier of the tariff rate was a violation of its contractual obligations with the Claimant. The Arbitral Award granted the loss of income claimed by the Claimant but denied the claim for future losses, as they are speculative and immeasurable. The Arbitral Tribunal rejected that contention of the Respondent that a *force majeure* clause allowed it to change the multiplier of the tariff rate. In fact, the contract was vague as to whether it is merely an interim agreement. Despite legislation, the multiplier rate

---

1 *Nykomb Synergies Technology Holding AB v Republic of Latvia*, SCC Case No 118/2001.

2 *Nykomb Synergies Technology Holding AB v Republic of Latvia*, IIC 182 (2003).

3 *Id.* at para 1.1.

4 *Id.* at para 1.2.3.

5 *Id.* at para 1.3.

should have continued for the 8 years after production as stipulated by the contract between the parties.[6]

The next case involved *Petrobart Limited* (Claimant), a company registered in Gibraltar, versus *the Kyrgyz Republic* (Respondent).[7] In February 1998, it entered into a contract with Kyrgyzgazmuniazat (KGM) for 120,000 tons of gas condensate. In March of the same year, Petrobart delivered the gas condensate and invoiced KGM for $2,457,620. KGM made the first 2 payments amounting to $951,976. It failed to settle the rest of the balance due to financial difficulties and subsequently suspended further deliveries.[8]

At the local Court in Bishkek, Petrobart obtained a debt judgment of $1,507,812. However, prior to this, in September 1998, KGM's assets were to be sold off by Presidential Decree to 2 other state entities. It subsequently was granted a stay of execution on the debt judgment for 3 months. During those 3 months, KGM sold off assets to 3rd party entities and was declared bankrupt. In 2003, Petrobart initiated arbitration proceedings under Article 26 of the ECT, which came into force in 1998 in Kyrgyzstan[9].

Petrobart claimed that Kyrgyzstan breached several obligations under the ECT. It claimed that the Respondent breached Article 10(1) of the ECT by not creating stable, favourable and transparent conditions. It claimed the Respondent's domestic law did not provide effective means for the assertment of claims and enforcement of rights with respects to investment, as required under Article 10(12). It claimed the breach amounted to an expropriation, contrary to Article 13(1). It lastly claimed that state owned entities did not act in a manner consistent with its obligations, in breach of Article 22(1). It requested compensatory damages of the debt judgment, plus interest, as well as for further loss of profits.[10]

The Kyrgyz Republic contested the arguments raised by the Claimant. It argued that Petrobart does not have an "investment" in the country as defined by Kyrgyz Foreign Investment Law. It asserts that the transferring of KGM's assets was part of a stabilisation programme, not to treat its creditors unfavourably. It claimed that the stabilisation programme complied with The Kyrgyz Investment Law. It also claimed that the Kyrgyz Republic did not act in bad faith, or to deprive the Claimant, and did not benefit from the bankrupty of KGM[11].

The Arbitral Tribunal accepted the arguments of Petrobart. It agreed that The Kyrgyz Republic breached Article 10(1) of creating a fair, equitable and transparent environment. This is due to the various Presidential decrees, changes to domestic law and direct government intervention in the affairs of KGM. These created unstable and inequitable conditions for Petrobart. By requesting and being granted a stay of execution of the debt judgment, it failed to ensure Petrobart could by effective means assert its rights in Court. It also violated Article 13(1), as the acts related to making KGM bankrupt effectively lead to an expropriation of Petrobart's investment. Petrobart was granted

---

[6] *Id.* at para 4.2.

[7] *Petrobart Limited v The Kyrgyz Republic*, SCC Case No. 126/2003.

[8] *Id.* at 5.

[9] *Id.* at 6.

[10] *Id.* at 25–35.

[11] *Id.* at 42–53.

compensatory damages of USD $1,507,812.60 and $2,376,339.60 as lost future profits, among other costs.[12]

Another case was between *Ron Fuchs* (Claimant) and the *Republic of Georgia* (Respondent).[13] The Republic of Georgia sought investments to develop its national energy infrastructure and develop a transit corridor that could transport oil and gas from Azerbaijan to the Black Sea (the Western Route). Meetings were held between the Claimants and representatives of the Georgian Government to discuss oil exploitation. The result of these meetings was that the Georgian Minister of Industry signed a Power of Attorney on 4 September 1991 with the Claimants through the company Tramex (International) Ltd, of which the 2 Claimants held equal shares. Two months later, the Respondents adopted Resolution No. 834, which authorized a joint venture between SakNavtobi (the Georgian state-oil company) and Tramex for the purpose of exploiting oil fields in the Georgian territories of Ninotsminda, Manavi and Rustavi, as well a license to export oil. The joint venture created GTI Ltd, of which Tramex and SakNavtobi held equal shares. Additionally, SakNavtobi held the rights to Georgia's main pipline known as Transneft.[14]

Transneft executed a Deed of Concession in favour of GTI for 30 years over Georgia's pipelines. This was signed by the parties, as well as ratified by the Minister of Fuel and Energy. GTI started some work on different parts of the pipeline projects whilst it was trying to secure financing for future projects. Meanwhile, 13 multinational oil companies in December 1994 formed the Azerbaijan International Operating Company (AIOC) to invest in the area. The government of Georgia also created the Georgia International Operating Company (GIOC) to safeguard the national interests of oil in Georgia. During this time, the Claimants communicated that GTI had the exclusive rights over Georgia's pipelines and that any interference by AIOC or GIOC would result in liability for damages. On 20 February 1996, the Georgian cabinet of ministers adopted Decree No. 178 which essentially cancelled the Claimant's rights to the oil pipelines. It re-assigned these rights to the GIOC, which offered contracts to the AIOC. The Claimants then initiated claims for compensation due to the cancellation of its rights on Georgia's pipelines. The Government created a commission to assess how much compensation should be paid to the Claimants. Eventually, on 15 November 2004, the commission decided that there was no legal grounds for holding the Government liable for the claim.[15]

The main argument of the Claimant was that the Respondent had expropriated its property, in breach of Article 13(1) of the ECT. It contended that Respondents had breached the fair and equitable standard. It contended that the Georgian Government, through various executive instruments such as Decrees by the Georgian cabinet of ministers, caused losses for the Claimant in regards to oil pipeline rights as well as ongoing oil pipeline work. It invoked the concept of state Responsibility to support its claim that Georgia should be liable. Additionally, it held the government of Georgia responsible because SakNavtobi and Transneft are wholly owned and controlled by the Georgian State.

---

[12] *Id.* at 73–77.

[13] *Ioannis Kardassopoulos v. The Republic of Georgia*, ICSID Case No. ARB/05/18.

[14] *Id.* at para 69.

[15] *Id.* at paras 155–162.

It contended that despite 10 years having passed, it was not time barred from making the claim as it had to wait for the result of the Georgian commission for compensation before it could have reasonably filed for arbitration. It seeks compensation for expropriation, as well as damages for loss of earnings, future earnings and other damages.[16]

The Respondent argued the arbitration tribunal did not have jurisdiction *ratione temporis* because treaties do not have retroactive effect. It argued that the acts occurred prior to 3 August 1996, before the Georgia/Greece BIT entered into force, and that all that remained was a complaint that it had failed to compensate the Claimants.[17] It also argued that the Claimant was time-barred from seeking arbitration as there was a delay of 10 years between the alleged acts and the claim. It argued that the Georgian government, while liable for the executive instruments used to expropriate from the Claimants, was not responsible for the contractual commitments of SakNavtobi and Transneft. It argued that the granting of GTI's rights to Georgian pipelines under the joint venture agreement and deed of concession was invalid and unenforceable. It further argued that the Claimant's did little to no work on the pipeline after the Deed of Concession was executed and therefore can't expect to continue to hold these rights or not be bought out.[18]

The Arbitral Tribunal sided with the Claimants. It held that it had jurisdiction to hear the case. It held that the Claimant was not time barred as the delay was reasonable, considering that Claimants had to wait for the decision of the Georgian commission in regards to compensation. It also held that the acts of SakNavTobi and Transneft were attributable to the government of Georgia on the basis of Article 7 of the Articles on State Responsibility. Most importantly, the Tribunal held that the acts of the Respondent with the adoption of Decree No. 178 had directly expropriated GTI and therefore the Claimants, of its rights and interests. The Georgian government had therefore breached their obligations to provide investors with fair and equitable treatment. It awarded the Claimants approximately USD $45 million each in damages.[19]

There was also a case between *Limited Liability Company AMTO* (Claimant) and *the State of Ukraine* (Respondent).[20] AMTO had purchased significant shares of EYUM-10, a state owned company responsible for the construction of the Zaporozhskaya AES (ZAES) nuclear power plant. ZAES was run by the state-owned company Energoatom. EYUM-10 supplied services of reconstruction and technical rearmament to ZAES. By March 2003, the Claimant had purchased 67.2% of the total share capital in EYUM-10. ZAES acknowledged it was in debt to EYUM-10 in respect to 11 contracts between them. Between 2002 and 2003, EYUM10 commenced court proceedings in the Commercial Court of Zaporozhskya, obtaining judgment for a total amount of 28,377,858.04 UAH. It sought execution of the judgment but the judgment was stayed due to bankruptcy proceedings against ZAES. In July 2003, the Ukrainian Cabinet of Ministers adopted Resolution No. 1160 which created special measures to discontinue operations on 'highly hazardous enterprises'.

[16] *Id.* at paras 304–316.

[17] *Id.* at para 234.

[18] *Id.* at paras 282–303.

[19] *Id.* at para 693.

[20] *Limited Liability Company Amto v. Ukraine*, SCC Case No. 080/2005.

In July 2005, the Respondent passed Law No. 2711-VI which implemented measures to support the financial standing of fuel and energy sector enterprises. This included the ability of the state to use these enterprises as business entities and provisions on the interaction of state authorities in respect to debt repayment mechanisms. By August 2006, EYUM-10 and Energoatom signed an agreement in relation to the outstanding debts of the 11 contracts and 2 further debt judgments of 2005. Energoatom made some of the debt repayments to reduce its outstanding debt[21].

The Claimant argued that the Respondent breached its obligations under Articles 10(1), 10(12) and 22(1) of the ECT. It contended that AMTO was a registered company in Latvia, a signatory to the ECT and had substantial business activities in Latvia within the meaning of Article 17(1). It contended that Energoatom was a corporate entity controlled by the state. It argued that the Respondent had failed to "encourage and create stable, equitable, favourable and transparent conditions for investors". It submitted evidence that AMTO suffered intimidation, discrimination and constant obstruction by Energoatom after it found out about AMTO's intention to buy shares of EYUM-10. After AMTO invested in EYUM-10, the Claimant asserts that Energoatom consciously decided not to obtain funding to repay its debts to AMTO. The Claimant argued that as a direct punishment for its choice to obtain more shares in EYUM-10, the Respondent stopped ordering services from EYUM-10 and tried to destroy the company by attempting to obtain an injunction against EYUM-10's assets so that it could not make payments to its workers and service providers. The Claimant also alleged denial of justice on the grounds that Ukraine failed to provide EYUM-10 effective means to enforce its bankruptcy judgment, interfered in bankruptcy proceedings and actions of the Ukrainian court that prejudice the Claimant. It sought compensation for damages suffered and restoration of AMTO's investment in EYUM-10.[22]

The Respondent's first argument was that the Tribunal did not have jurisdiction under Article 26 of the ECT based on multiple grounds. It argued that AMTO's shares in EYUM-10 did not qualify as an 'Investment' under the Article 1(6) of the ECT as they were not associated with economic activity in the energy sector since EYUM-10's activities consist merely of electric installation, repair and technical re-equipment services to ZAES. Other grounds included that the Respondent did not consent to arbitration; the ECT does not cover actions in the pre-investment period; the dispute is a trivial commercial dispute between 2 Ukrainian juridical persons and not with the Ukrainian State; and that the actual dispute had been exhausted and therefore there was no basis for the present arbitration. It denied that it had breached its obligations under the ECT on the grounds that any alleged breach took place in the pre-investment period. Furthermore, it claimed that EYUM-10 is a Ukrainian entity and cannot be given protection meant for aliens. It argued that any breach of this standard requires the unfair treatment reach a minimum threshold of intensity that was absent in this case. It claimed that the alleged breaches were based on unsupported allegations.[23]

---

[21] *Id.* at paras 15–24.

[22] *Id.* at paras 27–31.

[23] *Id.* at para 26.

The Arbitral Tribunal dismissed the claims of the AMTO. It held that the Claimant did have an 'Investment' within the meaning of the ECT in the energy sector. It held that it did have jurisdiction to hear the case. In regards to claims of denial of justice, the Tribunal held that there was no denial of justice as the Claimant was able to initiate bankruptcy proceedings after it was not included in Energoatom's first 3 bankruptcy proceedings. Furthermore, there was no evidence that the Courts were improperly influenced by the government of Ukraine. The Tribunal further held that resolutions passed by the Ukrainian parliament (such as Resolution No. 765) affected numerous state enterprises, not just the Claimant's and did not constitute an *ad hoc* interference by the state. The Tribunal did not find any discriminatory conduct by Ukraine towards the Claimant.[24]

Another case was requested by *Europe Cement Investment & Trade S.A.* (Claimant) against *The Republic of Turkey* (Respondent) on 6 March 2007.[25] The Claimant is a Polish registered joint stock company that had allegedly purchased shares in 2 electric power companies: Cukarova Elektrik Anonim Sirketi (CEAS) and Kepez Elektrik T.A.S (Kepez). The company is linked to the Uzan family headed by Cem Uzan. On 11 June 2003, the Respondent terminated Concession Agreements that it had signed with the 2 companies in 1998 regarding the generation, transmission, distribution and marketing of electricity. This claim was subsequently filed against the Republic of Turkey (pg. 1, para 2). The Claimant had also filed numerous other claims in relation to shareholdings in CEAS and Kepaz, such as Cementownia, Libananco Holdings Co. Limited, Polska Energetyka Holding S.A. and Cem Uzan at the European Court of Human Rights (pg. 18, para 108). Interestingly, both parties eventually filed discontinuance of the case due to lack of jurisdiction on similar grounds.[26]

The Claimant asserted that it had purchased shares in CEAS and Kepez in May 2003. It claimed that in June 2003, the Respondent had unlawfully terminated Concession Agreements between the Turkish Government and CEAS and Kepez. Additionally, it claimed the Respondent raided the premises of CEAS and Kepez, seized documents, intimidated witnesses and harassed employees. In light of this, the Claimant argued that the Respondent had breached its duties under the Energy Charter Treaty (ECT), in particular Article 13, by expropriating its property unlawfully. It further made claims under Article 10(1) that the Respondent give it "fair and equitable treatment". It claimed damages exceeding $3,800,000.[27]

The Claimant switched course after the Respondent filed its request for relief. It claimed that it did not refuse the Tribunal's orders to produce authentic share transfer documents, however it was unable to do so unless given a year's time[28]. Therefore, it requested that the Tribunal dismiss the case "due to our company's inability to show the shares legally acquired by our company".[29]

---

[24] *Id.* at paras 101–108.

[25] *Europe Cement Investment & Trade S.A. v. Republic of Turkey*, ICSID Case No. ARB(AF)/07/2.

[26] *Id.* at para 81.

[27] *Id.* at paras 25–26.

[28] *Id.* at para 66.

[29] *Id.* at para 66.

From the outset, the Respondent claimed that the Tribunal had no jurisdiction to hear the case. It requested a suspension of the proceedings until documentary evidence of the 'investment' was produced before the Tribunal and examined for authenticity. It claimed that there was a potential abuse of process and that proceedings should not continue until the share transfer agreements were produced and verified. Eventually the Respondent submitted its request for relief. It first sought a complete dismissal of the case due to lack of jurisdiction, on the grounds that the Claimant had never proved it had an investment in CEAS and Kepez. Secondly, it claimed that adverse inferences should be drawn against the Claimant for failure to comply with the directions of the Tribunal. Additionally, in its Memorial on Jurisdiction, it claimed that the case should be dismissed as the claim was manifestly ill-founded and asserted using non authentic documents; that the Respondent should be compensated by the Tribunal and that it should be awarded all costs in the matter (pg 11 para 63-65). It also rejected the request for dismissal of the proceedings without prejudice, on the grounds that under Article 49(2) of the Arbitration (Additional Facility) Rules, discontinuance of a case could not occur unilaterally.[30]

The Respondent further asserted that any evidence produced by the Claimant of the share transfer agreements were fraudulent. It argued that the Claimant never actually owned any shares in CEAS or Kepez. It claimed through expert testimony witness that share transfers are subject to many requirements, including approval by multiple government authorities, which were never done. It questioned the Claimant's financial records filed with the Polish courts, which never make any mention of this purchase. These and other inconsistencies were pointed out by the Respondent.[31]

Firstly, the Tribunal considered that both of the parties had applied for discontinuance of the case but on different grounds. The Claimant admitted it could not produce the share transfer agreements as ordered in time for the Arbitration and that, therefore, the proceedings should be discontinued. The Respondent argued that the Tribunal should discontinue the proceedings because the Claimant was never able to prove that it had an 'investment' as defined under the terms of Article 26(1) of the Energy Charter Treaty. The Tribunal concluded that despite both parties agreeing on the outcome of the case (dismissal), this was not to be treated as mutual consent of discontinuance of the present proceedings, as they had different grounds for doing so.[32]

The Tribunal agreed with the Respondent that it did not have jurisdiction to hear the case on the grounds that the Claimant never produced any evidence of an 'investment' as required to initiate arbitration proceedings under the ECT. It awarded full costs plus expenses ($3,907,383.14) to the Respondent.[33]

In the case of *Plama Consortium Limited* (Claimant) and *The Republic of Bulgaria* (Respondent), Nova Plama was a 100% Bulgarian State owned company which owned an oil refinery from 5 September 1995. Under the First Privatization Act, it was sold

---

[30] *Id.* at para 68.

[31] *Id.* at paras 92–95.

[32] *Id.* at para 121.

[33] *Id.* at para 186.

to EuroEnergy Holding ("EEH").[34] Subsequently, EEH, with approval of the Bulgarian Privatization Agency, sold its shares to the Claimant ("PCL") on 18 December 1998 under the Second Privatization Act. The owner of PCL was a Mr. Vautrin. Within a year of the transfer to PCL, the company faced problems and initiated bankruptcy proceedings. The bankruptcy case was dismissed by the Bulgarian Supreme Court of Cassation. It was re-opened by the Pleven District Court in April 2006 and Nova Pluma underwent liquidation on 18 June 2007.[35]

The Claimant argued that the Respondent created numerous and grave problems for Nova Pluma, leading to its bankruptcy. It argued that the Respondent violated Article 10(2) of the ECT by failing to provide fair and equitable treatment, failing to create stable, equitable, favourable and transparent conditions for the Claimant's investment, unreasonable and discriminatory measures and actions amounting to expropriation.[36]

The Respondent denied the above claims and firstly claimed that the Claimant, PCL, was actually a fictitious entity and was misrepresented to the Bulgarian Privatization agency by Mr. Vautrin. Therefore, the contract between the Claimant and Respondent was void *ab initio*. It further claimed that it was entitled to deny advantages to Nova Pluma by virtue of Article 17(1), which allowed each contracting party to deny advantages if that entity had no substantial business activities in the Area of the Contracting Party in which it was organized.[37]

The Respondent argued that ICSID did not have jurisdiction to hear the case as it had exercised its right under Article 17(1) to deny advantages of the ECT to the Claimant. It argued that there was no evidence of ownership, control, or substantial business activity by a member of the ECT within Bulgaria. This supposedly made it impossible for the Claimant to pursue dispute settlement under the ECT. The Respondent also argued that it did not consent to jurisdiction by the MFN principle, because that obligation only applied in an agreed sphere of relations. Due to the lack of clarity of the identity of the Claimant, there was no real agreed sphere of relations for which Bulgaria needed to give most favoured treatment. Whether or not there was ownership or control by the Claimant was an issue not decided on, pending other cases related to the Claimant. The Arbitral Tribunal held that invoking Article 17(1) of the ECT was not relevant to the issue of jurisdiction to hear the case.[38]

As far as jurisdiction, the Claimant, although not having any substantial business activities in Cyprus where it is incorporated, was ultimately owned by Mr. Vautrin, a French national, whose country is a party to the ECT. Therefore it had jurisdiction to hear the case. In regards to the misrepresentation by the Claimant, the Arbitral Tribunal held that the Claimant, Mr. Vautrin, failed to prove that PCL had control over the Investment, as it was actually in essence controlled by Mr. Vautrin through various other entities that were all owned by him. The Bulgarian Privitization agency was relying on the financial stability of the consortium that apparently financed PCL. However, this contention was

[34] *Plama Consortium Limited v. Republic of Bulgaria*, ICSID Case No. ARB/03/24.

[35] *Id.* at paras 56–65.

[36] *Id.* at para 73.

[37] *Id.* at paras 85–87.

[38] *Id.* at paras 89–91.

never rebuked by Mr. Vautrin. The Arbitral Award held that the Respondent did not have the right to deny advantages under Article 17(1). However, the Award could not give protection of the ECT to the Claimant because he was a fraudulent contracting party. It would have been against the principles of International Law as well as Bulgarian Law to entitle the Claimant to these protections. In essence, the Arbitral Tribunal ruled in favour of the Respondent, pending other litigation in Switzerland by other creditors[39].

Another important case was between *Azpetrol International Holdings B.V. Azpetrol Group B.V. Azpetrol Oil Services Group B.V.* (Claimants) and the *Republic of Azerbaijan* (Respondent)[40]. The Claimants were a company registered in Netherlands but affiliated with a national in Azerbaijan. The Respondent is the Republic of Azerbaijan. On 13 July 2006, the Claimants requested arbitration by ICSID on the grounds of breach of the ECT, violation of Article 13 as to expropriation by the Respondent, as well as Articles 10, 14 and 22. After some delays, on 1 July 2008, a witness, who was a director of the Claimants, admitted in testimony to bribing officials in Azerbaijan for protection of certain unnamed individuals. Thereafter, both parties filed for an adjournment, seeking a procedural standstill to the arbitration.[41]

Afterwards, a series of exchanges of emails between the Claimant and Respondent's solicitors indicated that they intended to settle the matter on a "drop hands" basis, which essentially means the case is discontinued without either party paying costs to the other. Eventually on 16 December 2008, counsel for the Respondent sent a comprehensive email detailing the counter offer to settle. The terms were that:

1) The Claimant must withdraw the claim;
2) Nuisance payment of $1500 were to be made to the Claimant;
3) There was no admission of guilt or liability;
4) Azerbaijan must be able to disclose the terms of the settlement to the public;
5) The settlement is the full and final settlement of any claim.[42]

Eventually on 19 December 2008, counsel for the Claimant agreed to the counter offer after discussing it with the Claimant. Afterwards, several email exchanges occurred in which the Claimants sought to reverse the acceptance of the counter offer. The Respondent filed for conclusion and discontinuance of the arbitration as a binding settlement had been reached, while the Claimant filed a counter memorial.[43]

The Claimant argued that the arbitration should not be discontinued as the settlement reached was 'an agreement in principle' and not legally binding. They argued that (in accordance with English law of contracts) there was no intention to create legal relations; no meeting of minds on anything other than a standstill agreement; an incomplete offer and acceptance and no communications meaning to intend a binding agreement.[44]

---

[39] *Id.* at paras 279–284.

[40] *Azpetrol International Holdings B.V., Azpetrol Group B.V. and Azpetrol Oil Services Group B.V. v. The Republic of Azerbaijan*, ICSID Case No. ARB/06/15.

[41] *Id.* at, para 6.

[42] *Id.* at para 28.5.

[43] *Id.* at para 11.

[44] *Id.* at para 76.

The Respondent claimed that the exchange of emails was a binding legal document and that the case was settled after the offer and acceptance contained in the emails.[45]

The Arbitral Tribunal discontinued the arbitration. The Court considered Claimant's arguments as far as the issue of whether the exchange of emails constituted a final binding agreement. First it looked at the language of the most conclusive e-mail, that of 16 December and found that the words "offer of settlement" and "we hereby accept the offer" constitute a final binding settlement rather than a settlement subject to further arbitration.[46] Secondly, it looked whether there was an intention to create legal relations. The Claimant argued that the agreement was only 'an agreement in principle' not beyond the conclusion of an agreement to a standstill. The Tribunal concluded that if that were the case, there had to be evidence in the exchange of emails. No such wording was found in the exchange.[47] Thirdly, there was the question whether there was a meeting of minds. The Tribunal used the objective test of whether "a reasonable observer would conclude that the exchange of emails on 16-19 December would conclude that the parties intended to conclude a binding agreement to settle the proceedings". On this issue, the Tribunal sided with Respondent counsel that they intended to make a binding agreement to settle the case.[48] Lastly, the Tribunal considered whether the terms of the agreement were incomplete. The Tribunal concluded that terms of the agreement, such as a provision on governing law, a provision on dispute resolution, and a provision regarding the witness's protection from prosecution, were not indispensable terms. They did not consider those sorts of terms as perquisites to a binding agreement.[49]

The Tribunal examined the arguments of the Claimant but found that there was intention to create legal relations, a meeting of minds and a binding legal agreement. They looked, in particular, at the wording of the email exchanges, to which no 'agreement in principle' was explicitly stated – the wording was definitive. It therefore concluded that the proper procedure was to dismiss the case on the basis that there was no 'legal dispute' as required by Article 25(1), nor a dispute under Article 26(1,) and therefore the Tribunal had no jurisdiction to hear the case. It rendered its award accordingly to dismiss the case.[50] The Tribunal was bound to follow Rule 43(1) of the ICSID Arbitration rules that it should discontinue the proceedings if the parties agreed to a settlement.[51]

Furthermore, there was a case between *Cementownia "Nowa Huta" S.A.* (Claimant) and *Republic of Turkey* (Respondent).[52] CEAS and Kepaz are both electric generation and transmission utility companies. The Turkish government had some shares in both companies. In the 1950s, they were given concession rights for generation, transmission and distribution of electricity. Eventually, in 1992, the Turkish government decided to privatize their remaining shares by offering them to public bidding through a tender

[45] *Id.* at para 42.

[46] *Id.* at para 70.

[47] *Id.* at para 76.

[48] *Id.* at para 81.

[49] *Id.* at para 84.

[50] *Id.* at para 105.

[51] *Id.* at para 103.

[52] *Cementownia "Nowa Huta" S.A. v. Republic of Turkey*, ICSID Case No. ARB(AF)/06/2.

process. The winning bidders were Rumeli Elektrik Yatirim which was owned by the billionare Uzan family, who subsequently increased their shareholding in the company.[53]

In 1998, new Concession agreements were entered into which allowed Rumeli Elektrik Yatirim to continue its operations but the facilities would remain state property of the Turkish Government and would revert to the state at the end of the concession period. In Feb 2001, the Turkish government passed a new Electricity Market Law which effectively prevented Kepez and CEAS to do business and instead would have them give up their operations to Turkish Electricity Joint Stock Company. This was disputed in the Turkish Courts as well as Parliament. Nevertheless, the Turkish Government sent multiple warnings to the CEAS and Kepez that they needed to adhere to the conditions set out by the Electricity Market Law or face adverse actions by the Turkish Government. These warnings were not followed by the companies.[54]

The Turkish Government pressured CEAS and Kepaz to transfer ownership of its companies to the state owned electricity company in early 2003. On 30 May 2003, the Claimants allegedly purchased shares from Rumeli Elektrik Yatirim. On 15 April 2008, the premises of CEAS and Kepaz were raided; assets seized and employees removed. An arbitration case was filed in addition to other similar cases filed by other companies controlled by the Uzan family, which further caused suspicion.[55]

The Claimant argued that the Respondent violated Articles 10(1) of the ECT which provides investors with constant protection and security without unreasonable or discriminatory treatment. They also claimed expropriation by the Turkish Government of the assets of the Claimant in violation of Article 13 ECT. Strangely, the Claimant agreed with the Respondent that ICSID lacked jurisdiction to hear the case. It responded to the Respondent's claim for discontinuance of the case by seeking that the Tribunal dismiss the case due to Claimant's inability to produce authentic documents showing the share transactions.[56]

First and foremost, the Respondent rejected the jurisdiction of ICSID to hear the case because Claimant knew it did not own assets in the CEAS and Kepez; it did not record the share transactions until 3 years after they allegedly took place; the shareholding of that company was uncertain and that it was part of a greater effort by the Uzan family to "assert baseless claims" before various Tribunals.[57] The Respondent argued that Cementownia was a front company for fraud and abuse and to retain its assets in the face of Turkish laws. It argued that the share transactions were not actually conducted and that no evidence was produced that shares were exchanged. They claimed that Kemal Uzan, of the Uzan family, used the Claimant to shield its assets and protect them from being expropriated by the Turkish government. It sought from the Tribunal a declaration that the claim was "manifestly ill-founded and has been asserted using inauthentic documents".[58]

[53] *Id.* at para 8.

[54] *Id.* at para 10.

[55] *Id.* at para 16.

[56] *Id.* at paras105–108.

[57] *Id.* at para 151.

[58] *Id.* at para 108.

The Arbitral Tribunal found that the Claimant's conduct through evidence showed that the transferring of shares was fraudulent and "a transfer of national economic interests to a foreign company in an attempt to seek protections under a BIT". The Tribunal found that the circumstances in which the transactions allegedly occurred were suspicious and inconsistent. Transactions were carried out by phone conversations. Purchasing shares without reporting to the Ministry and following the procedure were allegedly carried out. Financial statements by the Claimant did not mention the purchasing of these shares, despite the Claimant mentioning other transactions in the same fiscal year.[59] The Claimant was trying to transfer assets to gain jurisdiction to the ECT but later realising it would not win its case, tried to absolve itself from any liability imposed by the Tribunal. The Tribunal followed the principle of "cost follows the event", which makes the losing party bear all costs. It followed this principle on the grounds that the Claimant has filed a fraudulent claim, failed on all its requests of relief, delayed the arbitration proceeding which incurred more costs, and never signed a Custody Agreement despite being advised to.[60] The Tribunal awarded the Respondent all of its costs in the amount of USD 4.9 million.[61]

Finally, there was the case between *Hrvatska Elektroprivreda, D.D.* (Claimant) and *Republic of Slovenia* (Respondent).[62] The Claimant (HEP) has been the national electric company of Croatia since 1994 and is completely owned by the Government of Croatia. The Respondent was the Republic of Slovenia. The relevant party involved in the dispute was Elektro-Slovenija, d.o.o. Ljubljana (ELES-GEN) which was a subsidiary of Elektro-Slovenija, d.o.o. (ELES), the national electric company of Slovenia. Together they formed a joint venture company named Nuklearna Elektrana Krško ("NEK"), each contributing 50% of the funds. They built the Krško NPP power plant. Since they were equal partners, they followed the "parity" principle and were to be equal in all aspects of the plant. Their partnership was regulated by 4 governing agreements signed between 1970 and 1984. By 1991, Croatia and Slovenia were separate countries.[63]

During the years after independence, the Slovenian Government took some measures that the HEP claimed were breaking the parity principle and basic provisions of the Governing Agreements. The Respondents disconnected the Claimant's electricity lines and ended electricity delivers to the Claimant on 30 July 1998. The Respondent also issued a "Governmental Decree" which the Claimant views as affecting its rights as an equal partner.[64]

In June 2001, the two countries entered into negotiations and concluded, "the 2001 Agreement". On restoring rights and deliveries back to the Claimant. They proposed to "wipe the slate clean" and no claims to electricity would be entertained up to 30 June 2002. The Claimant, however, argued that the Respondent failed to restore its rights or resume electricity deliveries until 19 April 2003, nearly 10 months late. It sought

---

[59] *Id.* at para 129.

[60] *Id.* at para 177.

[61] *Id.* at para 154.

[62] *Hrvatska Elektroprivreda d.d. v. Republic of Slovenia*, ICSID Case No. ARB/05/24.

[63] *Id.* at paras 7–10.

[64] *Id.* at paras 11–14.

compensation for the 10 months of failed electricity deliveries plus restoration of its role as equal partner.[65]

The Claimant argued that by not restoring electricity deliveries until 30 June 2002, the Respondent had violated Articles 10(1) and 13 of the Energy Charter Treaty (ECT). It only made claims for the period of 30 June 2003, to 19 April 2003, as any previous claims were to be dropped by virtue of the 2001 Agreement. The Claimant was also alleging a breach of contract based on the 2001 Agreement. Earlier tribunal judgments dismissed the ECT claims and the Claimant sought to restore or reverse the decisions to drop of that issue. It argued that its claims were made based on 2 legal bases, the 2001 Treaty between Croatia and Slovenia, and the ECT[66].

The Respondent's argument was that the two rounds of negotiations between the parties in June and November 2002 were considered to be acquiescence to liability for those claims and that the liability had been satisfied by the offers of electrical power made to the HEP during those negotiations. Further, it stated that the claims of the ECT were dropped vis-à-vis the 2001 Agreement, citing the *Wena Hotels Ltd v Arab Republic of Egypt* case.[67] The Respondent considered the Tribunal decision to be factually and legally correct. It asserted that the 2001 Agreement was a single compensation package and waived any other claims.[68]

The two parties went through several levels of arbitration before reaching the ICSID and this case brief reflects the final award. The results of those arbitrations were a financial settlement as of 30 June 2002 and waiving off all previous claims. It was however subject to the determination of several issues, whether liability was acquiesced to by the Claimant during these negotiation sessions and whether the liability was satisfied by the two offers of electrical power made to the Claimant. This case brief focused on the issue in regards to the dismissal of ECT by the previous Tribunal. The Arbitral Tribunal finally held that the ECT claims made against the Respondent were only alternative treaty bases of claim. These ECT claims automatically fell out of consideration once the 2001 Agreement came up with a single compensation package to satisfy the entire claim.[69]

III. Conclusions

The Energy Charter Treaty has played an important role in the settlement of disputes in the energy sector as can be seen from the relevant ECT articles and the discussed case law. The disputes that arise in the energy sector will likely remain a subject of international arbitration for a long period. The demand for energy has been increasing globally, due to which foreign investment has become much more crucial to the development and the exploration of the states in possession of abundant energy resources. In this regard,

---

[65] *Id.* at paras 14–15.

[66] *Id.* at paras 562–565.

[67] *Wena Hotels Ltd. v. Arab Republic of Egypt*, ICSID Case No. ARB/98/4.

[68] *Hrvatska Elektroprivreda d.d. v. Republic of Slovenia*, ICSID Case No. ARB/05/24, paras 566–570.

[69] *Id.* at paras 573–580.

the ECT may provide a stable framework that also offers compulsory protection for the investors of other countries.

The ECT has the ability to provide significant capital and advantages to the countries that have interests in the trade of energy products. It can also be said that the presence of the ECT may have the ability to provide security to the investor of other countries. The ECT can also provide resolutions for disputes between contracting parties, or disputes concerning foreign investors of contracting parties. The treatment standards of the ECT have much resemblance to the practices of the World Trade Organization, which provides a strong basis for this treaty.

Furthermore, the theoretical protection provided by the ECT is reinforced by the actual arbitral practice. It has been shown through examples that the arbitral tribunals interpreting the ECT tend towards a balanced approach, leveraging the correct extent of protection, especially in relation to questions of expropriation.

Balazs Horvathy*

OPINION 2/15 OF THE EUROPEAN COURT OF JUSTICE AND THE NEW PRINCIPLES OF COMPETENCE ALLOCATION IN EXTERNAL RELATIONS – A SOLID FOOTING FOR THE FUTURE?

Abstract

In economic terms, the Common Commercial Policy is the most important policy area in EU external relations, needing a solid and predictable framework in terms of allocation of competences and national sovereignty. This paper addresses these facets of Opinion 2/15, which – in the context of the EU-Singapore Free Trade Agreement (EUSFTA) – clarified the division of competences between the European Union and the Member States in relation to international trade policy.

I. Introduction

Cecilia Malström, the EU Commissioner for Trade, is strikingly active on social media networks and her concise comments on recent developments of the EU external trade policy always are inspirational for headlines. In May 2017, followers of her Twitter account were informed on Malmström's relevant observation straight after the Court of Justice announced Opinion 2/15 concerning the conclusion of Free Trade Agreement negotiated between the European Union and the Republic of Singapore (EUSFTA).[1] Commissioner Malmström claimed that the Court's "[o]pinion should put us on solid footing for the future [...]" and expressed her commitment to work with the Governments and the European Parliament to define the way forward,[2] indicating that the Court's Opinion clarifies all sort of questions regarding the Common Commercial Policy (CCP).

In economic terms, the CCP is the most important policy area in the EU external relations and therefore it is indisputable that the CCP would need a solid framework and clarity relating to its EU law setting. This 'solid footing' might be essential, especially to the Member States, as the competence in the CCP is conferred exclusively on the European Union, consequently the allocation and scope of the competence might raise concerns about sovereignty and national regulatory freedom as well. This paper aims at

---

* Research fellow, Hungarian Academy of Sciences, Centre for Social Sciences, Institute for Legal Studies (H-1097 Budapest, Toth Kalman u. 4.); associate professor, Szechenyi Istvan University, Faculty of Law and Political Sciences (H-9026 Györ, Aldozat u. 12.). E-mail: horvathy.balazs@tk.mta.hu.

[1] Opinion of the Court 2/15., ECLI:EU:C:2017:376.

[2] Tweet of Cecilia Malmström (@MalmstromEU), commissioner for trade (EU external trade policy). Available at https://twitter.com/MalmstromEU/status/864427382647738368 .

reviewing these aspects of Opinion 2/15 and assessing its implications on the competence allocation between the European Union and the Member States.

II. CCP and the 'New Generation' Free Trade Agreements

The EUSFTA is a new generation trade and investment agreement[3] that covers not only the standard free trade issues but also lays down provisions concerning investments and non-trade concerns, e.g. sustainable development and environmental protection. These agreements are definitely opening a new era in international economic relations and generate the need to rethink the concepts of state sovereignty and autonomy.[4] In EU policy, the 'new generation agreements' are rooted in the European Union's Global Europe strategy[5] that paved the way to an ambitious trade agenda and a new approach to the negotiations of trade agreements. It is notable for the current case of EUSFTA, that the investment chapter of these 'new generation agreements' usually lays down detailed provisions with regard to the investment activities, such as investment protection, obligations and regulatory leeway of the host states, principles of appropriation.[6] Moreover, procedural rules are also enshrined in these agreements in order to facilitate the enforcement of their provisions and reconcile disputes between the contracting parties (state-state dispute settlement, SSDS) as well between investors and states (investor-state dispute settlement, ISDS). The overall objective of these agreements is to provide legal certainty to investors operating in the EU or in third countries concerned. The EUSFTA follows this line and covers substantial provisions beyond trade in goods, therefore, in the terminology of the World Trade Organization (WTO), the EUSFTA encompasses both 'WTO+'[7] and 'WTO-x'[8] rules. The investment provisions included in Chapter Nine of EUSFTA address a relatively broad range of issues.[9] The 'new generation agreements', as

---

[3] For a comprehensive analysis of the new generation agreements *see* Ewa Zelazna, *New Generation of EU Regional Trade Agreements*, 1 Lund Student EU Law Review 1 (2012).

[4] Csongor István Nagy, *Free Trade, Public Interest and Reality: New Generation Free Trade Agreements and National Regulatory Sovereignty*, 9 Czech Yearbook of International Law, 197–216, 198 (2018).

[5] European Commission: Global Europe: Competing in the World, COM (2006) 567 final.

[6] In general, *see* Zoltán Víg & Slobodan Doklestić, Requirements of Lawful Taking of Foreign Property in International Law (2016).

[7] So called WTO+ (WTO plus) provisions: all commitments building on those already agreed to at the multilateral level, *see* Henrik Horn & Petros C. Mavroidis & André Sapir, Beyond the WTO? An anatomy of EU and US Preferential Trade Agreements 3–7 (2009).

[8] WTO-x (WTO extra) commitments dealing with issues going beyond the current WTO mandate, *e.g.* on labor standards. *See id.* at 4.

[9] The Commission, however, intended originally to negotiate an agreement without investment provisions and its mandate has been extended to an investment chapter only afterwards. See details below. The Chapter encompasses the provisions on investment protection, lays down the definition of investment, which is based on the standard concept enshrined in several BITs (every kind of asset which has the characteristics of an investment, including such characteristics as the commitment of capital or other resources, the expectation of gain or profit, the assumption of risk, or a certain duration). Moreover, EUFSTA covers also requirements concerning national treatment, fair and equitable treatment and full protection and security, as well as compensation for losses suffered owing to war or other events (armed conflict, revolution, a

EUSFTA is also indicating, are becoming more important and will gradually replace the Member States' BITs, as the founding treaty provides the European Union with exclusive competence in the field of foreign direct investments. Even though the Lisbon Treaty extended the competence of the CCP to new areas, including investments, the character and scope of the competence has left questions unanswered.

This ambiguity over the competences, however, has always been seen during the evolution of the CCP. At the very outset, the founding treaties remained silent on the competence over the CCP, and the Court's intensive case law was to establish the concept of exclusivity in the 1970s.[10] The underlying arguments behind the exclusive competence character were the establishment of the customs union, the common interest, and the requirement that the CCP should be based on uniform principles. This argumentation expressed the need for unity of action of the Member States in the area of the external trade, e.g. the unity of positions in trade negotiations. The line of reasoning on the 'uniform principles'[11] referred to the fact that the internal market and the customs union would be inoperable if the Member States would have retained the competence to implement different trade policies. Moreover, different trade policies could set off distortions in the internal market as well. Therefore the Court's extensive case law resulted in a shift of competence over trade policy, drastically limiting the autonomy of the Member States in this area.

The ECJ clearly established the exclusive nature of the competence in its case law but this only reflected on the vertical allocation of competences between the EU and Member States, and did not specify which subjects were covered by the EU competence. Therefore, it is also important to identify the extent of the competence because the EU can exercise its powers exclusively within the material scope of the CCP. The Treaty originally laid down an exemplificative list of subjects relating to trade in goods, where the Community was empowered to act. However, from quite early on, the Court has gone beyond this narrow scope. The Court recapped the CCP in a wide and dynamic interpretation and did not restrict the CCP to instruments intended to have an effect only on the traditional aspects of external trade. In line with this approach, international commodity agreements,[12] customs valuation,[13] or the Generalized System of Preferences introduced by the Community,[14] had to be regarded as part of the CCP, even if the founding treaty did not make any reference to these subjects. Later the Court limited this dynamism and took a more restrained view of the extent of the EU's competence. In Opinion 1/94,[15] the Court had

state of national emergency, revolt, insurrection or riot), provisions of expropriation, and specific ISDS mechanisms.

[10] *See* especially Case 8/73 *Hauptzollamt Bremerhaven v Massey-Ferguson*, ECLI:EU:C:1973:90; Opinion of 11 November 1975 in Case 1/75 *Local Cost Standard*, ECLI:EU:C:1975:145, Case 41/76 *Donckerwolcke v Procureur de la République*, ECLI:EU:C:1976:182.

[11] *See* Case 174/84 *Bulk Oil (Zug) AG v Sun International Limited and Sun Oil Trading Company*, ECLI:EU:C:1986:60, para 29.

[12] Opinion of 4 October 1979 in Case 1/78 *Natural Rubber*, ECLI:EU:C:1979:224.

[13] Case 8/73 *Hauptzollamt Bremerhaven v Massey-Ferguson GmbH*, ECLI:EU:C:1973:90.

[14] Case 45/86 *Commission v Council*, ECLI:EU:C:1987:163.

[15] Opinion of 15 November 1994 in Case 1/94 *WTO*, ECLI:EU:C:1994:384.

to give an Opinion whether the Community had the competence to conclude all parts of the WTO Agreement on an exclusive basis. Even though the ECJ verbally kept the open nature of CCP[16] and held that the Community had exclusive competence to conclude multilateral agreements on trade in goods, the Community's competence did not cover the most part of subjects related to GATS and TRIPS. Therefore the WTO agreement fell in part within the competence of the Community and in part within that of the Members States and had to be concluded as a mixed agreement. This limited approach was represented also in subsequent Treaty amendments but the Treaty of Lisbon finally made major progress on consolidating the exclusive competence character and transferred key external trade policy competences to the supranational level.[17] The new language of Article 207 TFEU encompasses not only trade in services and the commercial aspects of intellectual property but also foreign direct investments.[18] As a result, the scope of the CCP has been extended to negotiations by the EU on agreements covering investment issues. [19] The TFEU explicitly lays down that the EU has *exclusive* competence in the areas of the CCP[20] and even the objectives of the CCP refer to the FDI as well.[21]

It was important also for the EUSFTA that these provisions have not been fully clear about the extent of the new competences conferred on the European Union as the TFEU applies the term 'foreign direct investment' without any definition. It was argued that the notion of FDI obviously differs from the term established in the WTO terminology which uses 'trade related investment measures.'[22] Compared to this, the

---

[16] Opinion of 15 November 1994 in Case 1/94 *WTO*, ECLI:EU:C:1994:384, para 41.

[17] Marc Bungenberg, *Außenbeziehungen und Außenhandelspolitik*, 44 Europarecht Beiheft 1 (2009); Jan Ceyssens, *Towards a Common Foreign Investment Policy? – Foreign Investment in the European Constitution*, 32 Legal Issues of Economic Integration, 3 (2005); Christoph Herrmann, *Die Zukunft der mitgliedstaatlichen Investitionspolitik nach dem Vertrag von Lissabon*, 21 Europäische Zeitschrift für Wirtschaftsrecht 6 (2010); Steffen Hindelang & Niklas Maydell, *Die Gemeinsame Europäische Investitionspolitik – Alter Wein in neuen Schläuchen? in* Internationaler Investitionsschutz und Europarecht (Marc Bungenberg & Joern Griebel & Steffen Hindelang eds., 2010); Joachim Karl, *The Competence for Foreign Direct Investment – New Powers for the EU*, 5 Journal of World Investment & Trade 3 (2004); László Knapp, *Mixed Agreements and the Treaty of Lisbon in* COFOLA 2010 – The Conference Proceedings 1539–1553 (Nadezda Rozehnalová & Roman Onderka eds., 2010); Markus Krajewski, *External Trade Law and the Constitutional Treaty*, 42 Common Market Law Review 1 (2005).

[18] Article 207 (1) TFEU.

[19] It should be mentioned here that despite the lack of competence, the Commission made attempts to have the support of the Member States to include investment provisions already before the Treaty of Lisbon, *see* Niklas Maydell, *The European Community´s Minimum Platform on Investment or the Trojan Horse of Investment Competence in* International Investment Law in Context 73–92 (August Reinisch & Christina Kahr eds., 2008).

[20] Article 3 (1) (e) TFEU. In addition to the explicit competence, the EU holds also 'implied powers', *see* Article 3 (2) TFEU: "The Union shall also have exclusive competence for the conclusion of an international agreement when its conclusion is provided for in a legislative act of the Union or is necessary to enable the Union to exercise its internal competence, or in so far as its conclusion may affect common rules or alter their scope." Inclusion of this provision in the TEU, however, is merely a codification of a principle established by the ECJ alredy in 1971 in Case 22/70 *Commission v. Council* (*ERTA*), 1971 ECR 263.

[21] *See* Article 206 TFEU. The EU must contribute "[...] in the common interest, to the harmonious development of world trade, the progressive abolition of restrictions on international trade and on foreign direct investment, and the lowering of customs and other barriers."

[22] The Agreement on Trade-Related Investment Measures (TRIMs) has been adopted as a part of the Marrakesh Agreements. The EU was already empowered for topics that are covered by the TRIMs agreement even

standard interpretation of 'foreign direct investment' implies a much wider term covering not only trade related aspects but the whole concept of direct investment activities conducted by EU investors in third countries or conversely, by third country investors in the European Union.[23] Reference to "FDI" also indicates a terminological restriction, since FDI specifically refers to 'direct' investments. This poses the question which factors can determine whether an investment activity is 'direct'. The notion can be traced back to the internal market provisions regarding the free movement of capital.[24] The CJEU has also applied the distinction between indirect and direct investments in a number of cases.[25] According to these interpretations, 'direct investment' covers all cross-border investment transactions conducted by natural or legal person investors, where the investor makes capital available to an undertaking in order to establish or maintain lasting and direct economic ties with this undertaking. If the investment is carried out by acquisition of shares from an undertaking (company), only transactions can be regarded as 'direct investment', in which the shares enable the investor to participate effectively in the management of that undertaking or in its control. [26] Following these lines of arguments, it is plausible that 'foreign direct investments' do not cover portfolio investments when the investors want to get shares in a company only for reason of making short-term profits without any intention to control or manage the target company.[27] It means that the difference between direct and indirect investments lays in the intention of control of the undertaking. However objective criteria are also applied for making the distinction easier. The Court's case law follows the method elaborated by the IMF that considers all acquisitions in a company below 10% of shares necessarily as portfolio investment,[28]

---

before the Lisbon amendment, *see* Markus Krajewski, *External Trade Law and the Constitutional Treaty*, 42 Common Market Law Review 16 (2005), and commentary to Article 207, *in* Das Recht der Europäischen Union (Eberhardt Grabitz & Meinhard Hilf & Martin Nettesheim eds., 43th ed., 2011).

[23] According to Article 207 (1) TFEU, transactions carried out by EU investors in the EU internal market are not to be regarded as 'foreign' investments. These investments fall within the internal market competence. For further analysis, *see*: Christoph Herrmann, *Die Zukunft der mitgliedstaatlichen Investitionspolitik nach dem Vertrag von Lissabon*, 21 Europäische Zeitschrift für Wirtschaftsrecht 6 (2010), and Steffen Hindelang & Niklas Maydell, *Die Gemeinsame Europäische Investitionspolitik – Alter Wein in neuen Schläuchen? in* Internationaler Investitionsschutz und Europarecht (Marc Bungenberg & Joern Griebel & Steffen Hindelang eds., 2010).

[24] Council 88/361/EEC Directive of 24 June 1988 for the Implementation of Article 67 of the Treaty.

[25] The term 'direct investments' is also applied by the provisions on the free movement of capital in Articles 63–66 TFEU. The Court of Justice interpreted and defined this term in a number of cases, *see* for instance: Case C-446/04 *Test Claimants in the FII Group Litigation v. Commissioners of Inland Revenue*, ECLI:EU:C:2006:774; Case C-157/05 *Holböck v. Finanzamt Salzburg-Land*, ECLI:EU:C:2007:297, para 34; Case C-112/05 *Commission v. Germany*, ECLI:EU:C:2007:623, para 18; Case C-101/05 *Skatteverket v. A.*, ECLI:EU:C:2007:804, para 46; Case C-194/06 *Staatssecretaris van Financiën v. Orange European Smallcap Fund NV.*, ECLI:EU:C:2008:289, para 100; Case C-274/06 *Commission v. Spain*, ECLI:EU:C:2008:86; para 18; Case C-326/07 *Commission v. Italy*, ECLI:EU:C:2009:193, para 35.

[26] *See* the above cited case law, specifically: C-446/04, para 182; C-157/05, para 35; C-112/05, para 18; C-194/06, para 101; C-326/07, para 35.

[27] *See* the Court's definition of 'portfolio investments': "[...] acquisition of shares on the capital market solely with the intention of making a financial investment without any intention to influence the management and control of the undertaking ('portfolio' investments)." Joined Cases C-282/04 and C-283/04 *Commission v. Netherlands*, ECLI:EU:C:2006:608, para 19.

[28] *See* IMF, Balance of Payments Manual 86–87 (5th. ed., 1993): "[...] a direct investment enterprise is defined

although from the very outset, the Court applied additional criteria as well. Accordingly, the CJEU highlighted that not only the proportion of the shares can determine the nature of a transaction, but other factors, e.g. special forms of participation in the management, or particular provisions of the domestic company law, might also be decisive.[29] These interpretations, however, left important questions unanswered. Therefore the negotiations of the new generation trade agreements opened a debate over the scope of competences and their allocation between the EU and the Member States. The seminal case in this debate was the CJEU Opinion procedure on EUSFTA.

III. The EUSFTA and Lack of Clarity on the Scope of the Competence

The EUSFTA was the result of a five years long negotiation but the original idea to conclude a wider, regional agreement with the ASEAN countries (Association of Southeast Asian Nations), dates back to earlier times. In 2006, the Commission intended to open negotiations with ASEAN but this 'interregional' approach proved to be unsuccessful and the negotiations were suspended. Consequently, the Commission changed this approach and proposed bilateral agreements to be concluded with individual ASEAN countries. The Council adopted the Commission's mandate for negotiations with Singapore in 2009 and the negotiations were launched in 2010.[30] In the beginning, the mandate did not cover investments but the Council extended the scope of negotiations and added investments to the mandate in 2011. The text of EUSFTA was initialled in 2015.

It was not surprising that no compromise was found between the Council and the Commission on the competence distribution for the agreement, since the Treaty, as examined in the previous subchapter, was not fully clear about the scope of the EU exclusive competence. Therefore, the Commission submitted a request for an Opinion procedure before the Court on the allocation of competences between the EU and the Member States concerning the conclusion of EUSFTA. The Commission sought guidance from the CJEU on whether the EUSFTA had to be concluded as an agreement between the EU and Singapore, without participation of the Member States, or as a mixed agreement that requires ratification on behalf of the Member States as well.[31]

[...] as an incorporated or unincorporated enterprise in which a direct investor, who is resident in another economy, owns 10 percent or more of the ordinary shares or voting power (for an incorporated enterprise) or the equivalent (for an unincorporated enterprise). [...]" This requirement can give guidance also for the interpretation of the treaty, however it can be established only as a presumption (i.e., in certain cases, also an ownership interest below 10% can be understood as direct investment).

[29] *See* the above cited case law, C-446/04, para 182.

[30] The first country, the EU commenced negotiations with, was Singapore.

[31] The Opinion procedure related only to the issue of whether the EU has exclusive competence and the Court did not examine whether the content of the agreement is compatible with EU law. The Commission submitted the following four questions: Does the Union have the requisite competence to sign and conclude alone the Free Trade Agreement with Singapore? More specifically, which provisions of the agreement fall within the Union's exclusive competence? Which provisions of the agreement fall within the Union's shared competence?; Is there any provision of the agreement that falls within the exclusive competence of the Member States?

The Commission's main position was that the EU has exclusive competence to conclude the EUSFTA alone. The Commission argued, first, that most parts of the agreement come within the exclusive competence under Article 207 TFEU. According to the Commission, the competence covering other provisions not falling within the scope of Article 207 TFEU is also of exclusive nature resulting partly from a legislative act giving authority for that,[32] or from the fact that conclusion of the EUSFTA may affect common rules or alter their scope.[33] Similarly, the European Parliament shared the view that the Agreement should be concluded by the EU on its own. However the Council and the Member States[34] submitted observations in order to claim that the Member States should also be a contracting party to the Agreement for the reason that certain topics of the Agreement fall within the shared competence of the EU and the Member States and some parts remained even in the (exclusive) competence of the Member States.

IV. The Opinion of the Advocate General

Advocate General Sharpston submitted an analytical and detailed Opinion to the procedure on 21 December 2016[35] and took the view that the EUSFTA can be concluded only by the European Union and the Member States acting jointly. Even though the major part of the agreement fell into the exclusive competence of the European Union, the Advocate General found that the European Union's external competence was shared on several topics, including the provisions on types of investment other than foreign direct investment.

The Advocate General gave a very detailed insight into the Treaty provisions as well as the permanent case law with respect to the exclusive competences in the CCP and aimed at establishing the material scope of the EU competence. This framework was then applied to the text of EUSFTA. The Opinion analysed the agreement from chapter to chapter and suggested deliminations for the subjects falling within the exclusive EU competence, shared competences between the EU and the Member States, and the competences retained by the Member States at the domestic level.

According to the Advocate Generat, the subjects of the EU exclusive competence cover the standard matters of trade in goods, services (including rail and road transport services), commercial aspects of intellectual property rights and foreign direct investment. Regarding the meaning of FDI, the Advocate General relied on the concept established in the Court's case law.[36] Keeping in line with the Commission's submission, the Advocate General argued that the objectives and general provisions of EUSFTA also fell within the scope of the CCP as those provisions corresponded with the objectives laid down in Article 206 TFEU or were purely accessory and therefore these provisions were not

---

[32] *See* the first ground under Article 3 (2) TFEU.

[33] *See* the third ground under Article 3 (2) TFEU.

[34] All Member States submitted written observations with the exception of Belgium, Croatia, Estonia and Sweden.

[35] Opinion of Advocate General Sharpston in procedure 2/15, ECLI:EU:C:2016:992.

[36] *See* the previous sub-chapter above.

such as to alter the allocation of competences between the European Union and the Member States as regards the other provisions of the EUSFTA.[37] It was crucial from the perspective of EUSFTA whether the dispute settlement and other procedural provisions (mediation, transparency mechanisms) might be established on the basis of the EU competence. In the Advocate General's reasoning, the dispute settlement and mediation mechanisms are ancillary in nature. Consequently the allocation of competences in those fields should be done in the same way as the substantive provisions to which they relate.[38] The EU enjoyed exclusive competence in those fields in so far as those provisions applied to ancillary parts of the agreement falling within the scope of the exclusive competence. Along with the latter areas, the assessment of the Advocate General also touched upon the competences vis-à-vis competition and related issues. Sharpston's Opinion followed the arguments of the Commission and held that the link between international trade and competition policy might be reasonably established. This connection can be seen in certain provisions in the WTO agreements and the detailed analysis of the related chapters in EUSFTA showed, according to the Opinion, that the provisions are covered by the CCP. The Opinion also highlighted that the EU enjoyed competence even relating to those provisions of EUSFTA that required harmonization of competition rules in some degree. This was because these harmonization requirements stemmed from competition law provisions of EU law the agreement extended to Singapore, or provisions concerning cooperation and coordination in law enforcement that were all ancillary to the main substantive obligations set out in EUSFTA.[39] Moreover it is also notable, how the Advocate General evaluated the position of the 'trade and environment' issues. The EUSFTA lays down provisions regarding the investments in renewable energy sectors in a separate chapter[40] and in accordance with the major objectives of the 'new generation agreements', contains a complete set of rules on sustainable development.[41] Sharpston referred conceptually to the consistency requirement of the Treaty between the CCP and the general objectives and principles of EU external relations and made plausible that levels of environmental protection demonstrated links with international trade.[42]

Regarding investments in renewable energy sectors, the Opinion argued that these provisions in EUSFTA are limited to measures which may affect trade and investment that are primarily concerned with regulating commercial policy instruments and eliminating trade and investment barriers and have direct and immediate effects on trade. Therefore, the exclusive competence of the EU can be based on the CCP. Similarly, she found that to some extent, trade and sustainable development relate to commercial policy instruments, therefore these elements thereof establish the exclusive competence at EU level.[43]

---

[37] Advocate General's Opinion, para 136.

[38] Advocate General's Opinion, paras 523–529.

[39] Advocate General's Opinion, paras 459–465.

[40] EUSFTA, Chapter Seven.

[41] EUSFTA, Chapter Thirteen.

[42] 473–483.

[43] Advocate General's Opinion, paras 484–504. The Opinion found the same conclusion relating to the conservation of marine biological resources.

The competences shared with the Member States covered subjects that were partly related to the above issues, but were excluded from the scope of the exclusive competence. The provisions of the EUSFTA on trade in air transport services, maritime transport services and transport by inland waterway (including services inherently linked to those transport services), were not part of the trade in services competence. Even though the exclusive competence comprised government procurements as well, those relating to transport services and services inherently linked to transport services were exempted as falling within the scope of the shared competence.[44] Similarly, Sharpston emphasized that EU has exclusive competence with regard to foreign direct investments as well as commercial aspects of IP rights. However, in the fields of indirect investments and non-commercial aspects of intellectual property rights, the EU enjoys only competences shared with the Member States. Since the Opinion found the procedural provisions (ISDS, mediation, transparency mechanisms) as falling only partly within the exclusive competence, all aspects of EUSFTA's procedural provisions were based on competences shared with the Member States that apply to the parts of the agreement for which the EU enjoys shared external competences. Moreover, the Opinion divided also the sustainable development chapter with respect to the available competence. In the Advocate General's reasoning, the fundamental labor and environmental standards were not covered by Article 207 TFEU. Therefore these matters fell within the scope of either social policy or environmental policy – consequently the EU enjoyed only competences shared with the Member States.

It was significant from the perspective of the competence allocation and the position of the Member States that the Opinion found also a subject where the EU was not empowered. Sharpston held that the EU had no external competence to agree to be bound by that part of the EUSFTA which terminated bilateral agreements concluded between certain Member States and Singapore. In her view, that competence belongs exclusively to the Member States concerned.[45]

V. The Opinion of the Court of Justice

The Court delivered its Opinion on 16 May 2017 and held that EUSFTA cannot be concluded by the European Union alone; therefore EUSFTA implies a 'mixed' agreement signed and concluded by both the EU and the Member States. The assessment of the exclusive competence for conclusion of EUSFTA was based on the standard approach conducted by the Court in the well-settled case law. The Court held that the CCP belongs within the context of the Union's external action and thus the CCP relates to trade with non-EU countries.[46] It was emphasized that only the fact that the measure has implications for international trade is not quite enough for deciding whether the subject is covered by the CCP. It can be classified as falling within the scope of the CCP if it relates

[44] EUSFTA, Chapter Eight and Ten.

[45] *See* Advocate General's Opinion, para 563.

[46] *See* Case C-414/11 *Daiichi Sankyo and Sanofi-Aventis Deutschland*, EU:C:2013:520, para 50; Judgment of 22 October 2013, Case C-137/12 *Commission v Council*, EU:C:2013:675, para 56.

specifically to international trade, which means that the measure is essentially intended to promote, facilitate, or govern trade, and has direct and immediate effects on trade. In other words, the existence of a specific link between the measure and international trade between the European Union and Singapore has to be established.[47]

Even though it is not expressly argued in the Opinion, it is obvious that this investigation is rooted conceptually in the case law on principles of choice of legal basis. More precisely, the assessment whether the EUSFTA falls within the scope of the CCP can be regarded as not only a question of the competence allocation between the EU and the Member States, but also as a question of delimitation of the Union's policies. Therefore the Opinion is significant for both the vertical and the horizontal aspects of the competence allocation. This conceptual basis is also palpable behind the reasoning, when the Court aims at finding objective factors, e.g., the purpose and the content of matters laid down in EUSFTA. This approached follows a very similar logical pathway that the Court usually applies concerning the choice of legal basis, where a provision pursues two- or multifold purposes or objectives. Accordingly, the Court is looking intuitively for the main or predominant objective and identifies the competence character of EUSFTA on the basis thereof.

Similar to the view of the Advocate General, the Court also found that the most part of the agreement can be covered by the exclusive competence of the CCP. However, disagreeing with the Advocate General, the Court's Opinion scrutinized the status and competence character of certain EUSFTA chapters differently. These major differences are related to services (Chapter Eight), investment (Chapter Nine), government procurement (Chapter Ten), IP rights (Chapter Eleven), and environmental concerns (Chapter Thirteen). The position as well as the argumentation of the Court regarding these issues shall be discussed in some detail.

a) Services

The Advocate General held that major parts of the services were covered by the exclusive competence, including rail and road transport services, while other important areas were shared between the EU and the Member States (trade in air, maritime and inland waterway services). However, the Court did not fully share this view and reassessed the extent of the competence in this area. The Court did not differentiate between the types of activities covered by trade in services ('modes' in WTO

---

[47] Opinion of the Court 2/15., ECLI:EU:C:2017:376., paras 34–36. *See*, for related cases, inter alia, Case C-137/12 *Commission v Council*, EU:C:2013:675, para 57, and Opinion of 14 February 2017 in Case 3/15 *Marrakesh Treaty on Access to Published Works*, EU:C:2017:114, para 61. For a general analysis, *see* Marise Cremona, *Shaping EU trade policy post-Lisbon: Opinion 2/15 of 16 May 2017*, 14 European Constitutional Law Review 1, 231–259 (2018); Rumiana Yotova, *Opinion 2/15 of the CJEU: Delineating the Scope of the New EU Competence in Foreign Direct Investment*, The Cambridge Law Journal, 29–32 (2018); László Knapp, *The Doctrine of Implied External Powers and the EU-Singapore Free Trade Agreement in* The Influence and Effects of EU Business Law in the Western Balkans (Judit Glavanits & Balázs Horváthy & László Knapp, eds., 2018, forthcoming); Charlotte Beaucillon, *Opinion 2/15: Sustainable Is the New Trade. Rethinking Coherence for the New Common Commercial Policy*, 2 European Papers 3, 819–828 (2017).

classification)[48] and found that there was no reason to make a distinction between the provisions relating to the cross-border supply of services and the supply of services by establishment or by the presence of natural persons. Thus, the Court held that all four modes fell within the scope of the CCP.[49] As Article 207 (5) TFEU excludes the negotiation and conclusion of international agreements in the field of transport from the scope of the CCP, the Court examined specifically transport services regulated in the EUSFTA. Some of them were held to be 'business services' and not auxiliary services in the area of transport e.g., aircraft repair and maintenance services during which an aircraft is withdrawn from service; the selling and marketing of air transport services and computer reservation system services. The Court concluded that these three types of services were covered by the EU exclusive competence.[50] For maritime, rail, and road transport services it was decisive that under Article 3 (2) TFEU and in line with the permanent case-law, the Treaty grants to the EU exclusive competence to conclude also agreements which may affect common rules or alter their scope. Considering the provisions of EUSFTA regarding the maritime, rail and road transport services, the Court concluded that these areas were largely covered by common rules already and may affect also common rules or alter their scope, therefore the EU enjoys exclusive competence in these areas. Concerning the internal waterways transport services, the Court, consistently with the permanent case law, found that there is no need to take into account of the provisions of an agreement, which are extremely limited in scope.[51] As the provisions regarding those services were very marginal in EUSFTA, it did not imply the delimitation of the EU competence. For this reason the Court concluded that the EU had exclusive competence in respect of services (Chapter Eight) in its entirety.[52]

b) Investment

One of the most complex issue was the competence allocation in the area of investments. It follows from the above analysis that the Opinion of the Advocate General strictly delimited the competences for direct and indirect investments (falling within the exclusive and shared competences respectively), and also the competences regarding ISDS were split along this logic. The Court drew similar conclusions concerning investment

---

[48] Trade in services encompasses the following four modes of activities in the terminology of the WTO: the supply of a service from the territory of one WTO Member into the territory of another Member (mode 1); the supply of a service in the territory of one Member to the consumer of another Member (mode 2, the latter two modes are cross-border services); the supply of a service by a service provider of one Member through commercial presence in the territory of another Member (mode 3); and the supply of a service by a service provider of one Member through presence of natural persons of a Member in the territory of another Member (mode 4). This differentiation was also applied by the Court in its Opinion 1/94.

[49] Opinion of the Court, paras 54–55. *See* for related case: Opinion 1/08, 30 November 2009, *Agreements Modifying the Schedules of Specific Commitments under the GATS*, EU:C:2009:739, paras 4 and 118 and 119.

[50] Opinion of the Court, paras 64–68.

[51] Opinion of the Court, para 217.

[52] *See id.*, and Opinion of the Court, para 69.

protection and the competence nature of FDI and non-direct investment, but assessed the powers for ISDS differently.

The distinction between the two aspects of foreign investments was made on the basis of the permanent case law. Thus, the Court defined FDI as "[...] investments made by natural or legal persons of that third state in the European Union and vice versa which enable effective participation in the management or control of a company carrying out an economic activity."[53] On the other hand, non-direct investment concerns, *inter alia*, acquisition of company securities with the aim of making a financial investment without any intention to influence the management and control of the undertaking (portfolio investments).[54] For the reason that the Treaty (Article 207 (1) TFEU) explicitly lists FDI as part of the CCP, it is undebatable that the foreign direct investment provisions fall within the exclusive competence of the EU. It follows also from this provision that the Treaty does not intend to include other foreign investment categories in the CCP. Therefore non-direct investments (portfolio investments) are not covered by the CCP. The commitments in the EUSFTA relating to foreign investments, other than direct investments do not fall within the exclusive competence of the EU. The Court, however, assessed these investment activities to be covered by the movements of capital provisions (Article 63 TFEU). Consequently non-direct investments fall within the shared competence between the EU and the Member States pursuant to Article 4 (2) (a) TFEU.[55]

The Court did not share the view of the Advocate General regarding investor-state dispute settlement provisions of EUSFTA. Sharpston found that ISDS is ancillary to the investment protection provisions. Therefore ISDS provisions related to FDI could be concluded within the scope of CCP but ISDS provisions concerning non-direct investment fall under shared competences. Contrary to this view, the Court considered that the whole concept of ISDS falls outside of the scope of the exclusive competence. The Court's argument was that the ISDS regime removes disputes from the jurisdiction of the courts of the Member States. Therefore these provisions of EUSFTA cannot be of a purely ancillary nature. It follows that ISDS cannot be established without the consent of the Member States.[56]

The third major question regarding the investment chapter was, whether the competence over CCP empowers the EU to replace the BITs between the Member States and Singapore. The BITs concluded by the Member States with third countries are now authorized by a regulation adopted in 2012[57] that enables the Member States to maintain their BITs in force until the EU concludes an investment agreement with the same third country. The Advocate General held that the EU had no power to terminate these pre-existing agreements but the Court took a different view and found that provisions in the EUSFTA terminating the BITs concluded by the Member States with Singapore do

[53] Opinion of the Court, para 82.

[54] Opinion of the Court, para 227.

[55] Opinion of the Court, paras 240–242.

[56] Opinion of the Court, para 292.

[57] Regulation (EU) No 1219/2012 of the European Parliament and of the Council of 12 December 2012 Establishing Transitional Arrangements for Bilateral Investment Agreements Between Member States and Third Countries, [2012] OJ L351/40.

not encroach upon a competence of the Member States, in so far as that provision relates to a field in respect of which the European Union has exclusive competence. The reasoning of the Court was based on the argument that if the EU negotiates and concludes an agreement with a third country relating to a field in respect of which it is empowered with exclusive competence, the EU replaces the Member States. In light of the well-settled case law,[58] it was clear "[...] that the European Union can succeed the Member States in their international commitments when the Member States have transferred to it [...] their competences relating to those commitments and it exercises those competences."[59] The EU has exclusive competence to terminate these agreements with respect to those provisions falling within the scope of FDI.[60]

c) Government Procurement

Contrary to the Advocate General's Opinion, the Court held that the provisions of EUSFTA regarding government procurement should be based completely on the exclusive competence of the European Union. It was argued, that these rules specifically aim at laying down the requirements under which economic operators of each party of the agreement may participate in procurement procedures in the other contracting party. The Court emphasized, as those requirements are founded on considerations of non-discriminatory access, transparency and efficiency, they have direct and immediate effects on trade in goods and services between the EU and Singapore.[61] Therefore these provisions were regarded as covered by the scope of the CCP. For the provisions on government procurement in the field of transport services, the Court followed the same logic and found an overriding argument in Article 3 (2) TFEU: since those related areas are already covered by common rules, the exclusive external competence for the whole Chapter Ten on government procurement was established.[62]

d) Intellectual Property Protection

The Advocate General supported the position of some Member States and held that EUSFTA addresses both commercial and non-commercial aspects of intellectual property but the CCP conferred only competences regarding commercial aspects on the EU. The main argument was that the EUSFTA referred to multilateral conventions in the context of IP and copyright, which include also provisions relating to moral rights.[63] The Court opposed this argumentation and took the view that such reference by EUSFTA was

[58] This started early, *see* Joined Cases 21/72 to 24/72 International Fruit Company and Others, EU:C:1972:115, paras 10–18.

[59] Opinion of the Court, para 248.

[60] Opinion of the Court, para 247.

[61] Opinion of the Court, para 76.

[62] Opinion of the Court, paras 77 and 224.

[63] *See* EUSFTA Article 10.24.

not sufficient for the subject to be regarded as a component of the agreement. This reasoning suggests that only the content and inherent provisions of the agreement play a role in delimiting the competence of the EU. Other sources like conventions referred to by the text of EUSFTA, are irrelevant.[64] The agreement itself does not contain provisions relating to moral rights. Therefore the Court concluded that the Chapter covered only the commercial aspects of IP rights and as a result, the EU enjoys exclusive competence for conclusion of Chapter Eleven.[65]

e) Trade and Sustainable Development

Disagreeing with the Advocate General, the Court saw the issues regarding trade and sustainable development covered by the CCP and the exclusive competence of the European Union. The conceptual framework of the Court's reasoning in this respect was, first, underpinned by the Treaty provisions regarding horizontal principles and objectives of EU external relations. Those principles and objectives enshrined in Article 21(1) and (2) TEU include sustainable development linked to preservation and improvement of the quality of the environment and the sustainable management of global natural resources. The CCP must be 'guided' by these principles and objectives.[66] In view of the Court, these provisions establish an obligation on the EU to integrate these objectives and principles into the conduct of the CCP.[67] The Court's argument implies that the EU is obliged to include these provisions into the agreements to be concluded with third countries. The Court argued that the relevant provisions of the EUSFTA on trade and sustainable development have a direct and immediate effect on trade. The Court highlighted that in terms of a specific provision of EUSFTA it is undisputable that parties to the agreement did not want to encourage trade by reducing the levels of social and environmental protection in their respective territories below the standards laid down by international commitments or to apply those standards in a protectionist manner. The Court concluded that the sustainable development of the EUSFTA (Chapter Thirteen) falls within the CCP and, therefore, within the exclusive competence of the EU. [68]

VI. Conclusions

The Opinion of the Court on the EUSFTA has made a novel contribution to a more precise separation of powers in the CCP, specifically regarding new generation trade agreements of the European Union. Delimiting clearly the competences in the areas of the CCP is vital for the Member States, as the exclusive competence character implies their sovereignty and autonomy not only in theoretical terms. The competence allocation

[64] Opinion of the Court, para 129.

[65] Opinion of the Court, para 130.

[66] Articles 205 and 207 (1) TFEU.

[67] Opinion of the Court, paras 142–145.

[68] Opinion of the Court, para 167.

might have a number of practical consequences as well. Even though the TFEU already lays down the framework of competence allocation, it is obvious that the founding treaties can answer only the abstract-categorical questions concerning the separation of powers between the EU and Member States in the CCP. It is pressing, however, to reach beyond these abstract questions and define the scope of the CCP in several matters, which might determine even the future of the external trade relations of the EU. From this point of view, it is strikingly important, how the emerging EU policy will gradually take the place of the Member States' own investment policies, which are still anchored in their more than one thousand agreements concluded with third countries bilaterally.

Considering these expectations, the message of the Opinion seems to be clear. Despite the exclusive competence character of the CCP, the new generation agreements are not fully covered by the EU competence. Therefore these agreements will require also the ratification on behalf of the Member States. Early commentaries regarding the Opinion confirmed a victory of the Member States in the competence debate. However, in the view of the present author, the picture may be much more sophisticated. First, the Court made evident the exclusivity of the EU competence in a number of areas, from services, over government procurement, to trade and sustainable development, among which the latter is, probably, of great importance. It does not affect only trade and environment issues. The Court's argumentation pulls indeed the whole domain of horizontal principles and objectives into the center of the CCP, which evidently expresses the conviction, that the CCP is based not only on pure economic decisions, but it is guided by shared values.

The mixed nature of the new generation agreements is telling not only with respect to the sovereignty of the Member States. It points also toward their legitimacy. In this perspective, the mixity can improve the legitimacy of the new generation trade agreements, as those must also be assessed by the national parliaments and ratified by the Member States. It must not be neglected, however, that the domestic ratification processes might be slowed down and that unforeseeable events can influence their outcome (see Wallonia's rejection of CETA).

Since the FDI is undenyably covered by the exclusive EU competence, the status of the Member States' extra-BITs are not implied essentially by the Opinion. The authorization under Regulation 1219/2012 is still relevant and enables the Member States to maintain the bilateral investment agreements in force until the Union concludes an agreement with the same third country. Even though the EU has already finished investment negotiations – apart from Singapore – with Canada, Japan and Vietnam, the signature or ratification procedures are still pending at this time. Therefore the related BITs maintained by several Member States with the latter countries have not yet been replaced. Moreover, the Member States are able to open new negotiations on a BIT or to sign and conclude a new treaty with third countries even in the future, under the authorization of the Commission (until now, 17 extra-BITs or additional protocols have been signed by Member States). Even though these concerns indicate that it will take longer time to replace the Member States' agreements, the Opinion made clear an important aspect of the replacement: the Court held that the EU has exclusive competence to terminate these agreements with respect to those provisions falling within the scope of FDI.

The Opinion left also questions unanswered regarding new generation trade agreements. Specifically, the EU competences regarding the ISDS mechanisms are not fully clear yet. It was much disputed, whether Article 207 TFEU covers also the procedural aspects of the investment protection, i.e., whether the exclusive competence empowers the EU to participate in dispute settlement procedures established under the agreements. This issue implies also practical concerns, knowing that the investor-state dispute settlement (ISDS) mechanisms are *sine qua non* instruments of comprehensive investment protection. The Court only argued that the ISDS regime removes disputes from the jurisdiction of the courts of the Member States. Therefore these provisions of EUSFTA cannot be concluded without the consent of the Member States. However, the ISDS mechanism, as a specific forum, has not been assessed profoundly by the Opinion. Specifically, the Investment Court System introduced in CETA raises questions of incompatibility with EU law. Therefore the ongoing procedure of Opinion 1/17 is expected to be decisive on these aspects of the new generation trade agreements and to move the CCP toward a more solid footing.

Csongor István Nagy*

EXTRA-EU BITS AND EU LAW: IMMUNITY, "DEFENSE OF SUPERIOR ORDERS", TREATY SHOPPING AND UNILATERALISM

Abstract

This paper addresses three aspects of the relationship between extra-EU BITs and EU law. First, are disputes under extra-EU BITs concluded before the given country's accession affected (and suppressed) by EU law? Second, given the fact that Member States ceded parts of their sovereignty to the EU, would the "defense of superior orders" work in relation to Member State acts mandated by EU law? Third, will the suppression of intra-EU BITs intensify the use of extra-EU BITs in terms of treaty shopping?

I. Introduction

In recent years, various issues concerning the relationship between EU law and bilateral investment treaties (BITs) have emerged and reached the Court of Justice of the European Union (CJEU).

Earlier this year, the CJEU, in *Achmea*,[1] pronounced an arbitration clause in an intra-EU BIT non-compliant with EU law because it found that it endangered the stability of the EU's judicial architecture and encroached on EU courts' privilege to interpret EU law. While it is unclear what the judgment's holding is and whether it covers arbitration clauses different from the one that reached the CJEU,[2] it is certain that the ruling generated a huge pessimism as to the future of investment arbitration in intra-EU matters.

In parallel to this, Belgium submitted a request for an opinion to the CJEU concerning the EU law compatibility of the rules on resolution of investment disputes between investors and states of the Canada-EU Free Trade Agreement (Comprehensive Economic and Trade Agreement – CETA).[3]

---

* LL.M., Ph.D., S.J.D, dr. juris, professor of law and head of the Department of Private International Law at the University of Szeged, research chair and the head of the Federal Markets "Momentum" Research Group of the Hungarian Academy of Sciences, recurrent visiting professor at the Central European University (Budapest/New York), the Riga Graduate School of Law (Latvia) and the Sapientia University of Transylvania (Romania). The author is indebted to Wojciech Sadowski for his comments on this paper. Of course, all views and any errors remain the author's own.

1 Case C-284/16 *Slovakia v. Achmea BV*, ECLI:EU:C:2018:158.

2 Csongor István Nagy, *Intra-EU Bilateral Investment Treaties and EU Law after Achmea: "Know Well What Leads You Forward and What Holds You Back"*, 19(4) German Law Journal 981 (2018).

3 Opinion 1/17: Request for an Opinion Submitted by the Kingdom of Belgium Pursuant to Article 218(11) TFEU.

This paper addresses three aspects of the relationship between extra-EU BITs and EU law. Are disputes under extra-EU BITs concluded before the given country's accession affected (and suppressed) by EU law? Given that Member States ceded parts of their sovereignty to the EU, would the "defense of superior orders" work in relation to Member State acts mandated by EU law? And would the suppression of intra-EU BITs intensify the use of extra-EU BITs in terms of treaty shopping?

II. Are Rights Protected by Pre-Accession Extra-EU BITs Suppressed by EU law?

Notwithstanding the changes in the division of competences between the EU and Member States brought about by the Treaty of Lisbon, BITs involving an EU Member State and a third country have remained, in essence, intact.

On one hand, Regulation 1219/2012 establishing transitional arrangements for bilateral investment agreements between Member States and third countries made it clear that extra-EU BITs, concluded before the Treaty of Lisbon or accession, will remain valid "until a bilateral investment agreement between the Union and the same third country enters into force."[4] On the other hand, extra-EU BITs may be governed by Article 351 TFEU, which provides that rights and obligations arising from treaties with third countries that precede accession "shall not be affected by the provisions of the Treaties".

> *"Article 351*
> *The rights and obligations arising from agreements concluded before 1 January 1958 or, for acceding states, before the date of their accession, between one or more Member States on the one hand, and one or more third countries on the other, shall not be affected by the provisions of the Treaties.*
> *To the extent that such agreements are not compatible with the Treaties, the Member State or states concerned shall take all appropriate steps to eliminate the incompatibilities established. Member States shall, where necessary, assist each other to this end and shall, where appropriate, adopt a common attitude.*
> *In applying the agreements referred to in the first paragraph, Member States shall take into account the fact that the advantages accorded under the Treaties by each Member State form an integral part of the establishment of the Union and are thereby inseparably linked with the creation of common institutions, the conferring of powers upon them and the granting of the same advantages by all the other Member States."*

The CJEU established very early, in *Attorney General v. Juan C. Burgoa*,[5] that the purpose of Article 351 TFEU is to make sure that EU law does not affect Member States' duties to respects the rights of non-member countries emerging from an agreement concluded prior to accession.[6]

---

[4] Article 3.

[5] Case 812/79 [1980] ECR 02787, ECLI:EU:C:1980:231.

[6] This phrasing has been consistently followed in the judicial practice. *See* Case C-84/98 *Commission v.*

> *"[T]he purpose of that provision is to lay down, in accordance with the principles of international law, that the application of the Treaty does not affect the duty of the Member State concerned to respect the rights of non-member countries under a prior agreement and to perform its obligations thereunder. Although the first paragraph of Article 234 makes mention only of the obligations of the Member States, it would not achieve its purpose if it did not imply a duty on the part of the institutions of the Community not to impede the performance of the obligations of Member States which stem from a prior agreement. However, that duty of the Community institutions is directed only to permitting the Member State concerned to perform its obligations under the prior agreement and does not bind the Community as regards the non-member country in question.*
> *Since the purpose of the first paragraph of Article 234 is to remove any obstacle to the performance of agreements previously concluded with non-member countries which the accession of a Member State to the Community may present, it cannot have the effect of altering the nature of the rights which may flow from such agreements. From that it follows that that provision does not have the effect of conferring upon individuals who rely upon an agreement concluded prior to the entry into force of the Treaty or, as the case may be, the accession of the Member State concerned, rights which the national courts of the Member States must uphold. Nor does it adversely affect the rights which individuals may derive from such an agreement."*[7]

In *Commission v. Slovak Republic*,[8] the CJEU held that benefits accruing from a private law contract and protected by Slovakia's extra-EU BITs and the ECT antedating accession persist under Article 351 TFEU.

In 1997, ATEL, a Swiss company, was granted preferential access to the electricity grid in Slovakia. The Commission launched an infringement procedure against Slovakia due to discriminatory treatment. However, the CJEU held that "the preferential access granted to ATEL may be regarded as an investment protected by the [Swiss-Czechoslovakian BIT] and that, under the first paragraph of Article 351 EC, it cannot be affected by the provisions of the EC Treaty";[9] "even if it were to be assumed that the preferential access granted to ATEL were not compliant with Directive 2003/54, that preferential access is protected by the first paragraph of Article 351 EC".[10]

Accordingly, investment rights and privileges granted before accession to non-EU investors persist on the basis of Article 351 TFEU if they were converted into a treaty right before accession. It has to be taken into account that in *Commission v. Slovak Republic* not

---

Portuguese Republic, [2000] ECR I-05215, ECLI:EU:C:2000:359, para 53; Case C-216/01 *Budějovický Budvar, národní podnik v. Rudolf Ammersin GmbH* [2003] ECR I-13617, ECLI:EU:C:2003:618, paras 144-145; Case C-249/06 *Commission v. Sweden*, para 34.

7 Case 812/79 *Attorney General v. Juan C. Burgoa* [1980] ECR 02787, ECLI:EU:C:1980:231, paras 8-10.

8 Case C-264/09 *Commission v. Slovak Republic* [2011] ECR I-08065.

9 Para 51.

10 Para 52.

only the BIT but also the investment contract was concluded before Slovakia's accession. The situation may be different if the promise or benefit protected by the extra-EU BIT (investment contract) is made or granted after the accession. Would the pre-accession BIT, under Article 351 TFEU, equally save a Slovak promise made post-accession for preferential access? The BIT itself, as a treaty concluded before accession, would certainly benefit from the immunity granted by Article 351 TFEU but would a post-accession measure enjoy the same treatment? Can a post-accession private law right turn into a treaty right under a pre-accession BIT?

The answer appears to be negative. Article 351 TFEU applies to treaties and not to (investment) contracts. In *Commission v. Slovak Republic* it was the contractual rights confirmed and protected by the BIT that benefited from Article 351 TFEU: the promise of preferential access was lawful before accession and it also ossified under the Swiss-Czechoslovak BIT before accession. Nonetheless, a similar post-accession promise may not be susceptible of ossifying. Even though the BIT would keep on benefitting from Article 351 TFEU, its immunity would not extend to post-accession private law rights and contracts.

Not only would it be preposterous to sanction state aids granted to non-EU investors with reference to extra-EU BITs but such an interpretation would also be conceptually flawed. Notably, Article 351 TFEU does not protect private law rights but treaty rights. This implies, that no treaty right comes into existence if there is no valid private law right to be protected by the BIT. Due to the doctrine of supremacy, EU law suppresses all non-compliant rights under national law. Therefore, a benefit infringing EU law will not be a valid right. Hence, it cannot ossify under the BIT.

III. The "Defense of Superior Orders" in the Arbitral Practice

The EU's multilayered system of competences and the partial transfer of national sovereignty create an involute system where competences and also responsibilities are shared. This may cause complicated questions in cases where the impugned national act was mandated by EU law.

A few arbitral proceedings have dealt with Member State liability for implementing the commands of EU law, i.e. Member States' liability for violations mandated by EU law.[11] In these cases, the Member State promised benefits which were revoked later on as illegal under EU law. These cases dealt with intra-EU BITs but may provide guidance also in relation to the same question under extra-EU BITs.

The problem may appear to be ephemeral, as pre-accession benefits will sooner or later fall out, lifting the factual basis of the theoretical question whether a Member States may be called to account for acts mandated by EU law. Indeed, this issue emerged in intra-EU disputes in the arbitral practice, where the benefits were granted before the country's accession. A common feature of these investment cases is that EU law, in particular state aid law, nullified benefits granted before accession. The claimed benefits

[11] *Cf.* Thomas Eilmansberger, *Bilateral Investment Treaties and EU law*, 46 Common Market Law Review 383, 413 (2009).

were lawfully promised but subsequently became unlawful when the accession treaty entered into force. In these cases, the state entered into an agreement with an investor, or created a legitimate expectation, and it was established at or after the accession that this arrangement contained illegal state aid and had to be abolished.

Nonetheless, the above issue will persist as to Member State acts which were lawful when adopted but were made illegal by an amendment of EU law. In certain cases a Member State measure may be compliant with EU law when it is adopted but turn illegal by a change in EU law. In such cases, it may be convincingly argued that the nullification, i.e. the invalidity of benefits non-compliant with EU law, were not foreseeable for the investor, hence, its legitimate expectations were frustrated.[12] Given that, should the Member State be held to account for a promise it lawfully made but was outlawed later on by the EU?

The investment law liability for acts mandated by EU law raises issues of supremacy[13] and the question whether the "defense of superior orders" provides immunity to Member States. The Commission has championed the theory that benefits nullified by EU state aid law may give rise to no valid claims due to EU law's supremacy. On the other hand, tribunals have consistently rejected to judge the question on the basis of EU law's supremacy, though they adopted diverging approaches regarding the "defense of superior orders".

In *Electrabel S.A. v. Republic of Hungary*,[14] the Commission enjoined Hungary to put an end to the Hungarian national electricity company's (MVM)[15] long-term power purchase agreements because they contained veiled state aid. Though Hungary terminated the agreements through a legislative act, the tribunal established that Hungary was not liable as its act was mandated by the Commission's formal decision[16] ("defense of superior orders"). This may imply that the EU should have been sued instead (in fact, the EU could have been sued as the claim was based on the Treaty Energy Charter (ECT), which was ratified not only by the Member States but also by the EU itself). At the same time, the tribunal did investigate those elements of Hungary's conduct where Hungary had a certain leeway. These acts were regarded as Hungary's own acts despite being done to implement the Commission's decision.

---

[12] Thomas Eilmansberger, *Bilateral Investment Treaties and EU law*, 46 Common Market Law Review 383, 418–419 (2009).

[13] Tamás Kende, *Arbitral Awards Classified as State Aid under European Union Law*, 3(1) ELTE Law Journal 37, 48 (2015).

[14] ICSID Case No. ARB/07/19. Award of 25 November 2015.

[15] In the mid-1990s Hungary privatized its power plants. The claimant purchased the majority of the shares in Dunamenti power plant and invested considerable funds for the purpose of retrofitting. Dunamenti had a long-term power purchase agreement with MVM, the Hungarian national electricity company. Such contracts were common at that time and were meant to back the privatization of the power stations: these facilities needed significant retrofitting and the long-term power purchase contracts were meant, in economic terms, to guarantee the investors that they would be able to sell the electricity they produced (note that at that time MVM was the only purchaser of electricity in Hungary and remained a super-dominant undertaking also after the electricity market was opened).

[16] Commission decision on the state aid awarded by Hungary, C (2008) 2223 final.

The claimant's expropriation claim was summarily rejected – the power purchase agreement itself was not considered to be a protectable investment and its termination did not deprive the claimant's investment (the power plant) of its value.[17] Hence, the case centered around the ECT's "treatment" provisions.

The tribunal established that the relationship between the ECT and EU law is somewhat special and "the ECT should be interpreted, if possible, in harmony with EU law".[18] It held that "there can be no practical contradiction between the ECT and EU law in regard to the [Commission's] Final Decision" and "the ECT does not protect the claimant, as against the Respondent, from the enforcement by the Respondent of a binding decision of the European Commission under EU law."[19] However, the tribunal also noted that the EU itself is not immune from liability under the ECT.[20]

The tribunal also stressed that Hungary's immunity was due to the compelling nature of the Commission's state aid decision and, for this reason, it extended only to the point where it had no autonomy of action.[21] Details left to its discretion or not spelled out in the Commission decision came under Hungary's individual liability and were to be scrutinized by the tribunal.[22]

Contrary to the above, in *EDF International S.A. v. Republic of Hungary*,[23] which was launched by another investor but emerged from the same state aid matter as *Electrabel*, the tribunal decided for the claimant (in an *ad-hoc* arbitral proceeding conducted under the UNCITRAL rules).[24] Unfortunately, the award is not publicly available so the tribunal's arguments cannot be reconstructed.

---

[17] ICSID Award in Case No. ARB/17/19, Paras 6.53 and 6.57-6.58.

[18] Para 4.130. First, the EU and its Member States were closely involved in the adoption of the ECT, and since according to Article 207(3) TFEU the Council and the Commission have to ensure that "the agreements negotiated are compatible with internal Union policies and rules". Paras 4.135-4.136. Second, the ECT and the EU have similar objectives: the ECT "is an instrument clearly intended to combat anti-competitive conduct, which is the same objective as the European Union's objective in combating unlawful state aid." Para 4.133. *See also* paras 4.137 and 4.141. Third, the tribunal also established (para 4.142.) that the ECT implicitly recognized that Commission decisions are binding on all Member States. *See* Article 1(3) ECT: "A "Regional Economic Integration Organization" means an organization constituted by states to which they have transferred competence over certain matters a number of which are governed by this Treaty, including the authority to take decisions binding on them in respect of those matters."

[19] Para 4.169.

[20] Para 4.170.

[21] Paras 4.191 and 4.196.

[22] Paras 6.72 and 6.76. Hungary created a scheme for establishing the net stranded costs and for compensating the power plants for these (in case these had not been recovered). The tribunal found that Hungary's own acts were in line with the applicable standards; however, since the last stage of this scheme was still to be carried out at the time of the award, the tribunal reserved the right to decide on this in another award. Paras 6.108-6.109 and 6.118. *Cf.* Thomas Eilmansberger, Bilateral investment treaties and EU law, 46 Common Market Law Review 383, 413 (2009) ("The EC law origin of the measure cannot exculpate the host state if it had some discretion as to the interpretation or application of the EC law provisions in question. Relevant BIT investment protection guarantees oblige Member States to exercise this discretion in the most investor-friendly (and investmentsparing) way.").

[23] The award was rendered on December 4, 2014. The tribunal consisted of Karl-Heinz Böckstiegel (chair), Pierre-Marie Dupuy and Albert Jan van der Berg.

[24] *See* http://globalarbitrationreview.com/news/article/33251/edf-wins-claim-against-hungary/.

In *Micula Brothers v. Romania*,[25] the tribunal condemned Romania for withdrawing certain benefits due to EU state aid law. This case spectacularly presents the clash between BITs and EU law and demonstrates the vicious circle[26] encapsulated in this issue. After Romania provided compensation to the claimants (as ordered by the tribunal), the Commission established that the compensation stepped into the place of the illegal subsidy it was meant to make up for and, hence, qualified as a state aid and ordered Romania to recover the financial benefit provided. This was a controversial position as the benefits were withdrawn before Romania's accession to the EU, so the withdrawal was motivated but not compelled by EU state aid law.

The dispute emerged from Romania's introduction and subsequent revocation (during the accession negotiations) of certain economic incentives for companies operating in under-developed regions.[27] The tribunal established that there was no real conflict between the BIT and EU law as at the relevant moment Romania was in the negotiation stage and not subject to EU law.[28]

The tribunal held that although Romania's conduct was, for the most part, reasonable and "appropriately and narrowly tailored in pursuit of a rational policy" (i.e. EU accession), it did undermine the investors' "legitimate expectations with respect to the continued availability of the incentives" and, hence, qualified as unfair or inequitable and was not sufficiently transparent.[29] Romania, with the support of the Commission, sought the annulment of the award before the ICSID but its plea was rejected.[30]

IV. The Longing for Intra-EU BITs and Treaty Shopping

Extra-EU BITs may gain enhanced significance due to the CJEU's perceived suppression of intra-EU BITs in *Achmea*. Whatever the proper interpretation of the ruling may be,

---

[25] *See* SA.38517 *Micula brothers v. Romania* (ICSID arbitration award); IP/15/4725: European Commission – Press release, State aid: Commission orders Romania to recover incompatible state aid granted in compensation for abolished investment aid scheme. Brussels, 30 March 2015. Case T-646/14 *Micula and Others v. Commission* (pending).

[26] Tamás Kende, *Arbitral Awards Classified as State Aid under European Union Law*, 3(1) ELTE Law Journal 37, 50-51 (2015) (circularity argument).

[27] Claimants argued that they made substantial investments in the legitimate expectation that these benefits would persists for a 10-year period. During Romania's accession negotiations, the EU invited Romania to put an end to the subsidy schemes incompatible with EU state aid law; and Romania terminated the incentives in question as from February 22, 2005 (though they were supposed to persists until April 1, 2009); Romania's accession to the EU entered into force on January 1, 2007, so the incentives were terminated two and a quarter year before EU law became applicable in the host country. While the Commission's position expressed during the negotiations was clear, no formal decision required Romania to revoke the incentives; in fact, no such formal decision could have been rendered, since during the relevant period Romania was not a Member State; however, the Commission made the termination of the subsidies a pre-condition of accession.

[28] Para 319.

[29] Para 827. Romania failed "to inform the claimants in a timely manner that the regime would be terminated prior to its stated date of expiration" Para 872.

[30] *Ioan Micula, Viorel Micula and others v. Romania*, ICSID Case No. ARB/05/20, Decision on annulment, 26 February 2016.

the general feeling is that it made arbitration under intra-EU BITs very risky. This may incite investors to seek alternative ways of protection and one of the obvious options is treaty shopping – EU investors may make investments in other Member States via third countries (or transfer their interests to special purpose vehicles in third countries) and claim the benefits of extra-EU BITs in intra-EU matters.

While some have acknowledged these strategies with aversion, the vast majority of arbitral awards, in fact almost all of them, has been intensely dismissive of piercing the corporate veil in cases where the BIT contained no specific requirements of substantive link or denial of benefits clause. In reality, "it has become so easy for foreign investors to relocate to different jurisdictions that the contents of nationality have largely lost their essence."[31] Although piercing the corporate veil is a living doctrine, it is exceptional and applies only to abusive practices. According to the arbitral practice, the mere fact that the nationals of a country establish a company in another country is, in itself, not an abuse justifying the piercing of the corporate veil.

Notwithstanding the growing role of denial of benefits clauses,[32] a good part of BITs consistently accord protection to companies incorporated in the other country, without containing any requirements of substantive links. Arbitral tribunals have been constantly disinclined to pierce the corporate veil of shell (or mailbox) companies in the context of BITs. It is settled practice that absent a specific provision to the contrary, the tribunal will, in principle, refrain from looking into whether there is a substantive relationship between the company and the country of incorporation.[33]

---

[31] Julien Chaisse, *The Treaty Shopping Practice: Corporate Structuring and Restructuring to Gain Access to Investment Treaties and Arbitration*, 11 Hastings Business Law Journal 225, 228 (2015).

[32] Julien Chaisse, *The Treaty Shopping Practice: Corporate Structuring and Restructuring to Gain Access to Investment Treaties and Arbitration*, 11 Hastings Business Law Journal 225, 289 & 302-303 (2015). *See* Remarks by Gabriela Alvarez, Proceedings of the Annual Meeting (American Society of International Law), Vol. 103, International Law As Law (2009), pp. 328–330, 329 ("Another concern is treaty shopping by investors for the sole purpose of obtaining protection of BITs. Some of the new provisions included in the new model BITs address this problem directly. For instance, the new models include a Denial of Benefits Clause that allows a state to deny benefits of the treaty to an investor of the other party if 1) the enterprise has no substantial business activities in the territory of the other party, and 2) if persons of a nonparty, or of the denying party, own or control the enterprise (i.e., shell companies). The extent to which these provisions will avoid treaty shopping still remains to be seen. The application of this type of clause has already caused a number of treaty interpretation problems. In the Norway Model BIT, the requirement of substantial business activities is directly contained in the definition of investor, which leaves it to tribunals to delineate the concept of substantial business activities. Also, the new Canada Model BIT provides that Most Favored Nation ("MFN") treatment does not extend to treatment accorded under existing treaties, and thus the MFN guarantees are applicable only to future treaty provisions.").

[33] "These investment agreements confirm that states parties are capable of excluding from the scope of the agreement entities of the other party that are controlled by nationals of third countries or by nationals of the host country. The Ukraine– Lithuania BIT, by contrast, includes no such 'denial of benefits' provision with respect to entities controlled by third country nationals or by nationals of the denying party. We regard the absence of such a provision as a deliberate choice of the Contracting Parties. In our view, it is not for tribunals to impose limits on the scope of BITs not found in the text, much less limits nowhere evident from the negotiating history. An international tribunal of defined jurisdiction should not reach out to exercise a jurisdiction beyond the borders of the definition. But equally an international tribunal should exercise, and indeed is bound to exercise, the measure of jurisdiction with which it is endowed." *Tokios Tokeles*, para 36.

In *ADC & ADMC v. Hungary*,[34] Canadian investors made investments in Hungary through a mailbox company incorporated in Cyprus. The Hungarian government objected that the Canadian investors were led by the motivation to gain access to ICSID jurisdiction as Canada was (at the relevant time)[35] not a party to the ICSID Convention. The tribunal rejected to pierce the corporate veil, because the Cyprus-Hungary BIT provided

> *"in its Art. 1(3)(b) [...] that a Cypriot 'investor' protected by that treaty includes a 'legal person constituted or incorporated in compliance with the law' of Cyprus, which each Claimant is conceded to be. [...] As the matter of nationality is settled unambiguously by the Convention and the BIT, there is no scope for consideration of customary law principles of nationality, as reflected in Barcelona Traction, which in any event are no different. In either case inquiry stops upon establishment of the state of incorporation, and considerations of whence comes the company's capital and whose nationals, if not Cypriot, control it are irrelevant."*[36]

The tribunal refused to read any "genuine link" requirements into the BIT.

> *"While the Tribunal acknowledges that such requirement has been applied to some preceding international law cases, it concludes that such a requirement does not exist in the current case. When negotiating the BIT, the Government of Hungary could have inserted this requirement as it did in other BITs concluded both before and after the conclusion of the BIT in this case. However, it did not do so [...] The Tribunal cannot read more into the BIT than one can discern from its plain text."*[37]

In *Saluka Investments BV v. Czech Republic*,[38] which likewise involved a shell company (incorporated in the Netherlands and owned by Japanese investors), the tribunal also refused to read extra requirements into the BIT.

> *"To depart from that conclusion requires clear language in the Treaty, but there is none [...] The parties having agreed that any legal person constituted under their laws is entitled to invoke the protection of the Treaty, and having agreed so without reference to any question of their relationship to some other third state corporation, it is beyond the powers of the Tribunal to import into the definition of 'investor' some requirement relating to such a relationship*

---

[34] *ADC Affiliate Limited & ADMC Management Limited v. Republic of Hungary*, ICSID Case No ARB/03/16, Award of 2 October 2006.

[35] In Canada, the ICSID Convention entered into force on 1 December 2013. *See* https://icsid.worldbank.org/en/Pages/about/Database-of-Member-States.aspx.

[36] Para 357.

[37] Para 359.

[38] *Saluka Investments BV v. Czech Republic*, UNCITRAL, Partial Award of 17 March 2006.

> *having the effect of excluding from the Treaty's protection a company which the language agreed by the parties included within it."*[39]

> *"The predominant factor which must guide the Tribunal's exercise of its functions is the terms in which the parties to the Treaty now in question have agreed to establish the Tribunal's jurisdiction. In the present context, that means the terms in which they have agreed upon who is an investor who may become a claimant entitled to invoke the Treaty's arbitration procedures. The parties had complete freedom of choice in this matter, and they chose to limit entitled 'investors' to those satisfying the definition set out in Art. 1 of the Treaty. The Tribunal cannot in effect impose upon the parties a definition of 'investor' other than that which they themselves agreed."*[40]

Most importantly, the tribunal noted that the host state has been fully aware that the claimants were "special-purpose vehicles set up for the specific and sole purpose of holding those shares."[41]

The same conclusion was reached in *Yukos v. Russia*, where the claimant, Yukos Universal Limited, a company incorporated in the UK (Isle of Man), was claimed to be controlled by Russian nationals. The arbitral tribunal held that as the claimant was "a company organized in accordance with the laws of the Isle of Man, qualifies as an Investor for the purposes of" the Energy Charter Treaty.[42]

> *"The Tribunal knows of no general principles of international law that would require investigating how a company or another organization operates when the applicable treaty simply requires it to be organized in accordance with the laws of a Contracting Party. The principles of international law, which have an unquestionable importance in treaty interpretation, do not allow an arbitral tribunal to write new, additional requirements – which the drafters did not include – into a treaty, no matter how auspicious or appropriate they may appear."*[43]

In *Niko Resources v. Bangladesh and others,*[44] the arbitral tribunal came to the same conclusion as to the subsidiary (allegedly shell-company) of a Canadian oil and gas exploration company in Barbados.[45]

---

[39] Para 229.

[40] Para 241.

[41] Para 242.

[42] Para 417.

[43] Para 415.

[44] *Niko Resources (Bangladesh) Ltd v. People's Republic of Bangladesh, Bangladesh Petroleum Exploration & Production Company Limited ("Bapex") and Bangladesh Oil Gas and Mineral Corporation ("Petrobangla")*, ICSID Case No ARB/10/11 and 10/18, Decision on Jurisdiction 19 August 2013.

[45] Paras 174–208.

> *"The Respondents have not presented any authorities to support their view that a requirement of a "real connection", assuming it were applicable in diplomatic protection or in treaty claims, should apply to contract claims as in the present case. In the Tribunal's view such an additional requirement cannot be read into the text of the Convention; nor can the travaux préparatoires for the Convention justify the assumption that this had been intended. It is sufficient for a claimant to show that it has the nationality of another Contracting State by reference to one of the generally accepted criteria, in particular incorporation or seat."*[46]

The very same line of interpretation has been taken as to "round-tripping", when domestic investors establish a shell company in a foreign country so as to be protected by the BIT between their home country and the shell company's country of incorporation.

In *Tokios Tokelés v. Ukraine,*[47] the claimant was a Lithuanian company, 99% of its shares were owned by Ukrainian nationals who, allegedly, wanted to make use of the Ukraine-Lithuania BIT. Although with the dissenting opinion of one of the arbitrators, the tribunal found no reason not to apply the Ukraine-Lithuania BIT.

A similar approach was taken by the arbitral tribunal in *Rompetrol v. Romania,*[48] where a Dutch company owned and controlled by Romanian nationals relied on the Netherlands-Romania BIT.

In *Alpha Projektholding v. Ukraine,*[49] quoting *Tokios Tokelés v. Ukraine*, the arbitral tribunal pointed out that it is the respondent who bears the burden of proof that the consent to arbitration, expressed in the BIT, was "clearly [...] not intended" for the purpose of encompassing an entity such as the claimant.[50]

In *KT Asia v. Kazakhstan,*[51] the tribunal also confirmed that where a BIT extends the scope of protection to entities incorporated in the other contracting party, the tribunal cannot read more demanding requirements, such as real connection or *siège social*, into the BIT, neither can it read a denial of benefits clause into the BIT.

> *"Accordingly, simply reading this provision, a legal entity incorporated in a Contracting State is deemed a national of that state. Faced with this definition, the Respondent argues that the principle of real and effective nationality sets requirements that go beyond this definition. The Tribunal cannot follow this argument."*[52]

---

[46] Para 203.

[47] *Tokios Tokelés v. Ukraine*, ICSID Case No ARB/02/18, Decision on Jurisdiction, 29 April 2004.

[48] *Rompetrol Group NV v. Republic of Romania*, ICSID Case No ARB/06/3, Decision on Respondent's Preliminary Objections on Jurisdiction and Admissibility, 18 April 2008.

[49] *Alpha Projektholding GmbH v. Ukraine*, ICSID Case No ARB/07/16, Award, 8 November 2010.

[50] Para 345.

[51] *KT Asia Investment Group BV v. Republic of Kazakhstan*, ICSID Case No ARB/09/8, Award, 17 October 2013, paras 111-139.

[52] Para 114.

The very rare exception that goes against the above clear line of case-law is *Venoklim v. Venezuela*,[53] where the tribunal declined jurisdiction over a Dutch company's claim because the company was in fact controlled by Venezuelan individuals.

V. Conclusions

After acquiring new competences in the field of investment protection, the EU has started elaborating a scheme for the relations with third countries. This paper examined three aspects of the "Europeanization" process: the status and validity of old extra-EU BITs, the problems that may emerge as a result of the division of regulatory competences between the EU and Member States and the perspectives of treaty shopping.

Given the division of powers between the EU and the Member States, it would be essential to ensure that liabilities under investment protection law match legislative and regulatory competences. The emerging question of "defense of superior orders" may be relevant also in the context of extra-EU BITs: the growing regulatory competences of the EU may lead to situations where national measures mandated by the EU give rise to investment claims. Once the BITs shift to the EU level, the problem of matching liabilities with competences may also be raised the other way around, as it is may emerge that the EU, absent provisions to the contrary, could be held liable for the acts of the Member States. A cautionary tale is found in *Abitibi-Bowater*, where Canada paid C$130 million in compensation for expropriatory acts of Newfoundland and Labrador. While it was the provincial acts that gave rise to the investment claim, the investor launched proceedings against the federal government.[54]

[53] *Venoklim Holding BV v. Bolivarian Republic of Venezuela*, ICSID Case No ARB/12/22, Award, 3 April 2015.

[54] Sue Bailey, Williams Unrepentant as Taxpayers on Hook for NAFTA Deal with Abitibi, Globe & Mail Report on Business (published on 25 August 2010, updated on 2 May 2018), available at https://www.theglobeandmail.com/report-on-business/williams-unrepentant-as-taxpayers-on-hook-for-nafta-deal-with-abitibi/article1378194/.

Pavle Flere[*]

ARBITRABILITY OF COMPETITION LAW DISPUTES IN THE EUROPEAN UNION – BALANCING OF COMPETING INTERESTS

Abstract

This paper examines the issues caused by the entrance of competition law in arbitration and identifies any recent developments. It reports on what issues emerge when arbitrators tackle antitrust law, including the issue of arbitrability, the position of the arbitrator and the problems of recognition of the awards.

I. Introduction

Traditionally, concepts and regulations considered to be part of public policy considerations, such as antitrust, have remained outside of the reach of arbitration proceedings. Therefore, public policy considerations such as those related to antitrust have been deemed banned from arbitration proceedings. Despite that, antirust in the context of arbitration has not remained unexplored. However, the recent developments and trends in arbitration proceedings certainly deserve special scrutiny. The purpose of this contribution is to review the already settled issues caused by the entrance of antitrust into arbitration, as well as to identify any recent developments. The paper will report on what issues emerge when arbitrators tackle competition law. Consequently, the author will scrutinize the issue of arbitrability of antitrust issues. Moreover, the position of the arbitrator, when faced with an antitrust issue, will be further analysed. The problems of recognition of the awards, which touch upon competition law, deserve clarification in this context.

II. Arbitrability of EC Competition Issues

a) Declining Relevance of Public Policy

Traditionally, the concept of arbitrability was related to public policy and, consequently, disputes that somehow involved interpretation of public policy were considered banned from an arbitrator's jurisdiction. Traditionally, a dispute involving competition law would have been deemed inarbitrable. However, at present, it can be concluded that competition law disputes are indeed arbitrable and that arbitrators can establish

[*] LLB, LLM, Senior Legal Counsel, Triglav Group.

jurisdiction over disputes involving competition law matters.[1] However, it is not quite clear which competition law issues can be arbitrated and in which context. Not surprisingly, some competition law disputes are more suitable for arbitration than others. For instance, in the context of partners' disputes concerning the terms of long-term contracts of either a horizontal or a vertical nature, issues of pricing, exclusivity, territory or termination can be considered very much arbitrable. Similarly, in cases of transaction-by-transaction business practice, disputes over price discrimination, resale, tie-ins, resale or use restrictions, refusal to deal or other monopoly abuses are also clearly arbitrable. However, in contractual disputes alleged anticompetitive behaviour by one party committed together with a third party is less suitable for arbitration since an arbitration agreement does not encompass third parties. By the same token, tortuous behaviour, for instance an anticompetitive take-over or predatory pricing, is less likely to be covered by an arbitration agreement.[2]

What has caused changes in the policy of the courts so that they allowed the entry of competition law into arbitration proceedings? The great success of arbitration in the 2nd half of the 20th century is the main reason for this development because it has become the preferred method of settling international commercial disputes. In comparison to classical judicial proceedings, the most important advantages of arbitration proceedings are usually related by the wish of the parties to secure a neutral forum, privacy, as well as simpler and more efficient conduct of proceedings[3] – arbitrators have, basically, won the trust of judges.

In conclusion, the concept of public policy in the context of arbitrability is gradually retreating. Courts have opened the gateway for arbitration of disputes involving public policy issues.[4] It should be emphasized that public policy is not even a workable test for determining what is arbitrable. There are three issues:

1) The notion of public policy is very vague and there are no guidelines how to interpret it.
2) The concept of public policy may also be interpreted narrowly, with the consequence that only certain issues are not arbitrable.
3) The notion of public policy may be construed broadly, meaning that all issues that would require the application of rules of public policy are not arbitrable.

Under an overly broad interpretation of "public policy", very few issues would remain arbitrable, because very few disputes involve only rules that cannot be construed as rules of public policy in some extent.[5] Very few commentators advocate such a broad

---

[1] This contribution deals only with 'objective arbitrability', which encompasses restrictions connected to sensitive public policy issues where it is felt that they should only be dealt with by the judicial authority of the state courts. Furthermore, theory is also familiar with the notion of 'subjective arbitrability' determining which entities may be parties to arbitration proceedings. For instance, in some jurisdictions, states and state owned entities may not be parties to arbitration agreements. *See* Julian D. M. Lew et al., Comparative International Commercial Arbitration 188 (2003).

[2] Jan H. Dalhuisen, *The Arbitrability of Competition Issues*, 11 Arbitration International 151, 158 (1995).

[3] Antonie Kirry, *Arbitrability: Current Trends in Europe*, 12 Arbitration International 373 373 (1996).

[4] Mathias Lehmann, *A Plea for a Transnational Approach to Arbitrability in Arbitral Practice*, 42 Columbia Journal of Transnational Law 751, 766 (2004).

[5] Antonie Kirry, *Arbitrability: Current Trends in Europe*, 12 Arbitration International 374 (1996).

interpretation of public policy today. However, these trends do not mean that public policy has entirely vanished from the concept of arbitrability. Issues that are non-arbitrable *per se* are indeed based on the legislator's scepticism stemming from public policy considerations. Yet, the concept of public policy may not constitute a clear-cut rule for the demarcation of arbitrable from nonarbitrable issues. Thus, it is the author's opinion that legislative concerns based on public policy would be much better protected if introduced through the exclusive jurisdiction of the Courts. For those reasons, in almost all European jurisdictions the practice has tried to "soften" the legislative framework, which was historically influenced by the legislators' desire to control arbitration proceedings.[6] EC competition cases show how the legal practice "separated" the notion of arbitrability into strictly nonarbitrable cases (nonarbitrability *per se*), owing to public policy reasons, and fully arbitrable cases. Thus, the practical effect of the introduction of antitrust disputes before arbitral tribunals is that Member State (hereinafter MS) control has basically disappeared at least in the context of arbitrating EC competition law for, as will be shown later, states can only invoke their limited powers when it comes to enforcing or setting aside of awards before the MS Courts.

b) The Rise of Lex Mercatoria and the Retreat of Conflict of Laws Analysis

Initially one of the main controversies surrounding arbitrability dealt with determining the law governing arbitrability. Whereas this issue was only of minor importance when dealt with by the Courts, determination by the arbitrators of the applicable law for arbitrability was a much more difficult task.[7] Due to the fact that arbitrator powers stem from the arbitration agreement, it is traditionally deemed that the law governing the arbitration agreement is also the applicable law regarding arbitrability. However, not always do the parties determine the law applicable to their arbitration agreement. Consequently, the arbitrators ultimately designate the applicable law – this is where the problem arises.

For the above reasons, it is not much of a surprise that both the New York Convention of 1958[8] and the UNCITRAL Model law[9] basically incorporate the conflict of laws provisions when dealing with arbitrability and exclude any reference to the definition of arbitrability.

---

6 Vera Korzun, *Arbitrating Antitrust Claims: From Suspicion to Trust*, 48 New York University Journal of International Law and Politics 867, 891–897 (2015).

7 For the choice of law rule regarding arbitrability, the New York Convention offers a clear cut rule only in the post-award stage, i.e. when the award is the subject of recognition and enforcement by the Court. Not surprisingly it adopted a *lex fori* approach. However, arbitrability may be reviewed in at least two other situations in the pre-award stage: 1. before arbitrators themselves when trying to decide the scope of their competence, and 2. before a national court in the dispute whether to enforce the arbitration agreement. *See* Tibor Varady et al., International Commercial Arbitration: A Transnational Perspective 209 (2nd ed. 2002).

8 United Nations Convention on the Recognition and Enforcement of Foreign Arbitral Awards, June 10, 1958, 330 U.N.T.S. 38 [hereinafter New York Convention], Article V(1)(a) and V(2)(a).

9 United Nations Commission on International Trade Law (UNCITRAL) Model Law on International Commercial Arbitration, U.N. Doc. A/RES/40/72 (Dec. 11, 1985) amended by G.A. Res 61/33, U.N Doc. A/RES/61/33 (Dec. 18, 2006), Article 34(2)(b)(ii).

Unfortunately, as will be shown, the aforementioned instruments do not provide the safety and forseeability that parties should be entitled to expect, as they only vaguely regulate this problem.[10] Karl-Heinz Böckstiegel rightly observed that"Agreement on the conclusion that there is disagreement seems to be the only common denominator that one can find between arbitrators, courts and publicists regarding the question, which is the applicable law on arbitrability."[11] In this context, at least 5 conflict of law rules determining applicable law can be identified:

1) the law of the forum (*lex fori*)
2) the law chosen by the parties to govern the arbitration clause (*lex electionis*) or the contract (*lex contractus*)
3) the law of the seat of the arbitral tribunal (*lex arbitrii*)
4) the place of enforcement of the award (*lex executionis*).[12]

Unlike courts, arbitration tribunals do not have anything like national law at their disposal.[13] Whereas the courts designate the applicable law stemming from national conflict of laws rules, arbitration tribunals may apply the rules they deem appropriate.[14] It seems that arbitrators enjoy complete freedom in choosing the applicable law since choice of law rules are construed in such a way as to allow them liberty.[15] Usually arbitrators face this task by determining which law the arbitration agreement is most closely connected to irrespective of any conflict of laws rules, including those of its seat. In this context, at least 3 viable solutions have emerged:

1) the law governing the contract incorporating arbitration agreement
2) the law of the arbitration seat
3) the law of the place where the arbitration agreement is to be enforced.[16]

If one of the parties challenges arbitrability of the dispute before an arbitration tribunal, arbitrators most frequently invoke *lex situs* as the governing conflict of law rule in order to determine the applicable law for the issue before them. However, there are some difficulties with this solution. The seat of the arbitration tribunal is usually incidental

---

[10] Julian D. M. Lew et al., Comparative International Commercial Arbitration 189 (2003).

[11] Karl-Heinz Böckstiegel, *Public Policy and Arbitrability*, 3 ICC New York Arbitration Congress 178, 184 (1986).

[12] Homayoon Arfazadeh, *Arbitrability under New York Convention: the Lex Fori Revisited*, 17 Arbitration International 73, 73 (2001).

[13] Mathias Lehmann, *A Plea for a Transnational Approach to Arbitrability in Arbitral Practice*, 42 Columbia Journal of Transnational Law 757 (2004).

[14] International Chamber of Commerce (ICC) Arbitration Rules, effective from 1 March 2017 [hereinafter ICC Rules] Article 21 (1): "The parties shall be free to agree upon the rules of law to be applied by the arbitral tribunal to the merits of the dispute. In the absence of any such agreement, the arbitral tribunal shall apply the rules of law which it determines to be appropriate." Similarly, G.A. Res 40/72, United Nations Commission on International Trade Law (UNCITRAL) Model Law on International Commercial Arbitration, U.N. Doc. A/RES/40/72 (Dec. 11, 1985) *amended by* G.A. Res 61/33, U.N Doc. A/RES/61/33 (Dec. 18, 2006) (hereinafter UNCITRAL Model law) Article 28(2): " Failing any designation by the parties, the arbitral tribunal shall apply the law determined by the conflict of laws rules which it considers applicable."

[15] Natalya Shelkopyas, The Application of EC Law in Arbitration Proceedings 267 (2003).

[16] Antonie Kirry, *Arbitrability: Current Trends in Europe*, 12 Arbitration International 379 (1996).

to the dispute and has no connection with the subject matter of the dispute. In fact, choice of the place of arbitration proceedings is often a matter of pure convenience or is chosen on the basis of alleged neutrality and is not a place of business of either of the parties. Furthermore, the seat may be changed during the proceedings, and, the tribunal may not have any physical seat as the correspondence may be carried out by modern means of communication. Therefore, seat as the determining factor for this issue is an unfortunate solution.

The choice of law where the arbitral award is most probably to be enforced is even more controversial from both practical and theoretical aspects. This approach is based on the presumption that arbitrators are supposed to grant an award that is enforceable and useful to the (winning) party. In fact, this theory has received so much attention and even approval so that ICC Rules have expressly adopted it.[17] Nevertheless, there are many arguments countering this controversial solution. There may be many possible countries of enforcement of the award, depending on where the losing party has its assets. Therefore, arbitrators could be put in the position of choosing where the award will most probably be enforced. However, this is a difficult, if not an impossible task. Even more striking is that the tribunal would be put in the position of determining the losing party at the very beginning of proceedings, since the question of arbitrability is usually decided at the outset of the proceedings.[18] In this situation the arbitrators would be forced to go into the merits of the case in order to establish their jurisdiction. However, in seeking to avoid this position, arbitrators would at least be put in the awkward position of guessing the losing party. Finally, this approach does not allow the party that entered into the arbitration agreement to object to the jurisdiction, by relying on the fact that an arbitral award is not enforceable.[19]

It seems that there is a strong tendency in arbitration practice that, in cases when the parties have chosen the law applicable to the main contract, to apply that law for the arbitration agreement and consequently for the issue of arbitrability, unless, of course, the parties have agreed otherwise.[20] However, most probably this approach is not in conformity with the principle of separability recognizing an arbitration agreement as a separate contract, being independent and different from the main one. In fact, the validity and termination of the main contract do not necessarily affect the validity of the arbitration agreement and therefore do not affect the jurisdiction of the arbitral tribunal. Consequently, it is not clear why the same law should be applied automatically to the arbitration agreement and arbitrability. Furthermore, attaching the law applicable to the arbitration agreement to the governing law of the main contract does not take into account the special nature of the arbitration agreement, which is, in effect, of a

---

[17] Article 43 ICC Rules (In all matters not expressly provided for in the Rules, the Court and the arbitral tribunal shall act in the spirit of the Rules and shall make every effort to make sure that the award is enforceable at law.).

[18] John Murray, *in* Legal Reasoning and Judicial Interpretation of European Law: Essays in Honour of Lord Mackenzie-Stuart 109 (Angus I. L. Campbell & Meropi Voyatzi eds., 1996).

[19] Mathias Lehmann, *A Plea for a Transnational Approach to Arbitrability in Arbitral Practice*, 42 Columbia Journal of Transnational Law 757 (2004).

[20] Julian D. M. Lew et al., Comparative International Commercial Arbitration 107 (2003).

procedural nature only, excluding the general jurisdiction of the courts that would otherwise have jurisdiction to decide the case. Therefore, an arbitration agreement has no common denominators with definition of substantive rights and obligations, which are included in the main contract.[21]

In conclusion, it seems that there is a remarkable trend, which is most clearly noticeable in the sphere of antitrust in international commercial arbitration, that arbitrators, when tackling the arbitrability of antitrust, have abolished conflict of law analysis. Thus, arbitrators have started referring to case law and doctrine from jurisdictions that had no connection with the subject matter of the dispute. For instance, in ICC Case No. 8423[22], two Portuguese and one French company were involved in a dispute in Belgium over the validity of a contract clause restricting competition between them. In determining that the dispute was arbitrable, the arbitrators referred to French case law and the famous *Mitsubishi*[23] case. In fact, applying conflict of laws analysis would not have led to either French or American law whatsoever. Nor is it farfetched to say that these states had no interest in "extraterritorial application" of their laws in this particular case. The answer lies rather in the fact that arbitrability of antitrust has become so widespread that it has become a part of the *lex mercatoria*.[24] Therefore, it may be freely confirmed "...that the principle of arbitrability of disputes relating to competition law should be regarded as a transnational principle, which is directly applicable, without any confrontation with a national law."[25] These trends are not necessarily restricted only to controversies involving antitrust as the list of arbitrable issues has greatly expanded to include other disputes that are influenced by public policy considerations e.g., securities. Thus, the relationship between antitrust and arbitration can be subsumed within the scope of interplay of mandatory rules and arbitration.[26] However, competition law has had the most important and decisive influence on this definitely unique development.

III. The Duty of Ex Officio Application of EC Competition Law by Arbitrators

Probably the most serious concern, at least from the arbitrators' point of view, is whether they should raise the issue of violation of EC competition law on their own motion, i.e. *ex officio*, or whether they should leave the issue to be raised by the parties exclusively.[27]

21 Antonie Kirry, *Arbitrability: Current Trends in Europe*, 12 Arbitration International 380 (1996).

22 Award in ICC case 8423 (1994), XXVI Yearbook Comm. Arb'n 153 (2001). Similarly ICC Case No. 4604 (1984), reprinted in 111 J. Du Droit Int'l 973 (1985).

23 *Mitsubishi Motors Corp. v. Soler Chrysler – Plymouth, Inc.*, 473 U.S. 614, 617–23 (1985).

24 Mathias Lehmann, *A Plea for a Transnational Approach to Arbitrability in Arbitral Practice*, 42 Columbia Journal of International Law 761 (2004).

25 Herman Verbist, *The Application of European Community Law in ICC Arbitrations – Presentation of Arbitral Awards*, ICC Int'l Ct. of Arb. Bull., Spec. Supp., International Commercial Arbitration in Europe 35 (1994).

26 Luca G. Radicati di Brozolo, *Antitrust: A Paradigm of the Relations Between Mandatory Rules and Arbitration – A Fresh Look at the "Second Look"*, 7 International Arbitration Law Review 23, 23 (2004).

27 T. Diederik de Groot, *The Impact of the Benetton Decision on International Commercial Arbitration*, 20 Journal of International Arbitration 372, 372 (2003).

If they chose to stay within the ambit of the suit and ignore EC competition law, they bear the risk of a challenge to the award on the grounds of violation of public policy. However, if they choose to broaden the scope of the dispute and scrutinize the issues for violation of EC competition law, they may bear the risk of exceeding their mandate, bearing the consequences under art. V (1)(c) New York Convention.[28]

The ECJ has already dealt with the question of *ex officio* application of competition law by the MS Courts.[29] However, there is no obvious reason why those tests should be applied by analogy to the arbitration proceedings as well. The answer to the dilemma of *ex officio* application should be sought within the rules and principles governing international commercial arbitration. The fact that the jurisdiction of the arbitral tribunal is embedded in the arbitration clause, depending on the free will of the contractual parties, requires that the principle of freedom of disposition and the principle of judicial passivity be even more emphasized than in traditional civil proceedings before the MS Court. The two connected and interrelated principles ensure that the facts of the dispute will be proved and rebutted exclusively by the parties, whereas the interpretation of law is within the ambit of the arbitral tribunal. Therefore, the arbitrators cannot rule on an issue that was not submitted to them (*ultra petita*), nor may they choose to ignore an issue that was submitted to them (*infra petita*).[30] However, these two principles should not be understood in the absolute sense as meaning that arbitrators have absolutely no other powers than those conferred by the parties. In fact, they do have powers that are implied in the duty to produce an award that is final and enforceable.[31] It seems that the arbitrators tried to do exactly this in the case of ICC No. 7181 (1992), when the party alleged that one of the contractual provisions was not in conformity with Community competition rules. After declaring that the contractual provision did not violate competition rules, arbitrators scrutinized on their own initiative other contractual provision from the disputed contract and stated that "In view of the public policy character of Article 85 (now Art. 101), the Arbitral Tribunal does however have to examine ex officio whether 1.6 of the agreement is not caught by the provision of restrictive agreement."[32]

---

[28] Article V(1)(c) New York Convention: (Recognition and enforcement of the award may be refused .... [if] The award deals with a difference not contemplated by or not falling within the terms of the submission to arbitration, or it contains decisions on matters beyond the scope of the submission to arbitration, provided that, if the decisions on matters submitted to arbitration can be separated from those not so submitted, that part of the award which contains decisions on matters submitted to arbitration may be recognized and enforced.).

[29] Joined Cases C-430-431/93 *Jeroen van Schijndel v Sticting Pensionfonds voor Fysiotherapeuten* 1995 E.C.R. I-4705; Case C-312/93 *Peterbroeck Van Campenhout Cie ScS v Belgium* 1995 E.C.T.-4599. In *van Schijndel*, the ECJ declared that the MS Tribunals have a duty to apply EC competition law, even when the parties have not relied on it. But this rule is limited by domestic rules. Therefore, if domestic rules would require in a case that the judges abandon their passive role and go beyond the ambit of the dispute, Community law and especially the direct effect of Community law, does not require a national court to raise the issue ex officio. In *Peterbroeck*, the ECJ set aside a MS provision on time limitation, which made the exercise of Community law impossible or excessively difficult.

[30] Natalya Shelkopyas, The Application of EC Law In Arbitration Proceedings 267, 278 (2003).

[31] Assimakis P. Komninos, *Presentation of Case C -126, Eco Swiss China Time Ltd. v. Benetton International NV, Judgment of 1 June 1999, Full Court*, 37 Common Market Law Review 459, 475 (2000).

[32] ICC Case 7181 (1992), reprinted in XXI Yearbook Comm. Arb. 99 (1996).

Accordingly, hard-core violations of Community competition rules may be dealt with *ex officio*, and those contracts may consequently be declared illegal, void or voidable, depending on the applicable *lex contractus*. Otherwise, the tribunal would be put in the awkward position of rendering an award knowing that it is likely to be set aside or unenforceable. However, the arbitrators duty to deal *ex officio* with those issues should be conditional on two qualifications, both of which were recognized by Advocate General Saggio in his opinion in *Eco Swiss* by stating that Community law does not require arbitrators to raise on their own initiative questions of Community competition law, "if consideration of those questions would oblige them to abandon the passive role assigned to them, going beyond the ambit of the dispute defined by the parties and relying on facts and circumstances other than those on which the party with an interest in application of those provisions relied in order to substantiate his claim."[33]

Ex officio scrutiny should be conducted according to the facts submitted by the parties without making further investigations. The arbitrators must not exceed the powers conferred by the parties.[34] Thus, arbitrators can apply *ex officio* EC competition law, should the two above mentioned conditions be met. Hypothetically, if the parties explicitly agree that arbitrators shall not deal with the competition law aspects of the dispute, then arbitrators cannot rule on competition law matters. In the case that the contract is manifestly violating competition law, the only possible escape for the arbitrators is to decline the jurisdiction. It should be emphasized that, although the arbitral tribunal has a "duty" to render an enforceable award, there is no sanction when it renders an unenforceable award, except, of course, a moral one.

In conclusion, even though there is no doubt that *ex officio* application of antitrust raises different theoretical as well as practical considerations and elaborations, we hereby conclude that arbitrators have the implied duty to apply EC competition law.[35] Perhaps, this approach contravenes the "sacred" principle of party autonomy in international commercial arbitration.[36] However, the increased volume of arbitrable issues compels increased responsibility from arbitrators, who must have additional tools, e.g. the duty of *ex officio* application of EC competition law, in order to meet the expectations of an ever more globalized international economy.

IV. EcoSwiss and Balancing of Competing Interests

Public policy in the context of setting aside and enforcement proceedings is one of the most controversial in international commercial arbitration. It is a well settled issue that public policy has formal, procedural side as well as substantive or material aspect. Whereas

[33] Opinion of Advocate General Saggio in Case C-126/97, *Eco Swiss China Time Ltd v. Benetton Int'l*, 1999 E.C.R. I-3057, para 26.

[34] Renato Nazzini, Concurrent Proceedings In Competition Law, Procedure, Evidence and Remedies, 343 (2004).

[35] Yves Derains, *in* European Competition Law Annual 2001 18 (C.D. Ehlermann & I. Atanasiu ed., Hart Publishing, Oxford/Portland Oregon, 2003).

[36] Gordon Blanke, *The Role of EC Competition Law in International Arbitration: A Plaidoyer*, 16 European Business Law Review 169, 176 (2005).

the former encompasses issues of the most fundamental principles of civil procedure, such as notions of a fair hearing for both sides, equality of the parties before the tribunal etc., it is the latter which is relevant in the context of this paper.[37] Substantive public policy includes fundamental principles of law, actions not in conformity with the good faith principle and national interests/foreign relations etc.[38] However, this classification may not be universally accepted for it depends on the time, case, circumstances, country etc. Moreover, public policy is not something static but very dynamic, as it is prone to changes. The Courts have a duty to apply it *ex officio*.[39] The author emphasizes that only truly international public policy serves as grounds for refusal of recognition. Purely local public policy of a recognizing MS does not fall within this scope.

In this context it is unavoidable to analyse *Eco Swiss*[40], which thus far has been the most important European judgment in this field. Its factual background is rather complex. In 1986, Eco Swiss, Bulova and Benetton entered into a trade license agreement for 8 years. However, in 1991 Benetton gave notice of termination to Eco Swiss and Bulova. Eco Swiss and Bulova consequently commenced arbitration proceedings pursuant to the arbitration clause under the licence agreement. In 1993, an arbitral tribunal issued a partial arbitral award in favour of the two claimants, declaring the license agreement to be in full effect among the three parties. Eventually, Benetton started proceedings to set aside both awards, among other causes, alleging that the awards violated Art. 81 (now 101) EC Treaty. The proceedings finally reached the Dutch Supreme Court, which decided to refer the matter to the ECJ, which was asked five questions, two of which were especially important:

1) whether Art. 81 (now 101) EC Treaty should be included in the concept of public policy, the violation of which was grounds for refusing enforcement or setting aside the arbitral award under national law,
2) whether the principle of *res judicata* could preclude scrutiny of the arbitral award on grounds of public policy, including a possible violation of EC competition law.

The ECJ, faced with complex issues, answered the first question in a very straightforward way, while stressing its famous cases, in particular *Nordsee*,[41] that Art. 81 (now 101) EC Treaty "constitutes a fundamental provision which is essential for the accomplishment of the tasks entrusted to the Community and, in particular, for the functioning of the internal market". Furthermore, the judges stressed that EC competition law may be considered public policy for the purposes of Art. V of the New York Convention, even when, disregarding EC competition law in the domestic case

[37] T. Diederik de Groot, *The Impact of the Benetton Decision on International Commercial Arbitration*, 20 Journal of International Arbitration 372, 723(2003).

[38] Julian D.M. Lew et al., Comparative International Commercial Arbitration 723(2003).

[39] Tomaž Keresteš, *Pridržek javnega reda pri priznavanju tujih arbitražnih odločb po newyorški konvenciji, in* Podjetje In Delo [Company & Labour], 1636 (1999) (Slov).

[40] Case C-126/97, *Eco Swiss China Time Ltd v. Benetton Int'l*, 1999 E.C.R. I-3055. For more commentary on the case, *see* Assimakis P. Komninos, *Presentation of Case C-126, Eco Swiss China Time Ltd. v. Benetton International NV, Judgment of 1 June 1999, Full Court*, 37 Common Market Law Review 459 (2000).

[41] Case 102/81 *Nordsee v. Reederei Mond*, 1982 E.C.R. 1095.

would not be grounds for setting aside the award.[42] The answer to the first question does not seem to be very pro-arbitration while the answer to the second one seems to be, at least at first glance, very forward thinking. Thus, the ECJ answered that application of EC law does not require that the national court refrain from application of its national rules of procedure including rules of *res judicata*.

It is still not quite clear what the real impact of the Eco Swiss judgment is as it is difficult to extract meaningful guidelines.[43] The fact that disregarding EC competition law may be considered a violation of public policy for the purpose of setting aside or enforcement proceedings was foreseeable and in some countries, e.g., Germany and Austria,[44] it was well known even before *Eco Swiss*.[45] The nature of international commercial arbitration, which was well recognized in *Nordsee*,[46] in which the ECJ ruled that arbitration tribunals do not have the right to make reference to the ECJ, increases the possibility for divergent application of competition law. The ECJ allegedly recognized this problem by emphasizing that the parties may not be free to contract out the application of EC competition law by referral to arbitration.[47] Since the issue of arbitrability of EC competition issues is nowadays rather moot, it may be inferred that the ungrateful duty of ensuring uniform application of EC competition law was vested in the courts of the MS through the annulment and recognition and enforcement proceedings.

One of the main issues is the dilemma of the "depth" of review of the recognising court.[48] Should it review the facts/merits of the case, application of the law, and choice of law rules, or perhaps only the effects of the possible adoption of the foreign arbitration award? It seems that the ECJ in *Eco Swiss*[49] was suggesting the adoption of the well known "second look doctrine", which may be described as the trade-off between the arbitrability of competition law disputes and ex-post control reserved to the courts.[50] The doctrine is a consequence of the more expanded scope of arbitrability. On the one hand, the courts have allowed certain disputes that involve public policy issues to be decided by other institutions than themselves yet, on the other hand, the reviews of those awards should be somehow more stringent than the tests otherwise applicable.

---

[42] Even though the ECJ did not explicitly mention the distiniction between international and domestic public policy, the distinction has been very much debated in scholarly writings and less in practice. However, this judgement is a great example of how this distinction can be of practical importance.

[43] Shriya Maini, *Arbitration of Anti-Trust Claims in the United States and Europe: a Comparative Analysis*, Young ICCA Blog (13 April 2015), http://www.youngicca-blog.com/arbitration-of-anti-trust-claims-in-the-united-states-and-europe-a-comparative-analysis/, accessed on 8 June 2018.

[44] *Kajo-Erzeugnisse Essenzen GmbH v. DO Zdravilisce Radenska*, Oberster Gerichtshof, 20 October 1993 and 23 February 1998, 24 Y.B. Comm. Arb. 919, 919 (1999) (Austria).

[45] Tomaž Keresteš, *Pridržek javnega reda pri priznavanju tujih arbitražnih odločb po newyorški konvenciji, in* Podjetje in Delo [Company & Labour], 1641 (1999) (Slov).

[46] *Case 102/81, Nordsee v. Reederei Mond*, 1982 E.C.R. 1095.

[47] *Case 102/81, Nordsee v. Reederei Mond*, 1982 E.C.R. 1095. paras 14 and 15.

[48] Shriya Maini, *Arbitration of Anti-Trust Claims in the United States and Europe: a Comparative Analysis*, Young ICCA Blog (13 April 2015), para 6, http://www.youngicca-blog.com/arbitration-of-anti-trust-claims-in-the-united-states-and-europe-a-comparative-analysis/, accessed on 8 June 2018.

[49] Case C-126/97, *Eco Swiss China Time Ltd v. Benetton Int'l*, 1999 E.C.R. I-3055.

[50] Renato Nazzini, Concurrent Proceedings in Competition Law, Procedure, Evidence and Remedies, 328 (2004).

The relationship between the arbitrability of EC competition disputes and public policy (*ordre public*) hereby becomes salient. While it is true that the New York Convention refers to arbitrability and public policy as two different grounds for refusal of recognition of the arbitral awards, they are, nevertheless, very much interrelated. The latter is being squeezed, since the influence of public policy upon arbitrability is diminishing (and, consequently, the number of arbitrable issues is growing), while public policy for the purpose of setting aside and recognition of award is being extended.[51] A similar conclusion was reached by Komninos when he stated that "[public policy]... has been called an "appeal through the back door", but its mere existence and its deterrent effect allow at the same time, a more liberal approach in other matters, for example in the question of arbitrability."[52] However, the introduction of the "second look" doctrine does not, in effect, pave the way for a review of the merits of an arbitral award. Such an interpretation of the "second look" doctrine would represent a step back for international commercial arbitration. An analysis of the case law of the "home country" of the second look doctrine – the United States – shows that these kinds of concerns are far from being legitimate.[53] Ultimately control by the courts will be limited, even when antitrust is at stake.

1) If the arbitrators' award is convincing, there may never be *ex post* control by the Court, but the parties will voluntarily comply with the award.
2) Even if the enforcing Court somehow chooses to review the award on the merits, a well-reasoned award may significantly influence the decision of the judges.
3) International commercial arbitration awards that were set aside or enforcement refused in one country may, after all, be enforced in some third jurisdiction.[54]

The "second look" doctrine should not depart from the well known tests and standards of public policy applicable by Article V New York Convention. Here the emerging dilemma is how to strike the right balance among competing policies. The first priority is to assure uniform and correct application of EC competition law rules. The second policy is to safeguard arbitration as an efficient, private and self-sufficient system, at least, in comparison to the courts. The latter policy certainly requires that any review of merits

---

[51] However, there are opposing views on the relation between arbitrability and public policy. Thus, according to Robert von Mehren, "Simply because the jurisdiction of arbitrators has been expanded to antitrust does not create a new class of arbitration cases to which courts should apply a higher standard for recognition and enforcement under the New York Convention than is applied in cases in which no antitrust issue is decided." *See* R. von Mehren, *Some Reflections on International Arbitration of Antitrust Law and Policy, in* International Antitrust Law and Policy 413 (1995). Even though this statement may be manifestly correct from the doctrinal point of view, it seems that pragmatism compels the former conclusion. *See* Assimakis P. Komninos, *Arbitration and the Modernisation of European Competition Law Enforcement*, 24 World Competition 211, 237 (2001).

[52] Assimakis P. Komninos, *Presentation of Case C-126, Eco Swiss China Time Ltd. v. Benetton International NV, Judgment of 1 June 1999, Full Court*, 37 Common Market Law Review 234 (2000).

[53] Partick M. Baron & Stefan Liniger, *A Second Look at Arbitrability, Approaches to Arbitration in the United States, Switzerland and Germany*, 19 Arbitration International 27, 50 (2003).

[54] John J. Barcelo III, *Who Decides the Arbitrators' Jurisdiction? Separability and Competence-Competence in Transnational Perspective*, Vanderbilt Journal of Transnational Law 1115, 1123 (2003).

should be excluded from the setting aside and recognition or enforcement proceedings. Interestingly, it can be inferred from *Eco Swiss* that:

1) The ECJ nowhere suggests that review of awards on grounds of public policy should involve a reopening of the case or a review on the merits.
2) The procedural bar to scrutiny is in conformity with Community law as long as those procedural rules do not "render excessively difficult or virtually impossible" the application of the rights conferred by Community law.[55]

Therefore, the ECJ suggested that there may exist rules expressing certain values that can prevail over the values enshrined in EC competition law. The ECJ was most probably implying that the MS Courts should be enabled to conduct such analyses as to allow them to take cognizance of any dispute or (non)application of the law that leads or might lead to conflicts with public policy embedded in EC competition law.[56] In fact, this is nothing but the introduction of the "second look" doctrine into European jurisprudence.

Naturally, the recognizing courts have a duty to conduct public policy review *ex officio*, even if none of the parties have invoked the reservation of public policy. Similarly, it is a well known fact that judges should not go into the merits but should only conduct the tests if the inclusion of the arbitral award within a certain jurisdiction would produce effects that may harm objectives protected by public policy. This approach may be appealing in theory, but how does it work in practice? The exclusion of a review of merits certainly does not mean that the judges' scrutiny is limited only to the dispositive part of the arbitral award[57] – the reviewing judge of the MS Court should be satisfied that the arbitrators have duly taken into account issues arising out of EC competition law. A preliminary question before the court should be whether there exists a sufficiently clear connection between the disputed transaction and EC or MS competition law rules. If this is true then MS courts should be satisfied that arbitrators have applied or have at least taken into consideration the relevant antitrust rules or have provided a sufficiently persuasive explanation for not applying them. An exceptional review of merits could be accepted only after establishing that the arbitrators have failed to give due regard to antitrust in the abovementioned manner, where the applicability of antitrust rules could not have been in any way ignored e.g., manifest and hard core violations of EC competition law, i.e. price fixing, market sharing etc.[58] It is the author's opinion that the approach outlined above satisfies the criteria for balancing of conflicting interests.

---

[55] Case C-126/97 *Eco Swiss China Time Ltd v. Benetton Int'l*, 1999 E.C.R. I-3055, para 45.

[56] Renato Nazzini, Concurrent Proceedings in Competition Law, Procedure, Evidence and Remedies 333 (2004).

[57] Natalya Shelkopyas, The Application of EC Law In Arbitration Proceedings 381 (2003).

[58] Luca G. Radicati di Brozolo, *Antitrust: A Paradigm of the Relations Between Mandatory Rules and Arbitration – A Fresh Look at the "Second Look"*, 7 International Arbitration Law Review 29 (2004).

V. Conclusion

In conclusion, the concept of arbitrability in the context of antitrust has evolved from a mainly domestically governed concept, which was greatly influenced by conflict of laws rules and public policy consideration, to a concept governed by substantive law. Moreover, the arbitrability of EC competition cases has become so widespread that it has become part of *lex mercatoria*. However, the role of public policy in the context of arbitrability has not disappeared, but has rather been transformed. The position of arbitrators in tackling potential violations of antitrust rules is rather peculiar, since they have virtually an implied duty to apply EC competition law to their own motion, despite the fact that they are not state authorities nor are obliged to protect fair competition.[59] Applicability of EC competition law by arbitrators is mainly governed by the fact that they need to produce enforceable arbitral awards. Furthermore, it can be concluded that arbitration institutions and practitioners have become *de facto* governments and courts of international trade, whereas the states themselves have very limited control of the process, except when they are involved in the stage of recognition and enforcement.

[59] Thomas E. Carbonneau & Francois Janson, *Cartesian Logic and Frontier Politics: French and American Concepts of Arbitrability*, 2 Tulane Journal of International and Comparative Law L 93, 222 (1994).

Enforcement and recovery

Yue Ma[*]

EXECUTION OF ICSID AWARDS AND SOVEREIGN IMMUNITY

Abstract

The execution of ICSID awards is a weak point of the post-award stage of ICSID arbitration. The ICSID Convention provides no protection to facilitate the execution of ICSID awards but leaves it under the control of domestic laws. An ICSID award may be rejected execution due to the host state's sovereign immunity defense. This article examines the rationale of the ICSID execution mechanism and evaluates how difficult it is to execute ICSID awards in practice under the recent backlash against investment arbitration. Based on analyses of the Convention text, the drafting history and the changed circumstances in today's global market, incompatibility between the ICSID execution mechanism and current reality is detected. This implies that there will be increasing challenges with the execution of ICSID awards than expected by the initial drafters. The Chapter further examines the legal systems and the case laws of selected jurisdictions, which shows that, not mentioning the recalcitrant host states, even in the pro-arbitration states, investors seeking to execute ICSID awards will face a number of obstacles before overcoming the hurdle of sovereign immunity. This situation may aggravate along with the backlash against the investment arbitration and cast the effectiveness of ICSID arbitration into serious doubt.

I. The Execution of ICSID Awards and the Recent Backlash Against Investment Arbitration

In 1966, the International Centre for Settlement of Investment Disputes (ICSID) was established as a branch of the World Bank. ICSID provides an international forum for private investors to sue host states in their own names through arbitration. Nowadays, ICSID arbitration has become one of the most important devices to resolve investment disputes. Thanks to its distinctive 'semi-public' feature, i.e., the involvement of both private and public parties in the arbitration process, the ICSID is equipped with some particular characteristics. Compared to commercial arbitration between private parties, the ICSID arbitration system provides a more advantageous protection to its awards in the review and enforcement proceedings. Once a commercial arbitration award is rendered, it will be subject to court review in the setting-aside proceedings as well as the enforcement proceedings. The court of the seat can review and set aside the award according to the

[*] LL.B, LL.M, S.J.D, possessing a China law license and admitted to the New York State Bar. I'm grateful to my doctoral advisor, Professor Tibor Varady, for his guidance and comments on the writing of the earlier draft of this paper. Email: mayuepeggy@gmail.com.

local law. As for the enforcement proceedings, courts can refuse to enforce an award if one or more of the enumerated grounds in the 1958 New York Convention Article V are met. By contrast, after an ICSID award is rendered, it is merely subject to internal review carried out by ICSID *ad hoc* committees in the annulment proceedings.[1] The award may be annulled merely due to egregious procedural violations enumerated in the ICSID Convention.[2] If the respondent party refuses to comply with the award, the prevailing party can bring the award to a national court of any ICSID member state for enforcement; the court should recognize the award as final and binding and enforce the pecuniary obligations therein within the state's territory as if it were a final court judgment of that state.[3] The annulment, recognition and enforcement proceedings shield ICSID awards, to a large extent, from external interventions by national courts at the post-award stage, in order to preserve the finality and enhance the efficacy of ICSID arbitration.

Nevertheless, protection against national court intervention does not extend to the execution of ICSID awards, which means that, when a court is asked to collect the money judgment after an ICSID award is confirmed enforceable, the court will make decisions based on the state's domestic law. According to the ICSID Convention, if a final domestic court judgment should not be executed in the forum of execution according to its municipal law, an ICSID award should not be executed either.[4] Furthermore, the respondent state can plea sovereign immunity to avoid some of its assets from being seized.[5] Sovereign immunity is not a matter involved in the execution of commercial arbitration, where only private parties are concerned. However, sovereign immunity becomes an unavoidable issue when an ICSID award is presented for execution because of the involvement of a public party in the ICSID arbitration. Even if an ICSID award survives all the challenges through the annulment, recognition and enforcement proceedings, it may still end up with no payment owing to the state's defense of sovereign immunity. Therefore, the execution mechanism of ICSID arbitration is called the 'Achilles' heel' of the ICSID system.[6] From the perspective of states, immunity from execution is the last bastion for them to protect their sovereign assets from being collected to fulfill an ICSID award. Thus, the execution proceeding can be deemed as the frontal battlefield between the effectiveness of ICSID arbitration and the national interest of sovereign states.

More difficulties and uncertainty as to the realization of ICSID-granted relief will be brought up by the recent backlash against investment arbitration. Over the past years, investment arbitration has been undergoing growing opposition and severe criticisms,

---

1 Regarding the ICSID annulment proceedings, *see* Article 52 of the ICSID Convention.

2 The annulment grounds listed in Article 52 of the ICSID Convention include (a) that the tribunal was not properly constituted; (b) that the tribunal has manifestly exceeded its power; (c) that there was corruption on the part of a member of the tribunal; (d) that there has been a serious departure from a fundamental rule of procedure; (e) that the award has failed to state the reasons on which it is based.

3 *See* Article 53-54 of the ICSID Convention.

4 *See* ICSID Convention, Article 54(3): "Execution of the award shall be governed by the laws concerning the execution of judgments in force in the state in whose territories such execution is sought."

5 *See* ICSID Convention, Article 55: "Nothing in Article 54 shall be construed as derogating from the law in force in any Contracting State relating to immunity of that state or of any foreign state from execution."

6 Michael Waibel, Sovereign Defaults Before International Court and Tribunals 321 (Cambridge University Press, 2011).

mostly from sovereign states. Some major developed countries, such as the US and Australia, used to be firm supporters of investor-state arbitration, as they are the home Sates of many transnational investors. However, along with the changing landscape of the global market, developed countries absorb more and more foreign capital and thus gain a dual-role, combining both home state and host state as to international investment. Accordingly, they also face the risk of being sued in the international forum by foreign investors. As a result, some developed countries start to assume a more cautious position towards investment arbitration. In 2004 and 2012, the US government revised the Model BIT[7] twice, restraining the investment arbitration jurisdiction to some extent.[8] The Australian government made a policy change in 2011 through that year's Trade Policy Statement, where it proclaimed that Australia will no longer include investor-state dispute settlement (ISDS) provisions in future trade agreements.[9] Although the 2013 government change in Australia partially reverted the above policy statement, the revealing of cautiousness or even hostility against investment arbitration still drew attention.[10] The European Commission (the "Commission") has also been opposing investment treaty arbitration for years. In December 2017, the negotiation of the FTA between the EU and Japan was finalized; however, investor-state arbitration is not included in that agreement.[11] In March 2018, the Court of Justice of the European Union (the "CJEU") issued a judgment in *Slovak Republic v. Achmea B.V.*, holding that the arbitration clause embedded in the 1991 Netherlands-Slovakia BIT is incompatible with EU law.[12] As the first precedent regarding the incompatibility of EU law and investor-state arbitration clauses contained in intra-EU BIT, this judgment reveals the EU's attitude against investor-state treaty arbitration and will probably have profound influence on future cases about investor-state arbitration based on intra-EU BITs.[13]

[7] Since the 1980s, the US government initiated the Model BIT program, which aims to provide a basic model for the negotiations of BIT with another country. The 2012 Model BIT is aviable online and in World Trade and Investment Law 113-138 (Frank Emmert ed., Indianapolis 2018)

[8] *See* Lise Johnson, *The 2012 US Model BIT and What the Changes (or lack thereof) Suggest about Future Investment Treaties*, 8(2) Political Risk Insurance Newsletter (2012), available at http://ccsi.columbia.edu/files/2014/01/johnson_2012usmodelBIT.pdf, accessed on June 1, 2018.

[9] *See* Leon Chung and Jamie Stollery, *Australia Goes Against the Trend with Investor-State Dispute Settlement*, http://www.lexology.com/library/detail.aspx?g=1b4fc432-f5d3-4a57-9d0c-f8edc6a2d992, accessed on June 1, 2018.

[10] Since the change of government in 2013, the Abbott Government reverted to the position that considering the inclusion of ISDS on a case-by-case basis. In fact, ISDS has been incorporated in the FTA between Australia and Korea (KAFTA, signed on April 8, 2014).

[11] The text of the agreement submitted for the approval of the European Parliament and EU Member States is available at https://eur-lex.europa.eu/resource.html?uri=cellar:cf1c4c42-4321-11e8-a9f4-01aa75ed71a1.0001.02/DOC_2&format=PDF#page=511.

[12] Case C-284-16 *Slovak Republic v. Achmea B.V.* The Dutch insurance company Achmea brought an arbitration claim against Slovakia under the Netherlands-Slovakia BIT Article 8. After the arbitral award was rendered, Slovakia initiated setting-aside proceedings before a German court, arguing that the arbitral tribunal lacked jurisdiction because Article 8 of the BIT was incompatible with the EU law. The German court rejected Slovakia's argument and referred the question about compatibility of the arbitration clause in the BIT with EU law to the CJEU for a preliminary ruling.

[13] It is noteworthy that, as pointed out by Csongor István Nagy, while *Achmea*'s anti-arbitration attitude may

Compared to the relatively measured changes in developed countries, some developing countries in Latin America took more radical countermeasures against investment arbitration. From 2007, a series of denunciation of the ICSID Convention, starting with Bolivia and then Ecuador and Venezuela,[14] hit the news in the circle of international investment, which attracted close attention and heated controversies. Along with the denunciation, condemnation of the ICSID system was also expressed by some government officials. For example, the Bolivian President Morales claimed that "the governments of Latin America and I think the world, never win the cases. The multinationals always win" and thus "[We] emphatically reject the legal, media and diplomatic pressure of some multinationals that…resist the sovereign rulings of countries, making threats and initiating suits in international arbitration."[15] Although the statistics of ICSID case outcomes and some scholars' empirical research show that investors were not better treated by ICSID tribunals,[16] the Bolivian President's statement represents some Latin American countries' strong dissatisfaction with the investor-state arbitration regime.

A historical overview of the Latin American countries' attitude towards investment arbitration may provide some explanation of their anti-ICSID position. In the late 19th century, the Calvo Doctrine was created and proliferated in Latin America, which essentially requires all disputes involving private individuals conducting business in a foreign country to be resolved by local remedies rather than international legal remedies.[17] Under the guidance of the Calvo Doctrine, Latin American countries generally rejected the jurisdiction of investment arbitration tribunals. During the 1960s and 1980s, many Latin American countries, notably Argentina, Brazil and Mexico, carried a massive debt burden.[18] In order to restructure debts and avoid financial panic, the Latin American countries turned to foreign banks for new loans. One condition attached to the loans was to sign treaties with provisions of foreign investor protection. Under this situation and along with the global wave of neoliberalism, many countries in Latin America became members of the ICSID Convention and signed hundreds of BITs including ICSID

guide feature cases, its holding is very narrow and the precedential value is questionable. *See* Csongor István Nagy, *Intra-EU Bilateral Investment Treaties and EU Law After Achmea: 'Know Well What Leads You Forward and What Holds You Back'*, 19(4) German Law Journal 981 (2017).

14 Bolivia, Ecuador and Venezuela withdrew from the ICSID Convention in 2007, 2009 and 2012 respectively.

15 *See* Diana Marie Wick, *The Counter-Productivity of ICSID Denunciation and Proposals for Change*, 11(2) Journal of International Business and Law 239, 245 & 245 fn 46 (2012). When Bolivia denounced the ICSID Convention, the Bolivian Ministry of Foreign Affairs released articles on its website elaborating reasons of the government's withdrawal, which include bias of ICSID arbitrators towards investors, lack of appellate proceedings and deficient transparency in arbitration hearings. *See* Investment Treaty News (ITN), May 9, 2007, http://www.iisd.org/pdf/2007/itn_may9_2007.pdf, accessed on 10/2/2013.

16 *See* Susan Frank, *Development and Outcomes of Investment Treaty Arbitration*, 50(2) Harvard International Law Journal 435 (2009).

17 Charity L. Goodman, *Comment Uncharted Waters: Financial Crisis and Enforcement of ICSID Awards in Argentina*, 28 University of Pennsylvania Journal of International Law 449. p. 469–470.

18 The debts rose sharply from USD 75 billion in 1975 to USD 315 billion in 1983. *See* Institute of Latin American Studies, The Debt Crisis in Latin America, page. 69.

arbitration as a dispute settlement option.[19] Recently, however, Latin America's resistance against investment arbitration began to rebound. This shift happened along with the soaring ICSID caseload against Latin American countries and the mounting damages waiting to be paid. According to UNCTAD data of the total number of investment treaty arbitration cases until 2015, Latin American countries occupy four seats among the top 10 respondent states,[20] and Argentina sits in the first place with 56 cases.[21] The large number of ICSID cases was by and large owing to the regional economic situation and governmental actions against foreign investment. For example, in 2001, a financial crisis swept across Argentina and caused economic collapse. To deal with the crisis, the Argentine government adopted several emergency actions, including a currency control manner called 'pesification', through which the government reduced the constant outflow of capital from banks by forbidding withdrawal of more than US$250 per week and limiting the transfer of funds abroad.[22] Foreign investors suffered severe losses and many brought claims against the Argentine government before ICISD based on investment contracts or BITs. As a result, Argentina had to face over fifty ICSID cases and the damages awarded against the government have amounted to tens of billions of dollars.[23] It is a huge burden for these countries to fulfill the awarded obligations under weak economic conditions. Hence, it is conceivable that some host states might be reluctant to comply with ICSID awards against them and take some measures to hinder the enforcement and execution of the awarded damages.

In summary, the design of the ICSID arbitration system and the changed attitude of some states towards investment arbitration raise questions regarding the execution of ICSID awards. The ICSID Convention does not provide any protection to facilitate the execution of ICSID awards but leaves it completely under the control of national laws. This execution mechanism allows the respondent states that refuse to comply with ICSID awards to bring up the sovereign immunity defense to prevent forcible collection of their assets. Moreover, the public backlash against investment arbitration reflects a change of the landscape in the global market and is the result of states' weighing their national interest in different aspects. In this situation, some analysis is needed to examine the rationale of the ICSID execution mechanism and evaluate how difficult it is to execute ICSID awards in practice. The following discussion will focus on these two aspects. Section two discusses, under the ICSID Convention, what specific hurdles should be expected by investors who wish to execute ICSID awards and Section three

---

[19] According to UNCTAD statistics, Latin American States did not engage in BITs until the late 1980s, while by the end of 1990s, Latin American States had entered into 300 BITs. *See* Wenhua Shan, *From "North-South Divide" to "Private-Public Debate": Revival of the Calvo Doctrine and the Changing Landscape in International Investment Law*, 27 Northwestern Journal of International Law & Business 632 (2007).

[20] *Id.* at 632.

[21] Mexico is not a signatory member of ICSID Convention; thus cases against Mexico before ICSID are under the Additional Facility proceedings.

[22] Silvia Karina Fiezzoni, *Study on the Challenges and Countermeasures of Latin America against ICSID*, Dalian Maritime University, PhD Thesis, 2011, 2.

[23] Oscar Lopez, *Smart Move: Argentina to Leave the ICSID*, Cornell International Law Journal Online (January 7, 2014), available at http://cornellilj.org/smart-move-argentina-to-leave-the-icsid/, accessed on June 1, 2018.

focuses on the attitude of several states toward the execution of ICSID awards under the current backlash against investment arbitration. Since the host state may have assets in different places, which include its own territory, the investor's home state or a third state and the host state is directly involved in the ICSID arbitration case while the home state or a third state is not, the analysis of the second question will distinguish two scenarios regarding ICSID execution: one is in the forum state, which refers to the home state or a third state; and the other is in the host state.

II. Hurdles Before the Execution of ICSID Awards

As stated above, the ICSID Convention provides that execution of ICSID awards is governed by the domestic law of the state where execution is sought. The national laws of most civilized countries set a procedural bar – sovereign immunity – to hinder forcible execution against a sovereign state unless some exceptions apply. Specifically, sovereign immunity has two subcategories i.e., immunity from jurisdiction and execution. Immunity from jurisdiction protects states from being sued. When an arbitral award against a state is brought to a national court, immunity from jurisdiction would hinder the court from recognizing and enforcing the award unless the respondent state waives its immunity. According to the ICSID Convention, a state waives its immunity from jurisdiction once it consents to ICSID arbitration. However, even if immunity from jurisdiction has been waived, immunity from execution may still prevent forcible attachment of certain assets belonging to the respondent state.

The principle of sovereign immunity finds its roots back in the time when the initial nation states emerged with the Treaty of Westphalia in 1648.[24] Thereafter this concept became widely recognized based on a global consensus that immunity from other territorial jurisdictions is critical to the dignity and independence of a sovereign. For a substantial period of time, the application of sovereign immunity was in an absolute way, meaning that a nation state can plea immunity in any situation to avoid being sued in judicial proceedings. Since the twentieth century, the notion of sovereign immunity has gradually evolved from the 'absolute' version to a more restrictive one.[25] Although nowadays the absolute doctrine still dominates in a few countries such as China, many other countries accept the idea that the application of sovereign immunity should be exempted in some circumstances. The most commonly recognized exceptions are states' waiver of sovereign immunity and whenever the activity of the state is of a commercial nature or the sovereign asset at issue is used for commercial purpose.

Shifting from the absolute to the restrictive concept of sovereign immunity was by and large fueled by the changing role of states. Besides implementing public and political functions, states have been more and more involved in commercial activities and sometimes acted like private actors. In the situation where a state participates in commercial activities as private actor, if a state invokes sovereign immunity vis-à-vis the

[24] Craig S. Miles, *Sovereign Immunity, in* Enforcement of Arbitral Awards Against Sovereigns 35–71 (Doak Bishop ed., JurisNet 2009).

[25] *Id.*

private party in order to circumvent a judicial remedy, there will be unfair results. Thus the restrained application of sovereign immunity is in accordance with the changing reality of state activities and the basic legal principle of fairness and justice. As for investment arbitration between investors and states, the restrictive doctrine of sovereign immunity opens the door for investors to utilize the exceptions of sovereign immunity to seek forcible execution against states' assets. However, it does not mean that investors can overcome the sovereign immunity defense with ease.

Emmanuel Gaillard points out that sovereign immunity from execution is incompatible with the principle of the effectiveness of arbitral awards.[26] Arbitration is carried out only if parties voluntarily agreed to it. A legitimate expectation underlying this agreement is the principle of the effectiveness of arbitral awards, i.e., the awarded obligation will be carried out by the losing party.[27] However, if one party of the arbitration is a sovereign state, whether the award will be enforced is determined by the state due to the principle of immunity. In this sense, Bruno Oppetit asserts that incorporating sovereign immunity in the context of the execution of arbitral awards would lead to the situation where a state is conferred "an exorbitant prerogative...to hold itself to its obligations only when it is inclined to do so."[28] Then people may ask why the drafters of the ICSID Convention created such an execution mechanism that the ICSID awards are exposed to the risk of denied execution due to the defense of sovereign immunity. Regarding this question, the drafting history of the ICSID Convention will provide some clues.

The *travaux préparatoires* of the ICSID Convention show that incorporating sovereign immunity in the execution of ICSID awards was taken for granted by drafters and state delegates. When the Convention was drafted, the notion of absolute sovereign immunity still had stronger influence compared with restrictive sovereign immunity. At that time, exceptions to the immunity from execution were sporadic. In addition, there was an assumption during the drafting process that host states will voluntarily honor ICSID awards and thus there would be little need to trigger forcible execution against states. Most of the drafters believed that, once a host state loses an ICSID case, the government will not choose to default on the payment of damages because of the side effect of nonpayment e.g., impaired reputation as an investment destination, loss of future opportunity to get loans from the World Bank, potential risk of diplomatic protection measures, etc. While excluding sovereign immunity from execution would perfectly preserve the effectiveness of ICSID awards, this idea would be highly contested by states. Hence, to give full effect of the national laws concerning sovereign immunity was also a strategic compromise to avoid "determined opposition of developing countries" and to pursue wider ratification of the ICSID Convention.[29]

---

[26] Emmanuel Gaillard, *Effectiveness of Arbitral Awards, State Immunity from Execution and Autonomy of State Entities: Three Incompatible Principles, in* State Entities in International Arbitration 179, 181 (Emmanuel Gaillard ed., Juris Publishing 2008).

[27] *Id.*

[28] *Id.*

[29] *Id.* at 1154, citing Alan Broches, *The Convention on the Settlement of Investment Disputes Between States and Nationals of Other States*, 136 Recueil des Cours 331, 403 (1972-II).

Based on the above considerations, designing the ICSID execution mechanism did not encounter substantive objection. Nevertheless, the rationales underpinning the drafting of the ICSID execution mechanism have changed today. Firstly, absolute sovereign immunity has become loose and turned to a restrictive version and in most countries exceptions to sovereign immunity have been widely recognized. Secondly, there emerges a new trend that more and more countries have been changing from a unilateral role to a dual role as both the host state and home state for international investment. Investors and their home states wish to diminish the barrier of sovereign immunity and thus the developing countries' strong desire on utilizing sovereign immunity decreases when they act as the home state of their own nationals investing overseas. Thirdly, the Convention drafters' assumption that host states will in general comply with ICSID awards is not necessarily correct. Public hostility against investment arbitration and the fact that several ICSID awards are not complied with voluntarily deepens the worry that states may take advantage of the 'Achilles' heel' to hinder the execution of ICSID awards. These changed circumstances result in an incompatibility between the ICSID execution mechanism and reality. This incompatibility also implies that there will be more difficulties with the execution of ICSID awards than expected by the drafters. Three possible barriers to the execution of ICSID awards against sovereign states will be enumerated in the following.

Firstly, although many countries accept the restricted application of sovereign immunity, the exceptions to sovereign immunity are still very limited. For example, a commonly recognized exception is the 'commercial exception', meaning that if the sovereign assets or actions are of a commercial nature, the state's plea of sovereign immunity might be defeated, but the criteria of this exception are generally rigorous. Moreover, there is an "exception to exception" – if the assets at issue qualify as 'specially protected assets', which usually refers to the assets of a foreign state's central bank or those used for military purposes or diplomatic missions, sovereign immunity will prevent forcible execution against these assets even if commercial features are involved. This "exception to exception" is widely recognized in many countries.

Secondly, due to the inconsistency of the legislation and legal practices in different countries regarding sovereign immunity, it becomes even harsher for investors to seek execution of ICSID awards. In terms of the exceptions from sovereign immunity, municipal laws vary in different jurisdictions. Although most countries adopt the restrictive sovereign immunity concept and limit it with certain exceptions, some countries, such as China, still prefer the absolute theory.[30] As for the criteria for applying exceptions to sovereign immunity, states also employ different approaches. The endeavor to develop a uniform sovereign immunity law at the global level has not proved fruitful. Up to now, there is only one multilateral treaty – the European Convention on state Immunity – which is in force but merely ratified by eight states.[31] Another international treaty, the United Nations Convention on Jurisdictional Immunities of States and Their Property, has not

---

[30] Dahua Qi, *State Immunity, China and Its Shifting Position*, 7 Chinese Journal of International Law 307–337 (2008).

[31] *See* the website of the Council of Europe, http://conventions.coe.int/Treaty/Commun/ChercheSig.asp?NT=074&CM=&DF=&CL=ENG, accessed on 11 September 2014.

entered into force due to insufficient number of ratifying states.[32] The ICSID Convention provides that an ICSID award can be presented for execution in any member state of the Convention. However the various legislation and case law regarding sovereign immunity increase the uncertainty whether and how it will be possible to collect damages against host states in different countries.

Thirdly, the emerging backlash against investment arbitration reflects the reluctance of some states to honor ICSID awards and raises concern about forum states' attitudes towards the execution of ICSID awards. As stated above, some Latin American countries denounced the ICSID Convention and expressed aggressive anti-ICSID rhetoric. It is not a wild guess that some states may also take measures to avoid paying damages. The ICSID Convention builds a solid wall, despite some weak points, to repel external attacks on ICSID awards at the post-award stage. However, when it comes to execution, the door is wide open for national courts' intervention due to sovereign immunity from execution. Considering the hostility against investor-state arbitration expressed by some developed countries, uncertainty regarding the execution of ICSID awards in these states may also increase.

Therefore, owing to the matter of sovereign immunity, the execution mechanism set up by the ICSID Convention brings up a number of difficulties for investors to forcibly collect damages against host states. In this sense, the execution mechanism may impair the effectiveness of ICSID arbitration. In the following section, states' practice regarding the execution of ICSID awards will be examined to find out how the execution mechanism works in reality.

III. States' Practices Regarding the Execution of ICSID Awards

Since ICSID was founded, not many arbitral awards have been brought in third country courts for execution. Among those identified cases going through the post-award adjudicative proceedings, only three are related to the execution of ICSID awards[33] – *LETCO v. Argentina*,[34] *AIG v. Kazakhstan*[35] and *Benvenuti & Bonfant v. Congo*.[36] These three cases were respectively litigated in the United States, United Kingdom and France. The above three countries are global business centers and the home states of most international investors, where many other countries have assets that can be detected and possibly attached by prevailing investors. It is noticeable that, in the above cases, the US, the UK and France are not the investment's host states and thus they are the

[32] *See* the website of the United Nations Treaty Collection (Oct. 29, 2014), https://treaties.un.org/Pages/ViewDetails.aspx?mtdsg_no=III-13&chapter=3&lang=en, accessed on October 29, 2014.

[33] Most of the published court decisions regarding enforcement of ICSID awards do not touch the matter of attachment of assets to execute ICSID awards. For instance, the US cases *Siag v. Egypt* (2009 WL 1834562 (S.D.N.Y)) and *Blue Ridge v. Argentina* (735 F.3d 72) do not concern the issue of execution.

[34] *Liberian Eastern Timber Corporation v. The Government of the Republic of Liberia*, 650 F. Supp. 73, (SDNY 1986)

[35] *AIG Capital Partners Inc and another v. The Republic of Kazakhstan and The National Bank of Kazakhstan* [2005] EWHC 2239 (Comm).

[36] *See* ICSID Reports Vol. I, 368–376.

'forum states' as defined above. A forum state can be the home state of an investor or a third state as a member of the ICSID Convention. For the convenience of discussion, this section distinguishes the forum state and the host state in terms of the execution of ICSID awards. As for the forum states, the US, the UK, France and China will be discussed. Despite that China has no decided cases regarding the execution of ICSID awards yet, it has become the biggest emerging capital-exporting state that may have execution cases in the future. Hence China will also be under discussion. Additionally, the scenario of executing ICSID awards in the host states will be analyzed. Up to now, there has been no execution case litigated in the host state. The execution proceeding comes into play only when the respondent states are reluctant to pay; thus it is conceivable that executing an ICSID award in the recalcitrant host state will not be easy.

a) Execution of ICSID Awards in the US

According to Article 55 of the ICSID Convention, immunity from execution entirely depends on domestic laws. The US statute governing sovereign immunity is the Foreign Sovereign Immunity Act (FSIA). The FSIA provides that in principle a foreign state should be immune from attachment arrest and execution. An exception applies when a two-tiered test set forth in §1610 (a) is satisfied.[37] To meet the first-tier test for the exception of immunity from execution, the sovereign assets at issue must be used for a commercial activity in the United States. To satisfy this test, several elements need to be demonstrated, namely, the commercial nature of the state's activity, the commercial purpose of the sovereign property, and the location of the property (must be in the US). The burden of proof is on the investors who seek execution. However, due to the information-asymmetry between sovereign states and private individuals, it is usually very difficult for investors to collect evidence regarding the host state's assets.

Besides the "commercial activity" test, there is also a second-tier test, i.e., one of the seven requirements listed under §1610 (a) must be met. Among others, two requirements deserve particular attention. According to §1610(a) (2) and (6), claimants need to prove that the property to be attached is or was used for the commercial activity upon which the claim is based, which is called the 'linkage requirement' or that the judgment is based on an order confirming an arbitral award rendered against a foreign state. As for §1610(a) (2), it is a heavy burden for investors to locate certain assets and demonstrate the nexus between the property and the claim. The 2004 UN Convention on Jurisdictional Immunities of states and Their Property eliminates this linkage requirement, which represents a trend to facilitate execution against states. Unfortunately, this Convention has not been ratified by any country. However, the satisfaction of the §1610(a) (6) requirement can be achieved more easily. Considering the US courts' pro-arbitration stance, recognition of an ICSID award as final and binding will face little resistance. Once the 'commercial activity' test and the §1611(a) (6) requirement are satisfied, the

[37] 28 US Code § 1609: "subject to existing international agreements to which the United States is a party at the time of enactment of this Act the property in the United States of a foreign state shall be immune from attachment arrest and execution except as provided in section 1610 and 1611 of this chapter."

investor can establish an exception to the immunity from execution. Hence, § 1611(a)(6) is a step toward facilitating execution of ICSID awards in the US.

As stated above, although many states accept exceptions to sovereign immunity, their national laws also recognize some "exception to exception", which widens the application of sovereign immunity again. Under the US law, one 'exception to exception' is the 'specially protected assets'. Even if the two-tiered test has been met, execution of ICSID awards may still be impeded if the assets fall under the category of 'specially protected assets'. Under the FSIA, three kinds of sovereign assets are specially protected from forcible executions. The first one is the property of those organizations designated by the President as being entitled to enjoy the privileges, exemptions and immunities provided by the International Organizations Immunity Act.[38] The second one is the property of a foreign central bank or monetary authority held for its own account.[39] This immunity can be explicitly waived by such bank or its parent foreign government.[40] The third one is military property – the property shall be, or intended to be, used in connection with military activity and is of a military character or under the control of a military authority or defense agency.[41] The last two categories of assets are also widely recognized as specially protected assets in several other jurisdictions, including the UK, Canada and Australia. Furthermore, the Vienna Convention on Diplomatic Relations shields the property used for diplomatic purposes under diplomatic immunity. The issue of diplomatic immunity was discussed in *LETCO v. Liberia II* before the US court, which will be analyzed below.[42] All in all, investors will face another hurdle to seek execution in the US if the assets at issue fall under the 'specially protected assets' category.

Up to now, only two cases regarding the execution of an ICSID award were litigated in the US.[43] Both cases are between the Liberian Eastern Timber Corporation ("LETCO") and Liberia, generating two separate decisions, *LETCO I*[44] and *LETCO II*,[45] concerning different assets and regarding different issues of sovereign immunity under the US law. These two cases reflect the US courts' position regarding the execution of ICSID awards. Moreover, a recent case *NML v. Argentina* reveals some changes in the US courts as to the issue of sovereign immunity from execution. Although the *NML* case is not about the execution of an ICSID award, it may have some impact on the execution of ICSID awards in the future.

---

38 28 US Code § 1611 (a).

39 28 US Code § 1611 (b)(1).

40 *Id.*

41 28 US Code § 1611 (b)(2).

42 659 F.Supp. 606.

43 There are more U.S. cases regarding the enforcement of ICSID awards, for instance *Siag v The Arab Republic of Egypt, Sempra v Argentina, Enron v Argentina, Blue Ridge Investments, LLC as purchaser and assignee of the Award rendered in favour of CMS in the case CMS v Argentina*, but the cases regarding execution matters are only *LETCO I* and *LECTCO II*.

44 *LETCO v. Liberia I*, 650 F.Supp. 73 (S.D.N.Y 1986).

45 *LETCO v. Liberia II*, 659 F.Supp. 606 (D.D.C 1987).

(1) *LETCO I*

In *LETCO I*, the critical issue was the 'commercial activity' test. LETCO had a concession agreement granted by the Liberian government for harvesting Liberian timber. Liberia terminated the concession and LETCO initiated ICSID arbitration against the host state. The ICSID tribunal rendered an award in favor of LETCO, which was later sought to be enforced by LETCO in the US Federal Court for the Southern District of New York. The court entered a judgment and issued a writ of execution. The properties LETCO sought to execute were the tonnage fees, registration fees and other taxes that the Liberian ship-owners located in the US owe to the Liberian government. Liberia moved to vacate the judgment and enjoin the issuance of execution on the properties.[46]

Liberia argued that, under the FSIA, the ICSID award cannot be enforced through execution against the ship-owners and the agents.[47] The issue is, according to FSIA § 1610, whether the fees LETCO sought to attach were used for commercial activity in the United States.[48] Liberia contended that the fees were collected as taxes designed to raise revenues for the Republic of Liberia and, as such, were sovereign assets rather than commercial assets, which are immune from execution.[49] LETCO responded that, despite the indisputable fact that the properties are tax revenues ultimately payable to Liberia, 27% of the property was retained for operating and administrative expenses and profits by United States corporations or citizens who rendered services in collecting the funds, which made those payments constituting commercial activities.[50]

The court did not endorse LETCO's methodology of dividing the assets into commercial and non-commercial portions.[51] According to the court, the fact that Liberia employed US citizens instead of utilizing the services of its consular employees stationed in the US did not change the nature of the registration fees or taxes as sovereign assets – the method of collecting the amount due to the Liberian ship-owners does not destroy the nature of that collection. Accordingly, the court decided that collecting the registration fees and taxes were the exercise of sovereign power rather than commercial activity and thus enjoyed immunity from execution.[52]

(2) *LETCO II*

In the following year, LETCO attempted to execute on several bank accounts used for the functioning of the Liberian Embassy.[53] The court discussed whether the bank accounts at issue are covered by diplomatic immunity under the Vienna Convention on Diplomatic Relations. LETCO argued that only the funds maintained on the premises of the mission

46 *LETCO v. Liberia I*, 650 F.Supp. 73 (S.D.N.Y 1986), at 74–76.

47 *Id.* at 73.

48 *Id.* at 75.

49 *Id.* at 77.

50 *Id.*

51 *Id.*

52 *Id.*

53 *LETCO v. Liberia II*, 659 F.Supp. 606 (D.D.C 1987).

are to be afforded diplomatic immunity, because only property described in Article 22(3) of the Convention is exempt from attachment.[54] The court refuted LETCO's argument and concluded that, although no specific provision in the Convention affords diplomatic immunity to bank accounts of diplomatic missions, the bank accounts enjoy diplomatic immunity considering consistency with the agreement set forth in Article 25 as well as the intention of the parties to the Convention.[55]

The court further discussed whether the bank accounts at issue were immune from execution under the FSIA. LECTO employed the same segmentation methodology as used in *LETCO I*, arguing that some portions of the funds in the bank accounts are used for commercial activities, such as the transactions to purchase goods or service from private parties. The court stated that, if any portion of a bank account is used for a commercial activity, then the entire account losses its immunity; however, if the funds used for commercial activity are 'incidental' or 'auxiliary', they would not cause the entire bank account to lose its mantle of sovereign immunity.[56] The court held that the main portions of the embassy's banks accounts were utilized to perform diplomatic functions and thus the public nature of the embassy's bank accounts was not affected.[57] In addition, the court stressed some characteristics of the "commercial activity" test:

1) the concept of "commercial activity" should be defined narrowly because sovereign immunity, rather than the exceptions to it, remains the rule;[58]
2) the "rule of thumb" to distinguish commercial activity and public activity is that "if the activity is one in which a private person could engage, it is not entitled to immunity".[59]

Therefore, the court decided that the bank accounts of the Liberian Embassy do not meet any exception under the FSIA.

Viewed from the two LETCO cases, it can be seen that US courts are inclined to a relatively conservative position regarding sovereign immunity from execution. As for the "commercial activity" test, the courts of these two cases introduced some specific rules:

1) the method of collecting the property does not affect the nature of the collection activity
2) if some portion of the assets is used for a commercial activity, the nature of the entire assets will not change if the commercial activity is ancillary.

These two rules restrict the scope of the 'commercial activity' exception. With regard to property used for diplomatic missions, the court of *LETCO II* confirmed that the property at issue was covered by diplomatic immunity according to the Vienna Convention on Diplomatic Relations, even though the property is not enumerated under Article 22(3)

---

[54] *Id.*

[55] *Id.*

[56] *Id.*

[57] *Id.*

[58] *Id.*

[59] *Id.* citing *Practical Concepts, INC. v. Republic of Bolivia*, 811 F.2d 1543, 1549 (D.C. Cir. 1987).

of the Convention, which again reflects that the US courts tend to support sovereign immunity rather than the exceptions.

(3) Argentina v. NML and the 'Discovery Immunity' with Regard to Foreign Sovereign Assets

As aforesaid, due to information asymmetry, it is an arduous task for private creditors to locate the respondent state's assets that might be available for execution. Under the US legal system, judgment creditors usually need to seek discovery of the state's assets, i.e., to collect information from the state or third parties regarding the potentially attachable sovereign assets.[60] On June 16, 2014, the US Supreme Court decided the case *Republic of Argentina v. NML Capital*[61] where the court rejected Argentina's plea that the discovery of its assets should be prevented due to sovereign immunity.[62] This is a landmark case that raises close concerns in and outside the US. Some scholars assert that the *NML* case would change the rules of the game in terms of execution against foreign sovereigns.[63] This case does not relate to an ICSID award but may still have influence on the execution of ICSID awards in the United States.

NML Capital is a Cayman Islands-based offshore unit of the US hedge funds Elliot Management Corporation. It is one of the so-called "vulture funds", which refers to hedge funds that buy debts from the secondary markets for discounted prices and seek full repayment of the original loan from the debtor to make huge profits. They especially target financially distressed countries such as Argentina.[64] In the former Argentine President Christina Fernandez de Kirchner's speech addressed the UN General Assembly in 2014, she criticized vulture funds and said that some of them had made profits of 1600% within one year.[65] During the past years, the battle between Argentina and vulture funds has always been in the spotlight and provoked controversies.

In 2001, Argentina defaulted on its external debt for about $81 billion.[66] In 2005 and 2010, Argentina restructured the debts by offering a deal including a 70% bondholder "haircut". 93% of the creditors accepted this restructuring.[67] NML purchased some of Argentina's debts at a discounted price and then rejected the restructuring as one of

---

[60] Robert K. Kry, *Asset Discovery Against Foreign Sovereigns After NML*, 87 New York State Bar Association Journal 40 (2014).

[61] 134 S. Ct. 2250 (June 16, 2014).

[62] *Id.*

[63] Robert K. Kry, *Asset Discovery Against Foreign Sovereigns After NML*, 87 New York State Bar Association Journal 40 (2014). The US Supreme Court's decision raised high attention, and was covered in the Wall Street Journal, the Financial Times and the Washington Post.

[64] *See* Vulture Funds, Jubilee USA network, http://www.jubileeusa.org/vulture_funds (accessed on June 1, 2018).

[65] Video of Christina Fernandez de Kirchner's speech in the UN General Assembly can be accessed on https://www.youtube.com/watch?v=SdvhoDszwDs (accessed on June 1, 2018). It also says that NML can make a profit of over 1000% through the legal actions against Argentina in the US courts, *see Argentina Forced into A "Technical" Default*, LAB (2014), http://lab.org.uk/argentina-forced-into-a-technical-default (accessed on June 1, 2018).

[66] *Id.*

[67] *Id.*

the holdouts.[68] In New York courts, NML sued Argentina for full payment of the debts and prevailed in all eleven actions against Argentina.[69] In addition, the court enjoined Argentina from paying other creditors that restructured through certain American banks before the holdouts have been paid in full.[70] This judgment was issued on the day when Argentina planned to pay the other creditors, thus Argentina is said to be forced into "technical" default due to the enjoinment of the payment.[71]

Argentina did not comply with the court judgment to pay the holdout creditors in full[72] and NML sought discovery of Argentina's assets for execution of the judgment. In 2010, NML served subpoenas to two non-party banks in search of Argentina's assets.[73] The US District Court for the Southern District of New York denied Argentina's motion to quash the subpoena issued to one bank and granted judgment creditor's motion to compel non-party banks to comply with the subpoenas.[74] Argentina then appealed and brought the case to the Supreme Court. Generally, the US Federal Rule of Civil Procedure allows judgment creditors to obtain discovery from judgment debtors and any other person in aid of an execution.[75] However, Argentina argued that the scope of discovery in aid of execution should be limited in this case by principles of sovereign immunity.[76] Thus, the main issue in the Supreme Court proceeding was whether FSIA "imposes [a] limit on a United States court's authority to order blanket post-judgment execution discovery on the assets of a foreign state used for any activity anywhere in the world".[77]

Regarding the question whether sovereign immunity prevents discovery of a foreign state's assets, the US case law before the *NML* case is inconsistent. In *Rubin v. Islamic Republic of Iran*,[78] the court refused plaintiff's demand for discovery based on the finding that FSIA prevents blanket discovery regarding all of a sovereign's property and thus only discovery relating to the attachable property is allowed.[79] In the subsequent case *EM Ltd. v. Republic of Argentina*,[80] which shared a similar factual background with the

---

[68] *Id.*

[69] *See Republic of Argentina v. NML Capital*, 134 S. Ct. 2250 (June 16, 2014).

[70] *Argentina Forced into A 'Technical' Default*, LAB (Aug.2, 2014).

[71] *Id.*

[72] Argentina tried to avoid complying with the New York Court judgments and took several measures to pay the other creditors that restructured. Before December 15, 2013, the due date of Argentina's debt set by Judge Griesa's decision, Argentina negotiated with NML. The negotiation failed and Argentina defaulted on its debt. Thereafter, Argentina's Senate approved a debt-swap bill that allows Argentina to pay the restructured creditors and circumvent the US financial institutions. On September 29, 2014, Judge Griesa found Argentina in contempt of court.

[73] *Republic of Argentina v. NML Capital*, 134 S. Ct. 2250 (2014).

[74] *Id.*

[75] Federal Rule of Civil Procedure 69(a)(2) states that: "In aid of the judgment or execution, the judgment creditor [...] may obtain discovery from any person – including the judgment debtor – as provided in the rules or by the procedure of the state where the court is located."

[76] *Republic of Argentina v. NML Capital*, 134 S. Ct. 2250 (2014).

[77] *Id.*

[78] 637 F. 3d at 795.

[79] *Id.*

[80] 695 F. 3d 201 (2d Cir. 2012).

NML case, the court upheld plaintiff's claim for discovery into Argentina's assets all over the world.[81]

The US Supreme Court's decision of *NML* is in line with the *EM Ltd* case, i.e., allowing discovery regarding Argentina's assets. The Supreme Court reasoned that FSIA only contains two kinds of sovereign immunity–immunity from jurisdiction and immunity from execution and there is "no third provision forbidding or limiting discovery in aid of execution of a foreign-sovereign judgment debtor's assets."[82] Argentina argued that "if a judgment creditor could not ultimately execute a judgment against certain property, then it has no business pursuing discovery of information pertaining to that property",[83] thus the discovery of the assets that do not fall within an exception to execution immunity under the FSIA is forbidden.[84] The court disagreed with Argentina's argument and stated that the FSIA only immunizes the foreign sovereign's assets in the United States; thus even if there was a 'discovery immunity' as alleged by Argentina, it would not shield Argentina's assets outside the United States.[85] Therefore, the court denied that Argentina could invoke sovereign immunity under FSIA to ban the investors from collecting information in order to locate Argentina's assets worldwide.

The *NML* case can be deemed as a big step toward a more restrictive practice regarding sovereign immunity in the US, which may also have a potential influence on future cases about the execution of ICSID awards. Investors seeking execution of ICSID awards in the US may benefit from *NML* for easier discovery of the respondent state's assets. The worldwide discovery established by the *NML* decision is a potent tool for investors to locate host states' assets in any country and to easily gather much more related information. In addition, this ruling makes host states' resistance to the collection of their assets more burdensome. However, states still have many ways to block the discovery. The Supreme Court's decision in *NML* only tackles FSIA but the court pointed out that "other sources of law" might restrict the discovery.[86] For example, the host state may invoke the Vienna Convention on Diplomatic Relations to repel the discovery of its diplomatic assets. They can also invoke the "secret privilege" to withhold sensitive national security information.[87] In addition, according to the comity principle, states may rely on their own laws to hinder the discovery. Furthermore, the Supreme Court stressed in the *NML* decision that district courts have discretions and may consider comity interests as well as the burden that the discovery might cause to the foreign state when deciding the matter of discovery.[88] All in all, the *NML* case reveals a sharp restriction of sovereign immunity under US law, although with certain limitations, and may not be applied in other cases. After *NML*, the landscape of the execution on foreign sovereign assets in

---

81 *Id.*

82 *Republic of Argentina v. NML Capital*, 134 S. Ct. 2250 (2014).

83 *Id.*

84 *Id.*

85 *Id.*

86 *Republic of Argentina v. NML Capital*, 134 S. Ct. 2250 (2014).

87 Robert K. Kry, *Asset Discovery Against Foreign Sovereigns After NML*, 87 New York State Bar Association Journal 40, 42 (2014).

88 *Id.* at 43.

the US has changed more or less and will probably make the execution of ICSID awards in the US a little easier than before.

In summary, the above analysis shows the basic features of the US legal system with regard to the execution of ICSID awards. On the one hand, US law imposes some difficulties on investors to overcome host states' sovereign immunity defense when seeking execution of ICSID awards. For instance, there is a heavy burden of satisfying the 'commercial activity' test and further requirements, as well as the 'exception to exception' – the question regarding the specially protected assets. Furthermore, the two cases concerning execution of ICSID awards (*LETCO I* and *LETCO II*) reveal US courts' conservative attitude regarding sovereign immunity from execution. On the other hand, US law also embodies some pro-arbitration provisions that may facilitate the execution of arbitral awards, such as the rule in FSIA § 1610(a) (6). It is noteworthy that the recent case *NML v. Argentina* reflects the US Supreme Court's changing attitude towards a more restrictive sovereign immunity and may help investors to execute ICSID awards in the United States.

b) Execution of ICSID Awards in the UK

The UK law dealing with sovereign immunity from execution is the State Immunity Act (SIA). The SIA, like the FSIA, also provides that in principle sovereign immunity from execution should apply to a foreign state.[89] However, instead of the two-tiered test required by the FSIA, the SIA provides for two single-tiered exceptions to the immunity from execution, namely the 'waiver exception' and the 'commercial use exception'. Under the SIA, the waiver of immunity from execution must be explicit. As for the commercial use exception, Section 13(4) of the SIA states that "Subsection (2)(b) above does not prevent the issue of any process in respect of property which is for the time being in use or intended for use for commercial purposes". Thus the standard of the commercial use exception focuses on the purpose of the assets, which is different from the US criteria that stress the nature of the commercial activity. Section 13(5) further provides that the most significant evidence of the commercial or non-commercial use of a certain property is a certificate or declaration by the head of a foreign state's diplomatic mission in the United Kingdom or the person for the time being performing this function.[90]

UK law also recognizes 'specially protected assets' as the "exception to exception". The SIA provides that the property of a foreign state's central bank or other monetary authority is immune from execution. Further, the UK is also a signatory country of the

---

89 SIA Section 13(2) provides that "(a) relief shall not be given against a state by way of injunction or order for specific performance or for the recovery of land or other property; and (b) the property of a state shall not be subject to any process for the enforcement of a judgment or arbitration award or, in an action in rem, for its arrest, detention or sale".

90 SIA Section 13(5): "The head of a state's diplomatic mission in the United Kingdom, or the person for the time being performing his functions, shall be deemed to have authority to give on behalf of the state any such consent as is mentioned in subsection (3) above and, for the purposes of subsection (4) above, his certificate to the effect that any property is not in use or intended for use by or on behalf of the state for commercial purposes shall be accepted as sufficient evidence of that fact unless the contrary is proved."

Vienna Convention on Diplomatic Relations. Thus, properties used for diplomatic missions also enjoy diplomatic immunity in UK courts.

The case *AIG Capital Partners Inc v. Kazakhstan* is regarding execution of an ICSID award in the UK.[91] The primary issue of this case concerns execution into certain property of the Kazakh central bank. The claimant AIG engaged in a project in Kazakhstan to develop a residential housing complex in the country. After the construction began, the government of Kazakhstan announced that the project was canceled because the land was required for a national arboretum and thereafter seized the project property.[92] AIG initiated ICSID arbitration against Kazakhstan and obtained a favorable ICSID award. Since Kazakhstan refused to pay any part of the damage, AIG registered this award in the High Court of the UK and then tried to attach the cash and securities held by third parties ("AAMGS") in London (the "London assets") pursuant to a Global Custody Agreement with the National Bank of Kazakhstan ("NBK"), which is the central bank of Kazakhstan.[93] The issue was whether the London assets were immune from execution.

The claimant AIG argued that, although the assets were held by AAMGS in the name of NBK, they were ultimately held for the beneficial ownership of Kazakhstan. Thus they were not the property of the central bank.[94] Additionally, the assets were "for the time being, in use or intended for use for commercial purposes" under the meaning of Section 13(4) of the SIA.[95] Therefore, AIG contended that the "commercial use" exception applied to the London assets. Kazakhstan objected to the two arguments of AIG. Firstly, Kazakhstan argued that the cash accounts held by AAMGS represented a debt due by AAMGS to NBK and thus they were the property of the central bank.[96] Secondly, the London assets formed part of the National Funds of Kazakhstan, the purpose of which is "[to ensure] stable social and economic development of the country, accumulation of financial resources for future generations, [and] reduction of the vulnerability of the economy to the influence of unfavorable external factors".[97] Therefore, the funds were not used for commercial purpose but in exercise of sovereign authority and immune from execution.[98]

The court upheld Kazakhstan's counter-arguments and decided that:

1) the London assets held by AAMGS are property of NBK and therefore enjoy immunity from execution under Section 14(4) of the SIA;
2) even if the London assets do not constitute the property of a central bank pursuant to Section 14(4), they are still immune from execution because their purpose is not for commercial use.[99]

---

[91] *AIG Capital Partners Inc v. Kazakhstan*. [2005] APP.L.R. 10/20.

[92] *Id.* at 1.

[93] *Id.*

[94] *Id.* at 7.

[95] *Id.*

[96] *Id.* at 8.

[97] *Id.* at 3.

[98] *Id.* at 8.

[99] *Id.* at 20.

In summary, the legislation regarding sovereign immunity from execution in the UK is quite similar to the US, despite some divergence in the standards of commercial asset exception and some other aspects. As for the case law, the AIG jurisprudence indicates that investors cannot overcome the bar of sovereign immunity with ease – at least for the specially protected assets such as the central bank accounts of foreign states.

c) Execution of ICSID Awards in France

France is famous for its arbitration-friendly attitude. Under French law, recognizing and enforcing ICSID awards does not face significant difficulties.[100] Even so, there still are a number of challenges for investors to execute ICSID awards due to the defense of sovereign immunity. There is no statutory provision in French law regarding the issue of sovereign immunity. In practice, sovereign immunity is regulated by court-defined rules.[101] Compared to the sovereign immunity acts in the US and the UK, the judge-made rules in France are more flexible and easier to evolve. They are also more favorable to facilitate the execution of arbitral awards.

In principle, sovereign assets of foreign states are immune from forcible execution in France, except for two situations:

1) immunity from execution is exempted;
2) the state has waived its immunity from execution.[102]

Under the first situation, certain sovereign assets can be seized if its origin and intended use are private and a nexus between the assets and the underlying claim can be demonstrated.[103] However, French courts have not developed consistent criteria to decide whether the property is for private use – some courts considered the nature of the activity, while other courts looked at the nature of the assets.[104] Besides this private use exception, the case *Republique Democratique du Congo*[105] also developed a new rule that certain foreign asset is not immune from execution if they are related to a civil operation.[106] In this case, Congo failed to pay the maintenance fee of a building used to house its personnel including diplomatic agents, against which the court granted

[100] Sarah Francois-Poncet, Branda Horrigan & Lara Karam, *Enforcement of Arbitral Awards Against Sovereign States or State Entities: France, in* Enforcement of Arbitral Awards Against Sovereigns 355, 355 (Doak Bishop ed., JurisNet 2009).

[101] *Id.* at 359.

[102] *Id.* at 358.

[103] *Id.* at 360 and 373.

[104] *Id.*

[105] Civ. 1, January 25, 2005, *Republique Democratique du Congo v. Syndicat des coproprietaires de l'mmeuble Residence Antony Chatenary*, 9 Rec. Dalloz 620 (2005).

[106] Sarah Francois-Poncet, Branda Horrigan & Lara Karam, Enforcement of Arbitral Awards Against Sovereign States or State Entities: France, *in* Enforcement of Arbitral Awards Against Sovereigns 355, 361 (Doak Bishop ed., JurisNet 2009).

judicial sale of the building in favor of the co-owners' association.[107] This development reflects that exceptions to immunity from execution in France have more flexibility to change through case law.

Under the second situation, it is confirmed by French cases that a state may waive its sovereign immunity from execution. Contrary to the common practice in most other countries, some French courts decided that a state's consent to arbitration not only means a waiver of immunity from jurisdiction, but also extends to immunity from execution.[108] In the case of *Bec Freres I*,[109] the court decided that "by agreeing to arbitration, [...] the [State] accepted the common rules of international trade and thereby waived its immunity from jurisdiction and, given that agreements must be executed in good faith, its immunity from execution".[110] In the subsequent case *Creighton* regarding challenges against an ICC arbitral award, the *Cour de Cassation* followed the same vein and stated that, when a state enters into an ICC arbitration agreement, it undertakes to carry out the resulting award in accordance with Article 24(2) of the ICC Rules and accordingly waives its immunity from execution.[111] Despite being in favor of the execution of arbitral awards, the *Bec Freres I* and *Creighton* decisions suffered severe criticisms because they contradict with the widely accepted view that a state's consent to arbitration does not mean a waiver of immunity from execution. Under the pressure of the criticism, a subsequent case adopted a new rule that "an agreement to arbitrate may be deemed as a waiver of immunity from execution, such waiver will not constitute a blanket authorization to enforce against any and all state assets. Some assets, such as those used for sovereign activities and by diplomatic delegations, would still be immune from execution".[112]

As for the "exception to exception", French courts consider the assets of a foreign central bank as being immune from execution regardless of commercial or non-commercial use.[113] As a member state of the Vienna Convention on Diplomatic Relations, France admits that the assets used for diplomatic missions enjoy diplomatic immunity.[114]

When execution of an arbitral award against a constituent subdivision or entity of a state is requested, difficulties may arise if the award was rendered against the state rather than the state entity. Regarding this question, the general rule is that the assets of the state entity can be attached only if the entity is an emanation of the state. In *Benvenuti & Bonfant v. Congo*, a French case concerning the execution of an ICSID award, this situation was at stake. Benvenuti & Bonfant ("B&B"), an Italian company, sued the Republic of Congo in ICSID and obtained a favorable award. After being granted an exequatur in French

[107] *Id.*

[108] *Id.* 370.

[109] CA Rouen, June 20, 1996, *Societe Bec Freres v. Office des cereales de Tunisie*, 1997 Revue de l'arbitrage 263 (1997).

[110] Sarah Francois-Poncet, Branda Horrigan & Lara Karam, Enforcement of Arbitral Awards Against Sovereign States or State Entities: France, *in* Enforcement of Arbitral Awards Against Sovereigns 355, 370 (Doak Bishop ed., JurisNet 2009).

[111] *Id.*

[112] *Id.* at 372.

[113] *Id.* at 363–366.

[114] *Id.* at 366–369.

court, B&B attempted to attach the funds held by a French bank on behalf of the Banque Commmerciale Congolaise ("BCC"). The issue is whether BCC is an emanation of the State of Congo and thus liable for payment of the award against Congo.[115] Regarding the issue of state emanations, the general standard employed by French courts, is that, if an entity has no separate legal personality and is merely an administrative organ of the state, the entity is deemed to be an emanation of that state.[116] In this case, B&B claimed that BCC is under the control of Congo, which makes it a part of the state.[117] Moreover, as contended by B&B, BCC received funds from the Congolese Treasury, which shows that BCC is an emanation of Congo. The *Cour d'appel* disagreed with the arguments raised by B&B. The court stated that the control exercised by a state over an entity is not sufficient to enable dependent entities to be an emanation of that state.[118] Considering that BCC is a limited liability company performing commercial banking operations on its own account, on behalf of third parties, or as part of a consortium, the court held that BCC is not an emanation of Congo and thus has no obligation to pay the damages granted in the ICSID award.[119] The B&B case shows that, in spite of the pro-arbitration stance, the French court decision does automatically favor the investors seeking execution of an ICSID award. The consideration behind this strict approach is probably to protect private properties from being unduly attached as public property by some investors.

The above analysis of French law and relevant cases shows that the judge-made laws regarding sovereign immunity in France are complex and inconsistent and the investors seeking execution of ICSID awards do not have an easier life in France. However, compared to the sovereign immunity act in the US and the UK, the French law has more flexibility to develop and the exceptions to immunity from execution indeed have been expanded in past years. More evolutions in favor of execution of arbitral awards are probably to be expected in France in the future.

d) Execution of ICSID Awards in China

Despite that no ICSID award has been brought to China for execution, there might be some cases in the future due to the increasing number of Chinese investors going abroad. In this sense, it is worth investigating whether China is a preferable forum for investors seeking execution of ICSID awards.

Unlike the above countries with an explicit endorsement of a restrictive approach regarding sovereign immunity, China is still deemed as a staunch advocate of the absolute sovereign immunity concept.[120] In fact, there is barely any legislation in China specifying

[115] *Benvenuti & Bonfant v. Banque Commmerciale Congolaise and Others*, ICSID Rep. Vol 1, 373 (1987).

[116] Sarah Francois-Poncet, Branda Horrigan & Lara Karam, Enforcement of Arbitral Awards Against Sovereign States or State Entities: France, *in* Enforcement of Arbitral Awards Against Sovereigns 355, 374 (Doak Bishop ed., JurisNet 2009).

[117] *Benvenuti & Bonfant v. Banque Commmerciale Congolaise and Others*, ICSID Rep. Vol 1, 373 (1987), at 374.

[118] *Id.*

[119] *Id.*

[120] Dahua Qi, State Immunity, China and Its Shifting Position, 7 Chinese Journal of International Law 307–

the issue of sovereign immunity, except for one statute in 2005 addressing the immunity from attachment enjoyed by the assets of foreign central banks.[121] Besides, no case up to now has been brought in Chinese People's Courts regarding the sovereign immunity issue.[122]

However, although in Mainland China the issue of sovereign immunity has not been touched in practice, a case regarding the execution of an arbitral award against the Republic of the Congo was brought in a Hong Kong court. This case reveals that absolute immunity in China is supported in practice.

Before analyzing the case, it is worth explaining the unique legal system in Hong Kong prior to and after the transfer of sovereignty from the UK to the People's Republic of China (PRC) in 1997 (usually referred to as "the Handover"). Before 1997, Hong Kong was under British rule for 99 years and its legal system was based on the English common law and rules of equity. At that time, the UK *State Immunity Act* (SIA) applied in Hong Kong, pursuant to which a restrictive approach to sovereign immunity was adopted. After the Handover, Hong Kong became a Special Administrative Region (SAR) of the PRC under the model of "One Country, Two Systems", meaning that Hong Kong has its own Constitution – The Basic Law of the HKSAR – enjoys a high degree of autonomy, and retains its current political, social, commercial and legal systems for 50 years after the Handover. The exception is foreign and defense affairs which are already controlled by the PRC Central Government.[123]

As for Hong Kong's position regarding sovereign immunity after the Handover, it remained unclear for a long time owing to the absence of specific legislation addressing this matter.[124] This situation lasted until 2011 when the Hong Kong courts decided the case *FG Hemisphere Associates LLC v. Democratic Republic of the Congo & Ors*.[125] Along with this case, it became clear that absolute sovereign immunity applies in Hong Kong.

FG Hemisphere, an American hedge fund, is the assignee of two ICC arbitral awards, held initially by a Yugoslav company Energoinvest, against the Democratic Republic of Congo (DRC).[126] After successfully obtaining the order for enforcement of the two

---

337 (2008); Guo Yanxi, *中国关于主权豁免问题的对策* (*Sovereign Immunity – China's Future Policy*), *法学* (*Jurisprudence*) (Vol.3, 1995), 38–39; Zeng Tao, *中国在国家及其财产豁免问题上的实践及立场* (*China's Practice and Position in Relation to Immunity of States and Their Property*), *社会科学* (*Social Science*) (Vol.5 2005), 51–55; Huang Jin & Ma Jingsheng, *Immunities of States and Their Property: The Practice of the People's Republic China*, 18 Hague Yearbook of International Law 163–181 (1988); Wang Houli, *Sovereign Immunity: Chinese Views and Practices*, 1 Journal of Chinese Law 23–32 (1987).

[121] *Id.* at 316. The statute is the Law of the People's Republic of China on Immunity of the Property of Foreign Central Banks from Compulsory Judicial Measures, adopted by the National People's Congress on October, 2005.

[122] *Id.* at 317.

[123] *See* the *Basic Law of the HKSAR*, Article 5, 11, 12, 17, 19.

[124] Mayer Brown, *Sovereign Immunity and Enforcement of Arbitral Awards: Navigating International Boundaries*, http://www.mayerbrown.com/files/Publication/2e0f7077-9b25-430e-8b70-6a8f8c1a9d76/Presentation/PublicationAttachment/1be4c54c-bfc2-4d78-9403-85e37c560f43/12270.PDF (accessed on June 1, 2018).

[125] FACV Nos. 5, 6 and 7 of 2010, dated 8 June 2011 and 8 September 2011.

[126] Hong Kong / 10 February 2010 / Court of Appeal, In the High Court of the Hong Kong Special Administrative Region / *FG Hemisphere Associates LLC* [HK] *v. Democratic Republic of the Congo et al.* / CACV 373/2008 &

awards from a Hong Kong court, FG Hemisphere sought to attach US$104 million, which was the entry fee for an agreement about mineral exploitation rights due from a consortium of Chinese enterprises to the DRC.[127] The Court of First Instance upheld the non-commercial nature of the transaction and stated that no further discussion regarding sovereign immunity was necessary.[128] During the appeal, the Court of Appeal addressed the matter of sovereign immunity and decided that the restrictive doctrine applies in Hong Kong because this is a rule of customary international law and thus should be recognized in Hong Kong.[129]

Before the Court of Final Appeal made its decision, the Standing Committee of the National Peoples' Congress (SCNPC) issued an interpretation of the *Basic Law* Article 13 and 19. The interpretation confirmed that the Central People's Government (CPG) had the power to determine the rules or policies on state immunity to be applied in Hong Kong and concluded that Hong Kong must adopt absolute sovereign immunity to be consistent with the stance adopted by the PRC.[130] In accordance with this interpretation, the Hong Kong Court of Final Appeal reasoned that, although the common law applies in Hong Kong, it must be subject to such modifications, adaptations, limitations or exceptions as are necessary to bring its rules into conformity with Hong Kong's status as a Special Administrative Region of the PRC and to avoid any inconsistency with the Basic Law.[131] Moreover, the Basic Law provides that the CPG is responsible for foreign affairs relating to Hong Kong, thus the matter of sovereign immunity that is deemed as "foreign affairs" within the meaning of Article 19 of the Basic Law should be subject to the CPG's determination.[132] Therefore, the court concluded that absolute sovereign immunity applies and denied the attachment.

After the *Congo* case, the Hong Kong courts' position in favor of the absolute doctrine of sovereign immunity has been recognized internationally. This is not a good sign for investors who wish to execute arbitral awards in Mainland China and in Hong Kong. Although scholars have been calling for a shift from the absolute to the restrictive notion regarding sovereign immunity,[133] and the SCNPC and the CPG's actions suffered severe criticisms for interfering in Hong Kong's judicial process, currently investors still face substantial obstacles before the execution of arbitral awards in China.

CACV 43/2009, New York Convention Guide, http://www.newyorkconvention1958.org/index.php?lvl=notice_display&id=686&seule=1, accessed on June 1, 2018.

[127] Mayer Brown, *Sovereign Immunity and Enforcement of Arbitral Awards: Navigating International Boundaries*, 10.

[128] *Id.*

[129] *Id.* at 11. The dissenting opinion in the Court of Appeal's decision stated that the restrictive doctrine had gained popularity in the international community, but there had been insufficient uniformity and consistency required to attain the status of customary international law.

[130] *See* the *Interpretation of paragraph 1, article 13 and article 19 of the Basic Law of the Hong Kong Special Administrative Region of the People's Republic of China by the Standing Committee of the National People's Congress*, adopted at its 22nd Session on 26 August 2011.

[131] *Democratic Republic of the Congo & Others v FG Hemisphere Associates LLC* FACV No 5 of 2010 (8 June 2011)1 & (8 September 2011)2 CFA.

[132] Mayer Brown, *Sovereign Immunity and Enforcement of Arbitral Awards: Navigating International Boundaries*, 11.

[133] *E.g.* Dahua Qi, State Immunity, China and Its Shifting Position, 7 Chinese Journal of International Law 307–337 (2008).

e) Execution of ICSID Awards in the Reluctant Host States

Forcible execution of an arbitral award only happens when the respondent party refuses to pay. Thus, it is not a wise choice for investors to seek execution in the national courts of reluctant host states. In fact, all of the known cases regarding the execution of ICSID awards were carried out in the home states or a third state, rather than the host states. Assuming that an investor wishes to execute an ICSID award in the host state, some obstacles can be envisaged.

The first obstacle might be the difficulty of obtaining a court judgment declaring the enforceability of the ICSID award. Although Article 53 of the ICSID Convention requires a host state to recognize an ICSID award and enforce the pecuniary obligations immediately, some host states may still have strong motivations to hinder the enforcement. Without a court judgment confirming the enforceability of an ICSID award, it is barely possible for investors to obtain local court assistance to collect the damage. Secondly, even if the investor obtains an order conforming the enforceability of the ICSID award, more resistance during the execution proceedings should be anticipated. Given that municipal law controls the execution of ICSID awards, the host state will probably invoke sovereign immunity to repel forcible attachment of their sovereign assets. Besides sovereign immunity, there might be additional barriers set up by the municipal law. For example, the Argentine law imposes some procedural conditions on the attachment of state assets. According to the Argentine Complementary Law on Budget ("CLB"), all funds, securities and other means aimed at covering the national budget or making the disbursements provided for in the national budget cannot be subject to attachment and the freedom to use, transfer or dispose of those funds, securities and means cannot be limited in any way.[134] CLB also provides that, if a state or its agencies is required to make payment pursuant to a judgment, the amount is paid only if sufficient funds were budgeted.[135] Therefore, even if the court decided that a certain amount of damage is payable by the state to the investor, the real payment is still subject to the availability of funds in the national budget.

Even though some obstacles to the execution of ICSID awards in host states can be predicted, there is no real case affirming host states' resistance as such. Contrary to the conjecture about some host states' hostility towards investment arbitration, there are also some voices negating this assertion. For example, in the 2014 UN General Assembly meeting, Argentine President Cristina Kirchner claimed that it is an untrue condemnation of developed states that Argentina will default on the debts it owes to foreign investors and that Argentina will honor the international arbitral awards against it. Disregarding the complex political issues between different countries, investors are advised to seek execution of ICSID awards in the home state or a pro-arbitration third state to avoid unpredictable results of the execution proceedings in the host states.

---

[134] Decree No. 1, 110/05, *see* Javier Robalino, *Enforcement of Foreign Awards Against Sovereigns in South America: the Cases of Argentina and Ecuador, in* Enforcement of Arbitral Awards Against Sovereigns 425, 434 (Doak Bishop ed., JurisNet 2009).

[135] *Id.* at 435.

IV. Summary

Based on an inaccurate assumption that respondent states would not default on ICSID awards, the ICSID Convention leaves the execution of ICSID awards entirely under the control of domestic laws, including the laws regarding sovereign immunity. As a result, an ICSID award will be executed only if the investor overcomes the respondent state's plea of sovereign immunity. The investigation of the legal systems and the case laws of selected jurisdictions shows that, not mentioning the recalcitrant host states, even in forum states with pro-arbitration rules, investors will face a number of obstacles to overcome the hurdle of sovereign immunity. Although the deadlock for executing ICSID awards is not a striking problem at the moment, it may keep growing along with the backlash against investment arbitration. In this situation, the effectiveness of ICSID arbitration will be cast into serious doubt.

However, it is worth noting that restricting sovereign immunity and promoting the execution of ICSID awards is not the straightforward answer. Sovereign immunity is never a purely legal issue but tangled with economic, political and international relationship considerations. Currently, several recalcitrant states that refuse to comply with ICSID awards are suffering from a distressed domestic economy. Sovereign immunity is a necessary shield to protect their national interests especially during economic hardship. If the forum courts take a pro-execution stance and deny sovereign immunity without considering the host state's financial difficulty, the host state may face greater hardship, which could prevent it from recovering from the crisis and regaining the capacity to pay back other creditors. Therefore, the balance between investors and host states should be borne in mind when considering the issue of execution of ICSID awards.

Orsolya Toth*

THE NEW YORK CONVENTION – CHALLENGES ON ITS 60TH BIRTHDAY

Abstract

The 1958 New York Convention on the Recognition and Enforcement of Foreign Arbitral Awards is arguably the most successful international convention in the field of arbitration. Its 60th birthday is a time for celebration and reflection. This paper considers some of the key challenges the Convention faces on this landmark anniversary by examining the risk of bias by domestic courts towards their own nationals, the problems of enforcement against states and the status of awards set aside at the seat. The application of the Convention is uncertain before domestic courts and the paper argues that efforts must be made to reduce these inconsistencies.

I. Introduction

There are few international instruments in the field of arbitration that have enjoyed success comparable to the New York Convention on the Recognition and Enforcement of Foreign Arbitral Awards ("the New York Convention" or the "Convention").[1] It has been rightly praised time and again for having contributed to the peaceful settlement of disputes through arbitration by laying down a harmonised enforcement regime.[2]

The significance of the Convention is difficult to overstate. The 'end game' in every arbitration is enforcement.[3] It is with a view to enforcement that claimants commence an arbitration, formulate their case strategy and obtain the required funding. In an international dispute, a future award creditor needs assurances that an award obtained in one country will be enforceable in another. Without this reassurance, parties would be

---

* MJur, MPhil, DPhil (Oxon). Assistant Professor in Commercial Law, University of Nottingham.

1 New York Convention on the Recognition and Enforcement of Foreign Arbitral Awards, 1958 (adopted 10 June 1958, entered into force 7 June 1959) 330 UNTS.

2 For an analysis of the Convention *see* Emmanuel Gaillard, George Bermann, Yas Banifatemi and other contributors, The UNCITRAL Secretariat Guide on the Convention on the Recognition and Enforcement of Foreign Arbitral Awards (*New York, 1958*) (United Nations 2016) available at http://newyorkconvention1958.org/pdf/guide/2016_Guide_on_the_NY_Convention.pdf accessed on 28 July 2018; Albert Jan van den Berg, The New York Arbitration Convention of 1958, Towards a Uniform Judicial Interpretation (Kluwer Law International 1981); Marike Paulsson, The New York Convention in Action (Kluwer Law International 2016); a compilation of publications on the Convention is available at http://www.newyorkconvention.org/publications/bibliography accessed on 28 July 2018.

3 Unless there are unique business or strategic considerations by the claimant, which is not the typical case, however.

less likely to resort to arbitration to resolve their cross-border commercial or investment disputes.

As is well-known, it is the New York Convention that provides these vital assurances to parties. Amongst others, the instrument sets out the conditions for recognising and enforcing a foreign award and the circumstances under which enforcement may be refused.[4] The key advantage to parties is that they are offered legal certainty – the intricacies of domestic laws in the country of enforcement cannot interfere with their right to recover the amount due to them under the award.[5] This mechanism increases the parties' trust in arbitration and adds credibility to the entire process.

Since its adoption, the Convention has been undeniably successful and extremely useful in promoting arbitration and offering parties much-needed legal certainty during enforcement. At the same time, it is a fact of life that the world has changed significantly over the past six decades. The way in which parties conduct their business dealings and settle their disputes has become ever more complex and sophisticated. The relationship between investors and states has also transformed over time. States are becoming more aware of their rights and, decades after attracting the initial investments, the bargaining power appears to have shifted from the investor to the state. The investor now has much to lose whilst the state has already reaped many of the benefits of the initial agreement.

The drafters of the New York Convention did not, and could not, foresee many of the complexities the instrument must face today. Whilst it is important to acknowledge the achievements of the Convention, the time is ripe to consider certain challenges that the instrument, domestic judges and parties engaged in arbitration must overcome. For the purposes of this discussion, three central issues will be examined that present significant challenges to the New York Convention on its 60th birthday. The first two problems stem from salient developments in the practice of arbitration whilst the third issue is a theoretical question, albeit with practical implications.

II. Three Birthday Challenges

The first issue to be addressed is the geographical expansion of the contracting states of the Convention. Today, the Convention has 159 contracting states and counting. This is a considerable increase compared with the 24 original signatories in 1958. This development is a natural result of the expansion of arbitration itself, which is now a truly global method of dispute settlement, with mushrooming arbitration centres world-wide. It is also a reflection of the success of the Convention which, at the same time, attracts unique challenges. As will be argued, this expansion brings with it greater scope for domestic courts to favour their own nationals in certain circumstances. In addition, it leads to further difficulties in terms of the interplay between domestic procedural rules and the rules of the Convention.

---

[4] Particularly Articles I-IV and Article V, respectively.

[5] On the role allowed for domestic law, *see* Article VII(1), which provides that a party will not be deprived of any right 'allowed by the law ... of the country where [the] award is sought to be relied upon.' For a discussion *see* MARIKE PAULSSON, THE NEW YORK CONVENTION IN ACTION Chapter 8 (Kluwer Law International 2016).

The second matter to discuss is the increasing involvement of states and state-owned entities in arbitration. This largely results from the growth of investment treaty arbitration designed to settle disputes between private investors and sovereign states.[6] It also stems from the desire of states to enter into commercial contracts with foreign investors, where the bargaining position of the parties often leads to an agreement to commercial arbitration within the territory of the host state. The growing importance of states in arbitration and during the enforcement of arbitral awards is perhaps the greatest challenge to the proper functioning and continued success of the New York Convention.[7]

Finally, the third topic to consider briefly is the on-going debate about the status of awards that have been set aside at the seat of arbitration. In theoretical terms, this debate has been cast as a dichotomy between 'internationalism' and 'territoriality'.[8] According to 'internationalism', what happens at the seat is irrelevant for the purposes of enforcing the award in another jurisdiction, because the award is not the product of the law of the country where it was rendered. Indeed, this is the approach followed in France, established in leading cases such as *Egypt v Chromalloy*[9] and *Putrabali v Rena Holding*.[10] By contrast, 'territoriality' holds that the courts of the enforcement state must defer to the courts of the seat, as required by international comity. An important argument of the territorial approach is that the court of the seat is the 'primary' jurisdiction, whereas the enforcement forum is the 'secondary' jurisdiction during enforcement.[11] Whilst this debate is not, strictly speaking, a new challenge to the effectiveness of the New York Convention, recent cases have shown increasing diversity on this issue. It will be submitted that new discrepancies have come to light in recent years that intensify the confusions

---

6 Generally *see* Rudolf Dolzer and Christoph Schreuer, PRINCIPLES OF INTERNATIONAL INVESTMENT LAW (2nd ed., OUP 2012); Meg N. Kinnear and others (eds), BUILDING INTERNATIONAL INVESTMENT LAW: THE FIRST 50 YEARS OF ICSID (International Centre for Settlement of Investment Disputes, Kluwer Law International 2015). Cases have been conducted notably before the International Centre for Settlement of Investment Disputes (ICSID), the Permanent Court of Arbitration (PCA), and as ad hoc proceedings under the UNCITRAL Arbitration Rules (UNCITRAL Rules).

7 As discussed *infra* in section IV.

8 The literature on these issues is voluminous, for divergent views *see*: Emmanuel Gaillard, *Enforcement of Awards Set-Aside in the Country of Origin: The French Experience, in* IMPROVING THE EFFICIENCY OF ARBITRATION AGREEMENTS AND AWARDS: 40 YEARS OF THE APPLICATION OF THE NEW YORK CONVENTION 505 (Albert Jan van den Berg (ed), Kluwer 1990); Jan Paulsson, *Arbitration Unbound: Award Detached from the Law of Its Country of Origin*, 30 International and Comparative Law Quarterly 358 (1981); Jan Paulsson, *Delocalization of International Commercial Arbitration: When and Why It Matters*, 32 International and Comparative Law Quarterly 53 (1983); Albert Jan van den Berg, *New York Convention of 1958: Refusals of Enforcement*, 18/2 International Court of Arbitration Bulletin 1 (2007); Albert Jan van den Berg, *The 1958 New York Arbitration Convention Revisited, in* ARBITRAL TRIBUNALS OR STATE COURTS: WHO MUST DEFER TO WHOM? 125 (Pierre A. Karrer (ed), Swiss Arbitration Association 2001).

9 *The Arab Republic of Egypt v Chromalloy Aeroservices Inc.*, Judgment (14 January 1997) 22 Y.B. Comm. Arb. 691 (CA 1997).

10 *PT Putrabali Adyamulia v. Rena Holding*, judgment (29 June 2007) 32 Y.B. Comm. Arb. 299 (Cass. 2007). *See also Pabalk Ticaret Limited Sirketti v Norsolor*, Cass Civ 1, Judgment (9 October 1984) 1985 Rev. Arb. 431; *Hilmarton v Omnium de Traitement et de Valorisation*, Cass Civ 1, Judgment (23 March 1994) 1994 ASA Bull. 445.

11 This terminology has been developed primarily by the US courts when applying the Convention. For a discussion, *see e.g.* Christopher Koch, *The Enforcement of Awards Annulled in their Place of Origin: The French and U.S. Experience*, 26 Journal of International Arbitration 267, 284-285 (2009).

present in the theoretical debates and it will be necessary to reconsider these debates to achieve more consistent decisions in practice.[12]

Before starting the discussion, a word of caution is needed. The fundamental basis of arbitration is party autonomy.[13] Although domestic laws vary in detail, the parties' right and obligation to arbitrate stems from their arbitration agreement.[14] This agreement compels parties to observe the award, regardless of the outcome. Indeed, the overwhelming majority of arbitral awards are voluntarily complied with.[15] Plainly, the involvement of domestic courts is antithetical to the nature and purpose of arbitration, since the objective of arbitration is precisely to avoid domestic courts.

The New York Convention regulates the sensitive process of court intervention in arbitration and it is burdened with the herculean task of balancing a wide range of conflicting interests. During enforcement, the interests of the parties must compete with the public interest and those of international comity which are, in substance, unrelated to the underlying dispute. To put it bluntly, court involvement is an irritant to arbitration, and judicial participation contaminates the parties' interests with a range of considerations that have nothing to do with them. At the same time, domestic courts are needed in the enforcement process to assist the award creditor and the drafters of the Convention have made a laudable effort to strike a balance between competing values.[16] Nevertheless, because of the antithesis between court proceedings and arbitration there will always be tensions and inconsistencies in the application of the Convention by domestic courts. Hence, the task sixty years after its adoption is to focus on the extent to which existing discrepancies in the Convention's application may be alleviated, rather than strive towards eliminating them.

---

12 Discussed *infra* in section V.

13 The extent to which party autonomy is fundamental has been debated. At one end of the spectrum are those who support de-localisation, and on the other are representatives of territoriality who argue that it is domestic law that gives any effect to the parties' agreement; for these views *see supra* n. 8. On either view, however, party autonomy is central to arbitration, it is only the extent of its relevance that is debated. Generally *see also* Peter Nygh, Autonomy in International Contracts (Clarendon Press 1999).

14 Domestic laws have been harmonised to a great extent thanks to the UNCITRAL Model Law on International Commercial Arbitration (1985) (United Nations document A/ 40/ 17, annex I), whilst international conventions deal with the parties' consent to investment treaty arbitration, such as the ICSID Convention and bilateral investment treaties.

15 *See* the discussion of relevant data by Maxi Scherer, *Effects of International Judgments Relating to Awards*, 43 Pepperdine Law Review 637, 637 n. 1 (2016) available at: http://digitalcommons.pepperdine.edu/plr/vol43/iss5/7 accessed on 28 July 2018.

16 Emmanuel Gaillard, George Bermann, Yas Banifatemi and other contributors, The UNCITRAL Secretariat Guide on the Convention on the Recognition and Enforcement of Foreign Arbitral Awards (New York, 1958) (United Nations 2016) available at http://newyorkconvention1958.org/pdf/guide/2016_Guide_on_the_NY_Convention.pdf accessed on 28 July 2018; Albert Jan van den Berg, The New York Arbitration Convention of 1958, Towards a Uniform Judicial Interpretation (Kluwer Law International 1981); Marike Paulsson, The New York Convention in Action (Kluwer Law International 2016); Emmanuel Gaillard, *The Urgency of Not Revising the New York Convention*, *in* 50 Years of the New York Convention, ICCA Congress Series 689 (Albert Jan van den Berg (ed.), Kluwer Law International 2009).

III. Geographical Expansion of the Contracting States of the Convention

Over the past sixty years, international arbitration has exploded geographically. In addition to the established centres in Europe (such as London, Paris, or Stockholm)[17], arbitration has gained significant momentum in the United States, Asia, the Middle-East, Latin America and Africa. New arbitration centres have emerged, some of which are now worthy competitors of the traditional locations. A number of high-quality institutions are offering their services to commercial parties with recently revised arbitration rules. Indeed, governments are seeking to make their jurisdiction attractive to parties by investing in new arbitral institutions, reforming their domestic arbitration laws and by acceding to the Convention.

Some of the most successful centres are in Singapore, Hong Kong, Dubai and New York.[18] Africa is also becoming more prominent on the global arbitration map, as disputes with parties from Nigeria and South Africa are on the rise.[19] The governments in Kenya, Rwanda and Mauritius are particularly active in supporting and promoting arbitration in their countries.[20] Arbitrating in exotic locations such as Mauritius or Malaysia may well have been wishful thinking during the adoption of the Convention. Today, it is reality.[21] If the recent efforts to modernise the arbitration laws of Fiji are considered, it quickly becomes clear that the expansion process is far from losing momentum.[22]

On one hand, these developments reflect the success of arbitration and the Convention. On the other, they present certain challenges during enforcement. With a growing number of signatories, the Convention will be interpreted and applied by a more diverse pool of domestic judges. To varying degrees, domestic courts may seek ways to favour their own nationals or they will place excessive emphasis on their own procedural rules, to the detriment of the Convention. This may be due to the fact that

---

17 Notable institutions, respectively, are the London Court of International Arbitration (LCIA), the International Chamber of Commerce (ICC) and the Stockholm Chamber of Commerce (SCC) all of which have their arbitration rules which are regularly updated, with the latest revisions recently implemented.

18 These are the examples of the Singapore International Arbitration Centre (SIAC), Hong Kong International Arbitration Centre (HKIAC), Dubai International Arbitration Centre (DIAC) and the New York International Arbitration Centre (NYIAC) respectively, all of which have updated arbitration rules.

19 Generally *see* Kwadwo Sarkodie and Joseph Otoo, *The Rise and Rise of Arbitration in Africa*, African Law & Business (2018), available at https://www.africanlawbusiness.com/news/8105-the-rise-and-rise-of-arbitration-in-africa accessed on 28 July 2018.

20 In support of the Nairobi Centre for International Arbitration and the Kigali International Arbitration Centre.

21 At the Kuala Lumpur Regional Centre for Arbitration in Malaysia, for example, recently renamed as the Asian International Arbitration Center (AIAC).

22 *See* Wilmer Hale, International Arbitration Group Assists Fiji in Adoption of UNCITRAL Model Law on International Commercial Arbitration (Client Alert, 25 September 2017) available at https://www.wilmerhale.com/en/insights/client-alerts/2017-09-25-international-arbitration-group-assists-fiji-in-adoption-of-uncitral-model-law-on-international-commercial-arbitration accessed on 28 July 2018: 'On 15 September 2017, the Parliament of the Republic of Fiji enacted the International Arbitration Act 2017 (the "Act"). The Act implements the United Nations Convention on Recognition and Enforcement of Foreign Arbitral Awards 1958 (the "New York Convention"), which Fiji ratified on 27 September 2010. It enacts a comprehensive, state-of-the-art legislative framework for international arbitration based on the UNCITRAL Model on International Commercial Arbitration 1985, with amendments adopted in 2006 (the "Model Law").'

they are naturally more familiar with their own law than with the provisions and purpose of the Convention. Another factor is that the operation of the judiciary is extremely slow in certain countries in comparison to others. If judges at the seat move slow with a set-aside application, this puts the courts of enforcement in a difficult position. During this time, the award has what may be termed an 'interim status'. Enforcement courts must find ways to tackle this interim period which will result in further divergences in applying the Convention.

In light of the overview of the challenges resulting from the geographical expansion of the Convention, it is appropriate to consider a few examples that illustrate these difficulties.

a) Risk of Bias Towards Nationals of the Enforcement State

An illustrative example of risk of bias during enforcement is offered by Fluor Transworld Services v Petrixo Oil (*Fluor v Petrixo*).[23] This case concerned the enforcement in the UAE of an ICC award rendered by a sole arbitrator in England. Fluor was a US company that succeeded in the arbitration with its claim for approximately US$ 11 million owed to it under a technical and consulting services agreement concluded with Petrixo. Petrixo was a UAE company and owned by a prominent Dubai businessman.

After obtaining the award in 2015, Petrixo applied to the Dubai Court of First Instance to have the award recognised and enforced in accordance with Article IV of the Convention. However, Petrixo resisted the enforcement and, amongst others, advanced the argument that enforcement should be refused because the arbitrator failed to submit the draft award for approval to the ICC Court in accordance with the ICC Rules of Arbitration. The Court of First Instance accepted this argument and refused to recognise the award. Fluor appealed this decision before the Court of Appeal and furnished proof that the award had in fact received the scrutiny and approval from the ICC Court.[24] However, this was not the end of the road for Fluor, because the Court of Appeal rendered an even more surprising judgment than the lower court. It held that in order for the award to be enforceable, both the UAE and the UK would have to be parties to the New York Convention but there was no proof on record showing that the UK signed the Convention. The UAE signed the Convention in 2006 but based on the 'principle of reciprocity' enshrined in the UAE's civil procedure rules, the award could not be enforced. In response, Fluor took the case to the Court of Cassation which overturned this ruling noting that the UK acceded to the Convention in 1975. On remand from the Court of Cassation, the Court of Appeal ultimately confirmed the award.

This case illustrates how the application of the Convention runs into difficulties in countries that have adopted it relatively recently.[25] Whilst the decision of the Court of Cassation is to be welcomed as it confirms the UAE's objective of being an arbitration

---

[23] For an overview *see Dubai Court Questions UK's Accession to New York Convention*, Global Arb. Rev. (7 April 2016).

[24] *Id.*

[25] The UAE adopted the Convention in 2006 and has not started applying it until 2010.

friendly jurisdiction, the decisions of the lower courts highlight the difficulties for the Convention to break through local peculiarities. The following observations can be made in connection with this case.

First, proof that the UK is a signatory to the Convention is publicly available.[26] Importantly, there is no burden of proof on the party seeking enforcement of the award under Article IV to supply evidence of the contracting states. Second, even if the UK had not been a party to the Convention, the UAE would still be obliged to enforce the award, because the UAE made no reservation of reciprocity when it acceded to the Convention. Third, it was therefore inappropriate for the court to rely on its own procedural rule of 'reciprocity'.[27]

The first natural reaction to this case is that the lower courts were biased in favour of Petrixo because its owner was a well-known Dubai businessman. The motivation of judges, however, is always difficult to decipher. It can be a combination of homeward bias, local traditions, cultural differences and lack of familiarity with the Convention. The issues raised in the Middle-East show that local peculiarities play an important part. For example, enforcement of an award has been refused on the basis that the witnesses were not sworn in before the arbitrator. Indeed, the conflation of domestic civil procedure rules with the rules of the Convention may, at least in part, result from a lack of terminological distinction under local law.[28]

Another case which illustrates the problem of bias is Corporacion Mexicana de Matenimiento Integral, S De RL De CV v Pemex-Exploracion y Produccion (*Commisa v Pemex*).[29] The case concerned the enforcement of an ICC award in the United States which was rendered and subsequently set aside in Mexico. The parties entered into a contract for the construction of offshore gas platforms in the Gulf of Mexico. Commisa was the Mexican subsidiary of a US corporation, whilst Pemex was a Mexican state-owned oil and natural gas exploration entity.[30]

---

[26] UN Treaty Collection website (https://treaties.un.org/), which provides formal evidence of the UK's status and the UNCITRAL website (www.uncitral.org/).

[27] *See Dubai Court Questions UK's Accession to New York Convention*, Global Arb. Rev. (7 April 2016), setting out criticism of the award by Marike Paulsson. In addition, the Court of Appeal decided to refuse recognition on its own motion which makes the decision even more vulnerable to criticism, *see* Hassan Arab, John Gaffney and Malak Nasreddine, Enforcing an ICC Arbitral Award in the UAE: Fluor Transworld Services vs. Petrixo Oil (2016) available at https://www.tamimi.com/law-update-articles/enforcing-an-icc-arbitral-award-in-the-uae-fluor-transworld-services-vs-petrixo-oil/ accessed on 28 July 2018.

[28] *See* the case of Qatar which has also been criticised because it relied on its domestic procedural law instead of the Convention. It has been explained that the same Arabic word, 'hukum' refers both to the enforcement of judgments and awards. This lack of distinction may be one reason for the confusion. *See Dubai Court Questions UK's Accession to New York Convention*, Global Arb. Rev. (7 April 2016).

[29] *Corporacion Mexicana de Matenimiento Integral, S De RL De CV v Pemex-Exploracion y Produccion*, (No 13-4022) United States Court of Appeals for the Second Circuit, Judgment (2 August 2016) (the *Commisa Judgment*).

[30] For a discussion of the case, *see* Steven Finizio and Santiago Bejarano, Annulled Commisa v Pemex Arbitration Award Enforced (12 October 2016) available at https://www.wilmerhale.com/en/insights/publications/2016-10-12-annulled-commisa-v-pemex-arbitration-award-enforced accessed on 28 July 2018; Marike Paulsson, *Comissa v. PEMEX The Sequel: Are The Floodgates Opened? The Russian Doll Effect Further Defined*, Kluwer Arbitration Blog (11 August 2016) available at http://arbitrationblog.kluwerarbitration.com/2016/08/11/reserved-pemex-decision/ accessed on 28 July 2018; Linda Silberman and Nathan Yaffe, *The US Approach*

In the arbitration, Commisa claimed wrongful termination of the contract and was awarded US$ 300 million in damages. Commisa then sought to enforce the award before the district court in New York.[31] Pemex opposed the application and initiated set-aside proceedings in Mexico. Pemex's efforts to set aside the award initially failed but it filed a constitutional action to annul the award on constitutional grounds which was ultimately successful. The Mexican appeals court held that the matters in dispute were not arbitrable, because they consisted of administrative acts of an entity of the Mexican government. The termination of the contract by Pemex was such an administrative act and therefore the administrative courts in Mexico had exclusive jurisdiction over the dispute. In its reasoning, the court applied a recently enacted legislation with retrospective effect which enabled it to reach this conclusion.

Meanwhile, the district court in New York confirmed the award. After the annulment in Mexico, the case came before the US Court of Appeals of the Second Circuit, which was called to rule on the enforceability of the award despite its annulment in Mexico. In assessing the case, the court confirmed its discretion to enforce an award set aside at the seat based on the word 'may' under Article V(1) of the Convention.[32] As for the extent of this discretion, the court held that it was entitled to exercise its discretion and enforce the award, because the annulment violated the requirements of fundamental fairness and public policy in the United States.[33] In particular, the annulment in Mexico violated fundamental principles of due process and justice. Amongst others, the court pointed to the fact that the Mexican legislation was applied retrospectively which was 'repugnant to United States law'.[34] Furthermore, the Mexican administrative courts which had exclusive jurisdiction over the dispute refused to hear Commisa's claim, because the 45 day limitation period to do so had expired. In the view of the US court, this deprived Commisa from a forum to hear its claim. In the court's view this would have resulted in 'a taking of private property without compensation for the benefit of the [Mexican] Government'.[35]

Commentators have reflected on this case because of its importance on the US stance towards the enforcement of annulled awards. The court's reasoning attracted praise on the basis that it strikes a proper balance between 'internationalism' and 'territoriality'.[36] It has also sparked criticism because it runs counter to the Convention's objective to promote

to Recognition and Enforcement of Awards After Set-Asides: The Impact of the Pemex Decision, 40-3 Fordham International Law Journal 799 (2017).

31 Before the US District Court for the Southern District of New York.

32 And based on Article 5 of the Inter-American (Panama) Convention which was applicable in this case, the wording of which is identical to the New York Convention.

33 The US court referred to previous cases such as *Baker Marine (Nig) Ltd v Chevron (Nig) Ltd.*, 191 F 3d 194 (2d Cir 1999) and *TermoRio SA ESP v Electranta*, 487 F 3d 928 (DC Cir 2007) and *Chromalloy Aerosevices, A Division of Chromalloy Gas Turbine Corp v Arab Republic of Egypt*, 939 F.Supp. 907 (DDC 1996). For a discussion *see* Linda Silberman and Nathan Yaffe, *The US Approach to Recognition and Enforcement of Awards After Set-Asides: The Impact of the Pemex Decision*, 40-3 Fordham International Law Journal 799 (2017).

34 *Commisa* Judgment 32.

35 *Id.* at 39.

36 *See New Thoughts on the New York Convention*, Global Arbitration Review (29 September 2016).

effectiveness. As has been argued, 'resurrecting annulled awards' is not effective.[37] Whilst these matters will be considered further,[38] another, largely neglected, aspect of the case deserves attention at this point.

It transpires from the court's reasoning that it practically applied US public policy as a standard against which it measured the Mexican judiciary. The US Court of Appeals has judged the Mexican court and the Mexican annulment judgment, rather than the award itself. What is more, the court relied on the merits of the underlying dispute in support of its decision to enforce the award. As set out above, the court was concerned that, without enforcing the award, the actions of the Mexican government would amount to the 'taking of private property' without compensation. This is a crucial part of the reasoning, because it confirms the correctness of the award on the merits. But how can the enforcement court take *any* view on the merits of the case? Has it heard the parties' submissions on the merits or reviewed the evidence adduced in the arbitration? The answer must be in the negative.[39] How is it, then, possible that the court was concerned that, without enforcing the award, the Mexican government would have committed expropriation?

The answer is between the lines and emerges from the facts. Commisa was the Mexican subsidiary of a US corporation and Pemex was a Mexican government entity. The US courts were concerned about the expropriation of 'US' property, rather than about the taking of 'private' property.

As for the retrospective application of the relevant Mexican legislation, the US court criticised Mexico on how it applied its *own* law. The court's finding that such an application was contrary to US public policy was one of the reasons that led to the enforcement of the annulled award. The question inevitably arises whether enforcement courts should be entitled to go as far as judging the application of the domestic law of the seat by their own courts. Again, had the relevant parties not been a US private corporation paired up with a Mexican government entity, it is unlikely that the US court would have been so ready and willing to undertake such an investigation and pass judgment on this issue. It is therefore submitted that the US court was motivated by homeward bias considerations and its desire to protect US property from expropriation by Mexico.

b) Interplay Between Domestic Laws and the Convention

Another consequence of the geographical expansion of the contracting states is that the Convention's application has to be reconciled with a growing number of domestic procedural laws. The increasing diversity of domestic laws presents challenges to the consistent application of the Convention.

---

[37] Marike Paulsson, *Comissa v. PEMEX The Sequel: Are The Floodgates Opened? The Russian Doll Effect Further Defined*, Kluwer Arbitration Blog (11 August 2016) available at http://arbitrationblog.kluwerarbitration.com/2016/08/11/reserved-pemex-decision/ accessed on 28 July 2018.

[38] In section V.

[39] If it were in the positive, that would show another grave deficiency of the enforcement process.

The first case to be discussed illustrates the interplay between US civil procedure rules and the Convention. In Thai-Lao Lignite (Thailand) v Government of the Lao People's Democratic Republic (*Thai-Lao Lignite v Laos*),[40] the US Court of Appeals for the Second Circuit upheld the lower court's decision of the reversal of its own earlier enforcement judgment. The award was rendered in an UNCITRAL arbitration at the Kuala Lumpur Regional Centre for Arbitration in Malaysia. The successful claimant, Thai-Lao Lignite applied to the District Court for the Southern District of New York to enforce the award. The district court granted a judgment enforcing the award. However, in the meantime, Laos applied to the Malaysian courts to set aside the award and was eventually successful before the Malaysian High Court. As a result of this annulment, the US district court 'de-enforced' the award – it reversed its earlier enforcement judgment pursuant to Federal Rule of Civil Procedure 60(b)5 which permits district courts to 'relieve a party ... from a final judgment' when the judgment 'is based on an earlier *judgment* that has been reversed or vacated'.[41] The case came before the US Court of Appeals which upheld the 'de-enforcement' judgment of the district court, after a long period of time.

A number of observations may be made about this case. First, it is submitted that the district court's application of Rule 60(b)5 confused the court's 'judgment' with the 'award'. It was not a 'judgment' that was 'reversed' or 'vacated'– it was an arbitral award that has been set aside at the seat. The confusion of the judgment of the seat's courts with the arbitral award is unfortunate and undesirable. Second, the appeals court noted in its judgment that 'we have held our ruling in this matter pending our decision and resolution of the petition in [Commisa v Pemex]'.[42] Awaiting the *Commisa v Pemex* decision was a reason for the court's delay in Thai-Lao Lignite. Whilst this delay may be justifiable from the perspective of the coherence of the US legal system, what do the parties in Thai-Lao Lignite have to do with the parties in Commisa? Absolutely nothing. Yet, the fate of their award was affected by the dispute of unrelated parties. In addition, as has been seen, the Commisa decision is not without its difficulties either.[43] Third, the added difficulty is that the Malaysian High Court's decision annulling the award was not final. It is open to appeal to the Federal Court in Malaysia. In case such an appeal succeeded, would the US district court reverse its 'de-enforcement' decision once again? If so, would that be a 'de-de-enforcement' or a 're-enforcement' decision? If it would decide not to change its decision, what would be its rationale?[44] How would that be consistent with international comity or, for that matter, with Rule 60(b)5?

---

[40] *Thai-Lao Lignite (Thailand) v. Government of the Lao People's Democratic Republic* (Nos 14597, 141052, 141497) United States Court of Appeals for the Second Circuit, Judgment (20 July 2017) (the *Thai-Lao Judgment*).

[41] Federal Rule of Civil Procedure 60(b)5 (extract, emphasis added); Id, at 3.

[42] *Id.* at 6.

[43] Also, in Commisa, the award was enforced despite annulment at the seat, whereas in Thai-Lao Lignite the opposite conclusion was reached.

[44] For the position in the UK, *see Malicorp Ltd v Government of the Arab Republic of Egypt and ors [2015] EWHC 361 (Comm)* which serves as a reminder that the fact that a foreign judgment is subject to a pending appeal will not, in itself, prevent the English court from recognising it as a final decision.

The second illustrative case is Anatolie Stati and others v The Republic of Kazakhstan (*Stati v Kazakhstan*)[45] where the English court adjourned the enforcement hearing pending the outcome of the set aside proceedings in Sweden. The judge found that there was a real prospect of success for Kazakhstan to set aside the award before the Swedish courts and that it would therefore be uneconomical to proceed with hearing the parties' arguments. He also noted that it was likely that the Swedish court would render its decision over the next few months, which would not prejudice the rights of either party. Importantly, the judge adjourned the proceedings on its own motion, citing international comity, public interest and the interests of case management. Amongst the latter category, it was noted that there would be a shortage of judges over the coming months due to court vacation. Accordingly, allocating the court's resources to solve the disputes of other court users was also in favour of the adjournment. As it turned out, the Swedish court did not set aside the award and the English courts eventually did have to conduct a full hearing on the enforcement application.

The *Stati v Kazakhstan* decision also serves to demonstrate how domestic considerations that have nothing to do with the parties, including court vacation, may affect the enforcement of a foreign award. In addition, the rationale of the adjournment in this case was to conduct the proceedings more economically, however, ultimately, it served only to delay the parties' dispute. The hearing eventually had to be conducted without saving any time, expense or court resources.

Finally, IPCO (Nigeria) Ltd v Nigerian National Petroleum Corpn (*IPCO v Nigeria*)[46] illustrates the interplay between English law on the provision of security and the Convention. As opposed to *Stati v Kazakhstan*, where the English courts were ready to adjourn enforcement partly in light of the expectation that the Swedish courts would rule speedily on the set aside application, the seat of arbitration was a less efficient jurisdiction. In IPCO v Nigeria, the English court noted the 'catastrophic delays' in the Nigerian proceedings which began some 13 years ago.[47] The judge predicted that it could take another 30 years until the Nigerian courts would reach their verdict and a stay of enforcement was lifted.[48] Indeed, this case illustrates how enforcement courts are adopting a different position during pending annulment proceedings at the seat depending on the efficiency of the judiciary of that country. The text of the New York Convention does not draw a distinction between 'efficient' and 'non-efficient' seats but this factor can make a significant difference in practice before the enforcement courts.

---

45 *Anatolie Stati and others v The Republic of Kazakhstan* [2015] EWHC 2542 (Comm).

46 *IPCO (Nigeria) Ltd v Nigerian National Petroleum Corpn* [2017] UKSC 16.

47 Tom Jones, *UK Supreme Court Hears New York Convention Appeal*, Global Arbitration Review (3 February 2017), reporting on the case.

48 The circumstances of the case were complex, however, as there was a consent order on adjournment which the claimant sought to set aside based on allegations of fraud and the interpretation of 'adjournment' was also at issue, *see IPCO (Nigeria) Ltd v Nigerian National Petroleum Corpn* [2017] UKSC 970–971.

IV. Increasing Involvement of States

The next modern day challenge to the New York Convention to consider is the increasing involvement of states in arbitration. With the growth of investment treaty arbitration and the sophistication of the legal framework regulating international investments through a global network of bilateral investment treaties and the adoption of multilateral agreements, such as the Energy Charter Treaty, the participation of states or state-owned entities in enforcement proceedings presents unique challenges. Investors and states are becoming more aware of their rights, and do not shy away from using arbitration or the enforcement proceedings for strategic purposes.[49] Inevitably, the current legitimacy crisis of investment treaty arbitration also negatively impacts the enforcement of awards under the Convention.[50]

a) Risk of Domestic Courts Favouring a Sovereign

As a result of the involvement of states in arbitration, there is a risk that domestic courts will afford preferential treatment to a sovereign, which prejudices the private party in the dispute. For example, the complex facts of *Thai-Lao Ignite v Laos* have arisen because the Malaysian courts allowed Laos to file its set aside application after the expiry of a time limit under Malaysian law.[51] Laos argued that it was unaware of this deadline and it was eventually granted permission to file the annulment application. The Malaysian court specifically mentioned that it was allowing this extension to a 'sovereign', suggesting that it would have been unwilling to give permission to a private party.[52] As discussed above, this permission had far-reaching consequences in terms of the enforcement of the award in the US.[53] The US courts, too, were unwilling to entertain the argument that Laos acted negligently before the Malaysian courts. International comity prevailed, arguably, to an extent that was hardly envisaged under the Convention.

---

[49] For example, in the context of the *Yukos* enforcement proceedings, *see infra* n. 55, Russia's former space agency, Roscosmos, threatened France with an investment treaty claim if its courts did not lift a freezing order over its assets. For another example of 'strategic use' of arbitration *see Chevron Corporation and Texaco Petroleum Corporation v. The Republic of Ecuador*, an UNCITRAL arbitration where Chevron initiated the proceedings at the PCA to block the enforcement of a judgment issued against it by the courts in Ecuador.

[50] In order to address the current deficiencies of the system, perceived or real, UNCITRAL Working Group III has been mandated with the scrutiny of 'Investor-State Dispute Settlement Reform' at an inter-governmental level. Their 35th Session took place between 23-27 April in New York. Materials from this and previous sessions showing the states' concerns and other issues are available at http://www.uncitral.org/uncitral/en/commission/working_groups/3Investor_State.html accessed on 28 July 2018.

[51] *Thai-Lao* Judgment 16–17.

[52] *Id.*

[53] Section III.1.

b) Sovereign Immunity Obstacles to Enforcement

Sovereign immunity as such is not a new challenge during enforcement, however, more recently, these defences have been raised by states more vigorously.

An example is the mammoth arbitration of Yukos Universal Limited (Isle of Man) v The Russian Federation (the *Yukos arbitration*).[54] The Yukos award is the largest known investment treaty award to date, in the amount of US$ 50 billion, arising out of an arbitration under the Energy Charter Treaty conducted before the Permanent Court of Arbitration at The Hague. The enforcement efforts of the claimants who succeeded against Russia have originally spanned six jurisdictions.[55] The enforcement proceedings affected a large number of entities, including the Russian Satellite Communications Company, Russian news agency RIA Novosti, and the Russian space corporation, Roscosmos.[56] When state assets are involved, it is often difficult to establish which assets are protected by sovereign immunity and which ones are available for seizure. During the *Yukos* enforcement, Russia repeatedly relied on the notion of sovereign immunity, whilst the claimants argued that the affected entities were merely an 'alter ego' of the Russian State and their assets should be used to satisfy the award.

With the growing involvement of states in enforcement proceedings, it may be expected that these arguments will be raised frequently before enforcement courts. The way in which domestic judges tackle these issues will affect the enforceability of awards under the New York Convention and local discrepancies may present parties with a pitfall during their efforts to collect on their award.

c) Huge Amount of Damages

With the growing worth of investments, it is a natural development that the value of the claims in investment disputes is also on the rise. As mentioned, in the *Yukos* arbitration, the claimants were awarded US$ 50 billion as compensation for the expropriation of their investment. The scale of the award was unprecedented and it amounted to about 20 per cent of Russia's annual budget.[57] The award in *Stati v Kazakhstan* amounted to US$ 500 million which is dwarfed by the Yukos award but it is still a huge setback to a country like Kazakhstan.

Whilst the often enormous amount of damages awarded to successful claimants may be understandable in light of the value of the investment, the difficulty is that extremely

[54] *Yukos Universal Limited (Isle of Man) v. The Russian Federation*, UNCITRAL, PCA Case No. AA 227.

[55] Belgium, France, UK, US, Germany and India. *See "Baiting the Bear": Yukos Enforcement Updates from Around the World*, Global Arbitration Review (19 April 2016).

[56] During the enforcement process in France, *Id.*

[57] *See e.g.* Ben Knowles, Khaled Moyeed and Nefeli Lamprou, *The US$50 Billion Yukos Award Overturned – Enforcement Becomes a Game of Russian Roulette*, Kluwer Arbitration Blog (13 May 2016) available at http://arbitrationblog.kluwerarbitration.com/2016/05/13/the-us50-billion-yukos-award-overturned-enforcement-becomes-a-game-of-russian-roulette/ accessed on 28 July 2018.

high awards will trigger the losing state to multiply its efforts to resist enforcement.[58] In addition, since public funds are at stake, the enforcement process may receive negative publicity and strengthen the already existing public 'backlash' against investment treaty arbitration. Accordingly, it may be more practical for parties and their advisors to consider this factor when formulating their claim, and perhaps, to lower the bar with an easier enforcement process in mind. This might appear to be a compromise in the short term but may well pay off in the long run, particularly at the enforcement stage. Similarly, arbitrators should also consider the impact of the amount of the award on enforcement when assessing damages.

V. Internationalism Versus Territoriality: the Status of Awards Set Aside at the Seat

Finally, it is appropriate briefly to consider the status of awards set aside at the seat. As mentioned, the current debate about enforcement of annulled awards is conducted within the framework of 'internationalism' versus 'territoriality'. In broad terms, 'internationalism' means that the annulment of the award at the seat does not affect enforcement elsewhere. By contrast, 'territoriality' means that deference must be given to the courts of the seat in this matter. The *Commisa v Pemex* case, in particular, has been appraised by commentators as striking the right balance between these two schools of thought.[59]

In *Commisa*, the US Court of Appeals for the Second Circuit confirmed the district court's discretion to enforce an award annulled in Mexico, because the annulment violated the requirements of fundamental fairness and public policy in the United States.[60] The US courts found that the way in which the Mexican courts applied Mexican legislation was 'repugnant to United States law.' The US courts, therefore, chose to enforce an award annulled at the seat. They did not defer to the Mexican courts' decision, therefore, this decision may be regarded as an example of 'internationalism'. A position based on 'territoriality' would have required the US courts to defer to the Mexican courts.

From the US courts' arguments in *Commisa*, however, it transpires that this dichotomy can be misleading. In theory, 'internationalism' would require a domestic court to focus on the award, rather than on a domestic judgment about the award. The task of the enforcement court is a scrutiny of the award, not the judicial system of another sovereign country. In its pure form, this theory would lead to the true 'de-localisation' of an award.[61] Arguably, 'delocalisation' is not fully supported by the New York Convention,

---

[58] Again, as demonstrated by Russia's efforts in the *Yukos* enforcement proceedings.

[59] *New Thoughts on the New York Convention*, Global Arb. Rev. (29 September 2016). For a critical appraisal of the impact of the decision, *see* Linda Silberman and Nathan Yaffe, *The US Approach to Recognition and Enforcement of Awards After Set-Asides: The Impact of the Pemex Decision*, 40-3 Fordham International Law Journal 799 (2017).

[60] Section III.1.

[61] *See* Jan Paulsson, *Arbitration Unbound: Award Detached from the Law of Its Country of Origin*, 30 International and Comparative Law Quarterly 358 (1981); Jan Paulsson, *Delocalization of International Commercial Arbitration: When and Why It Matters*, 32 International and Comparative Law Quarterly 53 (1983).

because, in Article V(1)(e), enforcement courts 'may' refuse to recognise an award if it has been annulled at the seat. Thus, a judgment about the award is not irrelevant but the Convention gives no specific guidance on the extent to which enforcement courts may (or should or could) take into account the annulment judgment at the seat.[62]

In this respect, the decision in *Commisa* was peculiar – the US courts have achieved a result which is seemingly 'internationalist', because they did not defer to the Mexican courts. However, in essence, the decision has confirmed 'territoriality', because the US courts enforced the award based on 'US public policy' considerations. In other words, the US courts have simply "re-localised" the award, rather than 'de-localised' it. Instead of giving 'priority' to the courts of the seat, they have given priority to themselves, i.e., to the courts of enforcement.[63] Care must be taken not to mistake apparent 'internationalism' with what in essence is merely covert 'territoriality' or 're-localisation'.

To alleviate at least some of these problems, it is submitted that the focus of the enforcement scrutiny should be on the award, rather than on the foreign courts' judgment about the award. This is not to say that the latter is irrelevant. Indeed, the extent to which it is to be taken into account is within the enforcement courts' discretion. However, focussing predominantly on the judgment of the courts of the seat will lead to a number of undesirable consequences. First, there is a real risk that domestic judges will sit in judgment of the judicial system of other countries. As discussed, *Commisa* illustrates this risk.[64] The enforcement of foreign arbitral awards should not turn into a process of 'judging the judges' of another country. Second, a 'hierarchy' of arbitral seats is emerging when it comes to enforcement. Enforcement courts may be more willing to defer to some seats than others, depending on their view of the quality of the judiciary of the relevant seat. Whilst there are divergences between domestic courts, the New York Convention does not envisage such a hierarchy. 'Selective' or even at times 'reverse' international comity is observable. Finally, it is discernible that these developments jeopardise legal certainty. The fate of the award may in practice depend on the 'reputation' of the judiciary of the seat, rather than on the consistent application of the Convention.

[62] This is why this issue is hotly and extensively debated in the literature. *See* Emmanuel Gaillard, *Enforcement of Awards Set-Aside in the Country of Origin: The French Experience, in* Improving the Efficiency of Arbitration Agreements and Awards: 40 Years of the Application of the New York Convention 505 (Albert Jan van den Berg ed. Kluwer 1990); Jan Paulsson, *Arbitration Unbound: Award Detached from the Law of Its Country of Origin*, 30 International and Comparative Law Quarterly 358 (1981); Jan Paulsson, *Delocalization of International Commercial Arbitration: When and Why It Matters*, 32 International and Comparative Law Quarterly 53 (1983); Albert Jan van den Berg, *New York Convention of 1958: Refusals of Enforcement*, 18/2 ICC International Court of Arbitration Bulletin 1 (2007); Albert Jan van den Berg, *The 1958 New York Arbitration Convention Revisited, in* Arbitral Tribunals or State Courts: Who Must Defer to Whom? 125 (Pierre A. Karrer (ed), Swiss Arbitration Association 2001).

[63] This is not to say that either jurisdiction enjoys priority over the other, as the text of the Convention does not envisage such a hierarchy.

[64] *See* section III.1.

VI. Conclusion

The New York Convention faces a number of challenges on its 60th birthday. Despite its successful life so far, it is appropriate to pause on this anniversary and consider some of the shortcomings of its application. The Convention is now being applied by more domestic judges than ever before. Instances of homeward bias are discernible, where courts favour their own nationals, consciously or subconsciously. There are also cases where domestic courts favour a foreign sovereign to the detriment of a private party during enforcement. The increasing involvement of states in international arbitration also draws attention to expected trends – the vigorous resistance by states at the stage of enforcement and possible negative publicity of the process which may further harm the perception of investment treaty arbitration which is already in a vulnerable state. The status of awards annulled at the seat remains controversial and fraught with uncertainties. There are terminological confusions as well as conceptual misunderstandings amongst domestic judges who are called upon to apply the Convention.

Solutions may take multiple forms, such as education of judges, and awareness of parties and their advisors of the most salient issues that they may face. Nevertheless, there is further work to be done by lawyers and policymakers if the aims of the drafters of the Convention are to be preserved, such as the purpose of increasing the credibility of arbitration by reassuring parties that they will be able to convert their award into tangible funds at the end of a hard-fought battle. Currently, it often appears that the Convention holds the promise of another battle, rather than the key to a final resolution.

Institutional issues: time for reform?

Zoltán Víg[*] & Gábor Hajdu[**]

INVESTMENT PROTECTION UNDER CETA: A NEW PARADIGM?

Abstract

Investment protection is a central element of many free trade agreements. However, this subject is provoking heated discussion in every corner of the world. There is a widely shared theory that provisions related to investment protection only serve the interests of the investors and not those of the citizens. The European Union-Canada Comprehensive Economic and Trade Agreement (CETA) has an exceptional importance for the European Union, as its provisions on the protection of investment can potentially reshape not only the environmental protection system of the European Union but its whole legislation. It is possible that the European Union would be reluctant to take socially and environmentally justified measures, because foreign investors would sue them if such measures harm their interests. Besides, large United States companies could "crawl" into the European Union through Canada and have the same advantages as Canadian companies. Therefore, it is important to scrutinize and interpret the investment protection system of the CETA, its potential future effects, and to make suggestions how to solve problematic issues.

I. Introduction

The European Union-Canada Comprehensive Economic and Trade Agreement (CETA) was the result of long negotiations between the European Union and Canada. There were plans for a comprehensive trade agreement between the parties already in 2002.[1] As an antecedent to the negotiation process, the Commission submitted to the Council of the European Union a proposal to entitle the Commission to start formal negotiations on an economic integration agreement with Canada. This was granted in 2009 and was amended in 2011 when the Commission received a mandate to negotiate on detailed investment protection issues and an investment related dispute settlement procedure. Both directives became partially public on December 15, 2015 with the decision of the Council.[2] The amendment of 2011 is of crucial importance for this work as it made it

---

[*] Associate professor, University of Szeged, School of Law and associate professor, Singidunum University, Faculty of Economics, Finance and Administratio (FEFA), Belgrade.

[**] Assistant research fellow and doctoral students, University of Szeged, School of Law.

[1] Panagiotis Delimatsis, TTIP, CETA, TiSA Behind Closed Doors: Transparency in the EU Trade Policy 11 (Tilburg Law and Economics Center, 2016).

[2] http://www.consilium.europa.eu/en/press/press-releases/2015/12/15-eu-canada-trade-negotiating-mandate-made-public/, accessed on May 12, 2018.

possible for the CETA to contain comprehensive investment protection rules. However, leaked information showed that the CETA draft already contained a chapter on investment protection in 2010. This chapter showed the influence of NAFTA, as it equated "fair and equal treatment" with the "minimum standard" of treatment of foreigners in international customary law. The term "like circumstances" used by NAFTA was also taken over in the provisions on national treatment and most favored nation treatment.[3] This influence of NAFTA and its concepts might be the result of Canada's influence and the Commissions' limited authority. Thus, the draft of the CETA received serious criticism from European Union-based interest groups because of the application of NAFTA's solutions, who were unwilling to accept such a system of protection. Because of this, the Commission partly changed its standpoint regarding the investment protection chapter in 2013 and tried to guarantee better protection for European investors' foreign investment abroad. However, these were only minor changes. Nevertheless, according to some opinions, the investment protection chapter of the CETA still shows the influence of the NAFTA.[4] The change of the Commission's position can be explained by the 2011 amendment, which gave a free hand to the Commission to negotiate investment protection issues related to the CETA. Furthermore, the 2008 economic crisis might have affected its position, as the European Union needed capital and the easiest way was to get it from North American investors. However, these investors wanted to have an investment protection system familiar to them, like that of NAFTA. The next step of the CETA's development was on October 18, 2013 when the President of the European Commission, José Manuel Barroso and Stephen Harper, Prime Minister of Canada, reached consensus regarding the most important parts of the CETA. However, working out of details still had to be resolved.[5] The Committee on International Trade of the European Parliament (INTA) received the text of the agreement as a classified document in August 2014.[6] The negotiations on the content of the agreement were closed in the same month. The next important step happened only two years later in July 2016 when the Commission made a formal proposal to the Council for signing the CETA.

Here the case of Belgium should be mentioned as the Vallon Regional Parliament was in the position to force Belgium to block the ratification of the CETA. This could have frustrated the conclusion of the agreement. In the end, Belgium and the European Union managed to handle the issue.[7] Thus, each member state gave consent on October 28, 2016 and the agreement was signed on October 30, 2016.[8] Subject to the decision of the Council, the CETA can be provisionally applicable. However, for it to enter into full force, the Council's decision, the European Parliament's consent and carrying out the

---

3 Filippo Fontanelli & Giuseppe Bianco, *Converging Towards NAFTA: An Analysis of FTA Investment Chapters in the European Union and the United States*, 50(2) Stanford Journal of International Law 231 (2014).

4 *Id.* at 232.

5 *Id.*

6 Panagiotis Delimatsis, TTIP, CETA, TiSA Behind Closed Doors: Transparency in the EU Trade Policy 12 (Tilburg Law and Economics Center, 2016).

7 http://www.bbc.com/news/world-europe-37731955, accessed May 13, 2018.

8 http://www.bbc.com/news/world-europe-37814884, accessed May 13, 2018.

ratification procedure in each member state is necessary.[9] Thus, the adoption of the CETA, on the side of the European Union, will be the result of a complex procedure, which is still not finished.

All in all, the CETA is the result of a long negotiation process and is a milestone of the new trade and investment policy of the European Union. However, national parliaments of the European Union still must approve the CETA before it can take full effect.

II. Investment Protection Standards of the CETA

Contracting parties tried to avoid ambiguity regarding definitions and tried to close loopholes that were present in some of the previous international investment protection treaties. Here, only the most important standards of the CETA will be analyzed.

The first standard that should be discussed is the already mentioned "fair and equitable treatment". The first section of article 8.10 of the Agreement explicitly states that contracting parties guarantee for the investors of the other party fair and equitable treatment and full protection and security.[10] Section 5 of the same article says "full protection and security" means the physical security of investors and covered investments.[11] Accordingly, "fair and equitable treatment" is dealt with in other sections of the agreement. Thus, Section 2 lists the measures that breach "fair and equitable treatment" requirement. These are

(a) denial of justice in criminal, civil or administrative proceedings;
(b) fundamental breach of due process, including a fundamental breach of transparency, in judicial and administrative proceedings;
(c) manifest arbitrariness;
(d) targeted discrimination on manifestly wrongful grounds, such as gender, race or religious belief;
(e) abusive treatment of investors, such as coercion, duress and harassment;
(f) a breach of any further elements of the "fair and equitable treatment" obligation adopted by the Parties in accordance with paragraph 3 of article 8.10.[12]

Item (f) is discussed in section 3 of the Agreement, which states that the parties to the Agreement shall regularly, or upon request of a party, review the content of the obligation to provide fair and equitable treatment. According to the same section, the Committee on Services and Investment may propose recommendations regarding such issues to the CETA Joint Committee which makes the final decision.[13]

Section 2 contains a seemingly exclusive list but its last item and section 3 of the same article makes it possible to extend the cases of breach of "fair and equitable treatment". It is important to emphasize that item (f) of section 2 together with section 3 allow

[9] http://ec.europa.eu/trade/policy/in-focus/ceta/, accessed May 14, 2018.

[10] CETA Section 1, Article 8.10.

[11] CETA Section 5, Article 8.10.

[12] CETA Section 2, Article 8.10.

[13] CETA Section 3, Article 8.10.

only extension, meaning that measures from items (a) to (e) cannot be excluded from applying this mechanism.

It is interesting to mention that in February 2013, the draft of the Agreement did not contain such an exhaustive list but relied on the application of general clauses. Finally, the parties diverged from the draft, with the aim to make the content of "fair and equitable treatment" clearer.[14] Instead of the general definition, the above analyzed combined solution – an extendable list – was applied. This is beneficial for North American investors, as treatment standards can be further extended.

Section 4 of article 8.10 is the next section which is worth examining regarding the analysis of "fair and equitable treatment". This section states that in case of dispute settlement, the Tribunal (the first instance investment protection court examined in the next part of this work) related to this treatment can take into account whether a party to the Agreement made a specific representation to an investor to induce a covered investment that created a legitimate expectation and upon which the investor relied in deciding to make or maintain the covered investment, but that the party subsequently frustrated.[15] Thus, CETA empowers the Tribunal to take into account potential bad faith conduct of the parties to the Agreement, like luring in foreign investors with certain benefits and later revoking such, causing damages to these investors. An excellent but extreme example is the *Veolia Propreté v. Egypt* case.[16]

Sections 6 and 7 should be mentioned in relation to article 8.10. Section 6 provides that a breach of another provision of CETA, or of a separate international agreement does not establish a breach of article 8.10.[17] Section 7 states that a measure that breaches domestic law does not, in and of itself, establish a breach of article 8.10.[18] These provisions aim to preclude avoidance of the application of rules stated in previous sections. Namely, if the Agreement made it possible to breach this article merely by the breach of another international agreement, or by the breach of other provisions of CETA, or by the breach of domestic law, the application of detailed rules laid down in section 1 could be avoided.

Related to the above-mentioned section 4 of article 8.10, article 8.9 of CETA should be discussed. Section 1 of this article states that the contracting parties keep their right to regulate to achieve legitimate policy objectives, such as the protection of public health; safety; the environment or public morals; social or consumer protection or the promotion and protection of cultural diversity.[19] Theoretically, this guarantees the right to regulate when it is needed for a public purpose, however, certain doubts might arise in comparison

---

[14] Günes Ünüvar, The Vague Meaning of Fair and Equitable Treatment Principle in Investment Arbitration and New Generation Clarifications 18–19 (OUP, 2016).

[15] CETA Section 4, Article 8.10.

[16] https://icsid.worldbank.org/apps/ICSIDWEB/cases/pages/casedetail.aspx?CaseNo=ARB/12/15, accessed May 14, 2018. Veola had entered into a 15 year contract for waste collection with the Governorate of Alexandria. It argued that the host country had breached legitimate expectations of the investior by refusing a re-negotiation of the terms of the contract after the adoption of new and burdensome labor legislation and the devaluation of the Egyptian currency.

[17] CETA Section 6, Article 8.10.

[18] CETA Section 7, Article 8.10.

[19] CETA Section 1, Article 8.9.

with section 4 of article 8.10. Sections 2 and 3 of article 8.9 further strengthens the right of states to regulate. Section 2 provides that the mere fact that a party regulates, including through a modification to its laws, in a manner which negatively affects an investment or interferes with an investor's expectations, including its expectations of profits, does not amount to a breach of an obligation under CETA.[20] Section 3 states that not issuing, renewing or maintaining a subsidy is not a breach, provided there was no specific commitment under law or contract to issue, renew, or maintain that subsidy or to the terms or conditions attached to the issuance, renewal or maintenance of the subsidy.[21] These provisions basically function as a counterbalance to section 4 of article 8.10, which tries to protect the investors against bad faith conduct of states while these try to protect the public interest-based legislation of states.

Three further elements should also be discussed which are important innovations of CETA. The first is that article 8.1 exactly determines who can be considered investor: A party to the Agreement; a natural person or an enterprise of a Party, other than a branch or a representative office, that seeks to make, is making or has made an investment in the territory of the other party.

CETA also defines what constitutes an enterprise of a Party. There is a requirement for it to be constituted or organized under the laws of that Party CETA also demands that it has have substantial business activities in the territories of that Party. This clause was evidently designed to exclude shell corporations and enterprises from the provisions of CETA. However, CETA also recognizes enterprises that are constituted or organized under the laws of that Party and are either directly or indirectly controlled or owned by a natural person of that Party or by an enterprise fitting within the other category mentioned above. This second category is more troubling, because it omits the "substantial business activity" clause and only requires the enterprise to be owned or controlled by a natural person of that Party or an enterprise fitting the previous definition.[22]

The next element which should be dealt with is article 8.7. This article lays down the Most-Favored-Nation (MFN) principle – if any party to the Agreement concludes an agreement with a third party and this agreement provides for more favorable treatment to the investors of this third party, such treatment should be granted to the other CETA party as well.[23]

According to the opinion of the authors, section 4 of the same article is also important. It states that substantive obligations in other international investment treaties and other trade agreements do not in themselves constitute treatment and thus cannot give rise to a breach of CETA.[24] Hence, in theory, this precludes investors to invoke more advantageous substantial provisions from other international treaties during the dispute settlement procedure.

---

[20] CETA Section 2, Article 8.9.

[21] CETA Section 3, Article 8.9.

[22] CETA Article 8.1.

[23] OECD, Most-Favoured-Nation Treatment in International Investment Law, 2004/02 OECD Working Papers on International Investment 2 (OECD Publishing, 2004).

[24] CETA Section 4, Article 8.7.

According to this section, an investor of a Party may submit a claim to the Tribunal that the other Party has breached an obligation under either Chapter 8 (chapter on investments) Section C (provisions on non-discriminatory treatment) of CETA or Section D (provisions on investment protection) if the investor suffered loss or damage as a result of the alleged breach.[25] This means that the breach of other provisions of CETA does not constitute standing for a dispute settlement procedure.

All in all, it can be said that CETA's chapter on investment is quite precise. It contains detailed, exact terms and standards. There is a clear aspiration to close up loopholes. At the same time, it should be noted, especially relating to section 4 of article 8.10, that considerable discretion was left to the Tribunal.

III. Procedural Provisions of the CETA

The other relevant part of the CETA is the investment dispute settlement procedure. This is the biggest innovation of the CETA as it establishes a permanent international tribunal for the settlement of investment disputes instead of *ad hoc* arbitration. The dispute settlement system established by the CETA is called Investment Court System (ICS), contrary to the Investor State Dispute Settlement (ISDS) system used for similar disputes before.[26] The competence and organization of the two tribunals and the procedure will be discussed. However, before this discussion, it should be mentioned that the CETA also contains two alternative disputes settlement methods: Consultation, provided for in article 8.19, and mediation, discussed in article 8.20. The parties to the dispute can resort to any of these at any time during the dispute, even during arbitral proceedings.[27] Presumably, these articles aim to help the parties to find a solution to their dispute effectively, in the least costly manner, and to reduce the load of the tribunals set up under the CETA.

According to article 8.18, an investor of a party may submit to a tribunal constituted under the CETA a claim only in cases where an obligation under section C or D of chapter 8 has been breached and where the investor has suffered loss or damage as a result of the alleged breach.[28] This excludes claims based on the breach other provisions of the CETA, in which cases typically the contracting parties should act in the dispute settlement instead of the investors.

The constitution of the first instance tribunal, "the Tribunal", is regulated in article 8.27. Section 2 states that the CETA Joint Committee shall, upon the entry into force of the Agreement, appoint fifteen members of the Tribunal, from which five are nationals of a member state of the European Union, five are nationals of Canada and five are nationals of third countries.[29] According to section 3, the Joint Committee may increase

[25] CETA Section 1, Article 8.18.

[26] http://ec.europa.eu/commission/2014-2019/malmstrom/blog/proposing-investment-court-system_en, accessed May 14, 2018.

[27] CETA Article 8.19, Article 8.20.

[28] CETA Article 8.18.

[29] CETA Section 2, Article 8.27.

or decrease this number, however, only with numbers divisible by three and on the same basis as provided for in paragraph 2.[30] Pursuant to these two sections, the Tribunal should always have the same number of EU, Canadian and third country members, to guarantee the neutrality and impartiality of the Tribunal. According to section 5 of the Agreement, seven arbitrators appointed immediately after the entry into force of the CETA will serve for 6 years. Otherwise, arbitrators are chosen for a 5 year term and this term can only be renewed once. Vacancies are filled as they arise. A person appointed to replace an arbitrator of the Tribunal whose term of office has not expired holds office for the remainder of the predecessor's term. A member of the Tribunal serving on a division of the Tribunal when their term expires may continue to serve on the division until a final award is issued.[31] This latter element was inserted to the Agreement to prevent interruption of procedures because of the expiry of the term of an arbitrator.

The service requirements for the members of the Tribunal according to section 4 of article 8.27 are as follows. The arbitrators have to possess the qualifications required in their respective countries for appointment to judicial office, or be jurists of recognized competence. They should have demonstrated expertise in public international law. It is desirable that they have expertise, in particular, in international investment law, in international trade law, and in the resolution of disputes arising under international investment or international trade agreements.[32] Article 8.30 imposes additional requirements: They have to be independent and not affiliated with any government; they shall not take instructions from any organization, or government with regard to matters related to the dispute; they shall not participate in the consideration of any disputes that would create a direct or indirect conflict of interest. In addition, upon appointment, they shall refrain from acting as counsel or as party-appointed expert or witness in any pending or new investment dispute, irrespective whether it is under the CETA or another international treaty.[33] Conflict of interest rules are laid down in detail in article 8.30.

The President and Vice-President of the Tribunal shall be responsible for organizational issues and will be appointed for a two-year term and will be selected by lot from among the Members of the Tribunal who are nationals of third countries. They shall serve on the basis of a rotation drawn by lot by the Chair of the CETA Joint Committee. The Vice-President shall replace the President when the President is unavailable. The Tribunal may draw up its own working procedures.[34] The reason for the selection of these office holders from third countries can be that the Agreement tries to strengthen with this the impartiality of the Tribunal, as these arbitrators are responsible for operational tasks.

The other tribunal established by the CETA is the second instance – the Appellate Tribunal. The CETA itself does not provide for the number of its members, composition

[30] CETA Section 3, Article 8.27.

[31] CETA Section 5, Article 8.27.

[32] CETA Section 4, Article 8.27.

[33] CETA Section 1, Article 8.30.

[34] CETA Section 8 and 10, Article 8.27.

and similar issues. Instead, section 3 of article 8.28 states that these issues, as well as the appointment of its members, are decided by the CETA Joint Committee.[35]

At the same time, the CETA stipulates some basic organizational issues, like conditions of appointment mentioned in article 8.27. The ethical and conflict of interest rules from 8.30 also apply to Appellate Tribunal arbitrators as well.[36] We suppose that the parties did not find the issue of the organization of the Appellate Tribunal as important as the first instance tribunal and this is the reason that they referred the majority of these issues to the competence of the Joint Committee, instead of regulating these issues in the Agreement.

Another provision that should be highlighted related to the Appellate Tribunal, is that the earlier mentioned Committee on Services and Investment periodically reviews its functioning according to the Agreement. It can make recommendations to the Joint Committee, which can revise its decisions related to the functioning, composition, etc. of the Appellate Tribunal.[37] Thus, two committees can be linked to the functioning of the Appellate Tribunal.

The next element that should be discussed after organizational issues is the procedure of these two tribunals. First of all, the course of the procedure in front of the Tribunal should be examined, highlighting the most relevant elements. One of these is that the foreign investor can submit the claim not only on its own behalf but also on behalf of a locally established enterprise which it owns or controls directly or indirectly.[38]

The next issue are (f) and (g) items of section 1, article 8.22, according to which the investor cannot have an ongoing proceeding before a national or international tribunal or a court related to the same claim and waives its right to initiate a proceeding related to the same issue in the future if he or she wants to submit a claim to the ICS system.[39] This provision is aimed at eliminating concurrent procedures.

Another important provision of CETA explicitly prohibits an investor from submitting a claim if the investment has been made through fraudulent misrepresentation, concealment, or corruption.[40] This might have dissuasive power against proceedings in bad faith during the course of an investment.

The CETA provides the possibility for the Tribunal to dismiss a claim if the respondent files an objection about how a claim is manifestly without legal merit. Furthermore, the Tribunal may address and decide as a preliminary question any objection by the respondent that, as a matter of law, a claim or any part thereof, is not a claim for which an award in favor of the claimant may be made under CETA, even if the facts alleged were assumed to be true.[41] These two articles are aimed at making the Tribunal's work more efficient and quicker.

---

35 CETA Section 7, Article 8.28.

36 CETA Section 4, Article 8.28.

37 CETA Section 8, Article 8.28.

38 CETA Section 1, Article 8.23.

39 CETA items (f) and (g), Section 1, Article 8.22.

40 CETA Section 3, Article 8.18.

41 CETA Article 8.32 and 8.33.

Returning to the main elements of the procedure, it should be stated that the Tribunal hears cases in divisions consisting of three members, one of whom is a national of a Member State of the European Union, one a national of Canada, and one a national of a third country. The national of the third country chairs the tribunal. At the same time, the parties may agree that a case should be heard by a sole arbitrator appointed at random from the third country nationals. Such a request shall be made before the constitution of the division of the Tribunal.[42] This strengthens CETA's idea of ensuring impartiality of the tribunals through third country members and makes the procedure more cost efficient as well.

Tribunals cannot oblige states to amend or to revoke their legislative acts. Instead, they can be obliged to pay monetary compensation. Such compensation cannot exceed the damage suffered by the investor. The Agreement explicitly forbids punitive damages as used in the United States. The CETA also states that costs related to the proceedings shall be borne by the unsuccessful disputing party.[43] These provisions are primarily in the interest of states: preserving their right to legislate and putting the burden of paying for the costs on the losing party.

Finally, special procedural rules related to the Appellate Tribunal are highlighted. Similarly to organizational issues, the Joint Committee decides on procedural issues as well.[44] The most important provision related to the Appellate Tribunal is that it may uphold, modify or reverse a Tribunal's award based on:

(a) errors in the application or interpretation of applicable law;

(b) manifest errors in the appreciation of the facts, including the appreciation of relevant domestic law;

(c) the grounds set out in Article 52(1) (a) through (e) of the ICSID Convention, in so far as they are not covered by paragraphs (a) and (b).[45]

Thus, the Appellate Tribunal can examine factual as well legal issues.

The Appellate Tribunal is also constituted of three members, who are elected randomly. Regarding the award, the same rules apply as to the first instance tribunal.[46] The issue of transparency is also very important. The CETA essentially took over the UNCITRAL rules on transparency with certain digressions. For example, section 5 of article 8.36 states that hearings are open to the public. The reason for this might be that potential compensations are paid from public funds. At the same time, the CETA makes it possible to have a private hearing if the Tribunal determines that there is a need to protect confidential or protected information.[47]

Regarding the future of ICS, article 8.29 should be mentioned, according to which Canada and the European Union will aspire to establish a multilateral investment tribunal and appellate mechanism for the resolution of investment disputes with their other trading partners. Once it is set up, the CETA Joint Committee will decide how to fit the

---

42 CETA Section 6 and 9, Article 8.27.

43 CETA Article 8.39.

44 CETA Section 7, Article 8.28.

45 CETA Section 2, Article 8.28.

46 CETA Section 5 and 6, Article 8.28.

47 CETA Article 8.36.

"current" rules into that system.[48] This definitely represents the goals of the European Union in establishing a single international tribunal for investment dispute issues, based on the ICS in the CETA.

On the whole, it can be said that the CETA has introduced a new form of investment dispute settlement procedure. Instead of the earlier *ad hoc* ISDS, it has introduced the new ICS system, which is intended to be more stable and predictable.[49]

IV. "Regulatory Chill" and the Future of Investment Protection Arbitration

There are several issues related to investment protection arbitration, both in economic and societal aspects. This part of the paper deals with the issue of "regulatory chill" and its potential effects on the future of investment protection arbitration.

Legal disputes between foreign investors, who are usually multinational companies, and host states, are often decided by international arbitration panels due to provisions in international investment agreements. Critics fear that these arbitration panels favor multinational companies as they have the incentive – more cases, more fees. This would make governments reluctant to adopt appropriate policies. Reluctance to adopt socially desirable legislation due to such fear is called regulatory chill. In a wider sense, regulatory chill means that the given state's lawmaker will avoid making laws that might have negative effects on foreign investors and, in a narrower sense, it means that they will avoid making specific laws for certain investments.

There are a number of cases related to this issue: *Philip Morris v. Australia*[50]; *Philip Morris v. Uruguay*[51] (regulation related to public health); *Vattenfall v. Germany (*regulation related to environment) [52] and *Veolia v. Egypt* (regulation related to minimum wage)[53]. In order to highlight the controversies arising around ISDS and its supposed regulatory chill effects, the two *Vattenfall* cases mentioned above will be discussed. These cases significantly influenced German public opinion about investment arbitration and thus merit a deeper examination.

The first *Vattenfall* case[54] concerned a planned power plant in Hamburg in 2009. This power plant was to be coal-powered and was to be constructed by an investor named Vattenfall, a 100% government-owned Swedish utility company. However, problems arose where the local Hamburg government changed and the issuance of administrative permits related to emission controls, water quality and water usage were allegedly delayed by the new local government. Furthermore, Vattenfall also argued that the content of the permits themselves were not consistent with what was agreed upon with the previous local government. Thus, Vattenfall claimed that the local Hamburg

---

[48] CETA Article 8.29.

[49] http://europa.eu/rapid/press-release_IP-15-5651_en.htm, accessed May 15, 2018.

[50] UNCITRAL, PCA Case no. 2012-12.

[51] ICSID Case no. ARB/10/7.

[52] *See* the next section, below.

[53] ICSID Case no. ARB/12/15.

[54] ICSID Case no. ARB/09/6.

government and, by extension Germany, were in violation of the Energy Charter Treaty, specifically articles 10 (1) (fair and equitable treatment) and 13 (expropriation without compensation). Interestingly, the case never went before an arbitration tribunal as Germany instead decided to settle the case with Vattenfall. Unfortunately, the contents of this settlement were not revealed to the public and thus the agreement is unknown.[55]

This case, while it never went before an arbitration tribunal, still showcased the potential for conflict between international investment law and domestic regulation, environmental regulation in this particular case – currently one of the most sensitive legal topics. If the case had gone before an arbitration tribunal, the arbitrators would have had to decide whether the domestic environmental regulations were consistent with international investment law, specifically the Energy Charter Treaty. In this hypothetical scenario, the effects of regulatory chill could have potentially been observed, as Germany could have been essentially penalized, if it had lost, for adopting environmental regulation that was detrimental to a foreign investor. Furthermore, the first Vattenfall v. Germany case also highlights that regulatory chill is not restricted to national legislation. In this particular case, the primary problem lay with the conduct and decisions of the local Hamburg government, which means that regulatory chill can even affect local-level legislation or regulation.

The second *Vattenfall* case[56] also deals with conflict between the interests of a foreign investor and environmental regulation. However, the situation is fundamentally different as in this case German federal legislation was at the center of the proceedings. The case is still pending at the moment and could have significant implications on the future of German anti-nuclear legislation and thus environmental regulation. The background of this case lies with the Fukushima incident. In 2011, a tsunami caused significant damage to the Fukushima nuclear power plant, disabling its power supply and the cooling system of its reactors. This event led to the meltdown of the reactors and thus triggered a serious radioactive release.[57] While the event was caused by unforeseen complications with the power supply of the nuclear power plant, international public opinion sharply turned against the usage of nuclear power in general. This created the situation in Germany. Seeing the devastation of the Fukushima nuclear accident, the German parliament decided to amend the country's Nuclear Energy Act. The amendment ordered a more rapid phasing out of nuclear power in Germany and the scheduled deadline for the completion of this procedure was brought forward to 2022. Besides this element, the amendment also proscribed the immediate shut-down of the oldest nuclear reactors in Germany. Vattenfall, the same Swedish company, owns and operates two of these affected nuclear reactors: the Krümmel and Brunsbüttel nuclear power plants.[58] The initial situation

---

[55] Markus Krajewski, *The Impact of International Investment Agreements on Energy Regulation, in* European Yearbook of International Economic Law, 2013 19 (Christoph Herrmann, Markus Krajewski, Jörg Philipp Terhechte eds., Springer, 2013).

[56] ICSID Case no. ARB/12/12.

[57] http://www.world-nuclear.org/information-library/safety-and-security/safety-of-plants/fukushima-accident.aspx, accessed May 14, 2018.

[58] Nathalie Bernasconi-Osterwalder, Martin Dietrich Brauch, The State of Play in Vattenfall v. Germany II: Leaving the German public in the Dark 2 (International Institute for Sustainable Development, 2014).

in this case shows exactly how environment-minded legislation, or environmental policy, can conflict with the interests of foreign investors. Vattenfall alleged that this amendment and especially the immediate shut-down of two of its nuclear reactors, caused it a significant loss of profits. Thus, Vattenfall initiated arbitration proceedings against Germany within the International Centre for Settlement of Investment Disputes and also filed a lawsuit before the Federal Constitutional Court of Germany. The basis of these claims was the Energy Charter Treaty, under which Vattenfall was considered a foreign investor.[59] The compensation claimed by Vattenfall as a foreign investor is currently at 5.140 million USD.[60] It can be seen in this situation that environmental regulation harmful to a foreign investor's interests immediately prompted a reaction, namely a reference to international investment arbitration. While the case is still pending, it is undeniable that for Germany, the second Vattenfall case has been a troubling and tiresome exercise, with significant associated legal fees, which will remain even if the state wins the case. If Germany loses against Vattenfall, the economic fallout will be significant, even for the relatively large federal budget of Germany.

As mentioned above, while Germany is not particularly threatened by the damages awarded to foreign investors, its less wealthy counterparts are much more imperiled. A developing country might be more reluctant to introduce environmental legislation that might conflict with the interests of foreign investors, fearing costly arbitration. The regulatory chill effect is very likely to loom over such cases. A host country acting in the public interest is thus coming under threat.

This can be an issue with the CETA as well. Moreover, the definition of investor in the Agreement is too broad and almost every large US corporation has a Canadian subsidiary. They can try to challenge EU environmental and other standards which are generally higher than US standards via Canada, .

Article 8.9 of the CETA reaffirms the right of the parties to regulate "within their territories to achieve legitimate policy objectives, such as the protection of public health, safety, the environment or public morals, social or consumer protection or the promotion and protection of cultural diversity." Theoretically, investors without such provisions would have the right to sue their host state if the latter increases the minimal wages, creates more severe environmental protection rules, or just ceases granting earlier preferences, resulting in the investor suffering damages. Thus, it should be examined whether article 8.9 is suitable to preclude the above-mentioned issues from dispute settlement procedures. The answer to this question is not obvious. Section 1 of article 8.9 enumerates certain legitimate policy objectives. However, it does not define the concept neither in this article, nor in article 8.1 which deals with definitions. Therefore, it can be said that the determination of the content of this concept is entrusted to the courts established in the ICS system. This causes uncertainty and there are no precedents.

The "necessity test" could be the solution – the Tribunal should examine whether such measures are "necessary". However, the Agreement does not define this concept either and, thus, this causes more uncertainty for host states.

---

[59] *Id.*

[60] http://investmentpolicyhub.unctad.org/ISDS/Details/467, accessed May 14, 2018.

The second section of the same article tries to be specific by stating that the mere fact that a Party regulates, including through a modification to its laws, in a manner which negatively affects an investment or interferes with an investor's expectations, including its expectations of profits, does not amount to a breach of an obligation under the CETA. However, it is the Authors' opinion that this is not sufficient. The motivation behind the fact might amount to the breach of an obligation under the CETA and such motivation will be examined by the Tribunal, again an uncertainty factor. This might deter states in some cases from legislating, because the necessity of the legislation will be decided by the Tribunal. In addition, in the beginning there will be no precedents, which makes their decisions even more unforeseeable. Thus, this might lead to "regulatory chill"– states will avoid legislating in certain fields, being afraid of potential law suits and losses.

Article 8.10 deals with fair and equitable treatment, which is also related to the issue of regulatory chill. This principle is open, enumerated cases can be extended by the Joint Committee, and section 4 practically gives free hands to the Tribunal when applying the principle. Thus, this principle in fact strengthens the position of potential investors, that is to say, it can contribute directly to "regulatory chill".

Related to "regulatory chill", it is worth to deal with the issue of compensation. Although CETA prohibits punitive damages,[61] this is not enough to protect states. In the case of major investments, compensation for the loss suffered can be a considerable amount. This can be a serious issue for Member States of the European Union with scarce resources, for which even a compensation which has to be paid for a loss suffered can be a serious amount of money. This is enhanced by the fact that usually these are the states where there is need for new legislation in the social and environmental fields. Therefore, regulatory chill would cause the biggest harm to the most vulnerable countries.

This also leads to issues of fundamental rights, because, regulatory chill would potentially prevent the enforcement of second and third generation fundamental rights. These are, among others, related to the right to work, or from third generation rights, the right to a healthy environment, or the right to natural resources. Without legislation in these fields, the before-mentioned rights would be endangered. At the same time, there are two fundamental rights which would be presumably furthered by the CETA: The right to property as investment, strongly protected by the Agreement, is at the same time property. That is to say, protecting investment is also protecting private property and the right to economic development. There was a tremendous increase in the significance of foreign investment during the last few decades, especially in less developed countries. New foreign investment can strengthen the development of these EU Member Countries.

The definition of "'investors" may be problematic as defined in article 8.1. Although CETA excludes the possibility of establishing shell companies, the text, in our view, is not precise enough to exclude companies from non-contracting states having established a subsidiary in a contracting state. At the same time, smaller domestic enterprises are disadvantaged, in the sense that they do not have the means to use the above mentioned back door via establishment of a foreign subsidiary. Another problem might be that

[61] CETA Section 4,Article 8.39.

the procedure is asymmetrical. Only investors can initiate proceedings in front of the tribunal. However, states might also have justified claims against investors.

Overall, it can be said that CETA applies mostly American solutions, based on investment treaties (and the NAFTA) concluded by the United States, for investment arbitration and the main problem is the issue of regulatory chill.

V. Conclusions

In this paper, we have tried to find solutions to the issues raised by the wording and content of CETA.

Article 8.9 should be changed as it gives the right to the parties to regulate. CETA should define exactly what should be understood under "legitimate policy objectives". The current solution with examples is adequate. However, there should also be a general definition for this concept. Furthermore, it would be wise to add a concrete and unambiguous provision that the Tribunal is bound by this article. Thus, if an act of a state complies with the notion of "legitimate policy objectives", irrespective of the motivation, the Tribunal should not be able to establish a breach of CETA related to this issue. Such amendments could significantly improve upon the lack of balance between the investor and the host state. As a result, the host states would not only formally, but also factually, be guaranteed the right to enact necessary legislation.

An amendment is also advisable for article 8.10. The notion of "fair and equitable treatment" is far too broad and should be narrowed down. We would advise to replace the current open list with an exhaustive list. The provision which allows the CETA Joint Committee to extend the list should also be redacted, as well as the wide discretion given to the Tribunal in section 4 of the same article. Such actions would serve three goals: The end of confusion related to the notion of "fair and equitable treatment"; the currently too investor friendly interpretable principle would become more balanced and neutral and it would create stability and legal certainty both for the investors and the host states, as the investors would know exactly what to expect, while the states would be made aware of what legislation does and does not violate this principle.

It is also recommended to insert a general clause into this chapter of the CETA, which squarely states that investment protection cannot result in violation of basic rights. In addition to this, it would be necessary to regulate exactly the violation of which basic rights should be avoided. It should be made clear that the states would have the right to rely on these provisions during dispute settlement procedure and that the Tribunal would be obliged to take them into consideration. This clause would insure, beside the amended article 8.9, that the Tribunal will not undermine basic rights with its awards.

Thus, these measures could guarantee the avoidance of regulatory chill. Article 8.9 would reinforce the right to legislate and article 8.10 would precisely define the notion of "fair and equitable treatment". This would bring stability to both sides and strengthen the view that public interest is not harmed by investment protection.

With the intention to improve the balance between states and investors, there is also the possibility of introducing the initiation of legal action for states against foreign investors under the CETA. However, our opinion is that this would not be an ideal solution, as the primary function of the dispute settlement procedure is to protect investors and not host states against investors. Therefore,.the above said changes would be enough to protect the interests of states during dispute settlements.

At the same time, we would suggest the amendment of article 8.1. The definition of the term investor is not exact and lacks precision. This might provide an opportunity to misuse the Agreement. Therefore, it would be reasonable to expressly exclude subsidiaries which are under the control of third country investors or enterprises, or in which the majority owners are third country natural or legal persons. This might seem like a quite strict measure, but in our opinion, it is necessary to avoid the above-mentioned circumventions.

Similarly, it is necessary to solve the problem of domestic investors. Economically stronger investors can find ways to be treated as foreign investors under CETA. However, smaller domestic investors are at a disadvantage, because they do not have the means to use these loopholes. Therefore, we would suggest to make the CETA dispute resolution procedure accessible for domestic investors as well. In this case, there would be a need for special provisions. It would be particularly important to provide such possibility to domestic investors only as *ultima ratio*. That is to say, they should first exhaust domestic legal remedies before appealing to the Tribunal. This would presumably mitigate their disadvantageous situation. Furthermore, such a solution would fit into the concept of a multilateral investment protection court, an idea which is supported both by Canada and the European Union.

In conclusion, we can say that there is a need for certain amendments to the text of the CETA, in order to solve these issues. Although, in many respects the CETA is more advanced and more detailed than older BITs or other trade agreements, it also has certain imperfections and needs revision.

Author Biographies

Wasiq Abass Dar is a doctoral student in international business law at Central European University, Budapest. His doctoral research focuses on issues related to the public policy exception in international commercial arbitration. Before joining the Central European University in 2015, he practiced law in the State of Jammu and Kashmir, India. Wasiq holds a Bachelor of Laws degree (B.S.L. – Ll.B.) from the University of Pune, India (2010), and a Master of Laws in International Law (LL.M.) from the South Asian University, New Delhi, India (2014). He was admitted to the Bar Council of Delhi in 2010. He is also a member of the Young International Council of Commercial Arbitration. In 2017 (June-September), as the Central European University's Global Teaching Fellow, he introduced courses on international commercial arbitration and international investment law at the University of Yangon, Myanmar. He was a visiting scholar at Cornell Law School, New York, during the fall semester of 2017. In September 2018, he was invited to attend the Dickson Poon School of Law at King's College London as a visiting researcher. The research areas that interest him include international commercial arbitration, international investment law and investment arbitration, commercial mediation, bankruptcy law, secured transactions law, private international law and certain areas of public international law.

Dalma R. Demeter is an academic at the University of Canberra, an international arbitrator, and a legal practitioner with over twenty years of experience. She has a truly international background encompassing both civil law and common law education and practice, with law degrees from leading European and US universities, and Australian qualifications in higher education. She is teaching and researching in international law, primarily in international dispute resolution, international sales law, international trade law, as well as mooting and advocacy. She is also coaching and arbitrating for the Willem C. Vis International Commercial Arbitration Moot in both Hong Kong and Vienna. Her teaching is based on extensive research, and her excellence has been recognized by several teaching awards both locally and internationally. Combining teaching with practice, Dalma is also an arbitrator in international commercial disputes, a partner at the Australasian Dispute Resolution Centre, and the Deputy Chair of the UNCITRAL National Coordination Committee for Australia (UNCCA). She is a member of the Law Council of Australia International Division, and of numerous arbitral institutions and professional organizations globally. She is a contributor to law reform inquiries in private international law, alternative dispute resolution and international trade law, and fluent in English, Hungarian and Romanian.

Frank Emmert is a tenured professor at Indiana University Robert H. McKinney School of Law in Indianapolis and the Director of its Center for International and Comparative Law. He teaches international business transactions, international commercial arbitration, world trade law, international investment law, as well as European Union law, and has published more than 100 books and articles in these areas of law. Besides Indiana University, Professor Emmert has taught courses for credit at Cardozo, Tulane, Rutgers, and Stanford in the USA, St. Gall and Basel in Switzerland, as well as Amsterdam, Strasbourg, Sheffield, Prague, Warsaw, Tallinn, Guadalajara, Alexandria, Cairo, and several other universities. He frequently speaks at conferences around the world and serves as a consultant and arbitrator in international business disputes where he brings his dual background in civil and common law legal systems to bear. He is a Fellow of the Chartered Institute of Arbitrators and the founder and CEO of the International Smart Mediation and Arbitration Institute in Indianapolis (www.SmartArb.org). In 2017, he co-founded PrepayWay, a Swiss based company developing smart contracts for international real estate and other business transactions secured on the Blockchain (www.PrepayWay.com). For more information see www.FrankEmmert.com, as well as https://mckinneylaw.iu.edu/faculty-staff/profile.cfm?Id=166.

Begaiym Esenkulova is an Associate Professor of the Law Division of the American University of Central Asia. She has LL.M. (summa cum laude) and S.J.D (summa cum laude) degrees from Central European University. She served as a visiting scholar at Columbia Law School, New York, USA (2013) and as a visiting postdoctoral scholar at Indiana University, Bloomington, USA (2018). Her research interests include but are not limited to international investment law and sustainable development, international investment arbitration, international trade law, and environmental law.

Pavle Flere is a dual Slovenian and Serbian national. He was born in Novi Sad, Serbia in 1979. In 2003, he obtained a degree in law from the Faculty of Law of Maribor University, Slovenia. During his undergraduate studies, he was an exchange student at the Faculty of Law, Erasmus University Rotterdam. In 2004, he obtained a master degree in international business law from Central European University (with distinction). Thereafter, he passed the Slovenian bar exam. Besides being an affiliate member of the International Compliance Association, holding an advanced certificate in business compliance, he is a holder of the SDA Bocconi University UniCredit Risk Management Diploma. Mr. Flere is fluent in English, German, Serbian, Croatian and Slovenian. Mr. Flere is licensed as a judicial interpreter for Serbian language. Mr. Flere started his career in 2004 in the High Court of Maribor, Slovenia. Thereafter, he joined UniCredit Group. In 2018, Mr. Flere joined the Triglav Group as senior legal and compliance counsel. Mr. Flere is a regular speaker at conferences related to various legal and compliance matters. Moreover, in the capacity of legal advisor, he has been involved in many projects under the auspices of international institutions such as the World Bank and the European Commission. He publishes in the field of finance and insolvency law, including EU and international commercial arbitration.

Gábor Hajdu is a doctoral student in the Doctoral School of the Faculty of Law in the University of Szeged. He obtained his law degree from the Faculty of Law of the University of Szeged. During his studies, he took part in several research-based contests, and reached national first place in the OTDK contest, competing in the category of private international law. At the end of his studies, he received a certificate from his university for his contributions to scientific endeavors as a student. Gabor Hajdu's chief areas of interest include foreign investment protection and international trade law, especially issues relating to dispute settlement. He has been publishing in both English and Hungarian.

Balázs Horváthy is a research fellow at the Hungarian Academy of Sciences CSS Institute for Legal Studies (Hungary, Budapest) and associate professor at Szechenyi Istvan University, Faculty of Law and Political Sciences, Department for Public and Private International Law (Hungary, Győr). He obtained his Ph.D. from ELTE University (Hungary, Budapest) in protective measures of the Common Commercial Policy in 2009. He teaches courses in EU public law and policies of the EU, and international trade law. His current research interests include social policy conflicts of EU and international trade law and "trade and environment" issues. He participates in the "Lendület-HPOPs" Research Group of the Hungarian Academy of Sciences on "The Policy Opportunities of Hungary in the EU" since 2013. He has also carried out an individual research project on the environmental impact of international trade law in the frame of the Bolyai Research Scholarship of the Hungarian Academy of Sciences (2011–2014). He is a member of the Society of International Economic Law, the University Association for Contemporary European Studies (UACES), the Institute for the Danube Region and Central Europe (IDM) and the Hungarian Society of the International Federation for European Law (FIDE).

Rebecca E. Khan obtained her S.J.D., summa cum laude, from Central European University in Budapest, Hungary. Previously, she graduated with highest honors from the George Washington University Law School, obtaining a Master of Laws (LL.M.) in International and Comparative Law. A Fulbright scholar from the Philippines, Rebecca was also a Buergenthal scholar at GW Law. For more than a decade, Rebecca worked as government attorney, specializing in international litigation and arbitration, including trade and investment disputes. Her litigation experience includes arbitrations before the World Bank's International Centre for Settlement of Investment Disputes (ICSID), the International Court of Arbitration of the International Chamber of Commerce (ICC), as well as disputes brought before the World Trade Organization (WTO). Rebecca also has extensive experience in litigating cases before all levels of the Philippine judicial system, including the Supreme Court, the Court of Appeals and specialized courts such as the Court of Tax Appeals and the Sandiganbayan, where she handled several high-profile asset recovery cases. Aside from her litigation experience, Rebecca was tapped by the Philippine Supreme Court as a member of its drafting committee for the Rules of Court on Alternative Dispute Resolution. She was also a member of the Philippine delegation to the UNCITRAL Working Group that prepared the Rules on Transparency in Treaty-based Investor-State Arbitration. She has taught courses on public international law and international investment law in Manila and Budapest, and lectures frequently on the topic of international arbitration for various professional audiences.

Bálint Kovács is a researcher in the field of international economic law, focusing on international investment law at the University of Debrecen, Hungary. He is an adjunct professor of international commercial law at Sapientia University in Cluj-Napoca, Romania. After obtaining his LL.B. degree at Babeş-Bolyai University Law School, he continued his studies obtaining two LL.M. degrees in the field of private law of the European Union and European and international business law. The main focus of his Ph.D. research and of his upcoming dissertation is on the field of investment protection and investment arbitration. He currently works as a business consultant, also being involved in and running projects of civil society organizations dealing with human rights issues, as well as youth education. He is fluent in Hungarian, Romanian and English, and has a basic knowledge of German.

Yue Ma obtained her LL.B. from Shandong University and an LL.M. from Emory University. Afterwards, she enrolled in the doctoral program of law in Central European University under the supervision of Prof. Tibor Várady. Her research interests are in international investment arbitration and international commercial arbitration. Her doctoral thesis focused on the ICSID review and enforcement mechanisms and the backlash against investment arbitration. In 2016, she successfully defended her thesis with summa cum laude. She possesses a China law license and was admitted to the New York State Bar in 2013. She studied in Xiamen University and City University of Hong Kong in exchange programs. In 2013, she worked with Prof. John Barcelo as a visiting researcher at Cornell University.

Csongor István Nagy is professor of law and the head of the Department of Private International Law at the University of Szeged. He is recurrent visiting professor at Central European University (Budapest/New York), the Sapientia University of Transylvania (Romania) and the Riga Graduate School of Law (Latvia). He is admitted to the Budapest Bar and an arbitrator at the Court of Arbitration attached to the Hungarian Chamber of Commerce and Industry, Budapest. Csongor graduated from Eötvös Loránd University of Sciences (ELTE, dr. jur.) in Budapest, in 2003, where he also earned a Ph.D. in 2009. During his studies he was a member of the István Bibó College of Law and Political Sciences and of the Invisible College. He received Master (LL.M., 2004) and S.J.D. degrees (2010) from Central European University (CEU) in Budapest/ New York. As an exchange student, he pursued graduate studies in Rotterdam (the Netherlands), Heidelberg (Germany) and Ithaca, New York (Cornell University). He had visiting appointments in the Hague (Asser Institute), Munich (twice, Max Planck Institute), Brno (Masarykova University), CEU Business School (Budapest), Hamburg (Max Planck Institute), Edinburgh (University of Edinburgh), London (British Institute of International and Comparative Law), Bloomington, Indiana (Indiana University), Brisbane, Australia (TC Beirne School of Law, University of Queensland) and the China-EU School of Law, Beijing. He was a senior fellow at the Center for International Governance Innovation in Canada and Eurojus legal counsel in the European Commission's Representation in Hungary. He has more than 170 publications in English, French, German, Hungarian, Romanian and (in translation) in Croatian and Spanish.

Zebo Nasirova is a PhD candidate at the University of Canberra (Australia). She received her LL.B. (Bachelor of Laws) in 2005 and her LL.M. (Master of Laws) at the University of World Economy and Diplomacy (UWED) in Uzbekistan. During her studies, she combined study and work by starting her legal career as a legal assistant at the Department of Press and Information of Uzbekistan. After earning her LL.B., she worked as a legal consultant and then as a lawyer at the same place. Zebo studied and worked in civil-law jurisdictions and, therefore, was passionate about learning different legal systems. Therefore, she decided to study in a common law country and started her second LL.M. at the University of Canberra (2013-2014). After acquiring her second LL.M., she decided to get her PhD. She is currently teaching and researching in international business law, international e-commerce and contracts, with her Ph.D. focusing on the interpretation of international law through the lens of domestic law, with special focus on the uniform interpretation of the CISG.

Orsolya Toth is assistant professor in commercial law at the University of Nottingham. Orsolya specializes in international dispute resolution, commercial law and international investment law. Previously, she was a member of the International Arbitration Group at Allen & Overy in London, where she worked on numerous commercial and investment treaty arbitrations in a range of industry sectors. She has acted as counsel on arbitrations under the rules of ICSID, LCIA, ICC and DIAC. She has represented clients in various industry sectors, such as energy, construction, and telecommunications. She has written several articles in the fields of arbitration and legal harmonization. Her monograph, The Lex Mercatoria in Theory and Practice (Oxford University Press, 2017), has won the St. Petersburg International Legal Forum Private Law Prize 2018. Orsolya regularly speaks at conferences on the topic of international dispute resolution and arbitration. She was educated at Keble College, Oxford where she obtained her DPhil, MPhil and MJur degrees.

Zoltán Víg teaches business law at the Faculty of Economics, Finance and Administration (FEFA) in Belgrade and subjects related to international economic relations at the Faculty of Law, University of Szeged. He obtained a degree in law (Masters equivalent) at the Szeged University Faculty of Law. He holds LL.M. and S.J.D. degrees in international business law from Central European University in Budapest. During his studies in Budapest he worked as teaching assistant to Professor Stefan Messmann. He conducted research at Max Planck and Asser Institutes, as well as at Humboldt, Hamburg, Emory and Yale Universities. In 2006, he was appointed assistant professor, and in 2012 he was promoted to associate professor at Singidunum University. During his career he has taught corporate law, EU company law, EU law and environmental protection law. He has published several books and articles in Serbian, English, German and Hungarian. Dr. Víg also gained additional practical work experience by working for Freshfields Bruckhaus Deringer international law firm. He currently works as an advisor for DBP Advokati law office in Belgrade and as a research fellow at the Hungarian Academy of Sciences.

Dildar Frzenda Zuber Zebari is an Iraqi Kurd lawyer and doctoral researcher at the University of Szeged. His fields of specialization are investment and energy law. He has an LL.M. from the University of East London, United Kingdom and a B.A. in Law from the College of Law and Politics, Dohuk University, Iraq. From 2012 until 2014, he worked as legal adviser for the Iraqi Crown oil service company and at the same time was director of legal affairs at Duhok Polytecnic University in Iraq, where he taught civil law and scholarly research. Since October 2014, he has been a doctoral student at University of Szeged. He published numerous papers and contributed to several conferences. As of October 2017, he has been international coordinator and legal adviser at Hevestherm Kft. in Hungary. He is fluent in English, Arabic, Kurdish and Persian.

Published by the Council on International Law and Politics

International Business and Trade Law:

Talia Einhorn & Frank Emmert: International Business Transactions – Documents,2nd rev. ed., Chicago 2013, ISBN 978-09858156-2-2

Joseph E. Miller: Changing Our Approach to Changing the World – Encouragingand Enhancing American Engagement in International PhilanthropyThrough Tax Law Reform, Chicago 2013, ISBN 978-09858156-3-9

Frank Emmert (ed.): Corporate Social Responsibility in Comparative Perspective, Chicago 2014, ISBN 978-09858156-4-6

Frank Emmert (ed.): World Trade and Investment Law – Documents, Indianapolis2018, ISBN 978-0-9858156-7-7

Csongor István Nagy (ed.), Investment Arbitration and National Interest,Indianapolis 2018, ISBN 978-0-9858156-8-4

Islamic Law Library:

Ahmed M. El Demery: The Arab Charter of Human Rights – A Voice for Sharia inthe Modern World, with a Foreword by Prof. M. Cherif Bassiouni, Chicago2015, ISBN 978-0985815653

Ahmed A. Altawyan: International Commercial Arbitration in Saudi Arabia,Indianapolis 2018, ISBN 978-0-9858156-9-1

Rakan F. Alharbi: The Development of Saudi Women's Rights – Theory, Practice,Challenges, and Solutions – a Critical and Analytical Study of the Impact ofCultural Norms on the Recognition of Women's Rights of Employment and Freedom of Movement, Indianapolis 2019 (forthcoming)

Mohammad M. Bayoumi Ibrahim: Women's Rights Under International, American,Islamic and Egyptian Law: An Irresolvable Conflict?, Indianapolis 2019(forthcoming)

All publications of the Council on International Law and Politics are available on Amazonand from leading booksellers.

Academic
excellence.
Professional
opportunity.
You'll find both at
Indiana University
Robert H. McKinney
School of Law,
located in metropolitan
Indianapolis—the heart
of Indiana government
and business.
ROBERT H. McKINNEY
SCHOOL OF LAW
INDIANA UNIVERSITY
Indianapolis
mckinneylaw.iu.edu
What Matters. Where it Matters.

Made in United States
Orlando, FL
04 November 2026

90209059R00131